Collins

Webster's

175 YEARS OF DICTIONARY PUBLISHING

easy learning

COMPLETE ENGLISH

HarperCollins Publishers
Westerhill Road
Bishopbriggs
Glasgow
G64 2QT

First edition 2012

Reprint 10 9 8 7 6 5 4 3 2 1 0

© HarperCollins Publishers 2012

ISBN 978-0-00-745064-0

Collins ® is a registered trademark of
HarperCollins Publishers Limited

www.collinslanguage.com

A catalogue record for this book is
available from the British Library

Typeset by Davidson Publishing
Solutions, Glasgow

Printed in Great Britain by Clays Ltd,
St Ives plc

HarperCollins does not warrant
that www.collinsdictionary.com,
www.collinslanguage.com or any other
website mentioned in this title will
be provided uninterrupted, that any
website will be error free, that defects
will be corrected, or that the website
or the server that makes it available are
free of viruses or bugs. For full terms and
conditions please refer to the site terms
provided on the website.

For the publishers:
Lucy Cooper
Kerry Ferguson
Elaine Higgleton
Lisa Sutherland

Based on:
*Collins Webster's Easy Learning Grammar
and Punctuation*
*Collins Webster's Easy Learning
English Spelling*
Collins Webster's Easy Learning Writing

Collins Webster's Easy Learning Complete English is a handy three-in-one book: spelling, writing, and grammar and punctuation in one volume. The book is ideal for anyone who wants to improve their English. Whether you are preparing for tests, need a quick look-up guide to English, or you simply want to browse and find out more about the English language and how it works, this book gives you all the information you need in a clear and accessible format.

Grammar & Punctuation: this section begins with a clear outline of the different parts of speech, and it then describes their forms and uses. All the main tenses of English are explained and exemplified, with emphasis on their function in everyday English.

Next, you will find a description of different types of statement and clause, with attention given to structures such as question forms, conditionals, and reported speech.

Finally, a guide to punctuation gives you clear and up-to-date information on important topics such as the use of the apostrophe, capital letters, and full stops.

Spelling: this section uses simple explanations, backed up with examples demonstrating each point, to describe the important features of English spelling. It also points out the most difficult words to spell, and offers ways of learning these.

The section begins with an explanation of how letters and groups of letters regularly correspond to certain sounds, and then looks at the reasons why the spelling of some words does not match the sound.

Next, it looks at recurring patterns, and rules you need to be familiar with in order to understand and predict how words are spelt.

The last part is concerned with words whose spellings are not easy to predict: it provides some practical advice on learning tricky spellings and then looks at difficult words themselves, showing why each can present pitfalls even to experienced users of English.

All of the difficult words that are examined in this section are listed in an alphabetical index at the end.

Writing: this section begins by reviewing all the things you need to know before you can write effectively. The topics covered here apply to all types of writing, and range from planning your writing to checking it at the end. Tricky issues such as how to show speech, abbreviations, and numbers are also covered. In addition, there is a comprehensive guide to style, looking at areas such as writing plain English, avoiding ambiguity, and writing with the appropriate level of formality.

The second part of the writing section takes a detailed look at different types of writing, from informal emails and letters to formal essays, reports, and presentations. It gives advice on structure, tone, and style, with examples of good practice, as well as providing suggestions for useful words and phrases to use in your own work.

The third part deals with common mistakes, and issues that people often disagree about. Expert practical guidance is given, so you can feel confident of making the right choice, whatever the situation.

The Collins Corpus forms the basis of all the points covered in this book, helping us to make accurate decisions about how the English language works in today's world. Explanations are fully illustrated with examples that remain close to the corpus, occasionally with small changes made so that they can be as clear and helpful as possible.

We hope you will enjoy learning about the English language and improving your skills. For more information about Collins language reference books, visit us at www.collinslanguage.com.

contents

1. Grammar & Punctuation

Grammar

Parts of speech

Sentences are made up of **words**. A sentence can be made up of any number of words.

> *He left us.*
> *The man in the corner lowered his newspaper.*
> *Whenever I see Tammy I worry about how I look.*
> *Until tomorrow then.*
> *Yes.*

We can put words together in many ways to make new sentences.

> *I can help you.*
> *Can I help you?*

Grammar describes how we put words together. Each word in a sentence belongs to a particular set or **class**, depending on how it is used. These classes are called **parts of speech**.

All sentences begin with a capital letter and end in either a period, a question mark, or an exclamation point. When we talk about these marks, e.g., commas, semicolons, periods, parentheses, and so on, we are talking about **punctuation**.

The term **clause** is used to describe a group of words that contains a verb, the **subject** of that verb, and, often, some other words such as an **object**.

> *I live in Vermont.*
> *...where I live.*
> *Jessica lived in Memphis at first.*
> *He was living in Rome that year.*
> *...when he had eaten breakfast.*

A sentence can contain one or more **clauses**.

I can help you if you will let me.
Whenever you need to talk to someone, just drop in and see
  if I'm here.

Many sentences are made up of a single clause. Single clause sentences are called **simple** sentences.

He arrived on Friday.
My brother loves his skateboard.

A clause always contains a **verb**.

run	*walk*
think	*believe*

A sentence, however, does not always have to be a clause. See p. 262 for more about clauses.

Certainly not.
Until tomorrow then.
Yes.
Why?

A **phrase** is just a **group** of words. The term is usually kept for words that go together naturally.

the other day
my friend Hank
in spite of
over the hill
would have been walking

Many words can refer to one thing only or to more than one. We use the terms **singular** and **plural** for this. A more general term is **number**. Pronouns and nouns can be singular or plural in grammatical number. See p. 204.

When we want to identify the speaker or the person spoken about in grammar, we use **first person** to mean the speaker, **second person** to mean the person who is spoken to, and **third person** to mean the person who is spoken about. For example, we talk about "first person plural" or "third person singular."

	singular	*plural*
1st person pronoun	*I*	*we*
2nd person pronoun	*you*	*you*
3rd person pronoun	*he, she, it*	*they*
nouns	*the man* *a girl*	*the men* *two girls*

A **verb** tells us about an action or a state of being. Ordinary verbs are called **main verbs**.

come	*go*	*think*
want	*economize*	*believe*

A special group of verbs are called **auxiliary verbs**. These can be put together with main verbs to form different tenses.

*I **am** thinking.*
*She **has** seen the movie already.*
*I **can** help you.*
*We **might** need to.*

A **noun** is a name for a thing or an idea.

table	*book*	*ugliness*
time	*animal*	*thing*

If we do not want to repeat the same noun in a sentence or a paragraph, we can replace it with a **pronoun**. A pronoun is a word that is used instead of a noun phrase or a noun.

> *Gary saw Sue so **he** asked **her** to help him.*
> *Ross was hungry so **he** stopped at a coffee shop.*

An **adjective** gives more information about a noun. Adjectives help us describe or pick out which particular thing among many is being referred to.

a man	*a **tall** man*
their TV	*their **new wide-screen** TV*
the cat	*the **fat black-and-white** cat*

A **determiner** is used to point more precisely to the person, thing, or idea that is being talked about. Examples of determiners are the **definite article**, the **indefinite articles**, and **possessives**.

***the** cat*	*a man*
***my** aunt*	*their TV*

An **adverb** gives information about the way that an action is carried out or when and where it takes place.

> *She ran **quickly** down the path.*
> *The children laughed **hysterically**.*
> *He lifted the box **carefully**.*

Some adverbs can also be used before adjectives.

> *He was a **rather** tall man.*
> *This cake is **quite** nice.*
> *It was **fairly** good.*
> *It's a **very** hot day.*

Other adverbs can be used to introduce a sentence.

> **Fortunately**, *the rain stopped.*
> **Honestly**, *I can't help it.*

Many adverbs are formed from adjectives by adding -ly.

A **preposition** is one of a small group of words that can be used with nouns and verbs. Prepositions give information about position, movement, time, manner, and other things.

> **on** *the bridge*   **with** *a knife*
> **in** *the morning*   **to** *the gates*

When a preposition is used in front of a noun, the two together do the work of an adverb or an adjective.

> *He is coming* **now**.
> *He is coming* **in the morning**.
> *a* **rabid** *dog*
> *a dog* **with rabies**

A **conjunction** joins two or more nouns or clauses to each other.

> *I went to the store* **and** *bought some bread.*
> *I bought some bread,* **but** *I forgot to get milk.*

Many words can act as more than one part of speech. It is not unusual for an English word to be a **noun** in one sentence and a **verb** in another sentence.

> *Jamal scored several* **runs**.
> *She* **runs** *half a mile each morning.*
> *I've been chosen for the school* **play**.
> *Chris and Art* **play** *golf together on Fridays.*

Parts of the sentence

Sentences consist of a number of parts. The most important parts of a sentence are:

- The **subject**, which is either a noun phrase (see p. 137) or a pronoun (see p. 203). Normally the subject comes before the verb phrase in a sentence.

  The girls had been swimming.
  The new teacher came in.
  They had finished.

- The **verb phrase**, which includes the main verb and which may have auxiliary verbs to go with it. See also pp. 32–90.

  The girls had been swimming.
  The new teacher came in.
  They had finished.
  She uses her skateboard quite a bit.
  Rajiv was reading a new novel.
  She is riding someone else's horse.

- The **object**, which is a noun phrase or a pronoun.

  She used her old skateboard.
  Rajiv was reading a new novel.
  Josh found it.

Not all verbs need an object. When there is one, the object normally comes after the verb phrase. Some verbs may also need an **indirect object**. See also p. 231.

  Hamid gave me a party invitation.
  Ruth gave Lauren a nice bunch of flowers.

- An **adverbial**, or **adjunct**, which is an optional part of the sentence.

This may be:

- a single word, which will always be an **adverb**.

    *Suddenly, it started to rain **heavily**.*

- an **adverbial phrase**, which is a group of words that functions as an adverb.

    ***In the morning**, the sky was clear.*
    *You probably won't notice it **after a while**.*

- an **adverbial clause**, which is a group of words including a verb that functions as an adverb.

    *I'll get some cookies for you **when I've poured the drinks**.*
    ***When I've poured the drinks**, I'll get some cookies for you.*
    *Mark played **while Mandy sang**.*

Though some adverbials have a fixed position, most can be added to a sentence in several places.

    ***In the winter**, the roads get very slippery.*
    *The roads get very slippery **in the winter**.*

A sentence can have several different adverbials, some working together and some independent of each other.

- A **complement**. With certain verbs, such as *be* and *seem*, a complement takes the place of an object. A complement can be either an adjective or a noun phrase. Complements provide further descriptive detail about the subject. See also p. 233.

    *He became **a doctor** in 2005.*
    *Andrew is **an auto mechanic**.*
    *He felt **a bit foolish** when he realized what he'd done.*
    *They became **good friends** despite the mistake.*

Direct and indirect objects

The **object** of a sentence (if there is one) normally comes after the verb phrase. Whether there is an object or not depends on the meaning of the verb. For example, if you want to talk about what someone is doing, you might say "She is writing", but if you want to talk about the point of the activity, you might say, "*She is writing a book.*"

> *She was riding.*
> *She was riding her horse.*
> *Erica was writing.*
> *Erica was writing a letter.*

An object that follows a verb like this is called the **direct object**.

> *Rory found a pen.*
> *Our cat doesn't like milk.*

Some verbs also have another sort of object, called an **indirect object**. An indirect object names the person for or to whom something is done. It is usually needed with verbs like *give*, *find*, and *owe*. For example, with *give*, we need to name both the thing that is given and the person (or sometimes, the animal) it is given to.

> *Mike owes Tom five dollars.*
> *Rob gave me a box of chocolates.*
> *Susan bought her rabbit some more food.*

Some verbs must always take a direct object, some never take a direct object; others sometimes take one and sometimes don't, depending on the meaning. When a verb has an object it is called a **transitive** verb.

> *Rowan bought a magazine.*
> *I don't like rap music.*

When it does not have an object it is called an **intransitive** verb.

> *Lynn fainted.*
> *Pavel screamed.*
> *Soon, everyone was shouting.*

Some verbs can be either **transitive** or **intransitive**.

> *Ann was reading (a letter).*
> *Kim was drawing (a picture).*

When a verb has both an indirect and a direct object it is called a **ditransitive verb**.

> *Amy owes* **Mark** *ten dollars.*
> *Sarina gave* **me** *some flowers.*
> *Katie bought* **her hamster** *a new cage.*

A direct object is needed where the meaning of the verb requires something to give it a focus. This is why we sometimes say that a direct object "complements" a verb.

- Some verbs must have an adverbial as well as a direct object, for example, to specify a place.

> *He placed* **the parcel** *on the chair.*
> *She put* **the umbrella** *in a corner.*

Verbs

Verbs are words that allow us to talk about activities, processes, states of being, and states of mind.

> *This basket **holds** a lot.*
> *Josh **was reading** Kaitlin's essay.*
> *Frieda **is preparing** a talk for next week's class.*
> *Helen **feels** much happier now.*
> *I **forgot** that it **was** your birthday.*
> *Paul **owned** several old motorbikes.*

Verbs can be divided into two major groups, according to the way they are used. Those in the larger group are called **main verbs**. The rest are called **auxiliary verbs**.

Verb phrase

A verb phrase can be a single word or a group of associated words.

> *he **walks***
> *he **is walking***
> *he **had walked***
> *he **can walk***
> *he **has been walking***
> *he **might have been walking***

When a verb phrase consists of a single word it is called a **simple** verb. Many verbs in English are made by combining an auxiliary verb and a main verb; this is called a **compound** verb.

- When we want to talk about all the parts of a verb, we use the term **verb phrase**.

Main verbs

Main verbs, or **lexical** verbs, are the verbs that we use to indicate actions and states. Most of the verbs in English are main verbs. Main verbs are divided or **classified** in several ways:

– according to whether they refer to **states**

> I *can* really *taste* the herbs in this omelet.
> This scarf *belongs* to me.
> He *hates* losing.
> She always *liked* boats and sailing.
> I already *feel* that I *have known* you for ages.

  or **actions**.

> Three boys *were kicking* a ball around in the yard.
> We *were running* across the football field.
> For six hours, Stuart *drove* across open desert.

– into **regular** and **irregular** verbs according to the spelling of their forms.

> regular: talk, talks, talking, talked
> irregular: swim, swims, swimming, swam, swum
> irregular: go, goes, going, went, gone

– according to whether or not they are followed by an object. That is, whether they are **transitive** or **intransitive**. See p. 84.

> I *can read*.
> We both *read* **the same authors**.
> *Don't tell* **me**.
> We both *ran* away.
> Sue *found* **a bracelet**.
> I *saw* **my best friend** on Friday.

Auxiliary verbs

These verbs are used in combination with main verbs in order to allow us to talk about different times or periods of time, different degrees of completion, and different amounts of certainty or doubt. There are several types of auxiliary verb. The primary auxiliaries help express time, and the modal auxiliaries help to express certainty and doubt. See pp. 39–78.

Tense

We use verbs to talk about actions and states. Verbs **tenses** allow us to talk about the time when the action or state takes place.

All main verbs have two simple tenses: the **present simple** and the **past simple**.

present simple	past simple
I walk	I walked
she sings	she sang
they come	they came
you bring	you brought

In these tenses the verb is used on its own without any auxiliary verbs.

English verbs also have compound tense forms. In these tenses the main verb is accompanied by one or both of the auxiliary verbs *be* and *have*. See p. 91 for more on tenses.

Aspect

The compound tenses of the verb express two **aspects**: **continuous** and **perfect**.

- The term **aspect** is used to talk about continuing actions versus completed actions or states. Simple tenses do not have aspect.

continuing actions	
I am walking	I was walking
she is singing	she was singing
they are coming	they were coming
you are bringing	you were bringing

completed actions	
I have walked she has sung they have come you have brought	I had walked she had sung they had come you had brought

We use these compound verbs when we want to talk about:

- the continuous nature of an action (using a form of the auxiliary *be* + *-ing*). This is called the **continuous aspect**.

> *I am still studying French.*
> *He was living in LA all that year.*
> *Jamal is helping out with the children this week.*
> *Sarina and Scott were looking for a new apartment at the time.*

- the completion of an action (using a form of the auxiliary *have* + a past participle). This is called the **perfect aspect**.

> *I have been a teacher for four years.*
> *He had lived in Dallas for a year before coming to Denver.*
> *Jamal has helped out before.*
> *Sarina and Scott had found their apartment by then.*

The two aspects of the verb can be joined so that we can talk about the duration and the completion of an action in the same verb phrase. See pp. 91–92 for more on tense and aspect.

> *I have been studying French for four years.*
> *I had been living in Dallas for four years when I met him.*
> *Jamal has been helping us this week.*

Simple tenses

Simple tenses show moments in time, timeless states, and habitual or repetitive actions.

> It *tastes* good.
> Julie *keeps* a diary.
> Adrian *went* home at midnight.
> She *heard* a strange noise in the night.
> Rob usually *walks* to school.
> Yesterday he *went* by car.

The **present simple** and the **past simple** of regular verbs are formed by using the base form of the verb. See pp. 97–101.

Continuous tenses

Continuous tenses show duration or continuity.

> It *is raining* hard this morning.
> It *was raining* when we came out of school yesterday.
> I'm *having* dinner. Can I call you back?
> He *was listening* to the radio when he heard the news.

The **present continuous** and the **past continuous** are formed from either the present or the past tense of the verb *be* + the **present participle** (or "*-ing* form") of the main verb. See pp. 102–105.

Perfect tenses

The present perfect tense can show that an action is completed but that it still has some importance in the present time. It can also show that a state began in the past and continues in the present.

> Ken **has walked** all the way from the station. (...and he's tired.)
> He **has** never **visited** me. (...and I'm feeling neglected.)
> She **has missed** the train. (That's why she's not here.)
> I **have lived** in Texas all my life. (I still live there.)
> My mother **has** always **believed** that I would succeed.
> (She still believes this.)

The **past perfect** is used to talk about something that happened in a time before a particular time in the past.

> He told us that he **had tried** it before.
> I **had** never **been** climbing before our activity holiday last year.
> She was late because she **had missed** her train.

The **present perfect** and the **past perfect** are formed using either the present or the past tense of the verb *have* + **the past participle** of the main verb. See pp. 106–109.

Perfect continuous tenses

Perfect continuous tenses show duration, completion, and importance in the present time or in the time referred to.

> I **have been working hard** in the garden all day.
> My mother **has been helping** me.
> My sisters **have been riding** this morning.
> I **had been working** in Italy that summer.
> Some of us **had been waiting** for two hours when the doctor appeared.

The **present perfect continuous** and the **past perfect continuous** are formed using either the present or past tense of the verb *have* + the **past participle** of *be* + the **present participle** of the main verb. See p. 110.

Other verb forms

Other verb combinations are used for positive or negative statements, or to express degrees of time and probability.

> *Do* you *like espresso coffee?*
> *I don't like fried food.*
> *Could I have a Coke, please?*
> *You will be in Atlanta within two hours.*
> *They will probably meet us at the airport.*

Types of main verb

Verbs of action

Most verbs describe an action such as *walking*, *running*, or *reading*.

> *John is running for the train.*
> *Haley has just bought a new camera.*
> *She is putting on an exhibition of her photographs.*
> *Ralph has seen the film already.*

- Action verbs can be expressed in all the tenses.

Verbs of state

Some verbs are used to talk about states of being or states of mind.

These include:

- verbs relating to the senses, e.g., *feel*, *hear*, *see*, *smell*, *taste*.
- verbs relating to emotions, e.g., *adore*, *fear*, *hate*, *like*, *love*, *want*, *wish*.
- verbs relating to mental activity, e.g., *agree*, *believe*, *expect*, *forget*, *mean*.
- verbs relating to possession, e.g., *belong*, *own*, *possess*.

> *I feel unhappy.*
> *I hate arguments.*
> *These flowers smell gorgeous.*
> *Raouf wishes he hadn't agreed to the plan.*
> *We mean you no harm.*
> *That car belonged to us once.*

- Verbs of state are not usually used in continuous tenses. When they are used in continuous tenses, they change their meaning.

  *I'm just **feeling** to see if the bone is broken.*
  *We **were tasting** some interesting New Zealand wines.*
  *Naomi **is expecting** a baby.*

There are some uses of the verb **be** that allow you to choose between a state or an action meaning. The word used as the complement makes an important difference.

  *Mark **is being** stubborn.*　　**but not** *Mark is being tall.*
  *Oscar **is being** nasty.*　　**but not** *Oscar is being intelligent.*

The verb **seem** has a limited number of adjectives that can be used as its complement.

  *Simon seems **happy**.*　　**but not** *Simon seems tall.*

The forms of main verbs

English verbs have up to five different forms. These are:

1 the base form, e.g.,   *pull*
2 the 3rd person singular,
   present simple tense, e.g.,   *pulls*
3 the past simple tense, e.g.,   *pulled*
4 the past participle, e.g.,   *pulled*
5 the present participle, e.g.,   *pulling*

- Regular verbs are all formed in the same way, by building on the **base form** (form 1). This is the form you normally find in a dictionary. Most verbs are regular.

- Irregular verbs have different forms, particularly forms 3 and 4. See p. 36.

Form 1:   The **present simple** tense has all but one of its forms the same as the **base form**.

Form 2:   When the **present simple** tense has a 3rd person singular subject, the verb is formed from the **base form** + *-s*.

Form 3:   The **past simple** is formed from the **base form** + *-ed*.

Form 4:   The **past participle** is formed from the **base form** + *-ed*.

Form 5:   The **present participle** is formed from the **base form** + *-ing*.

A special variation of the base form is the *to* **infinitive**. There are a number of uses of a verb where both the words *to* + the **base form** must be present.

> The base form is sometimes called the "bare infinitive."

As mentioned above, the 3rd person singular is formed from the **base form** + **-s**. Below are the exceptions to the rule:

Verbs ending in **-o**, **-ch**, **-sh**, **-ss**, **-x**, **-z**, or **-zz**: add **-es** to make the 3rd person singular, e.g.

veto	he veto**es**
catch	he catch**es**
focus	he focus**es**
push	he push**es**
miss	he miss**es**
box	he box**es**
buzz	it buzz**es**

Verbs ending in **-y** after a consonant:: change **y** to **i** and add **-es**, e.g.

carry	he carr**ies**
fly	he fl**ies**
worry	he worr**ies**

As mentioned above, the present participle is made up of the **base form** + **-ing**. There are some exceptions to the rule. Nearly all verbs that contain a short final vowel in front of a final consonant double the consonant before *-ing*, e.g.

sob	sobbing
bid	bidding
jog	jogging
run	running
stop	stopping
get	getting
put	putting

Irregular verbs

Irregular verbs are verbs that *do not* form the past simple tense and the past participle by adding *-ed* to the base form.

The three main groups of irregular verbs

In Group A, the base form, the past simple, and the past participle are the same:

1 the base form	*put*
2 the present simple tense	*puts*
3 the past simple tense	*put*
4 the present participle	*putting*
5 the past participle	*put*

A				
bet	*cut*	*let*	*set*	*spread*
burst	*hit*	*put*	*shed*	*thrust*
cast	*hurt*	*shut*	*split*	*upset*

In Group B, the past simple and the past participle have the same form:

1 the base form	*buy*
2 the present simple tense	buys
3 the past simple tense	*bought*
4 the present participle	buying
5 the past participle	*bought*

B1

base form	past form	base form	past form
bend	bent	hang	hung
bind	bound	have	had
bleed	bled	hear	heard
bring	brought	keep	kept
build	built	kneel	knelt
buy	bought	lay	laid
catch	caught	make	made
find	found	say	said

Some of the verbs in Group B have alternative spellings for the past participle:

B2   The past form may be either *a* or *b*.

base form	past forms a	b
burn	burned	burnt
dream	dreamed	dreamt
learn	learned	learnt
smell	smelled	smelt

The *a* forms are more common in American English.

In Group C, the base form, the past simple, and the past participle all have different forms:

1 the base form   *go*
2 the present simple tense   *goes*
3 the past simple tense   *went*
4 the present participle   *going*
5 the past participle   *gone*

C

base form	past forms		base form	past forms	
arise	arose	arisen	ring	rang	rung
awake	awoke	awoken	rise	rose	risen
bear	bore	borne	saw	sawed	sawn
begin	began	begun	see	saw	seen
bite	bit	bitten	shake	shook	shaken
blow	blew	blown	show	showed	shown
break	broke	broken	shrink	shrank	shrunk
fly	flew	flown	strive	strove	striven
give	gave	given	take	took	taken
know	knew	known	throw	threw	thrown
ride	rode	ridden	write	wrote	written

Auxiliary verbs

An auxiliary verb is a verb that is used together with a main verb to show time and continuity.

- *Be* and *have* are the **primary auxiliaries**. A primary auxiliary is used to construct compound tenses.

- *Be* is used to make present continuous and past continuous tenses.

  I am working.
  Randy is using the computer.
  We were all wondering about that.
  Kevin was teaching in Argentina in 1995.

  It is also used for the passive.

  These books are sold in supermarkets.
  Martin was arrested and held overnight.

See p. 44 for more on *be*.

- *Have* is used to make present perfect and past perfect tenses.

  Aaron has finished fixing the car.
  George and Alicia have seen the show already.
  Amanda had already eaten when we arrived.
  They had not expected to see us there.

See p. 48 for more on *have*.

- *Do* is the **supporting auxiliary**. It is used in forming negatives, questions, and emphatic statements.

  > I *do* not like hot dogs at all.
  > *Do* you like shrimp?
  > You *do* like shrimp, don't you?

See p. 52 for more on *do*.

See pp. 91–96 for more on simple and compound verb forms.

- *Will*, *may*, *might*, and the other verbs listed on pp. 57–58 are the **modal auxiliary verbs**, usually called, simply, **modal verbs** or **modals**. A modal verb allows us to talk about actions as possible, doubtful, or necessary.

  > Charlie *will go* home on Friday.
  > Charlie *may go* home on Friday.
  > Charlie *could go* home on Friday.
  > Charlie *must go* home on Friday.

Auxiliaries can be combined in a single verb phrase. For example, a verb phrase may consist of a **modal** + a form of *have* + a form of *be* + a form of a **main verb**.

  > I *could have been making* a bad mistake by trusting him.
  > Sara *will have been living* in New Mexico for 2 years next month.
  > You *must have been given* the wrong number.

The auxiliary verb, or if there is more than one of them, the first auxiliary verb, performs the following grammatical functions:

- it shows **tense** and is the **finite** part of the verb phrase.

  > I *have* seen it.
  > She *had* seen it.

*She **has** been thinking.*
*She **had** been thinking.*

- it shows **number** and **person** agreement with the subject.

*She **has** seen it.*
*They **have** seen it.*
*I **am** looking for it.*
*You **are** looking for it.*

- it will take any **negative** immediately after it.

*I **do not** want to do that.*
*She **has not** been concentrating.*

- it can come before the subject to make a **question**.

Do you want to help us?
Have you got a cell phone?

Contracted forms

Auxiliaries are very often used in contracted forms. In the case of *be* and *have*, the contracted form can involve linking the subject and the auxiliary verb into a single form, e.g. *I'm, I've, we'd* (*we had* or *we would*), *Sue's* (*Sue has* or *Sue is*).

We're back!
(We are back!)
I've found it.
(I have found it.)
They'd gone when I got there.
(They had gone when I got there.)
Tom's here.
(Tom is here.)

The contracted negative form **auxiliary** + *n't* is common with all the auxiliaries except *am*, e.g. *hasn't, wouldn't, don't*.

> She *isn't* (is not) trying.
> We *don't* (do not) live here.
> He *hasn't* (has not) seen it.
> I *can't* (cannot) come.

In standard English, the contracted form of *am not*, when it is part of a question, is aren't.

> *Aren't* I going to need some matches?
> I'm getting a ride with you, *aren't* I?

- Contracted forms are more informal than full forms. They are therefore more common in spoken English. Full forms are usually preferred in formal written English.

Auxiliaries are used in sentence tags.

> You had only had the carpet a week when the kitchen flooded,
>   *hadn't you?*
> It's Kaydance's birthday on Saturday, *isn't it?*
> You are joking, *aren't you?*

See p. 245 for more about sentence tags.

Auxiliaries are also used to make a short addition to a statement, such as:

- a positive addition to a positive statement, accompanied by so or too.

> I went to the park and Latoya *did too*.
> I loved the movie, and *so did* Fred.

- a negative addition to a negative statement, accompanied by *neither* or *nor*.

> *My dad never eats mussels and **neither do** I.*
> *I don't want to speak to Will now. – **Nor do** I.*
> *I can't understand it. – **Neither can** I.*

- Auxiliaries can be used in positive sentences to give emphasis. When they are emphatic they are never contracted.

> *You **have** made a mess!*
> *That **was** a nice surprise!*
> *I **am** proud of Kara. She's so clever.*

In the present simple tense and the past simple tenses the appropriate form of *do* is used to show emphasis.

> *I **do** like Pedro. – So do I.*
> *We **did** have a great time.*

> An auxiliary on its own can be used to give a short answer to a question. Whatever auxiliary is used in the question is used on its own in the answer. The main verb is not repeated. Short answers are very common in spoken English.
>
> > ***Do** you like avocados? Yes, I **do**. or No, I **don't**.*
> > ***Have** you read anything by Michael Crichton?*
> > *Yes, I **have**.*

Be

The verb *be* is used as an auxiliary verb and it can also be used as a main verb. See p. 32.

The verb *be* is irregular. It has eight different forms: *be*, *am*, *is*, *are*, *was*, *were*, *being*, *been*. The present simple and past simple tenses make more changes than those of other verbs.

I *am* late.	We *are* late.
You *are* late.	You *are* late.
He *is* late.	They *are* late.
I *was* late.	We *were* late.
You *were* late.	You *were* late.
She *was* late.	They *were* late.

The present participle is *being*.

He is *being* very helpful these days.

The past participle is *been*.

We have *been* ready for an hour.

- The present simple tense forms of *be* are often contracted in normal speech. Note that the contracted form of *they are* is spelled *they're*, and not *their*, which is the possessive form of *they*.

I'm here.	We're here.
You're here.	You're here.
He's here.	They're here.

Any form of *be* is made negative by adding *not* immediately after it. In speech, some forms of *be* also have contracted negative forms. Some of these forms emphasize the negative.

	emphasizes the negative
I'm not late. You aren't late. He isn't late. We aren't late. They aren't late.	You're not late. He's not late. We're not late. They're not late.
I wasn't late. You weren't late. He wasn't late. We weren't late. They weren't late.	

The major uses of *be* as an auxiliary verb are to form continuous tenses and the passive.

- **Continuous** tenses of main verbs use the appropriate form of *be*, present or past, followed by the present participle (or *-ing* form). See p. 102 and p. 110.

- The **passive** form of a main verb uses the appropriate form of *be* followed by the past participle. See p. 122.

The verb *be* is also used as a main verb. It is commonly found joining a subject to its complement.

As a **main verb**, *be* is used to talk about:

- Feelings and states. For this we use the simple tenses of the verb with a suitable adjective. See p. 91.

    I am delighted with the news but he is not happy.
    She was busy so she was not able to see me.

- People's behavior. For this we use the continuous tenses of the verb with a suitable adjective. See p. 100.

    I am not being slow, I am being careful.
    You were being very rude to your sister when I came downstairs.

- *Be* + the *to infinitive* is sometimes used to refer to future time. This is a somewhat formal use, which often appears in news reports. See pp. 132–136.

    The President is to visit Japan in October.
    The Archbishop is to have talks with the Pope next month.

- *It* + *be*: we use *it* as a subject when we are talking about time, distance, weather, or cost. In this use, *be* is always singular.

    Hurry up, it's eight thirty!
    Is it? I didn't know it was so late.

    It's thirty miles to Great Falls from here.
    Come and visit us. It's not very far.

    It's cold today but it isn't wet.

    It's very expensive to live in Boston.

- *There* + *is/are* is used to talk about something existing. In this use, the form that *be* takes may *be* singular or plural, depending on the number of the noun, and *be* is sometimes contracted.

    There's a spare toothbrush in the medicine cabinet.
    There was a cold wind blowing.
    There isn't enough gas for the trip.
    There are several gas stations on the way, aren't there?

To make the continuous tenses of the main verb *be* we have to use *be* twice, once as an auxiliary and once as a main verb.

> You *are being* so annoying!
> I know I *am being* childish, but I'm scared.

The question form of clauses with the verb *be* in them is made by putting the appropriate form of *be* right in front of the subject.

> *Are you* better now?
> *Is he* free this morning?
> *Was he* cooking dinner when you arrived?

Have

The verb *have* is used as an auxiliary verb –

> *She **has** finished writing her dissertation.*
> *Karl **had** read about the concert in the newspaper.*

and also as a main verb. See p. 28.

> *She is **having** a massage at the moment.*
> *The driver has **had** his breakfast, so we can go.*

The verb *have* has these forms: *have*, *has*, *having*, *had*. The base form of the verb is *have*. The present participle is *having*. The past tense and past participle form is *had*.

- The present and past forms are often contracted in speech, especially when *have* is being used as an auxiliary verb.

  The contracted forms are:

have = **'ve**	I*'ve* seen the governor.
has = **'s**	He*'s* gone on vacation.
	Jan*'s* behaved badly.
had = **'d**	You*'d* better go home.
	Jake*'d* left them behind.

> The form *have* contracts to *'ve*. This can sound rather like *of*, especially after other auxiliary verbs.
>
> > *She **would've** given you something to eat.*
> > *You **could've** stayed the night with us.*
> > *If he'd asked, I **might've** lent him my car.*
>
> Avoid the common mistake of writing *of* in sentences like the ones above.

As an **auxiliary** verb, *have* is used to make the **perfect tenses** of main verbs.

The **perfect** tenses of main verbs use the appropriate form of *have*, present or past, followed by the past participle. See pp. 106–113.

> *I **have read** some really good books over the holidays.*
> *I **had seen** that episode before.*

The negative of a clause containing a compound verb with *have* is made by adding *not* or another negative word immediately after the appropriate form of *have*. In speech, some forms of *have* also have contracted negative forms.

> *I **have never seen** such luxury.*
> *Rachel **had not been** overseas before.*
> *She **had hardly had** time to eat when Paul arrived.*

- Present tense and past tense forms that emphasize the negative element:

  I/we/you/they**'ve not**;   he/she/it**'s not**
  I/we/you/he/she/it /they**'d not**

  > *She**'s not** told me about it yet.*
  > *We**'ve not** been here before.*
  > *They**'d not** seen him for weeks.*

- Present tense and past tense negative forms that are used less emphatically:

  I/we/you/they **haven't**;   he/she/it **hasn't**
  I/we/you/he/she/it /they **hadn't**

  > *He **hasn't** found anywhere to stay on this trip.*
  > *We **haven't** been here before.*
  > *They **hadn't** looked very hard, in my opinion.*

As a **main verb**, *have* is used to talk about:

- states or conditions, such as possession or relationship.

- In these senses, continuous tenses are not used in standard English. With this meaning *have* is sometimes used alone, adding only *not* to make negatives, and adding nothing to make questions.

    > *I **have** something for you.*
    > *We **haven't** any reason not to attend.*
    > ***Have** you no sense of shame?*
    > *The driver **has had** his breakfast, so we can go.*
    > *We **had** a good time.*

It is also often used with forms of *do* to make negatives and questions.

> ***Do** you **have** a pen?*
> ***Does** she **have** my umbrella?*
> *She **doesn't have** any brothers or sisters.*
> ***Do** you **have** time to see me now?*

- **Have got** is an informal form of this main verb use of *have*, often used in speaking.

    > *I **haven't got** any brothers or sisters.*
    > ***Has** she **got** my umbrella? – Yes, she **has**.*
    > *She **hasn't got** any money.*

Notice that the participle is *got*, not *gotten* for this meaning (i.e, to show possession).

- activities, including those such as eating, and leisure.

This meaning of *have* sometimes uses continuous tenses. For simple tenses, negatives and questions are formed using one of the forms of *do*.

> *He was having a seizure when I phoned.*
> *I'm having lunch at twelve o'clock.*
> *Come and have a sandwich with me,*
> *No thanks. I don't usually have lunch.*
> *He's having a difficult day.*
> *Did you have a good vacation?*

Contractions and weak forms are not possible with this meaning. *Have got* is also not used with this meaning.

- to express obligation or necessity using *have to* or *have got to*.

> *I've got to go now, I'm afraid.*
> *Do you have to leave so soon?*
> *Have you got to leave so soon?*
> *The package has to go out today.*
> *The package has got to go out today.*

When *have* is a main verb, it makes perfect forms like all other main verbs. This means that it is possible to use *have* twice in present or past perfect sentences, once as an auxiliary verb and once as a main verb.

> *We have had enough, thank you.*
> *They had already had several warnings.*

Do

The verb *do* is used as an auxiliary verb.

I do not want it.	*We do not want it.*
You do not want it.	*You do not want it.*
He does not want it.	*They do not want it.*

I did not want it.	*We did not want it.*
You did not want it.	*You did not want it.*
She did not want it.	*They did not want it.*

Do can also be used as a main verb. See p. 32. When *do* is used as an auxiliary verb it is a **supporting verb**. Because a main verb cannot combine directly with negatives or make questions, *do* is used to support the main verb.

> *Don't talk!*
> *Don't run!*

It is also used to stand in for another verb to avoid repetition, as shown on p. 43.

The verb *do* is irregular. It has five different forms: *do*, *does*, *doing*, *did*, *done*. The base form of the verb is *do*. The past simple form, *did*, is the same for all persons, singular and plural. The present participle is *doing*. The past participle is *done*.

The present simple tense *do* and the past simple tense *did* can be used as an auxiliary verb. As an auxiliary, *do* is not used with **modal** verbs.

I do not want it.	*We do not want it.*
You do not want it.	*You do not want it.*
He does not want it.	*They do not want it.*

I *did* not want it.	We *did* not want it.
You *did* not want it.	You *did* not want it.
She *did* not want it.	They *did* not want it.

As an **auxiliary** verb *do* is used in the following ways:

- to help make the negative and question forms of present simple and past simple tenses.

> Oh dear, I **didn't feed** the cat this morning.
> **Do** you **know** what time it is?
> **Did** Tim **pay** for his ticket last night?

- to make the negative form of a command.

> **Don't** talk!
> **Don't** run!

- to make a command more persuasive. See p. 249.

> **Do** let me see it!

- to avoid repeating a main verb in additions, commands, sentence tags, and short answers.

> They go to the movies often, **and so do** we.

> Don't run on the road! Don't **do** it!

> You live in Sioux Falls, **don't** you?

> Do you play baseball? – No, I **don't**.
> Did they tell you the news? – Yes, they **did**.
> Jim likes jazz, I think. Yes, **he does**.

– in comparisons when the verb in the first clause is in a simple tense.

> She *sings* better than I *do*.

The positive forms of *do* cannot be contracted. In speech, the negative has contracted forms.

> I *don't* (do not) agree with you.
> She *doesn't* (does not) live here now.
> They *didn't* (did not) buy any food.

- Present tense negative forms:
  I/we/you/they *don't*; he/she/it *doesn't*

- Past tense negative form:
  I/we/you/he/she/it/they *didn't*

When *do* is a main verb, it has a range of meanings that includes *carry out*, *perform*, *deal with*, or *provide*. It is sometimes used in place of a more specific verb.

> I'll *do* the lawn now.
> (I'll *mow* the lawn now.)
> I'll *do* your hair.
> (I'll *arrange* your hair.)
> We don't *do* wedding receptions.
> (We don't *provide* wedding receptions.)

It is then used with the full range of tenses and forms. See also p. 97.

> *Are* you *doing* your homework?
> You *have been doing* well this semester.
> She *had done* enough, so she stopped.
> This *has been done* before.

The main verb use of *do* can be used to talk about:

- habits.

  > I *do* the dishes every evening.
  > This is what I usually *do*.

- behavior.

  > He *did* something pretty stupid.
  > I *didn't do* anything wrong.
  > What *are* you *doing*?

- plans.

  > What *are* you *doing* on Sunday?

As a main verb, *do* makes negatives and questions like all other main verbs:

- in the present simple tense with auxiliary *do*.

  > What *does* he *do* for a living?
  > *Do* I *do* it this way?
  > No, you *don't do* it like that at all.

- in the past simple tense with auxiliary *did*.

  > *Did* Hank *do* it, then?
  > *Didn't* Hank *do* it, then?
  > He *didn't do* it, you know.

This means that it is possible to use *do* twice in negative and interrogative sentences; once as an auxiliary verb and once as a main verb.

- As a main verb, *do* can be used with modal verbs.

    *They **will do** it for you, if you ask nicely.*
    *I **can do** it, but I **shouldn't do** it.*

Modal verbs

Modal verbs are a particular kind of **auxiliary**.

>*Look, I can do it! – Oh yes! So you can.*
>*Can I use your phone? – Of course you can.*
>*Do you think she will come? – I'm sure she will.*
>*I must get our tickets today.*

Modal verbs are used when you need to add special elements of meaning to a main verb, e.g.:

- to express different degrees of doubt and possibility about the action of the main verb.

>*I may not be able to do it.*
>*I think that I might have caught your cold.*
>*I could ask for you, if you like.*
>*You couldn't do it, could you?*

- to express degrees of future possibility, ranging from the definite future, *will*, to the possible future, *may*, and the conditional future, *could*.

>*You will be seeing her on Friday at Jackie's house.*
>*I may be late coming home tomorrow evening.*
>*I could bring some more bread home with me tonight.*

- to request or give permission for an action to take place.

>*May I come in?*
>*You can borrow my car tonight if you like.*

- to prohibit or discourage something, when used with a negative.

>*You shouldn't use this computer without permission.*
>*You cannot borrow my car tonight.*
>*He must not see this letter.*

- to speculate.

> *The weather's so bad the flight* **could** *be late.*
> *It* **might** *be all over by the time we get there.*
> *He* **may** *be really angry about all this.*

- to express obligation, necessity, or duty.

> *I* **must** *turn in my essay today.*
> *The clutch* **must** *be disengaged to start the engine.*
> *Helen* **ought to** *tell the truth.*

- to refer to typical behavior.

> *She* **can** *be very helpful on occasions like this.*

- to add politeness to a request that might otherwise sound abrupt.

> **Would you** *please close the door?*

- to make conditional sentences (see p. 276).

- in reported speech (see p. 282).

Modals can refer to a time range that reaches from the immediate present to some future time, so that they can all be used for future reference, especially when they are used with a time adverbial. See pp. 114–121.

> *You* **will be seeing** *her* **on Friday** *at Jackie's house.*
> *I* **may be** *late coming home* **tomorrow evening***.*
> *I* **could bring** *some more bread home with me* **tonight***.*

Some modals can refer to a time range that goes back from the immediate present to some indefinite past time. They can refer to habitual action when they are used with a time adverbial.

> *When I was little, I* **would** *ride my bike around and around the lawn.*

Form

Unlike other verbs, modal verbs have only one form, the **base form**, and only one tense, the present simple.

> You **will** be seeing her **on Friday** at Jackie's house.
> I **may** be late home **tomorrow evening**.
> I **might** go to visit Grandma **on Saturday**.

They do not have a **to** infinitive. They have no -s inflection in the 3rd person singular.

> **He will** be seeing her on Friday.
> **She may** be late coming home.

- Since modal verbs do not have past tense forms, you have to use other verbs to provide some of the modal meanings in the past. For example, past necessity is expressed by **had to** instead of **must**.

> I **must** visit Aunt May today.
> I **had to** visit Aunt May yesterday.

- The modals **shall** and **will** are usually contracted to **'ll** in spoken English. All the negative forms can be contracted to form a single word such as **can't**, **won't**, **wouldn't**. These contracted forms are common in both spoken and written English.

> I will/shall = **I'll**
> We will/shall = **we'll**
> You **mustn't** say things like that, Jane.
> John **can't** come to my party.

There are other contracted forms such as **he'll**, **we'll**, and **they'll**, that are common in spoken English but less common in written English.

- Several verbs act as modals sometimes and as full main verbs at other times. These are called **semimodal verbs**. Their forms vary depending on whether they are used modally or as a main verb.

> How *dare* he!
> He **dared** to ask me to do his laundry!
> She *need*n't come if that's how she feels.
> Monica **needs** a new raincoat.

Position

Modals come before any other auxiliary verb or main verb in the verb phrase.

- Modal verbs are followed by the **base form** of the verb if there is no other auxiliary verb present.

> Yes, you *can borrow* those earrings tonight.
> You *should try* that new restaurant in town.
> You *must come* over again some time.

If one of the auxiliary verbs *have* or *be* follows the modal verb, the main verb will take the appropriate present or past participle form.

> I *may have upset* him.
> You *could have looked* for it yourself.
> Janice *might be coming* too.
> Sunita *will have been worried* about her, I imagine.

- In negative sentences, *not* comes immediately after the modal verb and in front of all the other verbs.

> They *may not wait* for you if you're late.
> He *must not be* disturbed after 9 o'clock.

- *Can* cannot be combined with the auxiliary form *have*, but the negative form *can't* can be combined with *have*.

  They *can't have seen* him.   **but not** *They can have seen him*

Can and could

Both these verbs indicate ability in some respect. The use of *could* is usual in clauses that contain a reference to past time, and in these cases it may be helpful to think of *could* as the past form of *can*.

> *Morry can speak French quite well now.*
> *I couldn't play chess two years ago, but I can now.*

> *When I was younger I could play tennis really well.*
> *Winston is so strong he can lift me right off my feet.*
> *Can you get up the stairs without help?*
> *You can come over for dinner whenever you like.*

Can and *could* are used:

– to indicate that you know how to do something.

> *Mary can solve these equations.*
> *I couldn't draw very well when I was younger.*

– to show ability to do something. (Compared with *be able to*, *can* indicates ability in a more general way that includes "is allowed to.")

> *When I was younger I could ski really well.*
> *Greg can run ten miles in 25 minutes.*
> *Are you able to walk to the car?*

– to make polite requests or to ask for permission:

Could is more tentative than *can*. (Compare with *may*, which is more formal.)

> *Can I borrow the car tomorrow evening, Mom?*
> *Could I come with you on the trip?*
> *May I take this book home with me?*

– to express the possibility of an action in the future, especially when the possibility is related to plans or projects. (Compare with *may*, where the possibility referred to is still uncertain and in the future.)

> We *can* go to Paris next week since you are free.
> We *could* go to Paris next week if you are free.
> We *may* go to Paris, but it depends on our finances.

– to express the possibility of an action in the present.

> You *can* dive off these rocks; it is safe here.
> We *could* dive off the rocks, but we have to be careful.

– to talk about actions that were possible but did not happen, using *could* + the perfect form of *have*.

> Mariel *could have stopped* the fight but she didn't.

– using the perfect form of *have*, to speculate about actions that have recently taken place.

> Who *could/can have broken* the window?
> Who *would have guessed* that they were related?

A distinction between *can* and *could* is observed in conditionals. *Could* is used when the conditions are not met.

> If Louisa is coming, she *can* look after the children for a while.
> If Helen had more money, she *could* buy a computer.

When changing sentences from direct to reported speech *can* is usually changed to *could*.

> Bernard said, "I *can* do it for you, Stu."
> Bernard said that he *could* do it for Stu.

can
The negative form is: *cannot*.

> *I cannot understand why he did it.*

The contracted negative form is: *can't*.

> *I can't help it.*

could
The contracted negative form is: *couldn't*.

> *I couldn't help it.*

May and might

Both *may* and *might* can be used in requests and in expressions of possibility for the present and future.

> *Might I ask you your name?*

> *The weather **may/might** be better tomorrow.*
> *Craig **may/might** know his results soon.*
> *We **may/might** go to the movies tonight.*
> *"**May** I come with you?" Nicky asked.*

May and *might* are used as follows:

– *May* is used to ask permission in a more formal way than *can*.

> ***May** I have a drink, please?*
> ***May** I use your ruler? I've lost mine.*

Might is occasionally used in formal situations.

> ***Might** I suggest a different solution?*

– *May* is used to give permission, particularly when applied to *you*, *he*, *she*, *they* or a proper noun, to show that the speaker is allowing something to happen.

> *You **may** go now.*
> *Users **may** download forms from this website.*

– Both *may* and *might* are used to express the possibility of some future action; *might* is less certain than *may*.

> *The weather **may/might** be better tomorrow.*
> *Craig **may/might** know his results soon.*
> *We **may/might** go to the movies tonight.*

- *May* is often used for politeness, to make an order appear as a request; *might* is used to make the speaker less personally involved with the request.

> You **might** give that idea a bit more consideration.
> You **might** want to move a bit closer to the screen.

- *Might* is occasionally used when someone is trying to persuade another person to do something, perhaps with some degree of irritation. This use is a little old-fashioned.

> You **might** give me some cake too, Luke.
> Anna, come on, you **might** tell me what he said!

• When *might* is used in a conditional sentence, the *if* clause can be in the present or the past tense. Compare with *could*. See p. 62.

> If Lakesha **comes**, she **might** look after the children.
> If Lakesha **came**, she **might** look after the children.

When changing sentences from direct to reported speech may usually becomes *could*.

> "**May** I come with you?" Nicky asked.
> Nicky asked if she **could** come with them.

may
The contracted negative form is: **mayn't**

(Archaic only; not used in contemporary American English).

might
The contracted negative form is: **mightn't**.

> It **mightn't** be so hard to explain.
> **Mightn't** there be a better way to do this?

Must

Must is used to express obligation and necessity, and to give orders in a formal way. It can only be used for present and future reference. When the past is involved, you use *have to*.

Must is used:

- to express obligation.

    All students must bring a packed lunch tomorrow.

- to express necessity.

    The key must be inserted before you press the switch.

- to give orders firmly.

    You must go to sleep now.

- to speculate about the truth of something.

    She must be mad!
    You must be joking!
    There must be some mistake.
    Mr. Robertson is here; it must be Tuesday.

When this sort of statement is made in the negative or interrogative, *can* is used instead.

    Can Mary be joking? Can she really mean that?
    You can't be serious!
    It can't be true!

- *Must* can be used in the interrogative, but many speakers use *have to* instead.

  Must you go so soon?
  Must I invite Helen?
  Do you have to go soon?
  Do I have to invite Helen?

You can use *must* with a negative:

- to forbid someone to do something.

  You must not cross when the light is red.
  Passengers must not leave baggage unattended.

- to talk about an event or state that is unacceptable.

  There mustn't be any mistakes in your letter.
  The whale must not become extinct.

> Note that to express the fact that you are not obligated to do something, you use *do not have to*.
>
> Compare:
>
> *You must not come in here (you are forbidden).*
> *You don't have to come in here (if you don't want to).*

- It is necessary to change *must* to *have to* when changing sentences from direct to reported speech.

  "I must fill out those forms this evening," said Janos.
  Janos said that he had to fill out some forms.

must
The contracted negative form is: *mustn't*.

> You *mustn't* worry so much.

Shall and will

The normal way to express simple future time in English is using the modal verb *will* followed by the **base form** of a main verb.

> The modal verb *shall* is not used very much in modern spoken English, except in suggestions or offers of help.
>
> *Shall I help you?*
> *Shall I cook supper?*
> *Shall we go to the movies tonight?*

A distinction between *will* and *shall* is difficult to make in spoken English, since the contracted form, *'ll*, is used to mean both *shall* and *will*.

Shall is used:

— with questions involving *I* and *we* when the speaker is making a suggestion or offering help.

> *Shall I help you?*
> *Shall I cook supper?*
> *Shall we go to the movies tonight?*

— in many legal and formal contexts where authority is implied or where there is a legal obligation.

> **All visitors** *shall leave the park by 9 p.m.*
> **Both parties** *shall give three days' notice of any change in terms.*

Because *shall* was used frequently in earlier times, it still appears in many older texts that people memorize, such as poems, hymns, and nursery rhymes.

Will is used:

– with *I* and *we* to show intentions and to make promises.

> *Don't worry. I **won't** be late.*
> *We **will** be in touch.*
> *I **will** try to ensure that you get a good room.*

– with *you, he, she, it,* and *they,* to give reassurances.

> *Helen **won't** be late.*
> *He **will** be well treated.*
> *You **will** have your money next week.*

– to insist on something. Full forms are normally used, and are stressed in speech.

> *You **will** do what I tell you!*
> *Janet **will** go to Mary's even if I have to carry her there.*

– to make polite requests and to give invitations.

> ***Will** you help me look for my purse?*
> ***Will** you come to lunch on Friday?*

– to give orders.

> *You **will** finish your work before you watch TV, **won't** you?*
> *Luke, **will** you please be quiet!*

– to show prediction.

> *The match **will** be finished by now.*
> *I think it **will** probably rain tomorrow.*

– to show that someone persists in doing something. This use requires the full form with stress and is somewhat literary or old-fashioned.

> Oh! Tony **will** keep bumping me when I'm trying to write!
> No wonder you feel sick. You **will** eat chocolate all day long.

will
The contracted form is: **'ll**.

> He**'ll** be home soon.

The contracted negative form is: **won't**.

> Eve **won't** speak to Harriet.

shall
The contracted form is: **'ll**.

The contracted negative form is: **shan't**.

> I **shan't** say a word.

(Used mainly in British English; extremely rare in American English.)

Should

The modal verb *should* is used in the following ways:

- to talk about moral obligation. Compare *ought to* on p. 77.

  > They **should** do what you suggest.
  > People **should** report this sort of thing to the police.
  > She suggested we **should** visit Irene more often.
  > Rob insisted that we **should** think of others before ourselves.

- to give advice or instructions.

  > You **should** undo the top screws first.
  > You **should** keep your credit card separate from your checkbook.

- to suggest that something is probably true, though you have no way of knowing for sure.

  > They left here at 6 o'clock, so they **should** be home now.
  > The cherries **should** be in bloom when we arrive.

- to show politeness in a conditional clause. This use occurs in formal written communication.

  > If you **should** decide to go, please contact us.
  > **Should** you need more information, please call the manager.

- *Should* can be used with the main verb after certain set expressions such as *it is a pity that, it is odd that, I am sorry/surprised that*. This is a more formal use than the same expression without *should*, or than the same expression with *would*.

  > It's a pity that this **should** happen.
  > I was quite surprised that he **should** be doing a job like that.

- *Should* + the perfect form of the main verb can be used to express regret about something that was done or not done. Compare with *ought to*.

  > He *should have stopped* at the red light.
  > You *should have told* me you were ill.

- When changing sentences from direct to reported speech, *should* does not change.

  > Anna said that I *should* try to relax more.

In British English, *should* is sometimes used with *I* or *we* in conditional clauses, instead of the more common *would*.

> I *should* love to visit Peru *if I had the money*.
> We *should* hate to miss the play.

In this sense, *would* is more common in modern spoken English and the only form used in American English.

> I *would* love to visit Peru.
> We *would* hate to miss the play.

should
The contracted negative form is: *shouldn't*.

Would

The modal verb *would* is commonly used as follows:

– to make a polite request.

> *Would you mind moving your bag?*
> *Would you give me a hand with this ladder, please?*

– to offer something politely.

> *Would you **like** some tea or coffee?*

– together with *like* as a polite form of *want*.

> *We **would like** to see Mr. Brown now, please.*
> *My friends **would like** to see your garden.*

– to refer to habitual activity in the past, with the meaning of *used to*.

> *I remember Jeff; he **would** watch TV all day if you let him.*
> *Jessica was a kind girl; she **would** always go out of her way to help people.*

– to show that someone persisted in an activity in the past: ***would*** is sometimes stressed here.

> *John **would** keep nagging at her, though I asked him not to.*
> *She **would** go on and on until I lost my temper.*

– to express and ask about probability.

> *I saw a girl at the window. Who **would** that be?*
> *Oh, that **would** be his elder sister!*

- in conditional clauses, usually together with an **if** clause.

> *I **would** have taken it if it had been available.*
> *If you offered me some more I **wouldn't** refuse.*
> *Brian **would** have phoned the police if it he'd seen the accident.*

When changing sentences from direct speech to reported speech, **will** is usually changed to **would**.

> *Anna said, "Raymond **will** help you."*
> *Anna said that Raymond **would** help us.*
> *James said, "The car **won't** start!"*
> *James said that the car **wouldn't** start.*

would
The contracted form is: **'d**.

> *I'd have done it too, given the chance.*
> *We'd like to look at the garden.*
> *He'd be very angry if he knew about it.*

The contracted negative form is: **wouldn't**.

> *Even if he'd known about it, he **wouldn't** have been angry.*

Ought to

The use of *ought to* is similar to *should*, but it is not used as widely. It is usually more informal than should.

Like *should*, the verb *ought to* does not have a past form.

Ought to isn't typically used in questions and negatives, but there are some exceptions in formal and very informal language.

In negatives, *not* comes between *ought* and *to*. In questions, the subject comes between *ought* and *to*. This use is formal.

> I *ought not to* have said those things to her.
> *Ought we to* make such a sacrifice for the benefit of future
> generations?

The negative form *oughtn't* is used by some speakers; it is considered informal. When *oughtn't* is used, it does not always require *to* before the infinitive.

> I *oughtn't to* have said those things to her.
> You *oughtn't* be so friendly to strangers.
> *Oughtn't* we call first to see if they're open?

Ought to is used as follows:

- to express an obligation or an expectation that someone should do something.

> You *ought to* listen carefully.
> We *ought to* leave now.
> Linda *ought to* go by herself.
> People *ought to* be a bit nicer to us.

– to express the likelihood of something happening.

> *Anup **ought to** be here by now.*
> *The journey **ought to** take about 2 hours.*

– *Ought to* + *have* + **past participle of main verb** is used to express regret that something was not done or to reproach someone for doing or not doing something.

> *I **ought to have spoken up** earlier. I'm sorry.*
> *You **ought to have offered** to help.*
> *They **oughtn't to have told** us everything was taken care of.*

● In questions and negatives, *should* is frequently used instead of *ought to* because it sounds more natural.

> *__Ought I to__ report it to someone in authority?*
> *__Should I__ report it to someone in authority?*
> *__Ought we to__ make a start?*
> *__Should we__ make a start?*

ought to
The contracted negative form is: *__oughtn't (to)__*. It is used informally.

> *Oh dear, we **oughtn't to** have let that happen.*
> *Well then she ought to do something about it, **oughtn't** she?*

Dare and need

The two verbs *dare* and *need* have characteristics of both modal verbs and main verbs. Because of this, they are called **semimodals**. They sometimes behave like modal verbs and do not add *-s* to the form that goes with **he**, **she**, and **it**. This means that they have no 3rd person singular inflection. They are then followed by the **base form** of a main verb.

> *Need I say more?*
> *Dare I ask how the project's going?*

The past form *needed* is not used as a modal; *dared* is occasionally used as a modal.

The modal uses of these verbs are all **negatives** or **questions**.

> *Where will you all be today? –* **Need** *you ask?*
> *You* **needn't** *come if you're busy.*
> *Dare I suggest that we start a sign-up sheet?*
> *I* **dare not** *tell him the truth; he'll go crazy.*

Questions using these verbs are often set expressions such as *Need I/ you ask?, Dare I suggest...?* and *Need I/we say more?*

Dare and *need* sometimes behave like main verbs with *-s* inflection. In this case they are followed by the *to* infinitive. They can also use the auxiliary *do* and have the whole range of tenses appropriate to a main verb.

> *Lisa* **doesn't need to know**.
> *Does Paul* **need to go** *now?*
> *Paul* **needs to go**.
> **Dare to be** *different!*
> *They* **don't dare to mention** *it to him.*

When *dare* or *need* are used as modal verbs in a positive **statement**, there must be a word of negative meaning in the same clause. This word can be outside the verb phrase and may be a word with a negative sense, such as *only*, *never*, *hardly*.

> He *need only* ask and I will tell him.
> *No* sensible driver *dare* risk that chance.

As a modal verb, *dare* has forms as follows:

I *dare* not *go*.	I *dared* not *go*.	I *didn't dare go*. (informal)
He *dare* not *go*.	He *dared* not *go*.	He *didn't dare go*. (informal)

Dare I *do* it?
Dare he *do* it?

As a main verb, *dare* has forms as follows:

I *dare to do* it.	I *do* not *dare to do* it.
He *dares to do* it.	He *did* not *dare to do* it.
He *does* not *dare to do* it.	*Does* he *dare to do* it?
He *doesn't dare to do* it.	*Doesn't* he *dare to do* it?

As a modal verb, *need* has forms as follows:

I *need* not *go*.	*Need* I *go*?
He *need* not *go*.	*Need* he *go*?
He *needn't* go.	*Needn't* he *go*?

As a main verb, *need* has forms as follows:

I *need* it.	I *need to do* it.
He *needs* it.	He *needs to do* it.
I *do* not *need to go*.	I *do* not *need to do* it.
He *does* not *need to go*.	*Does* he *need to go*?

- Either of the two forms of *dare* and *need* can be used for sentences that have the same meaning.

> *Anna **didn't dare to jump** off the high fence.*
> *Anna **dared not jump** off the high fence.*
> *You **don't need to come** if you don't want to.*
> *You **needn't come** if you don't want to.*

Used to

The verb *used to* is a "marginal" modal verb. Unlike the other modal verbs, it is only found in the past tense. Therefore, when it is used with *do* to make negatives and questions, the form of the auxiliary verb is always *did*.

Used to is used as follows:

- to describe an activity or a state that happened many times in the past. For positive sentences the meaning is similar to the use of *would* for habitual past actions, as described on page 58.

   *Gerry always **used to** go for a run before breakfast.*
   *Peter **didn't use to** say things like that when I knew him.*

- to refer to an activity or state that was true in the past but is no longer true.

   *I **used to** like rock climbing when I was younger.*
   *You **didn't use to** be so stressed!*

Used to takes the following forms:

- the form *used to* is used with all subjects e.g., *I, we, you, he, she, it, they.*

I *used to*	We *used to*
You *used to*	You *used to*
She *used to*	They *used to*

   *I **used to** live in New Jersey.*
   *He **used to** deliver newspapers but he owns the paper now.*
   *Nancy and Bill **used to** live in California.*

There are two forms for a negative:

– *did not/didn't use to.*

> *We **didn't use to** have indoor plumbing when I was a child.*
> *Alan **did not use to** like children, but it's different now that he has his own.*

– *used not to.*

> *I **used not to** be able to watch myself on TV at all.*
> *We **used not to** worry much about money.*

To form a question, use *did* + **subject** + *use to* + **base form**:
i.e., *did he use to...?*

> *Did they **use to** visit you often? – Well, Mary **used to**.*

The contracted negative form is *didn't use to*.

> Do not confuse *used to* + **base form** with *be used to* +
> **present participle**, where *used to* means *accustomed to*.
>
> > *They lived in India for a long time, so they **are used
> > to eating** spicy food.*

Phrasal verbs

A **phrasal verb** is a type of verb that is created when a main verb is combined with either:

– an **adverb**,

>   *take off*   *give in*
>   *blow up*   *break down*

– a **preposition**,

>   *get at (someone)*   *pick on (someone)*

– or an **adverb** + **preposition**,

>   *put up with (something)*   *get out of (doing something)*

Type A. Verb plus adverb

Some Type A phrasal verbs have no object, i.e., they are **intransitive**. They make sense without any further addition to the verb.

>   *Mary went away.*
>   *Helen sat down.*
>   *The students came back.*

Others require an object, i.e., they are **transitive**.

>   *We could make out a figure in the distance.*
>   *He tried to blow up the aircraft.*
>   *Could you put your clothes away, please?*

If the object is a **noun**, many Type A phrasal verbs will allow the adverb to come either:

–   before the object,

>   I *picked up* Jim *on my way home.*
>   He *blew out* the candle.
>   She *put away* her things.

–   or after the object.

>   I *picked* Jim *up on my way home.*
>   He *blew* the candle *out.*
>   She *put* her things *away.*

If the object is a **pronoun**, it must come before the adverb.

>   I *picked* him *up.*
>   He *blew* it *out.*
>   She *put* them *away.*

Sometimes you can guess the meaning of these verbs from the meanings of the parts.

>   to *sit down* = sit + down
>   to *go away* = go + away

Sometimes you have to learn the new meanings, or use a dictionary.

to **make up** (an answer)	= invent
to **turn down** (an invitation)	= decline
to **work out** (a problem)	= solve
to **put up** (a visitor)	= accommodate

Type B. Verb plus preposition

Type B phrasal verbs always have an object. This is because prepositions always have an object.

> *He asked for* the check.
> *He asked for* it.
> *She listened to* the doctor.
> *She listened to* her.
> *They referred to* our conversation.
> *They referred to* it.

Sometimes there are two objects: the object of the verb and the object of the preposition.

> *He asked* the waiter *for* the check.

Type C. Verb plus adverb and preposition

Type C phrasal verbs are a combination of the two previous kinds of verb. All the parts of a Type C phrasal verb come before the object.

> *We are looking forward to* our vacation/it.
> *Don't put up with* bad behavior/it.
> *You must look out for* the warning signs/them.

- It is sometimes hard to tell adverbs and prepositions apart, because often the same word can be both a preposition and an adverb, depending on how it is used. For further information about prepositions see p. 220.

The following are examples of the three types of phrasal verb that are explained on p. 84.

Type A

Phrasal verbs made from a verb plus an adverb may be intransitive (do not take an object) or transitive (take an object).

some phrasal verbs that do not take an object	*some phrasal verbs that do take an object*
to break down	to blow something up
to carry on	to break something off
to fall down	to bring a child up
to get about	to bring a subject up
to get up	to call something off
to give up	to clear something up
to go away	to close something down
to go off	to give something up
to go out	to leave something out
to grow up	to make something up
to hold on	to pick someone up

Type B

Phrasal verbs made from a verb plus a preposition are all transitive.

to add to something	to hope for something
to agree with someone	to insist on something
to apply for something	to laugh at something
to approve of something	to listen to something
to arrive at something	to live for something
to ask for something	to look for something
to believe in something	to look into something
to belong to someone	to pay for something
to call on someone	to refer to something
to care for someone	to rely on someone
to come across something	to run into someone
to deal with something	to run over something

Some Type B verbs are doubly transitive, since both the verb and the preposition can have an object.

> to **add** insult **to** injury
> to **ask** a first responder **for** help
> to **check** your answers **with** the teacher
> to **pay** the clerk **for** your groceries
> to **refer** a customer **to** the manager

Type C

Phrasal verbs with an adverb plus a preposition all take a prepositional object.

to put up with something	to keep away from something
to carry on with something	to look back on something
to catch up with something	to look forward to something
to check up on something	to look out for something
to come up with something	to look up to someone
to cut down on something	to make up for something
to do away with something	to put in for something
to face up to something	to run away with something
to fall back on something	to run out of something
to get along with someone	to run up against something
to get out of something	to stand up for something
to go back on something	to walk out on someone
to go in for something	to watch out for something
to break in on someone	to lead up to something

Tense

Time reference

Verb forms help us make reference to time through their **tense**. Tense shows whether an action or a state took place in the past or takes place in the present.

> Jessica **works** at the post office.
> Laurence **worked** at the post office over the Christmas holidays.

English has two **simple tenses** and six **compound tenses**.

Simple tenses

Verbs in simple tenses consist of a single word.

There is a **present simple** tense

I like	I live
you like	you live
he likes	he lives

and a **past simple** tense.

I liked	I lived
you liked	you lived
he liked	he lived

The simple tenses of regular verbs

The **present tense** is the same as the **base form** of the verb, except that an -s is added to the verb when it has a noun or *he*, *she*, or *it* as a subject. This is called the 3rd person singular form.

> *he/she/it likes*
> *he/she/it lives*

The **past tense** of a regular verb is made from the **base form** of the verb with -*ed* (or -*d* if the verb already ends in -*e*) added. The spelling is the same for all persons.

> *I liked*   *I lived*
> *you liked*   *you lived*
> *he liked*   *he lived*

The simple tenses of irregular verbs

Most irregular verbs make the **present tense** from the **base form** of the verb just as regular verbs do.

> Present
> *I find*   *I go*
> *you find*   *you go*
> *he/she/it finds* *he/she/it goes*

- Irregular verbs make the **past tense** in a number of different ways. Sometimes the past tense is a completely different word. See pp. 36–38 for more on irregular verbs.

> Past
> *I found*   *I went*
> *you found*   *you went*
> *he/she/it found* *he/she/it went*

Aspect

When we use a verb, we often need to refer to more than the time at which an event took place. We sometimes need to refer to actions and states as completed or not completed. **Aspect** describes the way we think of verbal actions.

The **continuous aspect** is formed by using the appropriate form of the auxiliary be together with the *-ing* form (**present participle**) of the main verb.

We use **continuous aspect** to show that an action:

– is going on at the time of speaking.

> *I'm eating dinner just now. Can I call you back?*
> *I know what you are doing!*
> *Look! Someone's walking around in our driveway!*

– was going on throughout the time that you are referring to.

> *I was eating dinner when he called.*
> *I was waiting for her when she came out of the classroom.*
> *We were driving home when we saw the accident.*

– will be going on at the time that you are referring to.

> *We're going to Tennessee for vacation next year.*
> *They're coming to us for Christmas this year.*

The **perfect aspect** is formed by using the appropriate form of the auxiliary *have* together with the *-ed* form (**past participle**) of the main verb.

We use **perfect aspect** to show that an action:

- is complete at the time of speaking.

  I've finished the book. It was great.
  We've enjoyed having you all to stay.
  Jo has borrowed the book, so I can't look at it now.

- was complete at the time you are referring to.

  I had forgotten my promise to Aunt Jane.
  Sharon had lost her key, so she had to wait outside.
  Sue had seen the film three times already.

- began in the past and continues in the present. This usage is for verbs that show states or conditions rather than single actions.

  I've lived with diabetes since childhood.
  She's never appreciated country and western music.
  Jill has kept all of Grandma's old photos.

> It is possible to have a compound tense that shows both aspects, continuous and perfect.
>
> *Peter has been talking about you a lot recently.*
> *We had been waiting for 20 minutes and then three buses came.*

Compound tenses

The compound tenses are a combination of present or past **tense** (shown through an auxiliary verb) with continuous or perfect **aspect**. See also pp. 91–92.

> I'm *doing* my homework at the moment, so I can't come out.
> Ben *has seen* the camera that he wants.
> She *was listening* to the radio.
> Sandra *had invited* all her friends.

- The tense of the auxiliary verb shows whether the compound verb is **present** tense,

> I'm *eating* dinner just now; I'll call you back.
> We've *had* a fantastic stay; thank you.

or **past** tense.

> We *were dancing* around the living room and singing along.
> Mom *had gone* out and left us some snacks.

The choice of the **auxiliary** and the **participle** expresses the aspect of the verb.

- the auxiliary *be* and the *-ing* participle (the present participle) show the **continuous** aspect.

> My brother *is having* a party tomorrow.
> The kids *were running* wild when we got home.

- the auxiliary *have* and the *-ed* participle (the past participle) show the **perfect** aspect.

> Juanita *has walked* more than 500 miles for charity.
> Someone *had tied* up the dog to keep it from wandering off.

These are the main compound tenses:

present continuous   = present of *be* + *-ing* participle.

 Kerry *is waiting* until Jessica gets here.

past continuous   = past of *be* + *-ing* participle.

 Maria *was watching* TV when Jo called.

present perfect   = present of *have* + *-ed* participle.

 Sam *has seen* a few things that he'd like to buy.
 We've *bought* some better equipment.

past perfect   = past of have + *-ed* participle.

 She *had* really *believed* their story!
 Rory *had had* enough of their silly questions.

A compound verb can also combine both the continuous and perfect aspects, using **two auxiliary verbs** and a **main verb**. This produces the following combinations:

present perfect continuous
 = present of *have* + past participle of *be* + *-ing* participle.

 For the past two months, Zoe *has been visiting* us once a week.
 We've *been trying* to finish that job since Easter.

past perfect continuous
 = past of *have* + past participle of *be* + *-ing* participle.

 Vicky *had been hoping* for better news.
 I *had been traveling all day*, so I was exhausted.

The modal auxiliaries can be used in compound tenses.

>*She **might be babysitting** for us on Friday.*
>*We **would be sitting** here for hours if I told you everything.*
>*I **may have eaten** something that disagreed with me.*
>*I expect Nayeema **will have bought** something for supper.*

Modal auxiliaries come in first position in the verb phrase, so they are followed by:

- the subject and the rest of the verb in questions.

  >***Will** you **be going** shopping after work?*

- the negative *not* and the rest of the verb in negative statements.

  >*Marcus **may not have been** entirely truthful.*

- the subject, the negative *not*, and the rest of the verb in negative questions.

  >***Will** you **not be pushing** for that to be changed?*

However, if the contracted negative form of the modal is used, then it comes before the subject and the rest of the verb.

>***Won't** he **be visiting** us this evening?*

> Modals are not used with the supporting auxiliary verb *do*.

See pp. 62–83 for the meanings and uses of modal auxiliary verbs.

Responses

When you respond to a question that contains a compound verb phrase, you usually use just the first part of the verb phrase. That is, you use one of the auxiliary verbs.

If it is a simple tense you use the supporting auxiliary *do*.

> *Do* you *like* avocados? – Yes, I *do*.

If one of the forms of *be* or *have* is the first verb in the verb phrase, then use that as the response form.

> *Has* Claire *been* here yet? – Yes, she *has*.
> *Was* Sue Ellen *asking* for help? – Yes, she *was*.

If a **modal** verb is first in the verb phrase, some speakers prefer to use the modal and the auxiliary form together as the response form.

> Do you think he *might have left* the parcel somewhere? –
> Yes, he *might* or Yes, he *might have*.
> So Laurence *could be coming* with us then. – Yes, he *could*
> or Yes, he *could be*.

The present simple tense

This tense has only two typical forms: the base form, and the third-person singular form with added **-s**:

> *I know her.*
> *He knows her.*

The present simple tense of *do* is used as the supporting auxiliary when you want to:

- ask a question,

> ***Do** I know you?*
> ***Does** she know you?*

- make a negative statement using *not*,

> *I **do not** know her.*
> *She **does not** know you.*

- or give a short response.

> ***Do** you just **have** coffee for breakfast? – Yes, I **do**.*

We use the present simple tense to talk about:

- habits, likes and dislikes, and things that happen regularly.

> *I **like** coffee for breakfast but everyone else in my family **prefers** tea.*
> *I **don't take** sugar in my coffee.*
> *What **does** Jamie **usually have** for breakfast?*
> *They **often go** to the movies **on Saturdays**.*
> *I **don't usually watch** TV.*

(When we talk about habits, we often add adverbs such as *often*, *always*, *usually*, *sometimes*, or *never*, or adverbial phrases such as *on Sundays* or *in the summer*.)

– statements of fact that are scientific truths or that are about a permanent state.

> *The sun **rises** in the east.*
> *Birds **fly** south in the winter.*
> *We **live** in Iowa.*

– statements that indicate the speaker's opinions or beliefs.

> *I **think** he's a very good teacher.*
> *I **don't agree** with that at all.*

– for dramatic narrative to tell a story or describe an action vividly.

> *He **walks** slowly to the checkout and **puts** his bag on the counter.*
> *As the cashier **opens** the drawer he **pulls out** a gun…*

– or when giving a commentary on a sports event or public function.

> *… but Nadal **sees** it. He **runs** up to the net and **smashes** the ball.*

We can also use the present simple for planned future actions with a time adverb; for example, to talk about travel plans and schedules. See pp. 114–121 for more about future reference.

> *The train for Hartford **leaves** at 10:40 a.m. and **arrives** at 3:30 p.m.*

We use the present simple in conditional sentences about real possibilities that affect the future. See p. 276 for more on conditional sentences.

> *If I **lend** you my notes, I won't be able to review tonight.*

The present simple is typically used for verbs related to the things you do with your senses (i.e., hearing, smell, vision, etc.).

> I *smell* garlic.
> Do you *hear* that noise?
> I *see* several houses on the horizon.

The past simple tense

The past tense form is the same for all persons, and for singular and plural:

> I *met* her.
> They *met* him.
> I *went* there.
> They *went* there.

Because the past simple consists of one word only, the past simple tense of *do*, which is *did*, is used as the supporting auxiliary when you want to:

- ask a question,

> *Did* I *meet* him?
> *Did* they *meet* him?
> *Did* I *go* there?
> *Did* it *go* there?

- make a negative statement using *not*,

> I *did* not *meet* her.
> They *did* not *meet* her.
> I *did* not *go* there.
> They *did* not *go* there.

- or make a response.

> *Did* you *see* Jenny yesterday? – No, I *didn't*.
> *Did* Peggy phone you ? – Yes, she *did*.

We use the past simple tense to talk about:

- single actions in the past.

    > He *locked* the door and *left* the house.
    > I *went* out and *brought* the cat back in again.

- habitual actions in the past, often with *always*, *never*, or *often*.

    > In those days I *always went* to Juliano's for lunch.
    > I *cycled* in *every day* and that soon *made* me fit.
    > I *often visited* New York on business when I was in publishing.

- past actions where a definite time is mentioned. It is often used with a time expression such as *ago* or *last month*, when the action is seen as finished.

    > *Some time ago* now, I *went* to Aruba for a month.
    > *Once upon a time* there was a king in a faraway land.
    > I *saw* Roger *a little while back*.
    > I *bought* the microwave *a year ago*.

- points where the main action is broken. The rest of the sentence uses the past continuous tense to describe the past activity or action.

    > I was clearing out the garage when a car *came* up the drive.
    > We were leaving the house when the phone *rang*.

The present continuous tense

The verb *be* varies according to person in forms of the present continuous tense:

> *I am winning.*
> *He is winning.*
>
> *Am I winning?*
> *Is she winning?*
>
> *I am not winning.*
> *He is not winning.*
>
> *Aren't I winning?*
> *Isn't she winning?*
>
> *Am I not winning?*
> *Is she not winning?*

Some main verbs are not normally used in the continuous in standard American or British English, though they may be used this way in other varieties of English. These are generally verbs about states rather than actions, or verbs that pertain to perception and the five senses.

> *I am winning.*   **but not** *I am liking it.*
> *There is a bird singing.*   **but not** *I am hearing it.*

We use the present continuous tense to talk about:

– things that are happening now, at the time when we are talking.

> *Mom's **mowing** the lawn, but Ibrahim **isn't doing** anything.*
> *The children aren't asleep; they**'re messing around**.*
> *Come on; you**'re not trying**.*

– a temporary activity, even if it is not happening at the time when you are talking.

I'm studying German in college.
I'm thinking of getting a new car.

– a temporary situation in contrast to a permanent situation.

I'm living in Pittsburgh at the moment.
Francesca is working in the stables over the holidays.

– a changing state or situation.

My headache is getting better.
The daylight is slowly fading.

– the circumstances under which something is generally done.

I have to wear glasses when I'm driving.

– arrangements for future events along with a time adverb or phrase.

I am flying to New York next week.

See p. 114 for more on the future.

We also use it to express annoyance at a repeated action. In this case, one of the following adverbs is used with the verb: always, forever, constantly, continually.

She's always whining about something.
He's forever laughing and making dumb jokes.

When you give a short answer to a question, it is normal to echo (that is, repeat) the auxiliary but not the main verb.

Are you waiting for someone? – Yes, I am.
Is Hamid working in the library? – No, he isn't.

The past continuous tense

The verb *be* varies according to person in forms of the past continuous tense:

> *I was winning.*
> *She was winning.*
> *They were winning.*
>
> *Was I winning?*
> *Was she winning?*
> *Were you winning?*
>
> *I was not winning*
> *We were not winning.*
> *They weren't winning.*

Some main verbs are not typically used in the continuous in standard American and British English, though they may be used this way in other varieties of English. These are generally verbs about states rather than feelings and about perception and the five senses.

We use the past continuous tense in these ways:

– with a time expression, such as *at 6 p.m. yesterday*, to talk about an action that began before that time and finished after it. The exact length of time the action took is not important.

> *What **were you doing** at eight o'clock last night?* –
> *I **was standing** at the bus stop.*

– to talk about an interrupted action. Note that for the event that interrupts the action, we use the past simple tense.

> *We **were** all **sitting** in our places when the bell **rang**.*

– to talk about a short action that happened while a longer one was already taking place.

> I *dropped* my purse while I *was waiting* for the bus.

– to describe a scene in the past, especially in a story.

> It *was a dreadful morning. The snow **was still falling**, the wind **was blowing**, and the cars **were skidding** off the icy roads.*

The present perfect tense

The verb *have* varies according to person for the present perfect tense; it is often contracted:

> I *have finished*.
> He *has found* them.
> They*'ve finished*.
> They*'ve found* her.
> Listen! I*'ve heard* some great news; Jim*'s won*!
> They*'ve bought* a brand new car.
> You*'ve got* a lot of nerve!

> *Have* they *finished*? – No, they *haven't*.
> *Has* Mary *arrived* yet? – No, she *hasn't*.

> I *have* not *finished*.
> He *has* not *finished*.
> Ranee *hasn't found* her bracelet yet.
> They *haven't seen* her.

The contracted forms are:

has = **'s**	have = **'ve**
has not = **hasn't**	have not = **haven't**

The present perfect tense is used to talk about events that are relevant to the present but that happened in the past. It is also used to talk about an action that started in the past, without mentioning a specific time.

> Her daughter *has had* an accident.
> We *have seen* the Eiffel Tower and the Arc de Triomphe.

If the present perfect occurs more than once in a compound sentence, the second and subsequent instances of *have* can be left out.

> They *have bought* their tickets and *chosen* their seats.

- We can use *just* if we want to show that the action has very recently been completed.

> They **have just bought** their tickets.
> He **has just finished** his homework.

If an event did not take place but is possible in theory you can use *never* with the present perfect. If you want to find out whether something took place or not, you can use *ever*.

> **Have** you **ever been** to Greece?
> I**'ve never done** anything like this before.

- If we want to indicate a moment in time or a period of time, we can use expressions such as *recently, lately, this morning, today,* or *this week* with the present perfect tense.

> I **haven't been** to the movies **recently**.
> I**'ve waited a week** for your answer.

- In questions and negative sentences, the present perfect can be used with *yet*, meaning "at the time of speaking." In positive sentences, use *already*.

> **Haven't** you **finished yet**?
> **Have** you **bought** the tickets **yet**?
> I**'ve already seen** that movie.

The present perfect tense is often used to answer the question *How long...?* together with *for* to talk about a period of time, or *since* to talk about duration from a point in time.

> I **have lived** in Savannah **for fifteen years**.
> **How long have you lived** in Savannah?
> We**'ve had** this car **since** 2008.
> We **haven't spoken** to each other **since** the night of the argument.

The past perfect tense

The past tense form had, along with the past participle, is used to form the past perfect tense:

> I *had misunderstood*.
> She *had misunderstood*.
> I *had finished*.
> She *had found* them.
> She'*d gone*.
> They'*d found* her.

> *Had* I *misunderstood*?
> *Had* it *gone*?
> *Had* Mary *arrived* before Peter told you? – No, she *hadn't*.

> I *had not misunderstood*.
> He *had misunderstood*.
> I *had not finished*.
> It *had not worked*.
> I *hadn't realized* how serious the problem was.
> They *hadn't seen* her.

The contracted forms are:

> had = '**d**   had not = **hadn't**

The past perfect tense goes one step further back into the past than the present perfect.

> *Had* you ever *seen* her before then? – No, I *hadn't*.

The past perfect tense is used to talk about:

– an action that took place in the past before something else took place.

> *She **had just made** some coffee when I arrived.*

– an action or state that began before another action in the past and continued up to the time of the second action and perhaps even beyond that time.

> *Ashraf **had** already **known** my brother for two years when I met him.*

• It is often used in the main clause of a complex sentence, to set the scene for a past event.

> *We **had wanted** to visit Canada for a long time, so last*
> *year we decided to go.*

• It is often used with a time expression such as *always* or for *several days*.

> *We **had been** away for several days when the burglary occurred.*

The present perfect continuous tense

The present perfect continuous is formed with *have been* or *has been* followed by a present participle:

> *I have been waiting.*
> *I've been waiting.*
> *She has been waiting.*
> *She's been waiting.*
>
> *Have I been snoring?*
> *Has he been waiting?*
> *Have you been waiting long?*
>
> *I have not been waiting.*
> *She has not been waiting.*

We use the present perfect continuous tense to talk about:

- actions and states that began in the past and are still continuing at the time of speaking or writing.

> *I have been holding this ladder for ages. When are you going to come down?*

- actions and states that began in the past and have just finished.

> *Thank goodness you're here! I've been waiting for hours.*

- repeated actions.

> *I've been getting this magazine for years now.*
> *We've been attending church weekly since last fall.*

There is sometimes little difference between the meaning of the present perfect and the meaning of the present perfect continuous when they are used for long-term actions.

> *I have been working* here for three years.
> *I have worked* here for three years.

We usually choose the continuous form for more temporary actions or states.

> *I have been living* in Phoenix since I finished college.

... and the present perfect form for more permanent ones.

> *I have lived* in Phoenix since I was born.

- We cannot use this tense with verbs such as *be*, *know*, and *like*, which are not used in continuous forms. It is also not typically used for verbs that pertain to the five senses.

- We can use *for* and *since* with the continuous form in the same way as with the present perfect form.

> *I have been studying* English for three years.
> *I have studied* English for three years.

> *I have been living* in Phoenix since I finished college.
> *I have lived* in Phoenix since I was born.

See also pp. 102–105 for more about continuous uses of the verb.

The past perfect continuous tense

The past perfect continuous is formed with *had been* followed by a present participle:

> *I had been waiting.*
> *I'd been waiting.*
> *She had been waiting.*
> *She'd been waiting.*

> *Had I been talking nonsense? What had I said?*
> *Had he been waiting long?*
> *Had you been expecting to meet Mary at the airport?*

> *I had not been waiting.*
> *She had not been waiting.*
> *They hadn't been looking very carefully.*

The past perfect continuous tense is used to talk about an action which began before another action in the past and either:

– continued up to the time of the second action,

> *I hadn't been waiting long when a bus came up beside me.*

– or was completed before the second action happened.

> *I had been studying and decided to take a stroll to clear my mind.*
> *We had been cleaning the house for hours, so we stopped and had a drink.*

• The past perfect continuous is often used in the main clause of a complex sentence, to set the scene for an event.

> *I had been driving for about an hour when I heard a noise in the engine.*

the past perfect continuous tense **113**

- The past perfect continuous is often used to talk about a repeated action.

    *She **had been trying** to phone her mother all day.*

> Remember that you cannot use the past perfect continuous with verbs such as *like*, which are not used in the continuous. See p. 102.

Future reference

Verb forms

English has no future tense as such. However, several forms, especially the **modal** verb *will*, can be used to make future reference. These forms are summarized as follows:

1 *Will* + the **base form** makes the most direct form of future reference. See p. 70. The other modal verbs that express possibility make a more indirect reference to future time.

> It **will take** several years to finish.
> Jean **will take** care of the dogs while we're away.
> I'll **tell** her to mind her own business.
> We'll **see**.

2 *Be going to* + the **base form** is used to express intention and make predictions. See p. 116.

> He failed his exams last year; this year he **is going to work** harder.
> You'd better get the dogs in; it **is going to rain**.

3 The **present continuous tense** is used to talk about plans and arrangements in the future with a time adverb. See p. 102.

> Sarah and Harriet **are meeting at ten o'clock** on Tuesday.
> I **am flying** to Mobile **on Friday**.

4 The **present simple tense** is used with a time adverb to talk about future plans that are part of a schedule or previous arrangement. See p. 97.

> The main feature **starts at 2:45 p.m.**
> We **leave at 4 p.m. tomorrow**.

5   The **future perfect tense** (*will have* + the **past participle**) is used with a time adverb to talk about an action that will be finished at the time in the future that you are referring to. See p. 119.

> *I was hoping to meet James, but by the time I arrive he will have gone home.*

6   *Be about to* + the **base form** is used to talk about the very near future. See p. 120.

> *I'm sorry I can't stop and chat; I'm about to leave for work.*

7   The **future continuous tense** (*will be* + the **present participle**) is used to talk about future action in progress. See p. 121.

> *What will you be doing on Saturday morning? Oh, I'll be shopping as usual.*

8   *Be to* + the **base form** is used to talk about formal plans, especially in journalism. See p. 121.

> *The President is to attend the UN general assembly tomorrow.*

1   *will*

The modal verb *will* followed by the **base form** of a main verb is used to refer to the future.

> *I will come.*   *We will come.*
> *You will come.*   *You will come.*
> *She/he/it will come.* *They will come.*

Some older or more traditional speakers may prefer to use *shall* in the 1st person singular and plural. See p. 70 for more details.

- The contracted form is *'ll* for both *will* and *shall*, so there is no difference in informal speech.

    I'll probably be late, but I expect they'll be on time.

The contracted negative forms are **won't** and *shan't*. *Shan't* is not used in contemporary American English.

*We **won't** come.*

- If there are two verbs in the sentence, it is normal not to repeat the modal form before the second one.

    *I **won't** go see him or **speak** to him for six months.*

We use *will* (or rarely, *shall*) for future reference in the following ways:

- to talk about future facts.

    *I **won't** see Mary next week.*
    *I'll **be** on the plane this time tomorrow.*

- to make promises or reassurances.

    *I'll **be** home in time for supper.*
    *This **won't happen** again, I can assure you.*

- to announce a decision that the speaker has just made.

    *I'll **have** the pizza and a side salad, please.*
    *OK, I'll **ask** him, and see if his story matches yours.*

- to express negative intention, using **won't**.

    *I **won't** go there again. The service was dreadful.*

- to express refusal.

> I *won't put up with* any more of this silly behavior.
> I've tried to persuade her but she *won't come*.

- to talk about an event in the future, possibly in the distant future. A time clause may be used.

> People *will be* amazed when they hear about this in years to come.

- to refer to inevitable actions or events that will take place in the future.

> Christmas is past, but it *will come* again next year.

- to express an opinion about a future event after verbs such as believe, expect, hope, know, and think.

> I *expect* he'*ll be* home soon.
> I *hope* you'*ll be* very happy in your new home.

- to express a real possibility in conditional sentences. See p. 276.

> If you call after six I'*ll tell* you all about it.

2 *be going to*

Future reference can be made with *be* + *going to* + the **base form** of a main verb.

> I *am going to wait.*
> He *is going to wait.*
> I *am not going to wait.*
> He *is not going to wait.*
> *Is* he *going to wait?*
> *Are* they *going to wait?*

Be going to is used in the following ways:

- to express intention about the future.

    Mary isn't going to study art; she's going to be a nurse.

- to talk about things that have already been decided.

    Is Jim going to leave his job? – Yes, he is.
    Where's Mary? She said she was going to come early.

- to make a prediction about the future, often the very near future, based on something in the present.

    Watch the milk! It is going to boil over!
    Sally never does any work; she is going to fail her exams.

If the past tense of *be* is used, a past intention or prediction can be expressed.

    Judy was going to meet me, but she was ill and couldn't come.
    She was obviously going to get blisters with those new shoes.

> Note this difference:
>
> *Be going to* is usually used for future events where the speaker expresses his or her intention, often about something already decided.
> *Will* is used to express decisions made at the moment of speaking.
>
>> *I'm going to go to the movies on Friday; would you like to come?*
>> *Yes, I'll go if Chris goes.*
>> *No thanks, I'm going to visit my uncle this weekend.*

3 **Present continuous**

The present continuous tense is used to talk about plans for the future, or specific arrangements that people have made for future events.

> *The school **is having** a bake sale next week; I'm **organizing** it.*

It is often used in questions about future arrangements.

> *What **are you doing** on Saturday? – I'm **going** to a football game with Peter.*
> *When **are you leaving** college? – At the end of semester.*

If there are two verbs in the sentence, it is normal not to repeat the auxiliary before the second and subsequent ones.

> *We **are meeting** at 12:30 p.m., **having** a quick lunch, and **starting** work at 1:15.*

4 **Present simple**

The present simple tense is also used to talk about events that form part of a schedule or program.

> *The flight **leaves** Albuquerque at 10:10 a.m. and **arrives** in Baltimore at 5:20 p.m.*
> *These are the arrangements for Friday: doors **open** at 7 p.m., the Mayor **arrives** at 7:30 p.m., and the meeting **starts** at 7:45 p.m.*

5 **The future perfect** (*will have* + **the past participle of a main verb**)

This form is used to talk about an action that will be complete at a time in the future that you are talking about. It is often used with verbs relating to finishing or completing. The contracted positive form is *'ll have* or **will've**.

> *Can you come over next Saturday? – Yes, I'll have finished my exams by then.*
> *Dad will've made dinner by the time we get back.*

The contracted negative is won't have.

> *The essay is due on Tuesday, but I won't have completed it by then.*

In questions, the subject comes after will. The short answer to a question that begins with will is will without the past participle.

> *Will you have finished dinner by then? – Yes, we will.*

6 *be* + *about to* + **the base form**

The appropriate form of *be* + *about to* + the **base form** of a main verb is used to talk about events in the very near future.

> *Turn off the burner! The soup is about to boil over.*
> *Come on! The film's about to start!*

It is sometimes used with *just* following the *be* form to give even more immediacy.

> *I was (just) about to leave when the phone rang.*

Be about to can also be used in the **past** to suggest that someone is *on the point of* carrying out an action when it is interrupted. In this case it is usually followed by *when*.

*They **were** (just) **about to go** to bed **when** the fire started.*

7 The future continuous tense

This is made with *will* + *be* + the **present participle** of a main verb. *Will be* forms negatives, contractions, questions, and short answers in the usual way, as shown on page 71.

The future continuous is used in an informal way to suggest that something is about to happen or will happen at some time that is not clear or precise.

> *I'll **be seeing** you.*
> *We'll **be getting** in touch with you.*
> *They'll **be wanting** us to clean our own classrooms next!*
> *We **won't be seeing** Uncle John while we are in Tucson.*

It is also used to talk about an activity that will already be in progress at a particular time in the future.

> *Will you **be working** here next week?*
> *No, I won't. I'll **be starting** my new job.*
> *Just think! This time next week, we **will be flying** to Cancun.*

8 *be to* + the base form

The appropriate form of *be* + *to* + the **base form** of a main verb is used mainly in fairly formal English to talk about plans, arrangements, and instructions. It indicates that what will happen is part of an expected process, and is often found in journalistic texts.

> *Foreign ministers of the NATO countries **are to meet** in Brussels next week.*
> *The funeral **is to take place** on Saturday.*

Active and passive

Active sentences

In the following example, the verb is **active**.

> *The post office delivers thousands of letters every day.*

In a sentence with an active verb, the subject of the sentence carries out the action. This is sometimes called the active voice. We use the active voice when the subject of the verb is the doer of the action. The active is used in most English speech and writing, because we usually want to inform our listener or our reader who or what did something.

> *He hid the money under the bed.*
> *The car knocked over a pedestrian.*
> *I'm sending the book by courier.*

Passive sentences

In the following example, the verb is **passive**.

> *Thousands of letters are delivered every day.*

The subject in a passive sentence is not the person or thing that does the action of the verb. It is the person or thing that the verb acts on or does something to. Sentences with a passive verb use the passive voice.

> *The injured man was helped by first responders.*
> *The man was being questioned by the police.*
> *The patient was operated on by a team of five surgeons.*

The passive is made with the appropriate form of *be* + the **past participle** of the main verb.

- We use the passive voice to direct our listener's attention to a different part of our message. For instance, in the first example of this section we do not need to know who delivers the letters, so all mention of the letter carrier or the post office is left out.

- The passive can be used when we do not know who performs an action, or when it is not important to know. It is sometimes much more important to know what has happened than who or what did it.

> *The money **was hidden** under the bed.*
> *The book **is being sent** by courier.*
> *An elderly man **was run over** while crossing the road.*
> *Roger **has been given** his promotion.*
> *The patient **was operated on**.*

The passive allows us to select the parts of a sentence that we wish to draw attention to. It can be used when we want to focus on:

- the **agent**, i.e., who performed the action or brought it about. We show the agent with *by*.

> *The window was broken **by some boys**.*
> *My brother was given extra lessons **by his teacher**.*
> *The old man was run over **by a careless driver**.*
> *The patient was operated on **by a team of top surgeons**.*

- the **instrument**, i.e., what was used to make the action happen. We show the instrument using *by* or *with*.

> *The sorting is done **by machine**.*
> *The safe was blown open **with dynamite**.*
> *The old man was knocked over **by a bus**.*
> *I was showered **with presents** on my eighteenth birthday.*

- the **means**, i.e., what caused the action to happen. We show the means using *by* or *with*. There is sometimes very little difference between means and instrument.

> *The window was shattered by the explosion.*
> *He was exhausted with the strain of caring for his elderly parents.*
> *Spelling errors are marked with an X in the margin.*
> *He was taken to a hospital by ambulance.*

The subject of a passive verb

The subject of a passive verb is the word that would be its object in a sentence with an active verb. When a verb has two objects, either the indirect object or the direct object of the active verb may become the subject of the passive verb.

> *I've been offered a job in Kuwait.*
> *We were given a second chance.*

If the indirect object is mentioned after the passive verb, the sentence must use *to*.

> *The building has been sold to property developers.*
> *The medal is awarded to students who have shown academic excellence.*

Some verbs that are often used this way are: *give, offer, lend, promise, sell,* and *tell*.

Form of the passive

Passive verbs are made from a form of *be* + the **past participle** of a main verb. In the passive, the form of the auxiliary verb *be* indicates the tense.

> *They **sell** cheap computer games here.*
> *Cheap computer games **are sold** here.*
> *They **took** him to the police station for questioning.*
> *He **was taken** to the police station for questioning.*

- Some verbs are only or mostly used in the passive, e.g., *be born* and *be deemed*.

> *The movie **was deemed** unsuitable for younger audiences.*
> *My brother and I **were born** in Utah.*

The impersonal passive

This form of the passive sentence is useful when you want to report what is or was generally understood or accepted by a group of people.

> *The suitcase **was found** to be empty.*
> *The money **is thought** to be missing.*
> *The rumor **is believed** to be true.*

The form *it* + **passive** + **that** can be used when you do not want to mention the source of information.

> *It **is reported** that over a hundred people died in the explosion.*
> *It **is said** that his income is over $200 a minute.*

The passive with *get*

In informal English, a type of passive is sometimes made with *get* instead of *be*.

> *How did that teapot **get broken**?*
> *Our cat **got run over** last week.*

Get is also used to form a small set of passive verbs in contexts which are not informal (or "neutral"), e.g., *get dressed, get married, get lost*.

> *Harriet got lost in the subway.*
> *When are you two getting married?*

For both of these uses of get the usual past participle is gotten in American English.

> *He'd just gotten his hair cut when I saw him.*

The causative passive with *have*

There is another verbal group that is like the passive, because the person who carries out the action of the main verb is not the person who is the subject of the clause. It expresses the idea that the subject caused or ordered someone else to do something.

Compare:

Ralph repaired his car = Ralph did the work.
Ralph had his car repaired = He paid someone else to do the work.

> *We are having the garage door replaced.*
> *She had her hair cut short.*
> *They did not have the carpet cleaned after all.*

This construction has the form: *have* + **direct object** + **past participle**. A more informal version of this verbal group uses *get* + **direct object** + **past participle**.

> *We are getting the garage door replaced.*
> *She got her hair cut short.*
> *They didn't get the carpet cleaned after all.*

Finite and nonfinite verbs

In a sentence, there is normally at least one verb that has both a **subject** and a **tense**. When a verb has a subject and a tense, it can be referred to as a **finite** verb.

> *We want Charlie to act as club secretary.*
> *I like taking photographs of insects.*
> *Coming home last night, I saw a deer run across the road.*

Some forms of a verb are referred to as **nonfinite**. The **present** and **past participles** and the *to* **infinitive** are the most common of these. The base form is often used in a nonfinite way. Every verb can be used in a clause in either a **finite** or **nonfinite** way.

- A verb is finite if it is used in a clause in combination with a subject and a tense.

  > *I walked home.*
  > *We saw a deer.*
  > *They appreciate a little praise now and then.*

- It is nonfinite if it is used:

- without the verb having a tense.

  > *To open, tear off the tab.*
  > *Looking around, he noticed a letter on the floor.*
  > *Worn out by the heat, they stopped for a drink.*

- with no agreement between the subject (if there is one) and the verb.

  > *That plan failing, he gave up.*
  > *Our guest having departed, we felt a little depressed.*

A compound verb is actually made up of one finite part, which is always the first auxiliary verb, while the remaining nonfinite parts are the base form or the participles.

In the following examples the finite part of the verb phrase is in blue italic:

> I *may* have been joking *when I said that.*
> *Helen* **was** running *around screaming.*
> I *had* been living *in a dream for months.*
> *Olivia* **is** coming *over at 6 o'clock this evening.*

The present simple and past simple forms of a verb are always finite.

> I *sing*.
> *We* **tell** *stories at night.*
> *Maya* **laughed**.
> *The shelter* **collapsed**.

- A nonfinite verb is sometimes used immediately after a finite verb.

> I *like* to get up *early on weekends.*
> *Harriet really* **dislikes** cleaning *the oven.*
> *I certainly* **wouldn't want** to see *him again.*
> *We* **persuaded** *them* to join *us.*

Often a noun or pronoun can come between the finite verb and the nonfinite one. See p. 132 and p. 133 for more on this.

> *We* **want** *Charlie* to act *as club secretary.*
> *She* **saw** *houses* destroyed *by the tornado.*
> I *don't like* you cleaning *your boots over the sink.*

- When the second verb is an -*ing* form coming after a noun or pronoun, there can be a difference in grammar between two similar sentences. Both sentences below are acceptable, although the first example might seem ambiguous to some people. In the second sentence, the -*ing* form is used as a verbal noun, not a participle. See also p. 134.

  *She didn't like **him** cleaning his boots over the sink.*
  *She didn't like **his** cleaning his boots over the sink*

The nonfinite parts of the verb

Nonfinite parts of a verb are those that do not indicate number, person or tense. The common nonfinite forms are:

- the **base form** (sometimes called the **bare infinitive**)
- the **present participle** or -*ing* form
- the **past participle**
- the *to* **infinitive**

There are also other nonfinite forms, such as:

- the **continuous** *to* **infinitive**: *to be teaching*
- the **perfect** *to* **infinitive**: *to have taught*
- the **passive** *to* **infinitive**: *to be taught*

The base form

As well as serving as the verb form on which most of the other parts of the verb are based, the **base form** is frequently used as a nonfinite part of the verb. Because of this it is sometimes called the "*bare infinitive*" or the "*infinitive without to*."

The **base form** is used as a **nonfinite** part of the verb in these ways:

- after modal verbs.

    *You must **stop** at the curb before you cross.*
    *He should **think** before he speaks.*

- after *let's* (suggestion) and *let* (permission) and *make* (compulsion).

    *Let's **invite** Annette over for dinner.*
    *Let the cat **go**!*
    ***Make** him **stop**!*
    *Let him **finish** what he was saying!*

- after *feel*, *hear*, *see*, *watch* + an object.

  I heard him run downstairs.
  Later we saw them leave the house.

- after a *to* infinitive to which it is joined by *and*.

  I want you to sit and listen.
  Just wait and see.

- after imperatives *come* and *go*; these uses are informal.

  Go see who is at the door.
  Come sit beside me for a while.

- after *would rather* and *had better*.

  I would rather go out, but I think we had better stay home and
    finish the painting.

Verbs of perception may be followed either by the **base form** or by the
-ing form. There is often a difference of meaning between the two.

These verbs include: *see*, *hear*, *feel*, *smell*, *listen to*, *watch*.

  We watched her park the car = we watched the whole event.
  We watched her parking the car = we may only have seen part
    of the event.
  I heard a owl call = I heard just one call.
  We heard the birds singing = We heard part of the song of
    the birds.

The *to* infinitive

The *to* infinitive is used as follows:

– after an adjective of quality such as *small, tall, agreeable, pleasant, funny* that is used in combination with *too*.

> The child was **too small to reach** the switch.
> The knife was **too dull to cut** the string.

or (*not*) + adjective of quality + *enough*.

> The child was **not tall enough to reach** the switch.
> The knife was **not sharp enough to cut** the string.
> I was **stupid enough to go** walking in flip-flops.

– after adjectives of emotion such as: *angry, happy, glad, sad, sorry, surprised*, to express the reason for the emotion.

> I'm **glad to see** you.
> I'm **sorry to hear** your news.

– after a "behavior" adjective such as: *good, kind, nice, stupid, wrong,* (sometimes + *of* + another **noun phrase**).

> It was **good** of you **to come**, and **kind** of Jane **to have sent** those flowers.
> It was **stupid to shout** like that.
> It was **kind** of you **to call** me.

– after a **WH-** word such as: *how, what, where, whether, which, who, whom.*

> We have no idea **what to get** for Tim's birthday.
> I don't know **where to go**.
> I can't think **how to do** it.
> They were wondering **who to see** first.

- after a noun phrase such as *a good idea*, *a good thing*, *a mistake* (sometimes + **for** + another **noun phrase**).

  It was a mistake for Jim to buy that motorbike.
  It was a good idea to stop here.

- after an adjective such as *easy*, *difficult*, *hard*, *impossible* + *for* + **noun phrase**.

  It has never been easy for David to take exams.

- after a verb followed by for, e.g., *ask*, *wait* + *for* + **noun phrase**.

  They are waiting for us to decide.

- The *to* infinitive can be used to express purpose or necessity after a verb followed by a pronoun or a noun.

  purpose: I brought *it to read* on the flight = so that I could read it.
  necessity: There is *work to do*! = work that must be done.

  > Sometimes the particle *to* can be used alone; for example, in a short response when the whole verb form was used earlier.
  >
  > *Did you meet Tina? No, I wanted to, but she was wasn't there.*
  > *Are you going to visit the museum? Yes, we hope to.*

The *to* infinitive and the *-ing* form

The *to* infinitive and the *-ing* form (the present participle) can each be used after certain verbs.

Verbs followed by the *to* infinitive include: *agree, arrange, attempt, choose, decide, fail, hope, learn, manage, offer, plan, seem*.

> I **agreed to help** Shona with her homework.
> The driver **attempted to remove** the flat tire.
> I **hope to see** you again at the next meeting.

Verbs followed by an **object** + the *to* **infinitive** include: *advise, allow, command, forbid, force, invite, order, persuade, remind, teach, tell*.

> Peter advised Ron **to call the police**.
> Esther reminded her teacher **to assign some homework**.

Verbs that can be followed either directly by the *to* **infinitive** or by an **object** + the *to* **infinitive** include: *ask, expect, help, intend, like, love, hate, mean, prefer, want, wish*.

> I certainly intended **to go** to the party.
> We really expected **Samantha to pass** the exam.
>
> Note this difference:
> I want **to have** a cat = It will be my cat.
> I want **her to have** a cat = It will be her cat.
> Dad likes **to wash** the car = Dad washes the car.
> Dad likes **John to wash** the car = John washes the car.

Verbs followed by the *-ing* form include: *avoid, be used to, delay, dislike, escape, finish, forgive, give up, go on, imagine*.

> I usually **avoid going** into town late at night.
> Miriam **hates peeling** potatoes.
> Have you **finished reading** that book yet?

- Some verbs may be followed either by the *to* infinitive or by the *-ing* form with little or no change in meaning. These verbs include: *begin*, *start*, *cease*, *continue*, *intend*, *like*, *love*, *hate*, *prefer*.

  > *He began **to run** around.*
  > *He began **running** around.*
  > *She likes **to swim** in the sea.*
  > *She likes **swimming** in the sea.*
  > *I can't bear **to see** violence.*
  > *I can't bear **seeing** violence.*

- Some verbs may be followed either by the *to* infinitive or by the *-ing* form but the meaning of the sentence changes depending on the form that is used. These verbs include: *try*, *forget*, *remember*.

  > *I **remembered to turn** the lights off before we went out.* =
  >   *I turned the lights off.*
  > *I **remember turning** the lights off before we went out.* =
  >   *I specifically remember doing this.*

  > *She **tried to talk** to him, but his secretary wouldn't put the*
  >   *call through.*
  > *She **tried talking** to him, but he wouldn't listen.*

Particularly after verbs such as go and come, the to infinitive is understood to express purpose.

  > *She has **gone to do** the shopping.*
  > *They **came** here **to learn** English.*

Use of the verb followed by the *-ing* form concentrates on what happens. The second verb is really the object of the first one. These verbs include: *remember*, *forget*, *try*.

  > *I definitely **remember switching the lights off** before we went out.*
  > *She **tried talking to him**, but he wouldn't listen.*

Some **set expressions** (idioms) are followed by an *-ing* form.
These include: *it's not worth*, and *it's no fun*.

> It's **no fun going** out alone.
> It's **no use phoning** him; he's gone away.
> It's **worth trying** one more time.

The noun phrase

A noun phrase is a word or group of words that can function as the **subject**, the **object**, or the **complement** in a sentence.

> *The manager interviewed all the applicants on Tuesday.*
> *Lydia was the successful applicant.*

See pp. 22–23 and pp. 233–234 for more information about these functions. A noun phrase must always contain a noun or a pronoun.

A noun phrase may consist of only one word. That word will be either a noun or a pronoun.

> *Mary left late.*
> *She left late.*
> *Cheese is expensive.*
> *It is expensive.*

A noun phrase may consist of more than one word. One of these words, a noun or a pronoun, is the **headword** in the phrase. The other words describe or modify the headword.

> *the tall girl*
> *the very tall girl*
> *a strikingly beautiful girl*
> *the tall girl with green eyes*

Words that go before the headword are called **premodifiers**. A noun can be premodified by:

- a determiner. See p. 164.

> *the girl*   *that boy*
> *a spider*   *some rice*

- one or more adjectives. See pp. 164–194.

  tall girls
  tall dark girls
  tall dark handsome men

- a number, another noun, or the present participle or past participle of a verb.

  three days
  the *bus station* cafeteria
  an *annoying* habit
  an *overworked* man

Words that go after the headword are called **postmodifiers**. A noun can be postmodified by:

- a prepositional phrase (a noun phrase with a preposition in front of it).

  the person *in the corner*
  the view *across the valley*
  the house *beside the church*
  creatures *under the sea*

- a subordinate clause (usually one beginning with *who*, *which* or *that*). See p. 267.

  All the women *who had gathered there* finally went away.
  Milk *that has been kept too long* can go sour.

- less commonly, certain adjectives. See p. 164.

  an attorney *general*
  peaches *galore*
  the president *elect*

- Personal pronouns are only rarely premodified or postmodified. See p. 206.

> *Silly* me.
> *Poor old* you.

Types of noun

Nouns can be classified according to what they refer to.

- Nouns that are really names are called **proper nouns**. Proper nouns usually refer to a particular named person, place, or thing.

They include:

- the names of specific people.

Mohammed Belhaus	John Lennon
Takisha Everett	Mrs. Merton

- geographical items.

Spain	Mount Everest
China	Alaska
the Rio Grande	Calgary
Madison Square Garden	Sunset Boulevard

- days of the week, months, and annual Church festivals.

Thursday	June
Christmas	Easter

- patented products and company names.

Prozac	Tide
Toyota	Samsung

- newspaper and magazine titles.

The New York Times	Vogue
Science News	Wired

- stores, stadiums, theaters, buildings.

> *The Majestic*   *Macy's*
> *Wrigley Field*   *The Chrysler Building*

- titles (the polite or professional labels that we give to people).

> **Doctor** *Mahajan*   **Sir** *Elton John*
> **Professor** *James*   **President** *Sarkozy*

A person's title is usually placed before his or her name. Proper nouns and titles are always written with an initial capital letter.

- All the other nouns that refer to things or species are called **common nouns**.

> *I put the **tennis balls** in that **basket** there.*
> *My **brother** and **sister** visited my **mother**.*
> *The **anger** that John felt was overwhelming.*

Common nouns can be divided into the following groups, according to their meaning:

Abstract nouns. These refer to intangible items (that is, things that are not physical objects).

> *honesty*   *anger*
> *idea*   *time*
> *ugliness*   *behavior*

Concrete nouns. These refer to tangible items (that is, physical objects).

> *pig*   *granite*
> *table*   *farmer*
> *brother*   *sugar*

A concrete noun may refer to a living thing (**animate** nouns) or a physical object (**inanimate** nouns).

Collective nouns. These refer to collections of people or animals.

> *a **herd** of cows*
> *a **swarm** of bees*

Nouns may also be classified according to the words that they are used with, that is:

– whether or not the noun gives us information about **singular** and **plural number**.

– the other words that can be used in the same noun phrase.

This gives us a useful distinction between **countable nouns** and **uncountable nouns**.

Countable nouns refer to things that we can count: *one cat*, *two cats*, *seventeen cats*, and so on. They have singular and plural forms. They must be used with a determiner if they are singular.

> ***Dogs** ran wild in the streets.*
> ***The dog** is loose again.*
> *Bring **a chair** for Mandy, will you?*
> *We've bought **six new chairs**.*

Uncountable nouns refer to:

– things that are not normally thought of as countable.

> *John asked me for some **advice**.*
> *Anna gave us some more **information** about her **work**.*
> ***Homework** occupied much of Sonia's evening.*

– qualities or abstract ideas.

> Our **knowledge** of outer **space** is increasing daily.
> Troy gave **evidence** at the trial.
> **Anger** is a normal human emotion.

Uncountable nouns do not usually have a plural form. They are followed by a singular verb. They are not normally used with the indefinite article. (You cannot talk about "*an advice*" or "*a money*.") When it is necessary to think of an item as countable it has to be used with a **partitive noun**. See p. 145.

> He bought seven **yards** of cloth.
> Let me give you **a piece of** advice.

Some of the commonest uncountable nouns are: *advice, anger, beauty, behavior, conduct, education, evidence, furniture, happiness, information, knowledge, leisure, management, money, news, power, progress, research, safety, work.*

• Verbal nouns, sometimes called gerunds (p. 162), which are formed from the present participle of verbs, can also be used as uncountable nouns.

> Why don't you try **walking** to work?
> Brian was trying to stop **smoking**.
> The **ringing** in his ears continued.

> Note that nouns that are uncountable in English may be countable in other languages. See p. 146.

Mass nouns

Mass nouns refer to a substance that can be divided or measured but not counted, e.g., *sugar, water*. They do not usually have an indefinite article in front.

> *Meat is often less expensive than cheese*.
> *Sugar is quite cheap*.

Mass nouns only take a plural in special cases. They can be counted when they refer to:

- a particular type or types of the substance.

> *There was a buffet of bread and rolls, cheese, **cold meats**, and tea or coffee.*
> *Rosa brought out a tempting selection of **French cheeses**.*
> ***The principal sugars** are glucose, sucrose, and fructose.*

- a serving of the substance.

> ***Two sodas**, please.*
> *He went up to the bar and ordered **two beers**.*

- Mass nouns are often used together with a partitive noun.

> *There are only **two pieces of furniture** in the room.*
> *There are **three portions of meat** in this package.*
> ***Five pitchers of beer**, please.*

Partitive nouns

Partitive nouns, sometimes just called partitives, are commonly followed by *of*. They are used when we need to talk about a part of a mass noun or when we need to count the quantity of something that is referred to by an uncountable noun or a mass noun, especially when it is necessary to talk about:

- measurements and quantities with mass nouns.

  > *three **pieces** of toast*   *a **slice** of cheese*
  > *a **bit** of fluff*   *two **spoonfuls** of sugar*

- individual items with uncountable nouns.

  > *Two **pieces** of furniture needed major repairs.*
  > *We needed several **lengths** of string.*

- a collection of countable nouns.

  > *The road was blocked by a **flock** of sheep.*
  > *He has a small **herd** of dairy cows.*
  > *There was a **crowd** of football fans on the bus.*
  > *A **couple** of cats were fighting.*

> Many collective nouns can be used as partitive nouns. See p. 142.

Nouns that have both countable and uncountable uses

Most nouns are either countable or uncountable, as explained on p. 142.
Some nouns, however, behave like countable nouns in some sentences
and uncountable nouns in other sentences. They usually have different
meanings depending on how they are used. For example, *time*, *light*,
history, *space*, *laugh*, and *service* have more than one meaning.

> *Time passed slowly.*
> *She did it four times.*
> *Light travels faster than sound.*
> *The lights in this room are too bright.*
> *The rocket was launched into space.*
> *How many spaces are left in the parking lot?*

Some nouns that are countable nouns in other languages are used only
as uncountable nouns in English, e.g., *help*, *information*, *advice*.

> *He received all the necessary information.*
> *I don't need your help.*

Some nouns are used only in the plural form, even when we are talking
about one item, e.g., *pants*, *clothes*, *jeans*. We can use a partitive noun
with *of* when referring to a single item.

> *These slacks need cleaning.*
> *Put the scissors back when you have finished with them.*
> *I need a pair of pliers.*
> *Liz gathered up a bundle of clothes.*

Gender of nouns

In some languages, nouns have **gender**. This means that a noun causes other words such as adjectives to change their spelling according to certain rules. Grammatical gender often has no relationship with biological gender. English does not have **grammatical gender** for nouns.

On the other hand, the biological gender of the thing or person referred to does affect a few areas of English grammar.

> a cow... **she** or it a bull... **he** or it
> a girl... **she** a boy... **he**

Gender distinctions are relevant where personal pronouns (p. 206) and possessive determiners (p. 164) have to be decided on. These distinctions are only noticeable in **singular** nouns.

> **He** found **his** book.
> **He** had been looking for **it**.
> **She** found **her** book.
> **She** had been looking for **it**.

There are also special cases, such as the association of neuter gender with babies and small animals, or feminine gender with a vehicle.

> I just saw a **mouse**. **It** was running across the room.
> The **spider** was spinning **its** web.
> The **beetle** crawled into **its** hole.
> The **baby** threw down **its** rattle.
> I've got a new boat; **she's** a real beauty.

Nouns denoting male persons and animals are **masculine**. They are used with the pronouns and possessive determiners he, him, his.

Nouns denoting female persons and animals are **feminine**. They are used with the pronouns and possessive determiners she, her, hers.

*Barry saw Linda. **He** called out to **her** that **he** had found **her** book.*
*Marcia saw Paul. **She** called out to **him** that **she** had found **his** book.*
*Madeleine saw Kim. **She** said "Hello" to **her**.*

The pronouns and possessive determiners used to refer to common or **neuter** nouns are *it* and *its*.

> ***The truth** will emerge. **It** always does.*

Nouns denoting inanimate objects and abstract notions are also neuter and are referred to with *it* and *its*.

- Some nouns denoting people have the same form for masculine and feminine. Nouns used for a group, e.g., *government* or *team*, have **common** or **neuter** gender, even when we know that the group is made up exclusively of male or female members.

    > *The **government** has changed **its** policy.*
    > *The **team** has won **its** first medal at a major championship.*

With some nouns of common gender it might be possible to specify the gender if we had enough information. But if we do not have this knowledge, the choice of pronoun or possessive determiner becomes a problem.

> *a driver...he/she*
> *the cook...he/she*
> *doctor...he/she*

As a way around this problem, in informal and spoken English, **their** is sometimes used after a singular noun or an indefinite pronoun. See p. 205. Many people consider this grammatically unacceptable, but it is widely used to avoid repetitions of *his* or *her* or *him* or *her*.

> *Each **student** must apply to **his or her** tutor for an extension.*
> ***Everyone** must apply to **their** tutor for an extension.*
> ***Someone** has left **their** coat in my room.*

The specialized terms used to name male, female and neutered animals show a number of gender differences.

any animal	fertile female	fertile male	infertile male
horse	mare	stallion	gelding
–	cow	bull	steer
sheep	ewe	ram	wether

Gender differences are also shown in the nouns that indicate relationships.

parent	mother	father
child	daughter	son

- Many nouns denoting an occupation have no explicit gender.

engineer	doctor	programmer
mechanic	lawyer	driver

Some occupations and professions have a special feminine form for the noun.

> Call your branch **manager** today.
> Sue is **manageress** of a hairdressing salon.
> **Authors** from all over the state attended the ceremony.
> Here in the studio to talk about her new book is **authoress**
>   Mary Farrell.

Many people prefer to avoid these forms, regarding the distinction as unnecessary.

> Anne Tyler is a highly successful **author**.
> Meryl Streep is one of our finest **actors**.
> Michelle Stewart has been promoted to Office **Manager**.

Some speakers prefer to use a different form of the word or an entirely different word in order to avoid a gender-marked noun.

the chair**man**   the chair**person**   the chair

Many speakers use newer terms with a single name for professions or jobs that formerly used different terms for male and female.

steward	stewardess	flight attendant
mailman	mailwoman	letter carrier
waiter	waitress	server

If necessary, the gender of a common noun can be made clear by adding a descriptive term such as *woman* or *male/female*.

*Would you prefer to see a **woman** doctor?*
***Male employees** should use locker room B.*

> If we are discussing a country from an emotional, economic, or political viewpoint we sometimes use feminine gender.
>
> ***Poland** has made steady progress restructuring **her** economy.*

Showing possession through nouns

Possession can be shown in three ways:

– by using a possessive pronoun that refers to an earlier noun.

> The **man** was repairing **his** car.
> The **students** received **their** grades today.

– by adding -'s to a singular noun, or an irregular plural noun that does not end in -s.

> one dog   one boy   several children
> the **dog's** bones   the **boy's** books   the **children's** toys

– by adding -' to a plural noun.

> more than one dog   more than one boy
> the **dogs'** bones   the **boys'** books

There is also the *of* **possessive** (a noun phrase with *of* followed by another noun).

> the side *of* the ship   the end *of* the line

The *of* **possessive** is not just a different way of saying the same thing as the -'s possessive.

> the **boy's** pencil   **but not** the pencil *of* the boy

The -'s possessive is generally used only with nouns referring to tangible items and in time phrases.

> the **driver's** foot   the **dog's** nose
> the **woman's** house   the **company's** logo
> **today's** newspaper   a **week's** vacation

The *of* possessive is generally used with nouns referring to inanimate things (i.e., objects) and abstract ideas.

the leg *of the table*	the arm *of the sofa*
the wheel *of the car*	the foot *of the bed*
the world *of ideas*	the power *of thought*

The function of the possessive form in English is to:

– show possession.

the **boy's** books	the **dog's** blanket

– show a relationship, with a person either as the originator, or the user of the thing named.

her **parents'** consent	the **student's** letter
a **women's** club	the **children's** park

– indicate that a place is where someone lives.

the **Feezers'**	my **aunt's**

– show that something is a part of a whole.

the leg *of the table*	the **dog's** nose
the wheel *of the car*	the **girl's** shoulder

– add a descriptive element that premodifies a noun. It is a type of determiner. See also p. 164.

writer's cramp	A **Winter's** Tale

Rules for the formation of the possessive -'s (apostrophe -s) and -s' (-s apostrophe) are as follows:

– most singular nouns add an apostrophe + -s.

    a girl's ring   *a cat's face*

– most plural nouns add an apostrophe after the plural form -s.

    *the **boys'** football*   *five young **girls'** faces*

There are exceptions for the following:

– common nouns that end in -s in the singular. When these are made plural the choice of -'s or a simple apostrophe is optional.

    a cactus   *the **cactus'** spines*   *the **cactus's** habitat*

– plural nouns not ending in -s, such as those that have a plural ending in -*en*. In this case, add an apostrophe + s.

    children's   *men's*

– proper nouns and common nouns that end in -s. These usually add -'s in the singular unless the final sound of the basic word is [-iz], in which case, a simple apostrophe is enough.

    *Mrs. **Evans's** car*   *Mr. **Jones's** fence*
    ***Keats's** poetry*   *the **Bates's** cat*
    ***Dickens's** novels*   *Peter **Bridges'** car*

Compound nouns (see p. 155) put the -'s or the simple apostrophe at the end of the complete compound.

    my mother-in-law   *my **mother-in-law's** car*
    the runner-up   *the **runner-up's** trophy*
    the fact-checkers   *the **fact-checkers'** questions*

Noun phrases that are descriptive of someone's role or profession put the -'s on the headword of the phrase.

> *a stock market analyst's annual income*
> *the senior food inspector's monthly visit*

If they use an of construction the -'s or simple apostrophe usually goes on the last noun.

> *the governor of Iowa's official car*
> *the director of marketing's personal assistant*

Compound nouns

A compound noun is a noun that is formed from two or more words. The meaning of the whole compound is often different from the meaning of the two words on their own. Compound nouns are very common. The main noun is normally the last one.

teapot   *headache*
washing machine   *liquor license*
self-control   *C-note*

Compound nouns are commonly formed from the following word combinations:

– noun + noun
– verb + noun
– adjective + noun
– phrasal verb used as noun
– particle + noun

noun + noun:	*boyfriend*	*skinhead*
verb + noun:	*breakfast*	*grindstone*
adjective + noun:	*software*	*hardware*
phrasal verb:	*a break-in*	*a take-over*
particle + noun:	*onlooker*	*aftershave*

The term **particle** is used here for a word that can be either an adverb or a preposition.

Compound nouns can be written:

– as one word.

bookcase   wallpaper
birdcage   snowflake

– as two words.

post office   fire engine
eye shadow   cough drop

– with a hyphen.

anti-Zionist   air-conditioning
all-nighter   T-shirt

Consult a dictionary to discover how the word is normally written. There are often alternative forms to be found, for example, *drop down menu*, *drop-down menu*, and *dropdown menu* are all currently acceptable forms of the same compound noun.

Nouns as modifiers

The compound noun *girlfriend* names a special sort of *friend*. Nouns can also be used as **modifiers** without forming a compound noun.

a **concrete** slab   old **oak** beams
an **auto** mechanic   a **store** manager

A noun that is used as a modifier has the same function as an adjective. The first noun usually makes the second one more specific, but we do not think of it as part of a combination that forms a new word. See p. 190 for more on modifiers.

Number in nouns

Singular number is used when the noun refers to one item.
Plural number is used when the noun refers to more than one item.

Countable nouns have both singular and plural forms.

Uncountable nouns and **mass nouns** do not normally have a plural form. See p. 140 for more on the types of noun.

The regular plural ending of an English noun is -s.

    cat   *cats*

These are the exceptions to the normal pattern:

singular noun ending	*plural noun ending*
-s, -ss, -ch, -x, -zz	*-es*
focus	*focuses*
princess	*princesses*
church	*churches*
box	*boxes*
buzz	*buzzes*
-o	*-s or -es*
hero	*heroes*
taco	*tacos*
piano	*pianos*
potato	*potatoes*
consonant + y	*-ies*
baby	*babies*
hobby	*hobbies*
vowel + y	*-s*
key	*keys*
ray	*rays*

singular noun ending	plural noun ending
-f hoof dwarf thief roof	-s or -ves hoofs or hooves dwarfs or dwarves thieves roofs
-fe knife life	-ves knives lives

Irregular plurals

Some nouns have two plural forms.

fish   fish or fishes

Some of them have the same form in the singular and plural.

a sheep   ten sheep
a deer   seven deer

A few change a vowel to form the plural.

man   men
woman   women
foot   feet
mouse   mice

Some nouns form the plural with -en.

child   children
ox   oxen

Since it is not possible to give more than a selection of the irregular forms, you should check in a dictionary if you are unsure about a plural form. If the dictionary does not show the plural form, then you can assume that it is regular.

Compound nouns normally form the plural by adding -s to the last word of the compound.

a game console	*three game consoles*
a bookcase	*two bookcases*
a Mexican take-away	*two Mexican take-aways*

There are a few exceptions:

A compound noun formed from a noun and an adverb often makes the first word plural. However, a few of these plurals are formed regularly.

a passer-by	*several **passers-by***
a hanger-on	*several **hangers-on***
a break-in	*several **break-ins***
a play-off	*several **play-offs***

Compound nouns with *woman* as the first word make both words plural.

a woman doctor	*several **women** doctors*
a woman driver	*most **women** drivers*

A compound word which ends in *-ful* normally adds -s after *-ful*, but there is an alternative form with the *-s* following the base noun.

a cupful	*three **cupfuls/cupsful***
a spoonful	*two **spoonfuls/spoonsful***

Plural nouns with singular reference

Some nouns referring to clothes and tools where two equal parts are joined together, e.g., *pants*, *binoculars*, and *tongs*, are treated as being plural and are followed by a verb in the plural.

> My shorts **are** dirty.
> The scissors **are** on the table.

To talk about one of these items we can use the expression *a pair of...*

> John bought *a pair of jeans*.

To talk about more than one we talk about however many *pairs of...*

> Martina bought *five pairs of tights*.

- When they are used as ordinary numbers, words such as *dozen* and *million* have no plural form.

> **nine million** stars   **two dozen** glasses

When they are used to mean a large number, they do have a plural form, which can be used as a partitive.

> There are **millions** of pebbles on the beach.
> I saw **dozens** of children in the park.

Foreign plurals

Nouns that have come into English from foreign languages can:

- keep the plural form of the language they come from.

> an axis   two axes
> a phenomenon   two phenomena

– have plurals formed according to the rules for plural in English.

> *a thesaurus* *several thesauruses*
> (instead of thesauri)

– have two plurals: one from the foreign language and the other formed according to the rules for plural formation in English. The foreign plural is usually kept for scientific or specialized use.

> *an index* *some indexes/indices*
> *a formula* *some formulas/formulae*

Verbal nouns

A **verbal noun** is the *-ing* form, i.e., the present participle of the verb, used as a noun. It can be used in all the places that a noun can be used, but still keeps some characteristics of the verb. It is sometimes called a **gerund**.

> The **screaming** of the brakes terrified me.
> **Smoking** is prohibited.

The verbal noun normally functions as an uncountable noun, as above. However, there are some uses of the verbal noun that can be preceded by an indefinite article or used in the plural.

> He gave **a reading** from his latest volume of poetry.
> The movie was shot with alternative **endings**.

The verbal noun can be preceded by the definite article, by adjectives, and by possessives.

> Her fantastic **singing** won Helen the scholarship.

Just like any noun, the verbal noun can function:

– as a **subject**.

> **Driving** was impossible.

– as the **complement** of the verb *be*.

> **Seeing** is **believing**.
> His greatest pleasure is **working**.

– as an **object** after certain verbs. See also p. 134.

> Louisa likes **swimming** but Helen prefers **diving**.

– after **prepositions** to make a prepositional phrase.

> *Can you watch them **without laughing**?*

Verbal nouns are also used:

– after some phrasal verbs such as: *be for/against, give up, keep on, look forward to, put off.* See also page 143.

> *She was all for **leaving** immediately.*
> *Linda gave up **swimming** but she kept on **dieting**.*
> *They were looking forward to **writing** home.*

– after certain set expressions such as: *can't stand, can't help, it's no use/good.*

> *I can't stand **waiting** around.*
> *I can't help **getting** upset.*
> *It's no use **crying** over spilled milk.*

The **possessive determiner** can be used with the verbal noun, especially in formal English.

> *Anna left the house without **my knowing**.*

● The verbal noun also has:

– a perfect form: *having ...ed.*

> *Martin was accused of **having cheated**.*

– a passive form: *being ...ed.*

> ***Being asked** did not bother me.*

– a perfect passive form: *having been ...ed.*

> *The car showed no sign of **having been touched**.*

Determiners

Determiners are words that make the reference of nouns more specific. If I say "*this car*" it is clear that I mean a particular car that is near me. If I change it to "*my car*" I am saying something specific about ownership.

Determiners can be divided into several kinds according to:

- their meaning.

- what they may go with and where they may come in the noun phrase.

There are eight classes of determiner:

- the indefinite article *a* or *an*. See p. 166.

    A man came into the shop.
    An honest person would return the car to the owner.

- the definite article *the*. See p. 168.

    The dog chased the rabbit.

- the demonstratives *this*, *that*, *these*, *those*. See p. 172.

    This book is better than that one.
    These apples are redder than those ones.

- the possessives *my*, *your*, *his*, *her*, *its*, *our*, *their*. See p. 211.

    I gave my share to her sister.
    Shirona found his book in her car.

- the quantifiers *some*, *any*, *enough*, *no*, *all*, *both*, *half*, *double*, *several*, *much*, *many*, *more*, *most*, *few*, *fewer*, *fewest*, *a few*, *little* (meaning not much), *less*, *least*, *a little*. See pp. 175–181.

> I've got **some** coffee but I haven't got **any** sugar.
> Have you got **much** money on you?
> There were **no** witnesses to the accident.
> **Both** girls saw the attack.
> **Few** people know the answer to that.
> The safety net gives **little** help to those who need it most.

- the numbers, cardinal (*one*, *two*, *three*...), and ordinal (*first*, *second*, *third*...). See p. 180.

> There's **one** thing I need to ask you.
> The **two** boys grew up together in Manhattan.
> **Three** men were found hiding in the building.
> Their **second** child is due in October.
> She lost in the **third** round of the tournament.

- the distributives *each*, *every*, *either*, *neither*. See p. 182.

> **Each** child received a book.
> **Every** girl was given a number to wear.
> **Either** book should help you with the problem.

- the exclamatives *what*, *such*. See p. 184.

> **What** nonsense!
> **What** a shame!
> They make **such** a fuss over small things!

Generally, a noun phrase has only one determiner in it, or none at all. A few determiners, e.g., *all*, *both*, and the numbers, can be used together with another determiner. See p. 164.

The indefinite article

The indefinite article is *a* or *an*. The form *an* is used before a word that starts with a vowel sound.

> *a* girl   *a* cat
> *an* eight-year-old girl   *an* honor

The indefinite article is used with singular countable nouns:

– to refer to a person or a thing that you are mentioning for the first time in a conversation or a piece of writing.

> *A man was seen driving away in a black car.*

– to refer to a person or a thing that you do not want to be specific about.

> *I stopped off at a kiosk to buy a newspaper.*
> *You go past a gas station on the left, and then you'll see our street on the right.*

– to refer to a person or a thing that you cannot be more specific about because there is not enough information.

> *A man came by to see you this afternoon.*
> *There was a telephone call for you a minute ago.*

– in definitions.

> *An octopus is a sea creature with eight tentacles.*

– when you refer to a person's profession.

> *Her father is a dentist and her mother is a teacher.*

– to express the quantity *one*. If you wish to emphasize this quantity, then use *one* instead of the indefinite article. The equivalent for plural nouns is *some* or no determiner at all. See p. 164.

> *I want a needle and a thimble.*
> *Would you like a glass of wine?*
> *There is only **one** glass of wine left in the bottle.*
> *Guy has bought a skateboard.*
> *We've got three pairs of rollerblades and **one** skateboard.*

It is the sound, not the spelling, that decides where *an* is used. For example, although *unique* begins with a vowel, the sound at the beginning resembles a *y*- sound. *Honest*, by contrast, begins with a silent consonant and a vowel sound.

> *an idiot*   *an honest mistake*
> *a unicorn*   *a unique experience*

> There are a few words that begin with a silent *h-*, in front of which *an* should be used. They are: *heir*, *herb* (for some speakers), *heiress*, *hombre*, *honest*, *honor*, *hors d'oeuvre*, *hour*.

● Very formal or old-fashioned speakers also use the *an* form with some words beginning with an *h-* that is not silent, especially *historical* and *hotel*.

> *I waited an hour.*
> *They joined a historical society.*
> *They joined an historical society.*   *(old-fashioned English)*
> *They were staying at a hotel.*
> *They were staying at an hotel.*   *(old-fashioned English)*

The definite article

The definite article is *the*.

The definite article is used with singular and plural nouns. It is used both with countable nouns and uncountable nouns:

– to make definite or specific reference to a person or a thing that has already been referred to.

> *There's the man I was telling you about!*

– to refer to a person or thing that is already specific because those listening or reading know what you are talking about. In the first example below, *"the children"* would be members of our family and *"the swimming pool"* is the swimming pool we normally go to.

> *Let's take the children to the swimming pool.*
> *Did you switch the heating on?*
> *There were drinks in the fridge but the beer was soon finished.*

– to generalize about a whole class or species, usually of plants or animals. A singular noun is used for this purpose. The first example means *"The elephant species is still hunted for its tusks."*

> *The elephant is still hunted for its tusks.*
> *The snowdrop is the first flower to arrive in the new year.*

– when it is followed by an adjective used as a noun indicating nationality, or when generalizing about a whole class of people. *The Dutch* in the first example means *"Dutch people in general."*

> *The Dutch are very skillful engineers.*
> *The poor were crowding the streets of the capital.*
> *The homeless were sheltered in the church.*

– before the names of rivers, groups of islands, seas, oceans, and mountain ranges.

The Ohio	*The* Aleutians
The Caribbean Sea	*The* Pacific

- before the names of certain public institutions, most newspapers, and some magazines.

The Whitney Museum	*The* Hilton Hotel
The Lyceum Theater	*The* Capitol
The Washington Post	*The* LA Times
The Economist	*The* New England Journal of Medicine

- before the names of well-known institutions, even when a specific one is not named—usually because it is not important to know which one is meant.

  An ambulance took her to **the hospital**.
  His mom had to pick him up at **the police station**.
  They like to walk their dogs in **the park**.

- before parts of the body when these are referred to in an impersonal way.

  A stone struck him on **the hand**.
  Martin hit him on **the head**.

- The definite article is rarely used with titles when they are followed by a name. Proper nouns that refer to persons, such as *Sue* and *Ron*, and proper nouns used in conjunction with titles, such as *Queen Elizabeth*, *Doctor Thomas*, and *Captain Parry*, only take a definite article if:

- they stand for the name of a thing such as a boat.

  The *Queen Elizabeth II is on a long cruise.*

- a distinction is being made between people who have identical names. This use can give emphasis to the noun.

  Ah, no. **The David Parry I know** *lives in Minnesota.*
  I saw Paul Kay in town this morning. – Not **the** *Paul Kay?*

Nouns used without a determiner

Certain noun phrases do not have a determiner at all.

We usually leave out the determiner when we use a noun or a noun phrase in the plural to make a generalization.

> He sells **cars** for a living.
> **Tigers** are nearing extinction.
> **Onions** are good for you.
> **Grassy hills** rise on all sides of the town.

Singular nouns that are uncountable (including mass nouns) are used without a determiner when you are making a general reference.

> New **information** is now available.
> Do you like **jelly**?
> This shop sells **furniture**.

- This is particularly true when the uncountable noun is used for the first time in a general way in the course of a conversation or piece of writing. They can be used with a determiner when the reference becomes specific. For example, you can ask someone if they like *cake* as a rule, and then ask the person if she would like some of *your cake*.

> **The** information she gave me was inaccurate.
> Would you like some of **the cake** I made for the party?
> We don't let the dog climb onto **the** furniture.

There are a number of idiomatic expressions that usually omit a determiner. Examples are expressions that refer to:

- travel, when you proceed **by**: *bicycle, car, bus, train, ship, boat, plane, subway*.

> Anna went **by bicycle** but Lucy went **by taxi**.
> He was chased by police **on foot**.

- specific times (or events connected with them) with the prepositions *at*, *before*, or *by*, *dawn*, *sunrise*, *sunset*, *noon*, *midnight*, *night*, *breakfast*, *supper*, *dinner*, *day*, *night*.

> *Tomoko rose **at dawn** and went to bed **at sunset**.*
> *We swam in the pool **by day** and partied **by night**.*

- meals: to have *breakfast*, *lunch*, *brunch*, *supper*, *dinner*.

> *Jane had **breakfast** at home.*
> *She met Diana **for lunch**.*

- some institutions, with the prepositions *in*, *to*, *at*, or sometimes *from*: *church*, *college*, *jail*, *prison*, *school*, *work*.

> *John went **to college** in Wisconsin.*
> *Luella was sent home **from school** today.*
> *Ruth was **at home** all day.*

- seasons of the year, when you are generalizing, e.g.: *in spring*, *in summer*, *in autumn*, *in winter*. With *fall*, however, the definite article is usually used.

> *In spring, the potatoes are planted by machine.*
> *The place is packed **in summer**.*
> *In the fall, the grapes are harvested by hand.*

However, all of these words are used with the definite article when you are talking about a specific time, place, season, etc.

> *Philip traveled by **the same train** as Mehandra.*
> *Just look at **the wonderful sunset**.*
> *Pam works at **the prison**.*
> *I can't work well **in the summer**.*

Demonstratives

Demonstratives are used to specify the distance of something in space or time in relation to the speaker.

The **demonstratives** are: *this, that, these, those*.

This and *these* refer to objects near the speaker.

> *This apple looks ripe.*
> *These apples come from Oregon.*

The reference may be nearness in time, especially future time.

> *I'll stop by this afternoon.*
> *The festival ends this Thursday.*
> *This summer is the warmest I can remember.*

That and *those* refer to objects that are further away from the speaker.

> *I think that boy over there is lost.*
> *Can you see those people up on the hill?*

This and *that* are used before singular countable nouns and uncountable nouns.

> *I can take down this painting, but I can't reach that one.*
> *This book is mine, but that magazine isn't.*

These and *those* are used before plural countable nouns.

> *I'm peeling these potatoes to make hash browns.*
> *Those men are repairing the roof.*

Possessives

Possessives are used to specify the ownership of an item, or, if the noun refers to something living, to specify a relationship.

> *That is* **my** *car.*
> *Mr. Smith was* **my teacher** *in sixth grade.*

The form of the possessive changes according to the number and gender of the person or thing that possesses the item.

> **His brothers** *all came to the wedding.*
> **Their aunt** *lives in St. Louis, but* **their cousins** *live in Chicago.*
> **Your shoes** *are under* **your bed**.

person	singular	plural
1st	my	our
2nd	your	your
3rd (masculine)	his	their
3rd (feminine)	her	their
3rd (neuter)	its	their

> Possessive determiners, which can go into a noun phrase, are not the same as possessive pronouns (*mine*, *hers*, *yours*, etc.), which can stand alone. See p. 148.

Another sort of possessive is the **possessive phrase**. This acts just like a possessive word but is a noun or noun phrase ending in -'s or -s'. A possessive phrase acts as a possessive determiner, but may itself include one of the other determiners.

Robert's mother
the visitors' restroom
a good day's work
the President's press secretary

Sally's new job
the residents' dining room
my wife's cousin

Quantifiers

Quantifiers are used to indicate the amount or quantity of something referred to by a noun. They are different from numbers because they indicate an approximate amount rather than an exact amount. They can be grouped according to their use.

all, some, any, much, enough, no

- You can use *all*, *some*, *any*, or *enough* before a plural countable noun or an uncountable noun.

  > *Can I have **some** chips, please?*
  > *Anna gave me **all** her money.*
  > *Peter never has **any** time to visit us.*

You can use *no* before a singular or a plural countable noun or an uncountable noun.

  > *There were **no** pictures of the party.*
  > *There is **no** hospital in this town.*
  > ***No** information has been released yet.*

- *Some, any, much,* and *enough* are used to refer to a part of the item.

  > *Would you like **some** ice cream?*
  > *We didn't have **much** success.*
  > *I haven't seen **enough** evidence to convince me.*
  > *I couldn't find **any** fresh eggs at the supermarket.*

All and *no* refer to the whole of the item.

  > ***All** the milk has been used.*
  > *There is **no** milk in the fridge.*

- *Some* is used in positive sentences.

  > I've bought **some** chocolate.
  > I found **some** great deals in town this morning.

- *Any* is used in negative sentences.

  > I didn't buy **any** chocolate this week.
  > I haven't seen **any** birds in the backyard today.

- In questions, *any* is used when there is no particular expectation about the answer; *some* is used when the answer is expected to be positive.

  > Have you got **any** double-A batteries?
  > Has Paul heard **any** news about the accident?
  > Would you like **some** cake, Aisha?

- The use of *no* with *there is/are* is very common.

  > **There was no mail** today.
  > There are **no jobs** available for electricians at the moment.

half, double, both

- *Half* can be used with countable nouns and with uncountable nouns.

  > **Half the time** I didn't understand what was going on.
  > **Half the students** came from overseas.

- *Double* is used with uncountable nouns.

  > We're going to need **double the present supply** of water.
  > They want **double the money** they originally asked for.

- *Both* is used to define two things represented by a plural countable noun.

> *Both men were given another chance.*
> *Both dogs had to be put down.*

See p. 165 for more information about quantifiers when they are used with other determiners.

The following quantifiers are used to express **graded** amounts of an item (i.e., whether there is more or less of something).

> *Have you seen **many tourists** in town?*
> *Yes, I've seen **more tourists** than usual.*
> *I think **most tourists** just stay for a couple of days.*

> *I didn't put **much gas** in the car.*
> *I think we need **more gas**.*
> *The news caused **much excitement**.*
> ***Most information** about our services is available on the Internet.*

- *Many*, *more*, *most* are used with graded quantities of plural countable nouns.

> *Have you seen **many tourists** in town?*
> *Yes, I've seen **more tourists** than usual.*
> *I think **most tourists** just stay for a couple of days.*

- *Much*, *more*, *most* are used with graded quantities of uncountable nouns.

> *I didn't put **much gas** in the car.*
> *I think we need **more gas**.*
> *The news caused **much excitement**.*
> ***Most information** about our services is available on the Internet.*

- *Few, fewer, fewest* are used with graded quantities of plural countable nouns.

  Few people know the answer to this problem.
  Fewer loans are being granted than usual.
  Japanese workers take *the fewest holidays*.

- *Little, less, least* are used with graded quantities of uncountable nouns.

  There is *little chance* of rain today.
  This technique causes *less harm* to the environment.
  I need to get from one place to another with *the least inconvenience*.

Many speakers do not make the above distinction and use less and least with both countable and uncountable nouns. This is common but not technically correct.

- *A few*, and *a little* are different from *few* and *little* on their own because they have a positive sense. *Few* means "not many":

  Few buildings survived the earthquake.

but *a few* means "several."

  A few kind people helped the injured man.
  A few delays are inevitable.

Little means "not much":

  The students were given very *little help* with their projects.
  Edward got *little encouragement* from his parents.

but *a little* means "some."

> *I need a little help from my friends.*
> *Everyone needs a little encouragement now and then.*
> *Do you take sugar? – Just a little, please.*

Few and *little* are often used in a negative sense to suggest disappointment or pessimism, while *a few* and *a little* are used in a positive sense to suggest that things are better than they might have been.

Numbers

There are two common kinds of number:

Cardinal numbers are used in all forms of counting that involve a total.

one chair   *two* chairs
a hundred people   *ten thousand* dollars

Ordinal numbers are used to talk about where something is placed in an ordered sequence. They are often used right after the definite article or after a possessive.

The first horse to finish was disqualified.
He's celebrating his fifty-first birthday in August.
*The company has just celebrated its one hundred and fiftieth
    anniversary.*

Ordinals are mostly formed by adding *-th* to a cardinal number.

fourth   *twentieth*   *hundredth*
fifth   *forty-ninth*   *millionth*
sixth   *eighty-sixth*   *thousandth*
nine hundred and ninety-ninth

Some examples of exceptions are the words *first*, *second*, and *third*, and combinations which contain them, such as *twenty-first*.

Cardinal numbers can be used at the beginning of a noun phrase, like determiners.

one chair   *two* chairs
a hundred people   *ten thousand* dollars

or on their own, like pronouns.

> And then there were **three**.
> **Four** of them came toward us.
> The other **two** went to get help.

- Grammatically speaking, the words *next*, *last*, and *another* can also be regarded as ordinal numbers.

> It rained on the **last** day of our vacation.
> The **next** horse to finish was declared the winner.
> Oh no, not **another** birthday!

Ordinal numbers and the words *next* and *last* are sometimes called **postdeterminers**, since they come after the word *the* or a possessive.

> The **next** three days are going to be very exciting.
> The **last** three years have been difficult for everyone.
> We have to get off the bus at the **next** stop.

- An ordinal, as well as *next*, *last*, and *another*, can be used together with a cardinal number in the same noun phrase.

> The **first three** correct entries will win a prize.
> He scored **another two** goals before the end of the match.

- To show that a cardinal number is only approximate, the word some is often used before it.

> **Some two hundred** people gathered in the pouring rain.

Distributives

Distributives are determiners that are used to talk about how something is shared out or divided.

The distributives are *each*, *every*, *either*, and *neither*. They are used with a singular countable noun.

> *Each child was given a balloon.*
> *I remember every detail of our conversation.*
> *Either child could win the prize.*
> *Neither plan was successful.*

- *Each* and *every* are not used with proper nouns.

- *Each* is used to refer to separate persons or things in a group of two or more.

> *Four girls came and each one sang a song.*
> *Each ticket should have a number on the back.*

- *Every* is used to refer to all the persons or things in a group of three or more.

> *Every teacher has a key to the building.*
> *Katrina danced with every boy at the party.*

- *Every* can be used in front of ordinal numbers. "*Every second house*" means *the second house, the fourth house, the sixth house*, and so on.

> *I have to work every third weekend.*
> *Every fourth block has a fire hydrant.*

– *Either* is used to talk about one of two people or things.

> *They did not appoint either man as captain.*
> *Either restaurant would suit me.*

– *Neither* is used to exclude both of two people or things that are being referred to.

> *They appointed neither man as captain.*
> *Neither restaurant is cheap enough.*

Exclamatives

Exclamatives are used to introduce an exclamation of surprise, admiration, or a similar emotion.

The exclamatives are: *what*, *such*.

Exclamations introduced by one of these words consist either of:

- the exclamative in a noun phrase alone (usually with *What...*).

> *What a laugh!*
> *What awful weather!*
> *Such good manners!*

- the exclamative and its noun phrase in a complete clause.

> *He is such a nice man!*
> *You always wear such beautiful things!*
> *What a pleasant surprise this is!*

Noun phrases with several determiners

Most noun phrases contain only one determiner or none at all, but if there are more, they follow a definite order. Determiners can be divided into four groups, depending on what other determiners they can be used with and the order that they follow.

There are two large groups:

A *the*, *this*, *these*, *that*, *those*, *a(n)*, and the possessives *my*, *your*, *her*, *his*, etc.

> *a ripe orange*   *my young sister*
> *this ripe orange*   *our young sister*

B *another*, *some*, *any*, *no*, *either*, *neither*, *each*, *enough*, *a few*, *a little*.

> *each ripe orange*   *another sister*
> *some ripe oranges*   *enough money*

The words in groups A and B are known as the **central determiners**. A noun phrase will normally contain only one central determiner.

- The group A and group B words cannot be used together, with this exception: words in group B may be followed by a group A word if *of* is placed between them.

> *some* of *those* oranges   *neither* of *my* sisters

There are two smaller groups.

C   The smallest group consists of these words: *all*, *both*, *half*, *double*, and *twice*. These can be used on their own before a noun or before the group A determiners above. Some speakers of English prefer to insert *of* between *all*, *both*, or *half* and a central determiner.

> *All of the* visitors left the ship.
> *Half of the* oranges were thrown away.

- The words in group C are sometimes called **predeterminers**. The exclamatives *such* and *what* belong to this group. See p. 184 for more details about these.

D   The words in the fourth group are, *every*, *many*, *several*, *few*, *little*, *much*, *more*, *most*, *less*, the ordinal numbers *first*, *second*, *third*, etc., and *last*. These can be used on their own before a noun,

> *Every* move was carefully recorded.
> She did *many* kind things.
> She has *few* friends.
> *Last* call for Philadelphia. All aboard!

or after the A group of determiners.

> Your *every* move is being watched.
> The *many* kind things she did went unnoticed.
> Her *few* possessions had been stolen.
> The *first* thing she did was call her mother.
> I will always remember *these last few* days.

- Words in group A can be used in combination with determiners in groups C and D.

> *Both* girls were reading.
> *Both my* young sisters are really naughty.
> *All* visitors must now leave the ship.
> *All the* visitors left the ship.

Adjectives

Adjectives are used with nouns to make the meaning more specific. If you use the noun *"dog"* it can mean any animal of that species. As soon as you say *"a large, brown dog"* you have given two of its **attributes** (color and size). A noun is said to be **modified** by its adjectives.

Adjectives have two main features:

- most adjectives can go before a noun; this is known as their **attributive** use.

    a tall girl
    green grass
    four badly behaved little boys

- most adjectives can also go after a link verb such as *be* or *seem*; this is known as their **predicative**, or **predicate**, use.

    The roses are yellow.
    The girls are getting tall.
    These books seem really interesting.

Any word that can go into both of these positions is a normal adjective. When used predicatively (after a link verb), an adjective can either describe the **subject** of a sentence,

    The roses are yellow.
    The girls are getting tall.
    These books are really interesting.

or the **object** of the sentence. See also p. 15.

    Anna painted the room green.
    The children drove him crazy.

Adjective order

The order is normally:

- adjectives that describe feelings or qualities.

    pleasant childhood memories
    beautiful brown hands

- adjectives of size, age, temperature, or measurement.

    some hot biscuits
    a rectangular baking dish
    those nice young girls
    a big smile

- adjectives of color.

    the green hills of home
    stylish brown shoes
    her beautiful blue eyes

- adjectives of nationality or origin.

    those friendly Spanish girls
    both the small gray Irish horses
    an elegant French woman

- adjectives denoting the substance or material that something is made from.

    a large wooden door
    an elegant silver teapot

It is possible to use adjectives next to each other in English, but in practice more than four is uncommon.

> *a happy young blonde German* girl
> *beautiful old colonial brick* houses

- Adjectives before a noun are not usually separated by *and*, unless they are adjectives of color.

> *a green and white* striped shirt
> *a red and blue* flag

- Adjectives can themselves be premodified by adverbs of degree. See also p. 190.

> *an* **extremely** *intelligent* student
> *a* **very** *tall* man
> *a* **fairly** *messy* apartment

Some adjectives can only be used predicatively (i.e., after a link verb such as *be*). Many of the members of this group begin with *a-*:

> *abroad, afloat, afraid, alike, alive, alone, ashamed, asleep, awake.*

> *Our balloon was* **aloft** *at last.*
> *Charles is* **ashamed** *of what he did.*
> *The child is* **afraid***.*
> *The girls were* **asleep** *and were not* **aware** *of the noise.*

When an adjective is used predicatively it may have to be followed by a particular preposition if the phrase continues.

She was glad.	*She was* **glad** *to help.*
He was afraid.	*He was* **afraid** *for his life.*
I was free.	*I was* **free** *from guilt.*
It is **devoid** *of interest.*	*He was* **intent** *on revenge.*

There are some adjectives such as *devoid (of)*, *intent (on)* that always have to have a following phrase.

Although attributive adjectives usually come before the noun that they modify, there are some that can go immediately after the noun, particularly when they are used with plural nouns, e.g., *absent*, *present*, *involved*, *concerned*. When these adjectives are used in this position they may have a different meaning from the one that they have when they come before the noun.

> *Everyone **present** was offered juice.*
> *The **present government** took over four years ago.*
> *The **people absent** from work were all ill.*
> *Let us toast **absent friends**.*
> *The **dealers concerned** were sent to jail.*
> *There were letters from **concerned parents**.*
> *I prefer to have a **proper** introduction before we speak.*
> *Do you live in the city **proper** or a near suburb?*

- There are some set phrases that always have an adjective immediately after the noun. These are essentially noun phrases consisting of noun + adjective.

> *the **Surgeon General**   a **lion rampant***
> *the **president elect**   the **Attorney General***
> *a **court martial**   the **Prince Regent***

Premodifiers and postmodifiers

Adjectives, determiners, and other nouns can all be used to describe a noun more specifically; that is, they can be used as **modifiers**. Nouns can also be modified by prepositional groups (groups of words that begin with a preposition) and relative clauses added after the noun. See p. 273 for more about relative clauses.

To make it simpler to talk about any modifying word that comes in front of a noun, we can use the term **premodifier**.

a young man   *these* onions
my aunt's house   *the elephant* house

Those modifiers that come after the noun are called **postmodifiers**.

the young man **with the guitar**
the person **who met me**
the girl **I was standing near**
the people **involved**

Very few single-word adjectives in English are used only as **postmodifiers**.

riot police galore
flirting 101

Comparison

The **comparative** form of an adjective is commonly used to compare two people, things, or states, when you want to say that one thing has a larger or smaller amount of a quality than another.

- If the second part of the comparison is mentioned it follows *than*.

    *Anna is **taller than** Mary but Mary is **older**.*
    *Emma is much **thinner than** when I last saw her.*
    *Online learning is **less expensive than** conventional college courses.*

- Comparison in which you are considering whether two people or things are equal is shown by using *as...as* in the affirmative and *not as...as* or *not so...as* in the negative.

    *Helen is **as tall as** Linda, but **not as strong**.*

The **superlative** form is used for more than two people, things, or states, when one thing has qualities that exceed all the others. Superlative adjectives have ***the*** in front of them, but it can be omitted in predicative positions.

    *That is **the smallest** camera I have ever seen.*
    *He gave **the least expensive** gift to his sister.*
    *I'll have whichever is **ripest**.*

There are two ways in which the comparative and superlative forms of adjectives are formed:

- You add *-er* (comparative) or *-est* (superlative) to the adjective. Adjectives with one syllable usually take these endings.

	comparative	superlative
bright	brighter	the brightest
long	longer	the longest
sharp	sharper	the sharpest

- If the word already ends in -*e*, then only -*r* or –*st* is added. If a word ends in -*y*, it usually takes -*er* or -*est*, and the -*y* changes to -*i*.

	comparative	superlative
wise	wiser	the wisest
pretty	prettier	the prettiest
weary	wearier	the weariest

- You add the word *more* or *most* in front of the adjective. Adjectives with three syllables or more use *more* or *most* in front of the adjective.

	comparative	superlative
fortunate	**more** fortunate	the **most** fortunate
relevant	**more** relevant	the **most** relevant

Adjectives formed from participles use *more* or *most* as well.

	comparative	superlative
provoking	**more** provoking	the **most** provoking
enthralled	**more** enthralled	the **most** enthralled

To indicate the opposite of both the -*er/-est* and the *more/most* forms of comparison, *less* or *least* are always used.

	comparative	superlative
sharp	*less* sharp	the *least* sharp
fortunate	*less* fortunate	the *least* fortunate
interesting	*less* interesting	the *least* interesting
involved	*less* involved	the *least* involved

> Adjectives with two syllables (including those that already end in *-er*) can follow either pattern or sometimes both patterns. If you are doubtful about a two-syllable adjective, use the *more/most* pattern.

comparative	superlative	
shallow	shallower	the *shallowest*
or	*more* shallow	the *most* shallow
polite	politer	the *politest*
or	*more* polite	the *most* polite

A small group of irregular adjectives have quite different forms for the comparative and superlative forms.

comparative	superlative	
good	better	the *best*
bad	worse	the *worst*
far	further	the *furthest*

Far also has the regular forms *farther* and *farthest* but they are less common and typically used only where the meaning is about physical distances.

Adverbs and adverbials

When you want to add information about *how*, *when*, *where*, or *to what extent* something has happened, you can use an **adverbial**. Many adverbials are members of the group of words called **adverbs**, but adverbials are not necessarily just single words. They can also be word groups, prepositional phrases, or even clauses.

Adverbials generally modify the meaning of a verb,

> I *really* admire your courage.
> They changed *hurriedly* into their pajamas.
> Monica hummed *softly* as she washed the car.
> The firecracker exploded *with a loud bang*.
> He ran *across the lawn* toward the house.

an adjective,

> Harry is **totally** mystified by the result.
> You must admit that he can be **pretty** boring.
> That is **completely** unacceptable.
> Fears like that are **very** real to the sufferer.

another adverb,

> I thought about it **quite** seriously.
> The children are behaving **remarkably** well.
> Ali objected **very** strongly to the plan.

a whole sentence,

> **Frankly**, I think he is lying.
> **Nevertheless**, we must give him a chance.
> **Honestly**, I didn't mean to be rude to you.

or a prepositional phrase.

> *We are really in a no-win situation.*

Most adverbials are optional parts of a clause or phrase, but there are a few verbs that need an adverb to complete their meaning. See p. 85. Conditional sentences must also have an adverbial clause, usually one beginning with *if* or *unless*. See p. 270 for more about adverbial clauses.

Adverbials can be divided into:

– adverbials of **manner**, which express *how*: e.g., *slowly, with care, well.*

> *Two men were working their way **slowly** up the hillside.*

– adverbials of **place**, which express *where*: e.g., *there, here, up, in town.*

> *Two men were working their way **up the hillside**.*

– adverbials of **time**, which express *when*: e.g., *now, today, last night, lately.*

> *Two men were lost on the hills **yesterday**.*

– adverbials of **degree**, which express *to what extent*: e.g., *largely, extremely, much, by a hair.*

> *It was **largely** their own fault.*

– adverbials of **frequency**, which express *how often*: e.g., *rarely, often, sometimes, twice daily.*

> *Search parties went out **every hour**.*

Although adverbials change the meaning of clauses or phrases, they are usually optional parts of the group or clause.

> *He coughed* **nervously***.*
> **Really***, I think you are mistaken.*
> **In a fit of temper***, he slammed the door shut.*

They stand outside the word, group, or clause that they are associated with. For example, the same adverb can in one sentence be part of the description of a verb, while in another sentence, it may modify the whole clause.

> *I think she acted* **honestly***.*
> **Honestly***, who does she think she is?*

The exceptions are that:

– some verbs must be followed by an adverbial to complete their meaning.

> *Alice behaved* **wonderfully***.*
> *Sylvia acted* **unlawfully***.*
> *Justin sped* **down the corridor***.*

– some verbs require both an object and an adverbial to complete their meaning. See also p. 32.

> *Ranjit put the folder* **back***.*
> *Jamal stood the golf clubs* **in the corner***.*
> *Clare placed the cover* **over the crib***.*

• New meanings can be made by combining an adverbial with a verb to make a phrasal verb. See also p. 84 for more about phrasal verbs.

> *The car* **pulled** *out.*
> *Lydia* **went** *away.*
> *Things* **are looking** *up.*

Adverbials are classified according to the way they modify a word, group or clause. In addition to the uses given on p. 195, one important use of a special group of adverbials is to show how a sentence relates to what comes before it. An adverb used in this way is called a **sentence adverb**.

> *Nevertheless*, *we must give him an answer.*
> *However*, *it's good advice.*
> *On the other hand*, *we cannot turn him down.*

Another use of adverbials is to let your listener or reader know your point of view about a situation. This is called a **viewpoint adverb**.

> *Foolishly*, *I gave him my address.*
> *Clearly*, *he deserves our help.*
> *Actually*, *I don't mind.*

A further group of adverbials, all of them adverbs of degree, can only be used with adjectives or other adverbs. Examples are *very*, *fairly*, *rather*, *quite*, *really*, *too*, *somewhat*, and *pretty*, which is informal. These are sometimes called **submodifiers** because they can weaken or strengthen the descriptive value of the adjective.

> *She seems* **pretty** *nice.*
> *Antwon is a* **very** *good tennis player.*
> *Kim gave me this* **really** *expensive bag.*

They are used mainly with adjectives of quality. An adverb can also be submodified by another adverb.

> *She began to cry,* **very loudly***.*
> *Sometimes I think you're* **too easily** *impressed.*
> *It must have been done* **extremely recently***.*
> *The car was* **almost totally** *submerged in the flood water.*

There are certain adverbs (and adverbials) that can only be used with verbs and so cannot modify adjectives.

- Most adverbs can be used:

– before the verb phrase or the subject

> *Happily, she ran over the sand dunes.*
> *Tearfully, he told his brother the whole story.*

– after the verb phrase or the object

> *She ran **happily** over the sand dunes.*
> *He was telling the whole story **tearfully** to his brother.*

– between the auxiliary and the main verb.

> *She was **happily** running about over the sand dunes.*
> *He was **tearfully** telling the whole story to his brother.*

- Some adverbs can only come **after** the verb, e.g., *back, up, down, sideways, clockwise*.

> *Suddenly the frightened animal ran **back**.*
> *They hammered the wedge in **sideways**.*

- A few adverbs can come **before** the main verb, e.g., *barely, hardly, little, rarely, scarcely, seldom*.

> ***Scarcely had she spoken** when it came crashing down.*
> *He **had hardly eaten** anything.*
> ***Seldom** have I seen such ridiculous behavior.*

Notice that a subordinate clause beginning with one of these words has the same word order as a question: finite verb before subject. These are called **broad negatives**, because they give a negative meaning to a clause.

Compare:

> They *never noticed* her presence.
> They *scarcely noticed* her presence.

Some speakers take care not to place an adverb between the *to* and the **base form** of the verb in a "*to* **infinitive**." This is called a "split infinitive." There is no good reason to regard a split infinitive as an error; the choice is a matter of personal preference.

> I need to *really* think hard about this.
> I *really* need to think hard about this.

Adverbs with nouns and pronouns

While **adverbs** can modify most parts of speech, they normally do not modify **nouns** or **pronouns**. Much more common is the use of an adverb of degree to modify a whole **noun phrase**.

> Jason is *quite a skilled craftsman*.

There is a small group of adverbs that can modify nouns and indefinite pronouns.

> the *man downstairs*
> the *example above*
> *Almost everyone* brought a bottle to the party.
> *Most of the stores uptown* close at 6 p.m.

Form of adverbs

Most **adverbs** are formed by adding -*ly* to the end of the related adjective.

slow	slowly
clever	cleverly
annual	annually

Words that end in -*ble* drop off the -*e* before -*ly* is added. So do the words *true* and *due*.

sensible	sensibly
suitable	suitably
true	truly
due	duly

> A common spelling mistake is to add -*ley*. This mistake is often made when the adjective ends in the letter -*e*. Note the correct spelling of adverbs formed from adjectives ending in -*e*.
>
> | | |
> |---|---|
> | extreme | extremely |
> | divine | divinely |
> | free | freely |

Adjectives that end in -*y* change to -*i* before adding -*ly*, unless, like *sly* or *dry*, they have only one syllable.

happy	happily
greedy	greedily
sly	slyly

Some adverbs keep the same spelling as the adjective to which they are related. It is often difficult to tell at first whether the word is an adjective or an adverb. The general rule is to look at the other words that it occurs with. If it comes before a noun it is probably an adjective.

a short way   *a late meeting*
a long pause   *an early lecture*

If it relates to a verb or an adjective it is probably an adverb.

The lesson was cut short.
We met late at night.
Don't stay long.
He came in early.

Some adverbs have the same spelling as a preposition. They can be told apart if you look at the words they are found with. Prepositions are normally used in front of noun phrases, because prepositions must have an object.

He rushed in an attempt to catch his bus.
She hurried over her meal because she was late.

When the word is found without an object, especially at the end of a clause, it will usually be an adverb.

He rushed in.
She hurried over.

Just like certain adjectives, some adverbs have comparative and superlative forms and can be used with submodifiers.

Kim treated Sharon well, Karen less well and Janice the least well.
Malcolm walked the most slowly of all of them.
Tariq acted very kindly toward him.
You must behave much more sensibly in the future.
This graph shows that girls performed the best at math this year.

Superlative forms of adverbs are rare.

Pronouns

A **pronoun** is a word that is used in the place of a noun or a whole noun phrase.

Pronouns are commonly used:

- in place of a noun or a noun phrase that has already been mentioned.

> *Sam has to go to the airport. Can you give **him** a ride?*
> *The vice president and his wife came out onto the balcony.*
> ***They** waved to the crowd.*
> *The mechanic tested the starter. **It** would not work.*
> ***He** tried **it** again.*

- when we know who or what is referred to. When, for example, *I* use the pronoun I it is because it would be unusual to refer to myself by name.

> *I'm sorry I'm late.*
> *We'd better call and say **we're** not coming.*

- when the name of someone or something is not known.

> *He's the man who came to the house yesterday!*
> *Who's she?*

Types of pronoun

There are seven different types of pronoun, classified according to their meaning and use.

The **personal** pronouns can be used as subject or object in a clause.

> *He gave her a box of chocolates.*
> *We saw them both on Friday.*
> *I can see you!*

The **reflexive** pronouns are used in object position in sentences where the subject and the object refer to the same person or thing. You must use them with certain verbs.

> *The puppy entangled itself in the leash.*
> *I've just cut myself on a piece of glass.*

Reflexive pronouns are also used for emphasis.

> *Never mind. I'll do it myself.*
> *The professor himself did not know the answer.*

The **possessive** pronouns indicate ownership.

> *Give it back, it's mine.*
> *Perhaps it really is theirs after all.*

The **demonstrative** pronouns indicate items that are near to or far from us.

> *This is Betty's and that is Pedro's.*
> *These are nice. Where did you find them?*

The **relative** pronouns are used to link a modifying clause to a noun phrase or to a clause.

> *I don't know what you mean.*
> *That's the girl who always comes in first.*

The **interrogative** pronouns are used to ask a question about the noun phrase they stand in for.

> *What would you like for lunch?*
> *Which should I open first?*
> *Who was responsible?*

The **indefinite** pronouns are used for a broad range of reference when it is not necessary or not possible to use a personal pronoun.

> *Everyone had a compass and a whistle.*
> *Neither wanted to give in and apologize.*
> *Much needs to be done.*

Personal pronouns

Personal pronouns are used as the subject, object, or complement in a clause. They are commonly found taking the place of a noun phrase when it is mentioned for a second time.

person subject	object	singular subject	object	plural
1st	I	me	we	us
2nd	you	you	you	you
3rd masculine	he	him	they	them
3rd feminine	she	her	they	them
3rd neutral	it	it	they	them

The 1st person pronouns refer to the speaker or writer. The 2nd person pronoun *you* refers to the listener or reader. In the case of *you*, there is only one pronoun to cover the singular and the plural, so that it is sometimes necessary to use a form of words that will make clear who is being addressed.

> *You* should be ashamed.
> *All of you* should be ashamed.
> *You* must *all* stop writing now.

In informal and dialectal English, people use other forms to distinguish singular *you* from plural *you*.

> *Y'all* should be ashamed.
> *You guys* are late.

When more than one personal pronoun is used with a verb, the order is normally: 3rd or 2nd person before 1st person; 2nd person before 3rd person.

>*She and I do not get along very well.*
>*You and he should share the cost.*

When two pronouns or a personal noun and a personal pronoun are the joint subject of a verb, the subject form of the pronouns must be used. Avoid the common mistake of saying, for example, *Jerry and me are...*

>*Jerry and I are going to paint the house ourselves.*
>*He and I are going to paint it.*
>*Melanie and I are going shopping.*

When either two pronouns or a noun plus a personal pronoun are the joint object of a verb, the object form of the pronoun must be used:

>*They decided to help Jane and me.*

The object form of a pronoun is used after a preposition. Avoid the common mistake of saying, for example, *between you and I.*

>*Between you and me, I don't like this place.*
>*Wasn't that silly of me?*

The object form is usual in everyday spoken usage. In formal and old-fashioned English, the subject form is used:

— after the verb *be*.

It's me.	(informal)
It is I.	(formal/old-fashioned)
I saw at once that it was her.	(informal)
I saw at once that it was she.	(formal/old-fashioned)

— after *than* in comparison with *be*.

John is smaller than him.	(informal)
John is smaller than he (is).	(formal/old-fashioned)
Sylvia is smarter than me.	(informal)
Sylvia is smarter than I (am).	(formal/old-fashioned)

Otherwise, *than* + **object** pronoun is necessary.

> *She's probably done more than me.*

• The object form is also used to supply short answers to questions.

> *Who found Glen's watch? – Me. Aren't I clever!*

Reflexive pronouns

Reflexive pronouns are used whenever a grammatical object refers to the same person or thing as the subject in a sentence.

person	singular	plural
1st	myself	ourselves
2nd	yourself	yourselves
3rd masculine	himself	themselves
3rd feminine	herself	themselves
3rd neuter	itself	themselves
General	oneself	

I cut *myself* with the butcher knife.	(direct object)
John was surprised at *himself*.	(prepositional object)
John taught *himself* Latin.	(indirect object)

The reflexive form *oneself* can be used to refer to a person in general, though many speakers consider this formal and use *yourself* instead.

> The first golden rule is not to take *oneself* too seriously. (formal)
> The first golden rule is not to take *yourself* too seriously. (standard)

Oneself can also be used as a substitute for the 1st person singular. If it is used like this, the subject pronoun should be *one*. Most speakers also consider this formal and use the second person instead.

> One asks *oneself* whether it is worth the trouble. (formal)
> You ask *yourself* whether it is worth the trouble. (standard)

Some verbs take a reflexive pronoun only in particular uses of the verb.

> Jeremy introduced **himself**.
> The cat washed **itself**.

The reflexive pronoun can be left out if it is obvious that the subject was performing the action of the verb on him- or herself.

> Jeremy **washed** and **dressed**, then went out.

When a preposition is followed by a pronoun, the pronoun is normally in the object form.

> They all looked at **him** in silence.

If that pronoun refers to the subject of the main verb, however, it must be a reflexive pronoun.

> She looked at **herself** in the mirror.

- The reflexive can be used to make something you say stronger. To make a strong point, we sometimes use a normal subject or object pronoun and a reflexive pronoun as well.

> He told me **himself** that he was leaving.
> I'll do it **myself**.

- The reflexive can also be used with or without by meaning "alone" or "without help."

> I think you should try and do it **yourself**.
> Did she do that all by **herself**?

The compound pronouns *each other* and *one another* are not true reflexives. They are used when two or more subjects take part in the same action that affects both of them. They are sometimes called **reciprocals**.

> They should stop blaming **one another**.
> We will always love **each other**.

Possessive pronouns

Possessive pronouns are used when you want to indicate who owns or is associated with an item.

> *All those books are **hers**.*
> *Those suitcases are **ours**.*
> *Are you selling those books? I'd never sell any of mine.*
> *Those awful cousins of yours are here.*
> *This TV is really cheap. – Yes, **ours** was a bit more expensive, but better quality.*

There are separate forms for the singular and the plural except in the 2nd person. In the 3rd person singular the form changes to match the gender of the possessor.

> *I'm looking for Helen's sneakers. Perhaps these are **hers**.*
> *These are our seats and the ones in front are **yours**.*

possessive determiner	possessive pronoun
my	mine
your (singular)	yours
his	his
her	hers
its	(no form)
our	ours
your (plural)	yours
their	theirs

Note that none of these words should be spelled with an apostrophe. Avoid the common mistake of writing *it's* for the possessive form. *It's* is a short form for *it is*.

The demonstrative pronouns

The demonstrative pronouns are used instead of a noun phrase to indicate distance in time or space in relation to the speaker. They also indicate grammatical number (singular or plural).

	singular	plural
near	this	these
far	that	those

- The demonstrative pronouns are the same words as demonstrative determiners; how they are used determines which of these roles they fill. See also p. 164. Usually a demonstrative pronoun substitutes for a noun phrase that contains the same word being used as a determiner. In speech, demonstrative pronouns are often accompanied by a body movement that indicates the noun being talked about, or in a context where both listener and speaker know what object is being referred to and so need not name it.

  Would you like to share some of this pizza with me?
  *Would you like to share **this** with me?*
  I'd like you to put these things away before we go.
  *I'd like you to put **these** away before we go.*

- It is impolite to use a demonstrative pronoun to refer directly to a person, except when making introductions.

  *John, **this** is Harry Forbes, my colleague.*
  ***This** is my husband, Rob.*
  *Mom, **this** is my former teacher, Miss Evans.*

Relative pronouns

The relative pronouns are the words *who*, *whom*, *which*, and *that*.

	person	*thing*
subject	*who* or *that*	*which* or *that*
object	*whom* or *that*	*which* or *that*
possessive	*whose*	*whose*

The function of a relative pronoun is to link a subordinate clause to a main clause or to some other sentence element.

> **He might lose his job,** *which would be disastrous.*
> **Tim gave away all the money** *that was left.*

A subordinate clause introduced by a relative pronoun is called a **relative clause**.

Relative pronouns refer back to a noun phrase or pronoun that has just been mentioned. All relative pronouns must come as near as possible to the start of the clause that they are in. The only words that normally come before them in the clause are prepositions or conjunctions.

The choice of relative pronoun is influenced as follows:

– *that* is the most usual pronoun, but note that it never has a preposition before it. It can introduce both human and nonhuman subjects or objects.

> *This is* **the person** *that Annie was talking about.*
> *Here's* **the jacket** *that you forgot.*
> *This is* **the person** *about whom Annie was talking.*
> *That is* **a kind thought,** *for which I am most grateful.*

– *which* is not used for human subjects or objects. It can be used for nonhuman subjects even when there is no preposition involved, but *that* is more common.

> *That is* **the car** *which she has just bought.*
> *I have found* **a ring** *which you will love.*

– *who* and *whom* are restricted to human subjects or objects.

> *He introduced me to* **his friend,** *who had just returned from China.*
> *I liked* **the actor** *who was playing Oedipus.*

– in **defining** relative clauses (see p. 273), *that* can be used for all subjects. *Which* can be used for animals and inanimate things. For people you can also use *who* or *whom*.

> *I have found* **a ring** *that you will love.*
> *I have found* **a ring** *which you will love.*
> *She is* **the girl** *who was at Sam's party.*
> *She is* **the girl** *that was at Sam's party.*

The **object** form of the relative pronoun is used as the object of a verb or a preposition, but because *whom* is very formal, it is not often used: in everyday English, *who* is usually used instead.

> *The late* **principal** *of the school,* **whom** *we all remember with affection, died last week.*

> *I discovered who he was visiting.*   (standard)
> *I discovered whom he was visiting.*   (formal)

• In informal writing and speech, any preposition is placed after the verb phrase instead of before the relative pronoun.

> *The girl* **who** *Brian was talking* **to** *seemed nervous.*
> *The people* **that** *he had been working* **for** *that summer had offered him a permanent job.*

- A defining relative pronoun referring to the object of the clause may be left out entirely as long as the meaning is clear.

> *He is the **person** (that/who/whom) Annie was talking about.*
> *That is the **car** (that/which) she has just bought.*

Interrogative pronouns

The **interrogative pronouns** *who*, *whom*, and *whose* are used only for reference to people. The interrogative pronouns *which* and *what* are used for reference to things.

	subject	object	possessive
people	who	whom	whose
things	which what	which what	

Interrogative pronouns allow us to build a question around the thing that the pronoun refers to. See p. 240, where these pronouns are explained more generally under the heading of **WH-** words.

> **Who** *is dancing with Dontay?*
> **Which** *of these books would you recommend?*
> **What** *do you do when you're on vacation?*
> **Whose** *are these clothes?*

Who is used to ask questions about people in general.

> **Who** *is that man over there?*
> **Who** *did this?*
> **Who** *controls the day-to-day running of the business?*

What is used to ask questions about things in general. **What** can be either a subject or an object in a clause.

> **What** *happened next?*
> **What** *did you have for lunch?*

Which is used ask for identification of a particular person or a particular thing in a group.

>*Which do you prefer, working in theater or film?*
>*Which is your favorite Simpsons episode?*

Whose is the possessive form of the pronoun. It is used when a person is the possessor.

>*Whose is that sports car outside?*
>*Whose side are you on?*

- *Whom* is the object form of *who*. It is a formal word that most speakers avoid using in casual conversation, when *who* can be used instead. When writing, however, it is usual to use *whom*.

  Informal
  Who do you have in mind?
  Who were you speaking to?

  Formal
  Whom do you have in mind?
  To whom were you speaking?

- The object forms of the interrogative pronoun are used after a preposition. In informal and everyday usage, you can place the preposition at the end of the clause.

  Who does this belong to?   (standard)
  To whom does this belong?   (formal)

Indefinite pronouns

The indefinite pronouns are used when you do not know or do not need to say precisely who or what you are referring to. The noun phrase that they substitute for can refer to a person, a thing, or a group of people or things, in which gender and number are not made clear.

> *Someone* will have to tell her that she's failed.
> *Everybody* had a wonderful time.
> *Anything* is better than nothing.
> *Nothing* can make up for this loss.
> Some people like that sort of thing. *Others* don't.

The indefinite pronouns can be grouped according to meaning, as follows:

A General amounts and quantities: *most, some, none, any, all, both, half, several, enough, many, each*.

> *Many* find it impossible to cope.
> Congratulations from *all* at the club.
> Judging by the comments, *most* wanted her to stay on.
> Although we lost a lot of stuff in the fire, *some* was saved.
> *Enough* has been said on this topic to fill a book.

B Choice or alternatives: *either, neither*.

> Could you bring me one of those wrenches? *Either* will do.
> *Neither* was enthusiastic about a traditional wedding.

C Undefined singular or multiple persons and things:

someone	somebody	something
no one	nobody	nothing
anyone	anybody	anything
everyone	everybody	everything

Note the form of *no one*: it is always spelled as two words.

- The pronouns in group C that refer to people can cause problems concerning the **number** and **gender** of a following determiner or pronoun. Traditionally, only the use of a following **singular** form was permitted after all of these words. Today, common practice uses the plural form *their* in order to avoid awkward expressions like *his* or *her*.

> *Everybody* has *their* ups and downs.
> Has *anybody* finished *their* lunch yet?
> *No one* in *their* right mind goes on vacation there in January.

Many of these pronouns, especially those in groups A and B, have the same form as determiners. See p. 164.

- The way to tell a pronoun from a determiner is to see if the word on its own is used as a subject, an object, or the complement of a verb; if it is, it is a **pronoun**. If, on the other hand, it is used in front of a noun, it is a **determiner**.

> As a pronoun:
> *Both* were given life sentences.
> *Several* managed to escape.
> I've found *some*!

> As a determiner:
> *Both men* were given life sentences.
> *Several sheep* managed to escape.
> I've found *some scrap paper*.

- The pronouns in Groups A and B are often used like partitives, with *of* and a noun phrase or a personal pronoun.

> *None* of the children was hurt, but *most* of them were really upset.
> *Neither* of his parents remarried.

Prepositions

A preposition is a word that relates different items in a sentence to each other. Prepositions are very common and most of them are short words. Most English prepositions have a number of different meanings.

Simple prepositions consist of one word, e.g., *in, on, under*. Complex prepositions consist of more than one word, e.g., *due to, together with, on top of, in spite of, out of, because of*.

Prepositions enable us to express:

 - information about space and movement to or from a **place**.
 - information about **time**.
 - information about cause and purpose.
 - information about means or instrument.

Prepositions are normally followed by:

 - a noun phrase.

   in time   *over the edge*
   under the table   *together with my friends*

 - an *-ing* clause.

   Thanks for looking.
   He picked up some extra cash by working in a bar at night.

 - a relative pronoun (**WH-** word).

   He's married to Rachel, with whom he has one daughter.
   The inscription uses characters with which I am unfamiliar.

In everyday speech a preposition may end a relative clause rather than come before it. See also p. 274.

> *That's the girl we were talking **about**.*
> *That's the man (**who**) I gave the money **to**.*

A preposition needs an object—that is, a noun phrase that completes its meaning. A preposition and the noun phrase that goes with it is called a **prepositional phrase**.

A prepositional phrase can be used as an **adverbial**;

> *He put the flowers **on the table**.*
> *She shut the dog **in the kitchen**.*
> *He found the papers **in time for the meeting**.*

as a **postmodifier**;

> *The house **on the corner** has at last been sold.*
> *The flowers **on the table** are from Tim.*
> *A bird **with brilliant plumage** roamed the lawns.*

or as the **complement** of a verb or adjective.

> *Someone is **in the shed**.*
> *We were staring **at the accident**.*
> *I'm so sorry **for what I said**.*

- Prepositions combine with some verbs to make new meanings from the combination. These are one type of **phrasal verb**. See p. 84.

> *We **believe in** his innocence.*
> *I **stand for** justice.*
> *She **went through** a terrifying experience.*

The list below shows all the common simple prepositions. Some words can be either **prepositions** or **adverbs**, depending on how they are used and what they combine with. The words in *italics* are the prepositions that can also be used as **adverbs**.

> aboard, *about*, *above*, *across*, *after*, against, *along*, *alongside*, amid, among, *around*, as, at, atop, bar, *before*, *behind*, *below*, *beneath*, *beside*, *between*, *beyond*, *by*, despite, *down*, during, for, from, *in*, *inside*, into, like, minus, *near*, of, *off*, *on*, onto, *opposite*, *out*, *outside*, *over*, *past*, pending, per, plus, prior, pro, re, regarding, *round*, *since*, than, *through*, *throughout*, till, to, toward, *under*, *underneath*, unlike, until, unto, *up*, upon, via, with, *within*, *without*.

The example below shows adverbial uses.

> He went *in*.
> I put it *through*.

When a verb is followed by a preposition, there is often little or no choice as to which preposition to use, e.g., *rely on, speak to, give to*.

When there is a choice of preposition, the meaning changes with each:

> *check for, check on, check over; speak to, speak about; talk to, talk with*.

Prepositions allow us to express relationships. These are mostly to do with place and time. Some prepositions can be used with more than one meaning, depending on how we think about the time or place we are discussing.

Prepositions of location

Prepositions can indicate:

– the direction in which something is moving in relation to another person or thing: *toward, from, to, off*.

> They ran **toward** the police station.
> He took the road **from** the town **to** the state park.

– something or someone being enclosed: *within, in, inside, outside*.

> There is no wireless signal **within** the room.
> There seems to be something loose **inside** the control box.
> You have to stand **outside** the room while we make up some questions.
> Did you put the cheese back **in** the fridge?

– being at a certain point: *on, at, by, near*.

> Don't stand **on** the beds.
> I'll meet you **at** the library.
> There is a huge reservoir **near** where I live.

– movement over or onto a place: *over, across, on, onto*.

> Griffon jumped **onto** the back of the truck.
> He slid the package **across** the table.
> Tears flowed **over** his cheeks.

– location as a line: *along, over, on*.

> We walked **along** the bank of the river.
> Please sign **on** the dotted line.

Prepositions of time

Prepositions can also indicate:

- a point in time, a date, or a period of time : *at*, *on*, *in*, *during*.

> *The baby arrived at 9 p.m. on April 1st.*
> *They got married in June.*
> *I'll be with you in five minutes.*
> *During power outages we used wood for heat.*

- a period or point of time which marks a change: *before*, *after*, *since*, *until*.

> *We lived there before Mother died.*
> *I went to that school until I was sixteen.*
> *I usually go there after work.*

- the duration of some event (how long it lasts): *for*.

> *Helen stayed there for the whole of July.*

Prepositions of cause and purpose

Some prepositions indicate the reason something was done.

- cause or reason: *because of*, *for*, *from*, *through*.

> *The road was closed because of an avalanche.*
> *He did it for the money.*
> *They died from exposure to cold.*
> *She lost her way through carelessness.*

Prepositions of means or instrument

Some prepositions answer the question "how?" by telling us the way something was done or what was used.

– means or instrument: *with*, *by*, *without*.

> *We traveled by air to save time.*
> *He broke the door down with an ax.*
> *Can you find your way without a compass?*

Word order in sentences

The order of words in an English sentence is very important. A change in word order often results in a change of meaning.

Many other languages use **inflection**, a change in the form of words, to show how the parts of a sentence function. English has very few inflections, so the place that a word occupies in a sentence, its **syntax**, is the most important feature.

Neutral word order

Most sentences have a subject, and then something that is said about the subject, which is usually the rest of the sentence. This divides the sentence into the **subject** and the **predicate**.

> *John* (subject) *bought the tickets on Saturday* (predicate).
> *The wall* (subject) *was torn down* (predicate).
> *My elderly mother* (subject) *is completely deaf* (predicate).

Most English sentences put the information that they carry in this order, and so it is called neutral word order. When this neutral order is changed, the meaning of a sentence also changes.

> *The cat killed the dog.*
> *The dog killed the cat.*
> *The child watched the rabbit.*
> *The rabbit watched the child.*

Word order in simple sentences

Simple sentences are those that have only one clause. They are extremely common in all forms of written and spoken English. Simple sentences have a normal word order that varies according to whether the sentence is:

- a **statement**,

> I saw you at the theater on Saturday night.
> I didn't see you at the theater on Saturday night.

- a **question**,

> Did I see you at the theater on Saturday night?
> Didn't I see you at the theater on Saturday night?

- a **command**.

> You **should** buy a ticket now.
> You **shouldn't** buy a ticket yet.
> **Buy** a ticket now.
> **Don't** buy a ticket now.

Word order also varies according to whether the sentence is **negative** or **positive**.

Focusing

When we want to focus the attention of a reader or a listener on a particular word or phrase, we can use variations on neutral order, such as putting the subject last, splitting a clause into two, or repeating some part of the sentence.

Here are some variations of neutral word order that place emphasis on different elements of the sentence.

> We used to call him "Fuzzy."
> "Fuzzy," we used to call him.
> Didn't we use to call him "Fuzzy"?
> "Fuzzy" was what we used to call him.
> It was "Fuzzy" we used to call him.

Declarative, interrogative, and imperative statements

Each sentence in English provides some type of information. For example, a sentence can be a statement, a question, a request, a command, a denial or a response, etc. In English the choice and order of the parts of a sentence help us express these meanings.

Most statements and denials are in the **declarative**. An important feature of declarative sentences is that they have a subject that comes before the verb.

> *Our dog eats any old thing.*
> *Our dog won't just eat any old thing.*
> *The dog has already been fed.*
> *The dog hasn't been fed yet.*
> *We have already won several races.*
> *We haven't won any races yet.*

Most questions are in the **interrogative**. An important feature of interrogative sentences is that they normally have a subject that comes after an auxiliary verb.

> *Does your dog eat any old thing?*
> *Has the dog already been fed?*
> *Hasn't the dog been fed yet?*
> *Have you won any races yet?*
> *Haven't you won any races yet?*

If the subject does come first it will be a special question word.

> *Who won the race?*
> *Which team was it?*

- Exceptionally, we can ask questions using the declarative. We do this by using a special tone of voice.

You're telling me he has a new car? I don't believe it.
It's raining again? That makes three days in a row.

Many commands are in the **imperative**. Commands in the imperative have no word that acts as a subject, though the subject is understood to be you. Commands in the imperative can sometimes sound rude or impatient.

Eat up. We have to go!
Leave me alone.
On your marks, get set ... go!

- We can make a **request**, which is a type of command, sound more polite by using the interrogative.

Would you feed the dog, please?
Would you mind shutting the door?
Could I have that now? Thank you.

Not all imperative sentences are orders or commands. They can be social expressions whose purpose is to express a feeling or to convey information.

Have a nice day.
Get well soon.
Help yourselves to coffee.

There is also a **subjunctive** form. It may be used when you want to talk about an improbable or unlikely situation.

*If I **were** governor, I'd spend more money on education.*
*I'd take the offer if I **were** you.*

The declarative

The **declarative** is used to make statements. A statement is usually the expression of a fact or of an opinion. Statements can be both positive or negative.

> *Chana is working today after all.*
> *Conor wasn't reading your diary.*
> *Helen was talking about you.*
> *I'm not going on vacation this year.*

Declarative sentences always contain a subject and a following verb phrase.

The normal word order for declarative sentences:

subject + verb phrase

> *Chana is working.*
> *Conor was reading.*
> *Helen stared at me in surprise.*

subject + verb phrase + direct object

> *Ross is writing a letter.*
> *Pam borrowed three library books.*
> *Stephen ordered vegetarian lasagna.*

subject + verb phrase + adverbial

> *Dominic was eating very slowly.*
> *Lyndsey was studying in her room.*
> *Mikhail laughed nervously.*

subject + verb phrase + direct object + adverbial

> *Dominic was eating his lunch very slowly.*
> *Lyndsey had been reading a book in her room.*

Certain verbs must have following objects, e.g., *see, find, prefer, take*.

> *She saw **her friend**.*
> *He found **a camera**.*
> *They took **a resort brochure**.*

Other verbs need, or can have, both a **direct** and an **indirect** object, e.g., *give, buy, offer*.

> *Laura offered* **me** *another cookie.*
> *Scott's uncle bought* **him** *a new bike.*

The word order can be either:

subject + verb + indirect object + direct object

> *Sultan gave* **the dog** *a bone.*
> *Stuart bought* **Marie** *a birthday present.*

or, with the addition of a word that indicates the recipient:

subject + verb + direct object + *to/for* + indirect object.

> *Sultan gave a bone* **to the dog.**
> *Stuart bought a birthday present* **for Marie.**

Another group of verbs must be followed either by an object and an adverbial expression, or an adverbial expression on its own e.g., *put*, *place*, *stand*.

> *Richard placed* **the computer** on the table.
> *Diana put* **her jeans** in the drawer.
> *Michael stood* in the middle of the field.

A further type of declarative statement has the same basic order of subject and verb as the **subject + verb phrase + direct object** (example on p. 230), but with a **complement** replacing the direct object. See p. 233 for more about complements and p. 15 for more about objects.

> *Brad seems to have been* **really worried** *lately.*
> *This dessert is* **delicious**.

Complements

Some verbs such as *be*, *become*, *seem*, do not have an object but a **complement**.

The **subject complement** is a word or phrase that tells us more about the subject.

> Alan is *a nice person*.
> Rajiv is *a psychiatric nurse*.
> Alison seems *very well balanced*.
> Amber is *herself* again.
> That's *it*!
> This is *for you*.

The subject complement is linked to the subject by a verb, and the order is as follows:

subject + verb + subject complement

Subject complements may be either noun phrases, pronouns, adjectives, or even prepositional phrases.

- Most adjectives can be used after a group of verbs that includes: *appear*, *be*, *become*, *look*, *seem*, *smell*, *taste*, etc. An adjective that is used in this position is called a **predicative** adjective and it is functioning as a **complement**.

> The tickets seemed *expensive*, but the show was *excellent*.
> These little cakes are *delicious*.
> Soon afterward, Patrick became *ill*.
> Jackie appeared *friendly enough* when I first met her.

Less frequently we find an **object complement**. The object complement tells us more about the direct object. It relates directly to the object and is placed after it.

Verbs that can take an object complement with their direct object include *make*, *call*, and *appoint*. The word order is as follows:

subject + verb + direct object + object complement

Peter's phone call made **Maureen** happy.
She called **me** a **fool**.
They appointed **him** Director.

Word order in negative statements

In negative statements, the basic word order for subject and object is the same as in positive statements.

> *John has gone to school.*
> *John has **not** gone to school.*

The difference is that negative statements must contain *not*, and must have as part of the verb phrase, either:

- a **primary auxiliary** verb,

> *She **had not** arrived in time for lunch.*
> *Caitlin **is not** working this evening.*
> *Brandon **was not** reading your diary.*

- one or other of the **modal auxiliary** verbs, or

> *I warn you, he **may not** want to come.*
> *Ailsa **could not** see the road clearly.*

- a form of *be* used as a main verb.

> *That **is not** my book.*

The word *not* is added immediately after the first one of these auxiliary verbs. The main verb follows.

The word order is, therefore:
    subject + **auxiliary** + *not* + **main verb**.

A negative sentence may contain a modal verb and one or more auxiliaries as well.

> I **may** *not* **have** *gone by the time you arrive.*
> They **could** *not* **have** *seen her – they were asleep in bed.*
> They **should** *not* **have been playing** *in the road.*

In this case the word order is:
subject + **modal** + *not* + **primary auxiliary** + **main verb**.

If the verb phrase does not already contain one of these verbs, then it is necessary to add the **supporting auxiliary** verb *do*.

The present simple and the past simple tenses of main verbs take the appropriate form of *do*, and then add *not* followed by the base form of the main verb.

> *He runs.*
> *He **does not** run.*
> *He ran.*
> *He **did not** run.*
> *Lynn **does not** work overtime now.*
> *The bus **did not** run on Sundays.*

The word order is, therefore:
subject + *do-* **auxiliary** + *not* + **main verb**

See p. 238 for more on the supporting auxiliary.

• The contracted form of *not*, which is *n't*, can be used after any auxiliary verb except *am*. This is the most common spoken form.

> *He **doesn't** run.*
> *He **didn't** run.*
> *Lynn **doesn't** work on Sundays.*

She **hasn't** been to work all week.
He **isn't** going to come after all.
Bill went swimming but Ann **didn't** want to.

The full form with *not* tends to be used more in writing.

---

can + *not* is usually written *cannot*.

She **can't** come.
She **cannot** come.

- Other words with a negative meaning, *never*, *barely*, *hardly*, *scarcely*, *rarely*, do not change the order of words in a statement.

She **doesn't** buy *Vogue*.
She **never** buys *Vogue*.
He **barely** earns enough to live on.
I **hardly** think that is going to put them off.

The interrogative

The interrogative is normal for many questions. It contains a verb phrase that is followed by a subject.

There are two main types of question: those that can be answered *yes* or *no*, and those that have to be answered with a specific piece of information or a sentence such as *I don't know*. Each type of question has its own special word order.

Yes/no questions

Questions that expect the answer *yes* or *no* are called **yes/no questions**, or sometimes **polar questions**.

The **interrogative** is used to form yes/no questions.

The normal sentence order for the interrogative is:
modal/auxiliary verb + **subject** + **base form** of the **main verb**.

> *Were the dogs barking?*
> *Have you been dieting?*
> *Can Mahmoud come too?*
> *Must you go so soon?*
> *Would you like a chocolate?*

When a sentence does not contain a modal verb or an auxiliary verb, the question is formed by placing a form of the supporting auxiliary verb *do* before the subject and following it with the **base form** of the main verb.

> *Does he enjoy tennis?*
> *Do they play a lot?*
> *Did that surprise his mom?*

Yes/no questions also have a negative form. **Negative yes/no questions** are almost always contracted. The negative in its contracted form *n't* comes immediately before the subject.

> *Doesn't he like talking about his childhood?*
> *Can't Peter have one too?*
> *Don't you speak French?*
> *Wouldn't you like to know a bit more about this?*

If the full negative form *not* is used, it comes immediately after the subject. The full form is very formal.

> *Does he not like talking about his childhood?*
> *Do you not want to know what it was about?*
> *Can Peter not have one too?*

WH- questions

When you want to get a detailed answer, not just *yes* or *no*, you must use a **WH- question** (or **"nonpolar" question**), which allows for many possible answers. The words *who*, *whom*, *whose*, *what*, *which*, *when*, *where*, *why*, and *how* are used to form this sort of question. These words are referred to as **WH-** words. See pp. 240–243.

> **Yes/no:**
> *Did you phone the school? – Yes, I did.*
> *Was she all right in the end? – No/I don't know.*
> *Have you seen Alice yet? – Yes, I have.*
>
> **WH-:**
> *Who was that man? – He's my geography teacher.*
> *What did he say when you told him the news? – He was too surprised to say anything.*
> *When did you see Alice? – Last Wednesday.*
> *Where is Peter going? – To work.*
> *When did they arrive? – Yesterday.*
> *Why have you stopped going running? – The doctor told me to.*

WH- words

The **WH-** words are also called **interrogatives**. They are used for **WH-** questions. They can be determiners, adverbs, or pronouns.

WH- determiners

When used as determiners, *what*, *which*, or *whose* can be used to ask questions:

– about nouns

> *What book are you reading?*
> *Which plane is he catching?*
> *Whose jacket is this?*

– or about the pronoun *one* or *ones*.

> *Which one would you like?*
> *Which ones did Rudy want?*

- The determiner *which* can be used in questions about selecting. It can also be used together with the preposition *of* for the same purpose.

> *Which color shall we use?*
> *Which book sells the most copies?*
> *Which of these colors shall we use?*
> *Of all your novels, which of them did you enjoy writing the most?*

- The determiner *whose* asks about possession with reference to a person as the possessor.

> *Whose mother did you say she was?*
> *Whose bag is this?*

WH- adverbs

The adverb **WH-** words, *when*, *where*, *how*, and *why*, always make the sentence follow the interrogative word order.

– *When* asks about time.

> *When will they arrive?*
> *When shall I see you again?*

– *Where* asks about place.

> *Where are you going?*
> *Where have you been?*
> *Where is your coat?*

– *How* asks about manner or means.

> *How did you get here? – We came by train.*
> *How does this thing work?*
> *How did you manage to open the trunk?*

– *Why* asks about reasons and purpose. Questions with *why* are usually answered with a clause containing *because* to express reason, or with the *to* infinitive to express purpose.

> *Why is the baby crying? – **Because** she's hungry.*
> *Why are you saving your money? – **To buy** a bike.*

– *How much* implies reference to a quantity; *how many* implies reference to an amount or a countable number of things but may leave out the noun referred to.

> *How much money did they take? – All of it.*
> *How much does it cost? – $4.20.*
> *How many packs do you want? – Twelve, please.*
> *How many do you want? – Twelve, please.*

– *How* can also be used with adjectives such as *old*, *big*, *far*, or with adverbs such as *often*, *soon*, *quickly* to ask about degree, rate, or timing.

> *How far is it to the airport? – About five miles.*
> *How often does he come? – Not very often.*

WH- pronouns

The **pronouns** *who*, *whose*, *which*, and *what* can be the subject or object of a verb.

> *Who can help me?*
> *Whose is the new sports car outside?*
> *Which was your best subject in school?*
> *What happened next?*
> *What have you got to take with you to camp?*

The interrogative pronoun *whose* is used when the question is asked about a person as the possessor of something. See also pp. 204–205 on interrogative and relative pronouns.

> *Whose is the motorbike parked outside?*
> *Whose is this?*

• The form *whom* is used as the object of a verb or of a preposition in very formal or old-fashioned English.

> *Whom did you talk to?*
> *Whom would you rather have as a boss?*

Modern English usage prefers *who* instead of *whom* in all but the most formal contexts.

> *Who did you talk to?*
> *Who would you rather have as a boss?*

When *whom* is used as the object of a preposition, it normally follows the preposition.

> *To whom* did you speak?
> *With whom* did she go?

When *who* is used, the preposition is placed at the end of the clause.

> *Who* did you speak *to*?
> *Who* did she go *with*?

The **WH-** subject pronouns are found in the same sentence order as statements:
WH- subject pronoun + the main verb.

> *Who can help* me?
> *Whose is* that motorbike parked outside?
> *Which was* your best subject in school?
> *What happened* next?

The **WH-** object pronouns make the sentence take the word order of a question:
WH- object pronoun + primary or modal auxiliary + subject + base form of the verb.

> *What do you have* to take with you to camp?
> *What has Jonathan done* now?

- The exception to this is in informal spoken English, when the speaker wants to show shock or disbelief.

> *You did* **what**?

Sentence tags

Tags are short additions that look like questions, used at the end of a declarative sentence. They are sometimes called **question tags**, but many sentences ending with a tag are not real questions. They are usually used to check that the listener agrees with what the speaker has said. Sentence tags are very commonly used in spoken English, but not in formal written English.

The tag is added to the end of a sentence. If the auxiliary verb *be* or *have* or a **modal** verb is part of the verb phrase in the sentence, then it is used as the verb in the sentence tag.

> It *isn't* raining again, *is it*?
> You've *seen* the program, *haven't you*?
> Well, *we can't jump* over it, *can we*?
> You *will come*, *won't you*?

If the main verb is in the present simple or past simple tense, the tag is made using *do*.

> He certainly *likes* eating, *doesn't he*?
> I *slipped up* there, *didn't I*?

In negative tags, *n't* is added to the auxiliary. Note that this contracted form is always used.

> He certainly *likes* eating, *doesn't he*?
> I *slipped up* there, *didn't I*?
> They *went* with you, *didn't they*?

- The more formal forms such as *does he not*, *did I not*, *have you not*, are sometimes heard in some regional varieties of English.

The pronoun in the sentence tag must match the subject of the main verb.

> *You aren't listening, are you?*
> *He reads a lot, doesn't he?*

Sentence tags can be **negative**

> *They went with you, didn't they?*

or **positive**.

> *Your father doesn't belong to the VFW, does he?*

Normally, when the first part of the sentence is positive, the tag verb will be negative, and vice versa. Sentences in which both parts are positive are less common. These sentences must be used carefully as, with certain tones of voice, they can sound aggressive or judgmental.

> *So you think I'm a fool, do you?*
> *Oh! You smoke now, do you?*

- The same sentence tag may have different meanings depending on the tone of voice that is used with it.

> Falling tone: statement
> *She's gone out, hasn't she.*

> Rising tone: question
> *She's gone out, hasn't she?*

The sentence can be a statement of fact or a question, depending on whether your voice rises or falls at the end.

Sentence tags are used in the following combinations:

- To say something that the speaker expects the listener will agree with. This doesn't always sound like a question:

positive main verb + negative tag

> Mary *will pass* her driving test this time, *won't she*?
> Richard *seems* to have lost interest in everything, *doesn't he*?

or **negative main verb + positive tag**

> Jessica *didn't care, did she*?
> Kerry *hadn't done* enough preparation, *had she*?

- To point out or remark on something, often something that the listener cannot deny. This frequently sounds more like a question:

positive main verb + negative tag

> You've just *bought* a new car, *haven't you*?
> Henry *has been* away already this year, *hasn't he*?

or **negative main verb + positive tag**

> Dexter *hasn't been* to see you, *has he*?
> Paula *wasn't* in your class in school, *was she*?

- To show interest in something. This often repeats part of what the previous speaker has said:

positive main verb + positive tag

> You *saw* him in town, *did you*?
> So, you *come* from New Mexico, *do you*?
> So you've just *come back* from skiing, *have you*?

When a tag is used to show interest in something, the sentence is often begun with *So*. This type of tag can also be used in a challenging manner.

> *Oh, so you've been here all along, have you?*

After a command, a tag made with *will* or *would* makes an order more polite.

Make me a cup of tea, will you?
Just wait a minute, would you?

The imperative

Commands and orders

The **imperative** is used to give commands and orders. The form of the verb used for the imperative is the **base form** of the main verb, which is used without a subject.

> *Walk to the corner, turn right, and cross the road.*
> *Open your mouth and say "Aaaah."*

- Although the main feature of sentences in the imperative is that they have no **grammatical** subject, they do have an **understood** subject, *"you."*

The basic form of the imperative remains the same whether it is addressed to one or more people.

> *Come on, Mary; I'm waiting.*
> *Come on, girls; you're late.*

There is also a special type of imperative, using *let's*, that is used when you need to include the speaker. See p. 250.

The word order of a sentence in the imperative is:

verb + **object** (if needed).

The negative imperative is made with *do* + *not* or *don't*.

> *Don't lose that key.*
> *Do not come back without it!*

The uses of the imperative are as follows:

– to give an order.

> *Go away.*
> *Stop that.*
> *Keep quiet.*

– to give instructions.

> *Don't use this spray near an open flame.*
> *Apply the glue thinly and leave it for ten minutes.*

– to give advice or warnings.

> *Don't forget to take your passport with you.*
> *Be careful!*
> *Don't go on the ice.*

– to make an offer or an invitation.

> *Have a piece of cake.*
> *Come over and see me some time.*

The imperative of *do* + **a main verb** can be used:

– for polite emphasis.

> *Do take your coat off.*

– to be persuasive.

> *Do try to eat a little of this; it will be good for you.*

- Note that the imperative is not the only way to form a command or an order. You can also issue a command when you use a sentence in the declarative or the interrogative.

    I'm certainly not going to get it – you get it.
    Would you get it, then? I'm busy.

Making suggestions

Let's (*let* + *us*) + **main verb** is used in the 1st person plural only, especially when you are trying to encourage someone to do something with you.

It includes both the speaker and the hearer, so the subject that is understood is represented by the plural *we*.

    Let's visit Malcolm this weekend.
    Please let's go to the movies tonight.
    Let's pool our resources.

- Suggestions that start with *let's* often end with the sentence tag *shall we*?

    Let's call her now, shall we?
    Let's go for a walk after supper, shall we?

In ordinary English the negative is *let's not* + **main verb** or sometimes *don't let's* + **main verb**.

    Let's not worry about that now.
    Don't let's worry about that now.

In formal English, the negative is *let us not* + **main verb**.

    Let us not lose sight of our aims.

Do let's is the emphatic form.

> *It's a fantastic bargain; do let's buy it!*

- The uncontracted form *let us* + **main verb** is occasionally used in formal and written English.

> **Let us** *be clear about this.*
> **Let us** *hope that this will never happen again.*

The answer to a suggestion with *let's* is normally either, *yes, let's* or *no, let's not* or sometimes, *no, don't let's (...).*

> **Let's** *call her now, shall we?* – **Yes, let's**.
> **Let's** *call her now, shall we?* – **No, let's not**.
> **Let's** *invite Malcolm over this weekend.* – *No,* **don't let's** *do that.*

The vocative

The imperative is often used with a **vocative**, in which you mention a person's name or some other way of identifying the person to whom a command or request is being addressed.

> *David, come here!*
> *Come here, David.*
> *Hey, you, stop talking!*

The vocative can be a proper noun, the pronoun *you*, or a noun phrase. The vocative can come before or after the main clause. A vocative forms a part of many questions.

> *Peter, do you know where I put the DVD?*
> *Have you seen Chris recently, Jenny?*

A vocative is also combined with an interrogative clause to form a request.

> *Tony, would you pass me the hammer?*
> *Could I speak to you privately for a minute, Sunita?*

When a vocative is used with an imperative clause, the sentence is usually a command.

> *Sam, get off there!*
> *You, come back!*

A command can also be phrased as a request.

> *Would you stop talking now, darling, and go to sleep.*
> *Would you get off there, please, Sam.*

A practical reason for using a vocative is to supply the missing but understood subject, so that the right person will understand the command or request, and act on it.

Note the punctuation: there should be a comma between the vocative part of the clause and the remainder.

As part of a command, except for urgent warnings, the use of the vocative is considered rude or abrupt.

The subjunctive

The **subjunctive** is used in English for situations that are improbable or that express a wish, proposal, or suggestion. It occurs typically after certain verbs. These include:

ask	demand	insist
order	prefer	propose
recommend	request	require
suggest	urge	wish

It is also used in certain set phrases and in formal forms of speech and writing.

> Lord **have** mercy!
> God **bless** you!
> God **help** us!
> Heaven **help** us!
> Heaven **forbid** that that should happen to me.
> **Suffice** it to say he escaped with only a warning.

The present subjunctive

The form in the present tense is exactly the same as the base form in all persons of the verb. That is, there is no -s on the 3rd person singular.

The subjunctive is used in subordinate clauses that follow verbs expressing a desire, a demand, a formal recommendation, or a resolve.

> I only ask that he **cease** behaving in this extraordinary manner.
> It is vital that they **be** stopped at once.
> Is it really necessary that she **work** all hours of the day?
> I demand that he **do** something to make up for this.

The clause containing the subjunctive is linked to the main clause with *that*.

- American English uses the subjunctive fairly often. The subjunctive is not common in British English. British speakers usually take advantage of other ways of expressing the same message, especially in less formal speech. These forms are also acceptable in American English.

> I only ask that *he should cease* behaving in this extraordinary
>   manner.
> It is vital that *they are* stopped at once.
> It is vital *to stop* them at once.
> Is it really necessary *for her to work* all hours of the day?
> I demand that *he does* something to make up for this.

The past subjunctive

The past subjunctive form *were* is sometimes used with the 1st and 3rd person singular, in place of the normal past form *was*.

The past subjunctive may be used:

- after *if* or *I wish*, to express regret or longing

> If your father *were* alive he would help you.
> If I *were* rich I would buy a Ferrari.
> I wish I *were* taller.
> If only he *were* here now!

- after *as if/as though* and similar expressions, to express doubt or improbability.

> You talk to him as if he *were* your slave!
> Some people behave as though dogs *were* human.

Many people prefer to use the normal form of the past in this type of sentence. This is quite acceptable in ordinary spoken English but may be considered an error in writing.

If your father was alive he would help you.
If I was rich I would buy a Ferrari.
I wish I was tall.
If only he was here now!
You talk to him as if he was your slave!

Exclamations

Exclamations are short utterances that you make when you are very surprised or upset. They are not always whole sentences. Sometimes they are more like a noise than a word. In this case they are called **interjections**.

Ugh!   *Phew!*
Wow!   *Huh?*

Many exclamations consist of just one word.

Help!   *Nonsense!*
Dang!   *Hooey!*

Exclamations can also consist of:

– *what* or *such* + **noun phrase**

What a pity!
Such long fingers!
What idiocy!
Such impertinence!

– or *how* + **adjective**.

How silly!
How kind of him!

They may also have the form of a negative question.

Isn't *it a warm day!*
Aren't *they kind!*

- Another form of exclamation is when the hearer repeats part of the sentence that he or she has just heard. This is used when the hearer finds it hard to believe what has been said or is very surprised. This sort of exclamation is called an **echo**.

> *Richard's passed the exam. – **Richard's passed!** That's great!*
> *Salome's here. – **She's here!** What a relief!*

Responses

Responses are made in answer to a question or a statement by another person in conversation. Like exclamations, they may be full sentences, but can also be phrases or single words.

> *Yes.*
> *On Tuesday.*
> *I certainly will.*

Responses usually do not make sense on their own because their subject, predicate, or some other important piece of information is contained in what another person said.

Although a response may not have a subject or contain a main verb, it can be classed as a sentence, because a response uses our knowledge of what has just been said. The subject or the verb will usually be understood from the context.

> *Are you coming to the party tonight? –* **Yes**.
> *When are you going to Des Moines, then? –* **On Tuesday**.
> *Will you be doing some shopping? –* **I certainly will**.

- If the verb is in a simple tense you can use the supporting auxiliary *do* as the verb in the response.

> *Do you like zucchini? – Yes, I* ***do***.

- You usually just use the first part of the verb phrase in a compound verb to make a response. That is, the first **auxiliary** verb or the **modal verb** becomes the response form.

> *Has Tamsin been here yet? – Yes, she* ***has***.
> *Was Andrea crying? – Yes, she* ***was***.
> *Can we leave early? – Yes, you* ***can***.
> *Should I be doing this differently? – Yes, you* ***should***.

Some speakers prefer to use the modal and the auxiliary form together.

> *Laurence would be running if it weren't for his injury.*
> – *Yes, he* **would be**.

Sentences and clauses

A clause is a group of words that contains a verb. The verb in a clause can be finite

> *Use* this pan for the pasta.
> He *missed* the turnoff.

or nonfinite.

> *To cook* pasta, always use a large pan.
> *Dreaming* about Jenny, he missed the turnoff.

Simple sentences

Simple sentences consist of one clause, in which the verb is finite.

> *Ann* **went** to the bank.
> *She* **withdrew** $100.

Two or more clauses can be joined to make a **compound** sentence or a **complex** sentence.

Complex sentences

Complex sentences are those that contain a **subordinate** clause as well as a **main** clause.

> When he arrives, *I'll call you*.
> *He stayed at home* because he felt ill.

A **subordinate** clause is one that contains information about the main clause. It will usually be introduced by a **linking word** such as *when*, *if*, *because*, or *that*. The linking words are called **subordinating conjunctions**.

Most subordinate clauses can come before, after, or within the main clause. Usually, when one clause is of principal importance and the other clause gives information about the principal one, we have a complex sentence with one **main clause** and one **subordinate clause**.

- The position of a subordinate clause – that is, whether before or after the main clause – is determined mainly by what you want to emphasize in the sentence.

> *Since you seem to have made up your mind, I'll say no more.*
> *I stopped seeing her because she moved to Seattle.*

Compound sentences

A compound sentence is one that consists of two **main clauses**, joined by a word such as *and*, *but*, or *or*, called a **coordinating conjunction**. Each clause is of equal importance and gives information of equal value. The order of the clauses can be very important for the meaning. For example, the timing of an action can be described by the order in which the clauses follow each other.

> *He picked it up **and** ran over to her.*
> *He ran over to her **and** picked it up.*
> *I drove to Miami **and** went on to Key West.*

Compound-complex sentences

These have more than one main clause and at least one subordinate clause.

> *Angie came over **and** we decided to use my car **because** hers was acting up.*
> *He ran over to Julie, **who** was sitting at the end of the bench, **and** grabbed her handbag.*

Joining clauses

Coordination

The process called **coordination** joins two short clauses of equal importance with a conjunction. Each clause becomes a **main** clause in the new sentence.

> Ann went to the bank **and** withdrew $100.
> Dulcie goes to work **but** Courtney doesn't have a job.
> Brooke (**either**) stays at home **or** visits her family.

The clauses are linked by words called **coordinating conjunctions**, such as *and*, *but*, (*either*) *or*, *neither*, *nor*, or *yet*. Conjunctions come at the beginning of a clause.

- If the subject of both clauses is the same, it does not have to be repeated in front of the second verb.

> She came over **and** ~~she~~ gave me a hug.

The conjunction *and* is used:

- to join clauses where there is no contrast or choice.

- to join more than two clauses; the earlier clauses can be joined by a comma, but the last two must be joined by *and*.

> Ann got into the car, drove to the bank, withdrew $100,
>   **and** went shopping.

The conjunction *but* is used to join clauses where there is a contrast.

> She wanted to buy a new dress **but** she couldn't find one she liked.

The conjunction *yet* is used, mainly in written English, to join clauses where there is a surprising contrast.

> *He's a quiet man, **yet** he still manages to command attention.*
> *She was suffering from a knee injury **yet** she still won the match.*

- The conjunctions *and*, *but*, *or*, *neither*, and *nor* are also used to join two phrases of the same kind,

> *This book is useful for **planning and carrying out** research.*
> ***The former president and his wife** were there.*

or two words of the same class.

> *I use this chair when I am **reading and working**.*
> *Do you undertake **detailed or intricate** work?*
> ***Jack and Jill** went up the hill.*
> *This is a **complicated but intriguing** film.*

In particular, *and* and *but* are used to coordinate pairs of adjectives in a predicative position.

When there is a positive choice between the subjects of two clauses, you use the pair of words *either* and *or* to join the clauses.

> ***Either** you come to my place **or** I'll meet you at work. Which do you prefer?*

If the subject of the joined clauses is the same, the subject is used in the first of the joined clauses only. This is often also true of any auxiliary verbs that may be present.

> *Martin said he would **either** meet them for lunch **or** take them to dinner.*

When it is used in this way *either* must come in one of these places:

- before the subject in the first clause of the group.

- in front of the main verb and after any auxiliary verb.

You can use *either...or* to join more than two clauses if you repeat the use of *or*.

> *Tripp said he would (**either**) meet them for lunch,*
>   *(or) take them to dinner, or have them over for coffee.*
> *Fayssoux can (**either**) come with us or take a taxi later.*

The use of *either...or* emphasizes that the two clauses are alternatives and cannot both be true. Compare *and/or*.

> *Tripp said he would meet them for lunch, **and/or** have them*
>   *over for coffee.*

The word *either* can be left out if the sentence meaning is clear. Some writers treat all but the final *or* as optional.

> *Shut up **or** I'll throttle you.*
> *Choose a menu option, use a keyboard shortcut **or** use the cursor keys.*

> You can use *or* on its own to join two or more clauses,
> but *either* cannot be used on its own.

When there is a negative choice between the subjects of two clauses, you can use the pair of words *neither* and *nor* to join the clauses.

> *It is **neither** possible **nor** desirable to invite them.*
> *Jane was **not** a fool; **neither/nor was she** prepared to be blamed*
>   *for the error.*

The word *neither* can be used on its own to connect two clauses if the first clause contains a word with broad negative meaning such as *not*, *barely*, *hardly* or *scarcely*. If there is a subject in the second clause, question order must be used.

> There was **barely** enough meat for the children; **neither did they** have any bread.
> Eric **hardly** saw the fight; **nor did he** remember much about the incident later.

- The words *either* and *neither* can also be used as a pronoun or as a determiner. Each can then be used on its own; it does not then have a joining function.

> **Either** book will do. It doesn't matter.
> **Neither** book is at all suitable, I'm sorry.
> You can have **either**.

- *Either*, or, *neither*, and *nor* can be used as conjunctions inside a noun phrase or a verb phrase.

> You can choose to study **either** Shakespeare **or** Keats.
> **Neither** Vimala **nor** Katie knew the answer.
> She is **either** desperate **or** just stupid.
> He didn't know **whether** to stay **or** go.

Subordination

When two or more clauses are joined by a conjunction other than *and*, *but*, *or*, or *yet*, one of the clauses is the main clause; the other clauses are **subordinate** clauses. The different types of subordinate clause include **noun** clauses,

> What matters most is *that you treat everyone fairly*.

adverbial clauses,

> They went outside *as soon as the rain stopped*.

relative clauses,

> This is the problem *that we're facing* at the moment.
> We stayed in Telluride, *which is in the Colorado Rockies*.

conditional clauses,

> Maureen plans to live in Belize *if she can get a job there*.

and **reported** clauses.

> She told me *that Philip was in Providence*.

Each of the subordinate clauses is associated with an introductory word that signals what type of clause it is that follows.

> *After* she had read the diary, she returned it to the drawer.
> *As* they were going downstairs, the phone rang.
> They aren't coming *because* they've had an argument.

These words are called **subordinating conjunctions**. They include:

- the **WH-** words

- words like *since, if, when, because*

- the word *that*, either on its own or used with another word
  e.g., *so that* or *supposing that*

- a phrase ending in *as*, e.g., *as soon as, as long as*

- Each of the subordinating clauses has a preferred position. For example, most adverbial clauses usually follow the main clause, although they can also come before the main clause.

  > Shall I do the shopping **when I finish work?**
  > **When I finish work,** I could do the shopping for you.

  Reported clauses usually follow directly on from the main reporting clause. See p. 280.

Noun clauses

These are clauses that can be used as either the subject or the object of a sentence or in other places where a noun phrase is usually found. They are introduced by *that*

  > What I like about him is **that he always tries his best**.

or by a **WH-** word, e.g., *who, when, where*.

  > I don't know **where you live**.
  > **How the thief got in** is a mystery.
  > **Why she acts like this** is beyond me.

Word order after a **WH-** word is the same as in a statement.

> The subordinating conjunction *that* can often be omitted.
>
> I think **that he'll succeed**.
> I think **he'll succeed**.

Adverbial clauses

Adverbial clauses generally follow the main clause. The following are the main types of adverbial clause:

Time: sets the timing for the main clause.

> We should go *as soon as you are ready*.
> I'll call for you *whenever you like*.
> *Since she went away*, I haven't been able to sleep.
> *The moment he said it*, I started to feel better.

– may come before or after the main clause.

– introduced by *after, as, as soon as, before, once, since, till, the moment (that), until, whenever, when, while*.

Place: sets where the action of the main clause takes place.

> I put it *where nobody would find it*.
> He made an impact *everywhere that he went*.
> *Wherever you looked*, he was to be found.

– introduced by *where, wherever*, or *everywhere*.

Manner: sets out how the main clause was carried out.

– introduced by *as, as if, as though, how, just as, the way that*, or, informally, *like*.

> Mandy looked *as if she had seen a ghost*.
> Cameron wandered in, *the way that he does*.
> You have to fasten it *as though it was a shoelace*.
> The room was decorated *just as he had imagined*.
> Stop acting *like you own the place*.

Reason: sets out the thinking behind the action of the main clause.

> *I don't want to go **because I don't like old movies**.*
> ***Since no one was ready**, I sat down and turned on the TV.*

- may come before or after the main clause.

- introduced by *as*, *because*, or *since*.

Purpose: sets out what it was hoped would be achieved by carrying out the action of the main clause.

> *Put it right there **so that it holds the door open**.*
> *Leave a bit for Becky **in case she's hungry when she gets in**.*

- introduced by *so that*, *in order that*, *in case*, or *lest*.

• Purpose can also be indicated by *so as to*, *in order to* followed by the base form of a verb.

> *I'm living with my parents **so as to save money**.*
> *He put the chair against the door **in order to hold it open**.*

Result: sets out what happened when the main clause was carried out.

> *Ben was **so angry that he kicked the wall hard**.*
> *Nina is **such a generous person that she's often short of money**.*

- introduced by *so* + **adjective/adverb** + *that* or by *such a* + **noun phrase** + *that*.

Contrast: suggests that something else may need to be taken into account regarding the main clause.

> *However much you may want to spend your money*, try to
> save a little each month.
> *Although it had rained*, the ground was still very dry.
> We must try to do something for the environment, *even if we
> can't solve all the world's problems*.

– may come before or after the main clause.

– introduced by *although*, *even though*, *even if*, *however*, *much as*, or *while*.

Relative clauses

Relative clauses tell us more about nouns. They function somewhat like adjectives, and are found as **postmodifiers** in a noun phrase. The noun that is modified is called the **antecedent**. Relative clauses normally begin with *who*, *whom*, *whose*, or *that*.

These words are called **relative pronouns**. Note that some of them also function as interrogative pronouns. See also p. 213.

A relative pronoun can be the subject

> *The people **who live upstairs** are having a party.*
> *The dog **that bit me** had to be put down.*

or object

> *I don't like the music **that they are playing**.*
> *A man **whom I met on vacation** phoned last night.*

of the verb in the relative clause. If it is the object, the relative pronoun can be left out in ordinary informal speech and writing.

> *I don't like the music **they are playing**.*
> *A man **I met on vacation** phoned last night.*

Subject and object relative pronouns come at the beginning of the relative clause.

- A relative pronoun can also be the object of a preposition.

> *It was definitely Diana **to whom she was referring**.*
> *It's a great game **at which anyone can excel**.*

In informal English a relative clause can end in a preposition, especially if the relative pronoun is omitted.

> *It was definitely Diana **that she was referring to**.*
> *It's great game **which anyone can excel at**.*

Defining and nondefining relative clauses

There are two sorts of relative clause.

Some relative clauses act like an adjective by providing more information about a particular noun.

> *The people **who live upstairs** are having a party.*
> *I don't like the music **that they're playing**.*
> *The girl **who was on the bus with us** is called Sonia.*

These are called **defining** relative clauses or **restrictive** relative clauses. A defining relative clause is never separated from the noun by a comma.

The other type of relative clause adds extra information to the whole of the main clause. These are **nondefining relative clauses** or **nonrestrictive** relative clauses. This type of clause is separated from the main clause by commas. Note that this type of clause cannot begin with *that*.

> *The man next door, **who works from home**, kept an eye on the house for us.*
> *Thomas went home early, **which was a relief to us all**.*
> *We stopped in Estes Park, **which is a good place for a picnic**.*

Compare:

Defining.
My brother who lives in Canada is a lawyer.
(There are several brothers. The Canadian one is a lawyer.)

Nondefining.
My brother, who lives in Canada, is a lawyer.
(There is only one brother. He is a lawyer. He happens to
   live in Canada.)

Conditional clauses

Conditional sentences consist of a main clause and a **conditional clause** (sometimes called an *if-clause*). The conditional clause usually begins with *if* or *unless*. The conditional clause can come before or after the main clause.

> *We'll be late if we don't leave now.*
> *We'll be late unless we leave now.*
> *If we don't leave now, we'll be late.*
> *Unless we leave now, we'll be late.*

There are three main types of conditional sentence.

Type 1

The main clause uses *will*, *can*, *may*, or *might* + the **base form** of a main verb. The *if-clause* uses the present simple tense.

> *If you take the first bus, you'll get there on time.*
> *She'll be cold if she doesn't wear a coat.*
> *If you need more helpers, I can try and get some time off work.*

Type 1 sentences refer to the future. They suggest that the action in the main clause is quite likely to happen.

> *They will not finish their homework unless they start now.*
> *If you call early, you will get a seat.*

The use of the modal verb may or might in the main clause suggests that there is some doubt whether the main verb action will be achieved.

> *If you call early, you may get a seat.*
> *Mary might deliver your message, if you ask her.*

Type 2

The main clause uses *would*, *could*, or *might* + the **base form** of a main verb. The *if-clause* uses the past simple tense.

> *If Jim **lent** us his car, we could go to the party.*
> *We would save $5 a day if we **didn't eat** any lunch.*
> *If burglars **broke** into my house, they wouldn't find any money.*
> *Would you be very angry if I **failed** my exam?*

or the past subjunctive.

> *If I **were** you, I'd phone her right away.*

Type 2 sentences refer to an imaginary situation. They imply that the action in the *if-clause* will probably not happen.

> *If I won the lottery, I would buy a cabin in Montana.*
>   *(...but I don't think I'll win the lottery.)*
> *If you didn't spend all your money on lottery tickets, you could*
>   *afford a vacation.*
>   *(...but you do spend all your money on lottery tickets.)*

The past subjunctive is often used when giving advice to someone, especially about what the person should do.

> *If I **were** you, I'd tell them the truth.*

Type 3

The main clause uses *would, could,* or *might + have +* the **past participle** of a main verb. The **if-clause** uses the past perfect tense.

> *We could have had a longer vacation, if we **hadn't spent** so much money on the house.*
> *If I **had known** about the exam, I would have paid more attention in class.*

In Type 3 sentences the speaker is looking back from the present to a past time and event. The speaker is talking about what might have happened but did not, either because the wrong thing was done or because nothing was done. This type of sentence is used when making excuses, showing regret, blaming, or giving an explanation.

Type 3 sentences can usually be written without using *if*, by putting the auxiliary verb first in the **if-clause**:

> ***Had I known** about the exam, I would have paid more attention in class.*

Conditional clauses can also be used to talk about consequences, or to give an opinion about a situation in the following ways:

– The **if-clause** uses the present simple tense and the main clause uses the present simple tense. This is used to refer to universal truths.

> *If you **heat** water to 100°C, it **boils**.*
> *Plants **die** if they **don't get** enough water.*

– The **if-clause** uses the present simple tense and the main clause is in the imperative. This is used to give advice or orders for particular situations or sets of circumstances.

> *If the alarm **goes off, make** your way outside to the parking lot.*
> *If a red light **comes on** here, **switch off** the machine.*

– The *if-clause* uses the present continuous or present simple tense and the main clause uses a modal verb. This is used to make suggestions and give advice.

> *If you're thinking of buying a lawnmower, you could try mine first.*
> *You should turn down the radio if you don't want the neighbors to complain.*

– The *if-clause* uses *will/would* and the main clause uses a modal verb.

This is used to make a request or to give a polite order.

> *If you'll wait a minute, the doctor can see you.*
> *If you would sign here, please, I'll be able to send you the books.*

Note that a *'d* in the main clause is the contracted form of *would*. However, a *'d* in an *if-clause* is the contracted form of *had*.

> *I'd have gone if he'd invited me.*
> *I would have gone if he had invited me.*
> *I would've gone if he'd invited me.*

In the main clause the contracted forms of the modals used in speech and informal writing are:

I'd have	or	**I would've**
I could've		**I might've**

Reporting speech

There are two ways of writing down or reporting what was said on any occasion. We can repeat the actual words used (**direct speech**),

> *Monica said, "There's nothing we can do about it."*

or we can build the words into our own sentences (**reported speech**).

> *Monica said that there was nothing we could do about it.*

The words reported are normally accompanied by a **reporting verb**.

> *Monica said/declared that there was nothing we could do about it.*
> *"There is nothing we can do about it," Monica replied.*

Another name for reported speech is **indirect speech**.

Direct speech

Direct speech gives the actual words that the speaker used. It is common in fiction and other writing where the actual words of a speaker are quoted.

> *Monica said, "There's nothing we can do about it."*

The **reporting verb** may come before the words that were actually spoken, or after them, or at a natural pause inside the reported sentence.

> *Monica said, "There is nothing we can do about it."*
> *"There is nothing we can do about it," Monica said.*
> *"It's no good," Monica said, "we'll just have to ask for help."*

- The comma comes inside the quotation marks.

- Typical reporting verbs are: *agree, answer, ask, inquire, explain, reply, respond, say, tell,* and *wonder.*

The subject and the reporting verb are sometimes reversed.

> *"There is nothing we can do about it,"* **said Monica**.

The actual words spoken always begin with a capital letter, unless the reporting verb comes within a sentence. They are separated from the reporting verb by a comma, unless they are followed by a question mark or an exclamation.

> *"Why did you do it?"* she asked.
> *"Oh, mind your own business!"* he snapped.

- The words spoken are enclosed in double quotation marks.

> **"Have you been to the new shopping mall yet?"** enquired Shona.

> **"I've already seen it,"** John replied.

- Single quotation marks are used to set off a quotation within a quotation (see p. 302.)

Reported speech

Reported speech or **indirect speech** reports something that was said, but does not use the actual words that the speaker uttered.

> *Lynn asked whether Pryce had been to the new shopping mall.*
> *Pryce replied that she hadn't, but she had heard that there were some really cool shops there.*

Reported speech always has two clauses. The words that are spoken are put in a **reported clause**. There is also a **main clause** that contains a **reporting verb**. The main clause with the reporting verb usually comes before the **reported clause**.

> *Katie told me that Alison is going to resign.*
> *Peter asked whether Mandy was feeling better.*

The reporting verb in the main clause tells us how the sentence was uttered, e.g., *comment, remark, say, tell.* If the reported clause is a **statement**, the main clause is linked to the reported clause by *that*.

> *Mary said that her favorite actor was Matt Damon.*
> *John replied that he preferred Scarlett Johansson.*

If the reported clause asks a question, the main verb will be a question verb e.g., *ask, inquire, wonder, want to know.* The link between the main clause and the reported clause will be *if* or *whether*.

- The linking word *that* can be left out after most reporting verbs,

> *Jamie told Dad (that) he had passed his driving test.*
> *Lawanda said Alan had been accepted at drama school.*

but the links *if* or *whether* cannot be left out.

> *Miriam asked if she could borrow Leonie's mp3 player.*
> *Evelyn wondered whether the concert would be sold out.*

- Speech in a reported clause is not separated from the reporting verb by a comma, is not enclosed in quotation marks, and does not begin with a capital letter unless it is a proper noun. Reported questions are not followed by question marks.

Some writers put the main clause after the reported clause. In this case, no link is required. This is somewhat informal.

> *Harry Potter was on that night,* **Mary said**.

Reported clauses can also be used to express what is in someone's mind as well as what is actually spoken.

> *Evelyn* **wondered** *whether the concert would be sold out.*
> *Charlotte* **thought** *that she had better go and see her family.*

Changes in the reported words

When you use reported speech, the words put into the reported clause do not exactly match the words actually spoken.

> *"I'll leave here at 8:30 on Friday."*
> *She says* **that she will leave there at 8:30 on Friday**.
> *"I'm looking forward to seeing you."*
> *She says* **she's looking forward to seeing us**.

Pronouns and **possessive determiners** have to change in reported speech because of the change of speaker, e.g., I may become *she*; *you* may become *us* or *him*.

"I believe you."
She said that **she** believed **us**.

"I'm leaving you."
She said that **she** was leaving **him**.

"I've finished."
She said that **she had** finished.

Expressions of place and time may also have to change. *Here* may become *there* or *home*; *Friday* may become *in three days' time*.

"I've been here before."
She said that she **had been there before**.

"I'll see you on Monday."
She said that she would see him **in three days' time**.

Tense in reported clauses

The verb may also change, e.g., *must* becomes *had to* in reported speech. The most common change is a change of tense.

"Hello Jake? It's me, Shiloh. I've arrived here on time, and I'm going to take a bus to your place. There's one coming now, so I'd better run."

Shiloh called to say that **she'd** arrived **there** on time and **was going to** take a bus to **our** place. Then she said that one **was coming at that very moment**, so **she had to** run.

A reporting verb in the present tense can be used in the main clause when you report on a letter or on a recent conversation, such as a telephone conversation.

*"Hello, Jake? I've arrived here on time, and I'm going to take a
bus to your place."*
Shiloh has just phoned. She **says** that she has arrived on time
and that **she's coming** here by bus.

However, it is more common to use a past tense when reporting speech.

The changes of tense may be summarized as follows:

direct speech	reported speech
present simple	past simple
present continuous	past continuous
present perfect	past perfect
present perfect continuous	past perfect continuous
past simple	past perfect or past simple
future	conditional

Questions

Verb tenses in reported questions undergo the same changes as in
statements. See p. 282.

"Are you ready?"
He asked (us) if/whether we **were** ready.

"What time is it?"
He asked what time it **was**.
"Where has Jim gone?"
He wanted to know where Jim **had gone**.

Reporting verbs for questions include *ask, inquire, want to
know,* and *wonder.*

Direct **yes/no** questions are linked to the reporting clause by *if* or *whether*. **WH-** question words, e.g., *who*, *when*, *where*, are used in both direct and indirect questions.

> *"Are you ready?"*
> *He asked (us) if/whether we **were** ready.*
> *"What time is it?"*
> *He asked what time it **was**.*
> *"Where has Jim gone?"*
> *He wanted to know where Jim **had gone**.*

- The word order in a reported question is the same as that of a direct statement. Question order is not used in reported speech: no part of the verb comes before the subject.

Orders and requests

Orders are reported with *tell* + **object** + *to* **infinitive**.

> *"Stop calling me names!"*
> *She **told him to stop** calling her names.*

Requests for action are reported with *ask* + **object** + *to* **infinitive**.

> *"Please don't leave your things on the floor."*
> *She asked us **not to leave** our things on the floor.*

Requests for objects are reported with *ask for* + **object**.

> *"Can I have the salt, please?"*
> *He **asked for** the salt.*

- The reporting verb can be used in the passive.

> *"Don't park here, it's reserved for the doctors."*
> *I was **told not to park** there.*

Suggestions, advice, promises, etc.

A variety of verbs can be used for reporting suggestions and similar types of speech. Some of these are:

- *suggest, insist on*   + present participle

  > "Let's go to the zoo."
  > He *suggested going* to the zoo.

- *advise, invite, warn*   + direct object + *not* + *to* infinitive

  > "I wouldn't buy that one, if I were you."
  > She *advised* me **not to buy** that one.

- *refuse, threaten*   + *to* infinitive

  > "I'm not telling you!"
  > She **refused to tell** me.

- *offer, promise*   + *to* infinitive

  > "Don't worry; I'll help you."
  > He *offered* **to help** me.

Punctuation

The apostrophe (')

Misusing or omitting the apostrophe is one of the commonest punctuation errors.

Showing possession

The apostrophe (') is used to show that something belongs to someone. It is usually added to the end of a word and followed by an -s.

– -'s is added to the end of singular words.

> *a baby's stroller*
> *Hannah's book*
> *a child's cry*

– -'s is added to the end of plural words not ending in -s.

> *children's games*
> *women's clothes*
> *people's lives*

– An apostrophe alone (') is added to plural words ending in -s.

> *Your grandparents are your parents' parents.*
> *We're campaigning for workers' rights.*
> *They've hired a new ladies' fashion guru.*

– -'s is added to the end of names and singular words ending in -s.

> *James's car*
> *the octopus's tentacles*

- If the word is a famous name an apostrophe only, without the *s*, is sometimes preferred.

    Dickens' novels
    Sophocles' tragedies

– -'s is added to the end of people or their names to indicate that you are talking about their home.

    I'm going over to Harry's for dinner tonight.
    I stopped by Mom's this afternoon, but she wasn't in.

-'s can also be added to:

– whole phrases

    My next-door neighbor's dog was barking away like mad.
    John and Cath's house was on TV last night.

– indefinite pronouns

    Is this anybody's pencil sharpener?
    It's nobody's fault but mine.

– each other

    We're getting used to each other's habits.
    We kept forgetting each other's names.

When the possessor is an inanimate object (rather than a living thing), the apostrophe is not used and the word order is changed.

    the middle of the street (not *the street's middle*)
    the front of the house (not *the house's front*)

To test whether an apostrophe is in the right place, think about who the owner is.

the boy's books (= the books belonging to the boy)
the boys' books (= the books belonging to the boys)

Note that:

– An apostrophe is *not* used to form possessive pronouns such as *its*, *yours*, or *theirs*.

– An apostrophe is *not* used to form the plurals of words such as *potatoes* or *tomatoes*.

With letters and numbers

An apostrophe is used in front of two figures referring to a year or decade.

College students rioted in '68 (short for "1968").
He worked as a schoolteacher during the '80s and early '90s.

An apostrophe can be used in plurals of letters and numbers to make them more readable. It is sometimes used to show the plural of words and abbreviations spelled in all capital letters.

Mind your p's and q's.
His 2's look a bit like 7's.
She got straight A's in her exams.
He developed a scam to rob ATM's.

REMEMBER

it's = it is, e.g., *It's a holiday today.*
its = belonging to it, e.g., *The dog was scratching its ear.*

Contracted forms

An apostrophe is used in shortened forms of words to show that one or more letters have been left out. Contractions are usually shortened forms of auxiliary verbs.

be	have
I'm	I/we/they've (have)
We/you/they're (are)	He/she/it/one's (has)
He/she/it/one's (is)	I/we/you/he/she/it/one/they'd
(had)	

would
I/we/you/he/she/it/they'd (would)

or the negative *not*.

not
We/you/they aren't
He/she/it/one isn't
I/we/they haven't
He/she/it/one hasn't

In order to work out what the contracted forms *'s* and *'d* represent, you need to look at what follows them:

- If *'s* is followed by an *-ing* form, it represents the auxiliary *is*.

   She's reading a book about the ancient Egyptians.
   He's going to Cancun for his vacation.

- If *'s* is followed by an adjective or a noun phrase, it represents the main verb *is*.

   She's nervous about meeting my parents.
   He's brilliant at math.

- If *'s* is followed by a past participle, it can represent *is* as it is used in the passive,

    > He*'s* **portrayed** by the media as a kindly old grandfather.
    > It*'s* often **said** that rock stars are frustrated actors.

    or *has* as it is used in the present perfect.

    > She*'s* **broken** her wrist.
    > It*'s* **been** ages since we last saw you.

- If *'s* is followed by *got* or *gotten*, it represents the auxiliary *has*.

    > She*'s* **got** two brothers and one sister.
    > It*'s* **gotten** colder in the last few days.

- If *'d* is followed by a past participle, it represents the auxiliary *had*.

    > I*'d* **raced** against him before, but never in a marathon.
    > She couldn't believe what she*'d* **done**.

- If *'d* is followed by a base form, it represents the modal auxiliary *would*.

    > I*'d* **give up** now, if I were you.
    > When we were kids we*'d* **spend** hours out on our bikes.

- If *'d* is followed by *rather* or *better*, it represents the modal auxiliary *would*.

    > We*'d* **better** go home soon.
    > I*'d* **rather** not talk about that.

The comma (,)

The comma marks a short pause between elements in a sentence.

Separating main clauses

Main clauses that are joined together with *and* or *but* do not normally have a comma before the conjunction unless the two clauses have different subjects.

> *You go out of the door and turn immediately left.*
> *It was cold outside, but we decided to go out for a walk*
>   *anyway.*

Separating subordinate clauses from main clauses

Commas are normally used if the subordinate clause comes before the main clause.

> *If you have any problems, just call me.*
> *Just call me if you have any problems.*

Sometimes a comma is used even when the main clause comes first, if the clauses are particularly long.

> *We should be able to finish the work by the end of the week,*
>   *if nothing unexpected turns up between now and then.*

Separating relative clauses from main clauses

Commas are used to mark off nondefining relative clauses (see p. 274). This is the type of clause that adds to information about a noun or noun phrase.

> My next-door neighbor, who works from home, is keeping
>   an eye on the house while we're away.
> She moved to Los Angeles, where she was immediately
>   successful as a singer–songwriter.

Commas are not required in defining relative clauses (see p. 274), since these simply postmodify the noun.

> Let's make sure the money goes to the people **who need it most**.
> The computer **(that) I borrowed** kept on crashing.

Separating items in a list

Commas are used to separate three or more items in a list or series.

> She got out bread, butter, and jam.
> You can stay here, come with us, or come later with Heather.

Note that the comma is often not placed before the final *and* or *or*.

> They breed dogs, cats, rabbits and hamsters.

Separating common expressions and their abbreviations

Commas are used to separate expressions in sentences that indicate to the reader what follows or could follow. These expressions include *for example*, *that is*, and *and so forth*, along with their common abbreviations: e.g., *i.e.*, and *etc.*

> She got out bread, butter, jam, etc., and put them on the table.
> Several flavors are available, e.g., chocolate, caramel, strawberry,
>   and vanilla.
> His music is very accessible, i.e., easy to listen to.

Separating adjectives

Commas are used between adjectives, whether they come before the noun (i.e., used attributively) or after a linking verb (i.e., used predicatively).

> *It was a hot, dry, and dusty road.*
> *It's wet, cold, and windy outside.*

A comma is not usually used before an adjective that is followed by *and*.

With adverbials

When an adverbial such as *however, therefore* or *unfortunately* modifies a whole sentence, it is separated from the rest of the sentence by a comma.

> *However, police would not confirm this rumor.*
> *Therefore, I try to avoid using the car as much as possible.*

With sentence tags and short responses

Commas are used before sentence tags and after *yes* or *no* in short responses.

> *It's really cold today, isn't it?*
> *He's up to date with all his shots, isn't he?*
> *Are you the mother of these children? – Yes, I am.*
> *You're Amy Osborne, aren't you? – No, I'm not.*

With vocatives

Commas are used to separate the name of a person or group being addressed from the rest of the sentence.

> *And now, ladies and gentlemen, please raise your glasses in*
> *a toast to the happy couple.*
> *Come on, Olivia, be reasonable.*
> *Dad, can you come and help me, please?*

With discourse markers

Commas are used to separate discourse markers like *Well* and *Now then* from the rest of the sentence.

> *Well, believe it or not, I actually passed!*
> *Now then, let's see what's on TV tonight.*
> *Actually, I really enjoyed it.*

In reported speech

Commas are used to follow direct speech (if there is no question or exclamation point after the quotation), or to show that it comes next.

> *"I don't understand this question," said Peter.*
> *Peter said, "I don't understand this question."*
> *"You're crazy!" Claire exclaimed.*
> *"What do you think you're doing?" Dad bellowed.*

It is also possible to punctuate reported speech of the type *Peter said, "..."* using a colon instead of a comma.

> *Peter said: "Dream on."*

In dates

A comma must be used between the day of the month and the year, when the two numbers are next to each other.

> *March 31, 2011*

When a full date appears in a sentence it has both an internal comma and a comma after it.

> *As of March 31, 2011, your account will no longer be accessible via this website.*

Quotation marks (" ") or (' ')

Direct speech

Direct speech gives the actual words that a speaker used. It is common in novels and other writing where the actual words of a speaker are quoted (see p. 281).

The words spoken are enclosed in double quotation marks.

> *"Have you been to the new shopping mall yet?"* enquired Shona.

> *"I've already seen it,"* John replied.

- The comma comes inside the quotation marks.

Other uses

Double quotation marks are sometimes used:

- to suggest that the writer has some disagreement with use of the word or one of its meanings. These are informally called **scare quotes**.

> *I don't agree with this* **"mercy killing"** *business.*

- to indicate an unusual use of a word, or to show that a word you're using is new and not quite established.

> *She pointed out that the websites used for internet voting could be* **"spoofed."**

Single quotation marks are sometimes used:

- to draw attention to a word

   The word 'book' can be used as a noun or a verb.
   There is no such word as 'fubber.'
   Are there other acceptable spellings of 'kaballa'?

- when one quotation is contained within another

   "I heard him say 'Wait for me' but when I looked back he
      was gone," Lance said.

Capital letters

A capital (or upper case) letter is used to mark the beginning of a sentence.

When I was 20, I dropped out of college and became a model.

Capital letters are also used for the first letter in proper nouns. These include:

- people's names

    Javon Forbes   *William Doudi*

- days of the week

    Wednesday   *Saturday*

- months of the year

    August   *January*

- public holidays

    Christmas   *Yom Kippur*

- nationalities

    Spanish   *Iraqi*

- languages

    Swahili   *Flemish*

– geographical locations

Arizona	*Lake Powell*
Mount Everest	*The Mediterranean Sea*

– company names

Dyson	*HarperCollins*

– religions and systems of belief or thought

Islam	*Buddhism*

Capital letters are also used for the first letter in titles of books, magazines, newspapers, TV shows, films, etc. Where there are several words, a capital letter is usually used for all the main content words in the title (i.e., not the prepositions or the determiners, unless they are the first word in the title).

The Times	*Harper's*
Twelfth Night	*The Secret Garden*
Newsnight	*Mamma Mia!*

The period (.)

Periods are used:

– to mark the end of a sentence.

> *Let's have some lunch.*
> *I have to catch a bus in ten minutes.*

– to mark the end of a sentence fragment or sentence substitute.

> *Are you cold? – Yes, a bit.*
> *Do you like this sort of music? Not really.*

– in initials for people's names, although this practice is becoming less frequent.

> *J.K. Rowling*   *George W. Bush*
> *M.C. Hammer*   *Warren G. Harding*

– after some abbreviations, although this usage is variable and most abbreviations are clear without the period.

> *P.S. Do stop in next time you're passing through.*
> *She's moved to the I.T. department.*
> *R.S.V.P. to Helen Douglas on 555 2938.*
> *The U.S. government reacted strongly to the accusation.*

When an abbreviation consists of a shortened word such as *Soc.* or *Prof.*, a period is needed.

> *The Soc. of Retired Police Officers endorsed the decision.*
> *Prof. John Johansson will be speaking tonight.*
> *Flight UA 345: dep. 09:44 arr. 11:10.*

When an abbreviation contains the last letter of the shortened word, a period is also needed.

> **Dr.** McDonald   **St.** Mary's School
> 41 Douglas **Rd.**   the Akron Bar **Assn.**

- Note that periods are not used in many common sets of initials,

> Did you watch the game on **NBC** last night?
> Millions of people now call the **FBI** crimestopper line each year.

or at the end of headlines, headings and titles.

> Fear grips global stock markets
> Teaching grammar as a liberating force
> Wuthering Heights

Remember that a period, and not a question mark, is used after an indirect question.

> He asked if the bus had left.
> I wonder what's happened.
> She asked him where he was going.

> In British English, the period is called a full stop.

The question mark (?)

The question mark marks the end of a question.

> *When will we be arriving?*
> *Why did you do that?*
> *Does any of this matter?*
> *He's certain to be elected, isn't he?*

Question marks are used in direct questions, i.e., when the actual words of a speaker are used. A reported question should end with a period.

> *The lady said, "Where are you going?"*
> *The lady asked where she was going.*

Note that you put a question mark at the end of a question, even if the words in the sentence are not in the normal question order, or some words are omitted. Care is needed here as such a sentence can look, at first sight, like a statement rather than a question.

> *You know he doesn't live here any longer?*

A period, rather than a question mark, is used after an indirect question.

> *I'd like to know what you've been doing all this time.*
> *I wonder what's happened.*

The exclamation point (!)

The exclamation point (sometimes called the exclamation mark) is used after exclamations and emphatic expressions.

> *I can't believe it!*
> *Oh, no! Look at this mess!*

The exclamation point loses its effect if it is overused. It is better to use a period after a sentence expressing mild excitement or humor.

> *It was such a beautiful day.*
> *I felt like a complete idiot.*

The colon (:)

The colon indicates a break between two main clauses that is stronger than a comma but weaker than a period.

A colon is used:

– in front of a list.

> *I used three colors: green, blue, and pink.*
> *Make sure you wear clothes made from natural fibers:*
> *cotton, silk, or wool.*

– in front of an explanation or a reason.

> *Nevertheless, the main problem remained: what should*
> *be done with the two men?*
> *I decided against going away this weekend: the weather*
> *forecast was dreadful.*

– after introductory headings.

> *Cooking time: about five minutes.*
> *Start time: 10 o'clock.*

– to separate the hours from the minutes in expressions of time.

> *The conference call is scheduled for 10:45 this morning.*

– in more formal writing, between two main clauses that are connected.

> *It made me feel claustrophobic: what, I wonder, would happen*
> *to someone who was really unable to tolerate being locked*
> *into such a tiny space?*
> *Be patient: the next book in the series has not yet been*
> *published.*

– in front of the second part of a book title.

> *Farming and Wildlife: a study in compromise*
> *Beyond Single Words: the most frequent collocations in spoken*
>   *English.*

– to introduce direct speech, especially when the quotation is
  particularly long.

> *He said: "You owe me three dollars and twenty-five cents."*
> *The US Defense Secretary said: "There was agreement within*
>   *the administration that we didn't think we were far enough*
>   *down the road toward getting control of nuclear weapons*
>   *around the world to limit ourselves so explicitly."*

The semicolon (;)

The semicolon is used to mark a break between two main clauses when there is a balance or a contrast between the clauses.

Compare:

The engine roared into life. The propellers began to turn. The plane taxied down the runway ready for takeoff.

with:

The engine roared into life; the propellers began to turn; the plane taxied down the runway ready for takeoff.

A useful test to decide when to use a semicolon is to ask yourself whether the two clauses could be written instead as separate sentences. If the answer is "yes", then you can use a semicolon.

Note that it is acceptable to use a period in these cases, but a semicolon is preferable if you wish to express a link or continuity between the clauses in your narrative.

I'm not that interested in jazz; I prefer classical music. He knew everything about me; I had never even heard of him.

A semicolon is also used to separate items in a list, especially if the listed items are phrases or clauses that may already contain commas.

The trip was a disaster: the flight was four hours late; the hotel, which was described as "luxury," was dirty; and it rained for the whole week.

Parentheses ( )

Parentheses are used to enclose a word or words that can be left out and still leave a meaningful sentence.

> *The wooded area (see map below) is approximately*
> *4,000 acres.*
> *This is a process which Hayek (a writer who came to*
> *rather different conclusions) also observed.*

Parentheses are also used to show alternatives or options.

> *Any student(s) interested in taking part should e-mail me.*
> *A goat should give from three to six pints (1.4 to 2.8 liters)*
> *of milk a day.*

Note that when the structure of the sentence as a whole requires punctuation after a section enclosed in parentheses, the punctuation is given *outside* the parentheses.

> *I haven't yet spoken to John (I mean John Maple, my boss),*
> *but I have a meeting with him on Friday.*
> *For lunch we had sandwiches (pastrami on rye and so on),*
> *salami, coleslaw, fried chicken, and potato salad.*

Punctuation is given before the closing parentheses only when it applies to the enclosed section rather than to the sentence as a whole.

> *He's very handsome (positively gorgeous in fact!) and still*
> *single.*

Brackets [ ]

Brackets (also called **square brackets**) are used, usually in books and articles, when supplying words that make a quotation clearer or that comment on it, although they were not originally said or written.

> *Mr. Runcie concluded: "The novel is at its strongest when describing the dignity of Cambridge [a slave] and the education of Emily [the daughter of an absentee landlord]."*

Brackets are also used when you need to put a word or word in parentheses inside another set of parentheses.

> *The novel touches on aspects of colonial life in India (the author, E.M. Forster [1879–1970], visited there in the 1920s).*

The hyphen (-)

The hyphen joins words or parts of words.

Hyphens are used at the ends of lines where a word has been split, to warn the reader that the word continues on the next line. If the word you need to split is clearly made up of two or more smaller words or elements, you should put the hyphen after the first of these parts. Otherwise, you put the hyphen at the end of a syllable. Most computer programs that deal with text insert hyphens automatically in acceptable places. Consult a dictionary if you are not sure where to insert the hyphen in a word.

> wheelbar-row   inter-national
> listen-ing   compli-mentary
> infor-mation

It is best not to add a hyphen if the word is a short one, or if it would mean writing just one or two letters at the end or beginning of a line. For example, it would be better to write "unnatural" on the line below, rather than writing "un-" on one line and "natural" on the next.

Prefixes that are used in front of a word beginning with a capital letter always have a hyphen after them.

> a wave of anti-Mexican feeling
> a neo-Byzantine cathedral

A hyphen is used to join two or more words that together form an adjective, where this adjective is used *before* the noun it describes.

> an up-to-date account
> a last-minute rush
> a six-year-old boy

The hyphen is omitted when the adjective so formed comes after the noun or pronoun it describes.

> *The accounts are up to date.*
> *It was all rather last minute.*
> *He's six years old.*

Some common compound nouns are always written with hyphens.

> *mother-in-law*   *great-grandmother*

Hyphens can be used to split words that have been formed by adding a prefix to another word, especially to avoid an awkward combination of letters or confusion with another word.

> *co-owner*
> *re-covering furniture*
> *the re-creation of battle scenes*

Dashes

Printed books have two different kinds of dashes: the en dash (–) and the slightly longer em dash (—). These dashes can be created in most word-processing programs on computers, but in fact most people just use a hyphen where printed books use an en dash, and two hyphens (--) where printed books use an em dash. The information below applies mainly to the way dashes are used in printed books and professionally edited text.

The en dash (–)

An en dash is used:

– to indicate a range.

> *pages 26–42*

– between two adjectives or noun modifiers that indicate that two countries or groups are involved in something or that an individual has two roles or aspects.

> *Swedish–Norwegian relations improved*
> *the United States–Canada free trade pact*
> *a mathematician–philosopher*

– to indicate that something such as a plane or a train goes between two places.

> *the Anguilla–St. Kitts flight*
> *the New York–Montreal train*

The em dash (—)

An em dash is used:

- at the beginning and end of a comment that interrupts the flow of a sentence.

    Now children–Kenneth, stop that immediately!–open your books on page 20.

- to separate off extra information.

    Boots and shoes–all shapes, sizes and colors–tumbled out.

The slash (/)

The slash separates letters, words or numbers. It is used to indicate alternatives, ratios and ranges, and in website addresses. It is sometimes called a forward slash to distinguish it from a less frequently used character, the backslash (\).

> *he/she/it*
> *200 km/hr*
> *the 2011/12 accounting year*
> *http://www.abcdefg.com*

Punctuation in numbers

Dates

Slashes or periods are often used in dates.

	British usage
12/3/09	*3.12.09*
2/28/11	*28.2.11*

Abbreviations that indicate the era in which a date occurs are now usually written without periods after them, but periods are acceptable.

500 BCE	*January 13, 1520 A.D.*

Scientific usage

Periods are not used in metric system abbreviations.

12 kg	*50 cm*

Times

Colons are used in times. The letters *a.m.* and *p.m.* can be written with or without periods following them.

3:30 a.m.	*20:30*

Long numbers

Commas are used in numbers to mark off units of thousands, millions, billions, etc.

1,359   2,543,678

Decimals

Periods indicate decimal points.

1.5   25.08

2. Spelling

contents

contents

the basics of spelling

The basics of spelling

Spelling is the process of using letters to represent a word. For most words there is only one arrangement of letters that is accepted as the correct spelling. Using the correct spelling of a word means that you can be confident of being understood when you write English; getting the spelling wrong can make it difficult to be understood and can create a bad impression.

The alphabet

There are 26 letters that are used to spell words in English:

a b c d e f g h i j k l m n o p q r s t u v w x y z

Each of these letters can also be written as a capital letter. This form is used at the beginning of a sentence or a name, and in certain other places (see page 407–408).

A B C D E F G H I J K L M N O P Q R S T U V W X Y Z

Five of these letters (**A**, **E**, **I**, **O**, **U**) are **vowels**. These are used to represent sounds that are made when your mouth is open.

cat	*pen*	*sit*
dog	*cup*	

The other letters are called **consonants**. These are used to represent sounds that are made by closing your mouth or using your tongue.

pea	*see*	*do*

> The letter **Y** can act as a vowel in some words, such as *sky* and *crypt*.

Most words are spelled using a mixture of vowels and consonants. This is because in most cases we need to open our mouths between pronouncing different consonants. It is not typical to find more than two vowels or two consonants together.

Typical letter-sounds

Most consonants are strongly associated with a particular sound and represent this sound in virtually every word in which they appear. For example, the letter **B** nearly always makes the same sound.

big	*bad*	*bee*
cab	*club*	*robin*

Some consonants can represent different sounds in different words. For example, **C** can have a "hard" sound like a **K**.

cat	*cup*	*panic*

But it can also have a "soft" sound like an **S**.

city	*acid*	*place*

Combinations of consonants

Some consonants can be combined and still keep their typical sounds. The letters **L**, **R**, and **W** can come after some other consonants.

blob	*grip*	*dwell*
clip	*prod*	*twin*

The letter **S** can come before a number of other consonants.

scan	*skip*	*slip*

smell	*snip*	*spin*
squid	*stop*	*swim*

Some combinations of letters can appear in the middle of a word or at the end of a word, but not at the beginning of a word.

doctor	*left*	*golden*
milk	*help*	*belt*
lamp	*land*	*ring*
tank	*went*	*opt*

It is unusual, but not impossible, to have three or more consonant sounds together.

scrap	*split*	*extra*

Combinations that produce typical sounds

When some letters are combined with an **H**, they do not keep their own sounds but create a different sound. For example:

CH

chip	*chat*	*rich*

PH creates the same sound as the letter **F**.

phone	*elephant*	*graph*

SH

ship	*bishop*	*fish*

TH

thin	*anthem*	*path*

TH can also make a different, slightly softer sound.

this	*bother*	*seethe*

Simple vowel sounds

The vowels **A**, **E**, **I**, **O**, and **U** each have typical sounds when they appear on their own in short words.

cat	*rat*	*hat*
men	*pen*	*ten*
bit	*hit*	*sit*
dot	*lot*	*got*
but	*nut*	*hut*

The sound of a vowel changes from a "short" sound to a "long" sound when the consonant after the vowel is followed by the letter **E**.

date	*rate*	*hate*
scene	*cede*	*theme*
bite	*mite*	*like*
note	*lone*	*mole*
flute	*rule*	*brute*

Combinations of vowels

When two vowels are used together, they usually make a different sound rather than keeping the simple sounds they make on their own.

The letters **AI** have a characteristic sound when they appear together.

raid	*train*	*aim*

The letters **AU** have a characteristic sound when they appear together.

daub   *faun*   *haul*

The letters **EA** have a characteristic sound when they appear together.

read   *tea*   *eat*

When the letter **E** is doubled it produces a characteristic sound.
The sound is the same as the one typically produced by **EA**.

feed   *tree*   *bee*

The letters **IE** have a characteristic sound when they appear together.

tie   *fried*   *pie*

The letters **OA** have a characteristic sound when they appear together.

road   *goat*   *toad*

The letters **OE** have a characteristic sound when they appear together,
usually at the end of a word. The sound is the same as the one typically
produced by **OA**.

toe   *hoe*   *woe*

The letters **OI** have a characteristic sound when they appear together.

coin   *soil*   *oil*

When the letter **O** is doubled it produces a characteristic sound.

food   *moon*   *boot*

The double **O** can sometimes make a different, shorter, sound.

good   *wool*   *hood*

The letters **OU** have a characteristic sound when they appear together.

mouth *count* **out**

The letters **UE** have a characteristic sound when they appear together. The sound is the same as the one produced by **OO** in the word *food*.

true *sue* *glue*

Vowels followed by R

The letter **R** slightly changes the sound of most single vowels that come before it.

The letters **AR** have a characteristic sound when they appear together.

car *park* **art**

The letters **ER** have a characteristic sound when they appear together.

her *term* *herb*

The letters **IR** have a characteristic sound when they appear together.

sir *girl* *shirt*

The letters **OR** have a characteristic sound when they appear together.

sort *born* *for*

The letters **UR** have a characteristic sound when they appear together. The sound is the same as the one typically produced by **ER**.

burn *turn* *hurt*

Vowels followed by W or Y

When the letters **W** or **Y** come after a vowel, the letter usually changes the sound of the vowel, but it is not sounded itself.

The letters **AW** have a characteristic sound when they appear together at the end of a word or syllable. The sound is the same as the one typically produced by **AU**.

    paw   *claw*   *straw*

The letters **AY** have a characteristic sound when they appear together at the end of a word or syllable. The sound is the same as the one typically produced by **AI**.

    day   *stay*   *may*

The letters **EW** have a characteristic sound when they appear together at the end of a word or syllable. The sound is the same as the one produced by **OO** in the word food.

    flew   *yew*   *brew*

The letters **OW** have a characteristic sound when they appear together at the end of a word or syllable. The sound is the same as the one typically produced by **OU**.

    how   *growl*   *down*

These letters can also make the sound that is typically produced by **OE**.

    grow   *flow*   *own*

The letters **OY** have a characteristic sound when they appear together. The sound is the same as the one typically produced by **OI**.

    boy   *toy*   *joy*

why you need to work at spelling

Why you need to work at spelling

If every letter represented one sound and one sound only, you could write out words very easily once you knew which letter represented which sound. Some languages (such as Italian) are like this, and present few surprises with regard to spelling once you know how each sound is written.

But English uses about 44 different sounds to make up words, whereas there are only 26 letters to indicate these sounds. This means that some letters have to be used for more than one sound.

Moreover, there are certain other factors that mean it is not always easy to predict how an English word will be spelled. We will look at these factors in this chapter.

Some letters can have more than one sound

As we have just seen, there are more sounds in English than there are letters to represent them. This means that some letters have to represent more than one sound.

For example, the letter **T** usually makes the same sound when it occurs on its own.

    *t*in   *t*ank   pa*t*

But it makes different sounds when it is followed by **H**.

    *th*in   *th*is   pa*th*

More awkwardly, some letters have more than one sound, even though there are other letters that make one of the sounds. For example, the letter **G** typically has a "hard" sound.

*g*irl   ti*g*er   ru*g*

But in some cases it makes the same "soft" sound as the letter **J**.

*g*erm   *g*inger   pa*g*e

Similarly, the letter **S** has a characteristic "hissing" sound.

*s*ee   *s*it   ga*s*

But it can sometimes make the same "buzzing" sound as the letter **Z**.

ha*s*   hi*s*   plea*s*ant

The fact that letters can represent multiple sounds means that when you see a word you cannot automatically know how it will be pronounced.

Some sounds can be represented by different letters

A more significant issue for spelling is that, because some sounds can be represented by different letters or combinations of letters, you cannot automatically know how a word will be spelled when you hear it.

The vowel sound in the following group of words has the same pronunciation, but the letters used to represent the sound are different in each word.

m*ar*ch   *al*ms   bl*ah*   h*ear*t

The same thing can be true of most vowel sounds, as the following groups of words show.

*ai*sle	*guy*	m*igh*t	r*ye*
p*ai*d	d*ay*	pr*ey*	n*eigh*
b*ea*d	c*e*de	d*ee*d	k*ey*ed
z*oo*	d*o*	sh*oe*	y*ou*

Similarly, the consonant sound at the end of the following words has the same pronunciation, but is represented by different letters in each word.

if	*graph*	*rough*

The same thing can be true of other consonant sounds, as the following groups of words show.

*g*em	e*dge*	*j*am
*c*ap	dar*k*	*c*enter
*s*it	*c*enter	*sc*ene

So when you hear a word, you can't automatically work out how it is spelled, though you can often make a good guess.

Some words that sound the same are written differently

Because sounds can be represented by different letters, it is possible for two different words to sound the same but be spelled differently. This can lead to confusion between the two spellings.

For example, the words *there*, meaning "that place," and *their*, meaning "belonging to them," both have the same sound. Similarly, the words *stare*, meaning "to look intently," and *stair*, meaning "one of a set of steps," also share a single pronunciation.

It can be easy to confuse these words and use the correct spelling of one word when you are actually intending to write the other word.

English words come from many different languages

One of the most striking features of the English language is its readiness to accept words from other languages. At the heart of modern English are two completely different languages – Anglo-Saxon and French – which have two different spelling systems, but which both contributed thousands of words to English. In addition to this, English has borrowed words from many other European languages, such as Italian, Spanish, German, and Dutch. Furthermore, whenever scientists made new discoveries they turned to the classical languages of Latin and Greek to come up with names for the new things they needed to describe.

As communications between different parts of the world have become easier, more and more languages have contributed to English, including Turkish, Arabic, Hindi, Chinese, Japanese, and Russian.

Each of these languages has its own spelling system – many of which are quite different from the natural English system – and the words that English has borrowed from them often keep the spelling patterns of the original language.

For example, many words that come from French use **CH** where you might expect **SH**.

*ch*alet   *ch*ute   *ch*auffeur

Words that come from Greek usually use **PH** rather than **F**.

tele*ph*one   *ph*ysical   *ph*otogra*ph*

Words that come from Japanese use **K** rather than **C**.

karaoke   *karate*   *kimono*

So the pronunciation of a word might suggest to you any number of different spellings if you don't know which language the word came from.

Silent letters

Another thing that can be confusing is that some words contain letters that are not sounded when the word is pronounced.

Often these are letters that were sounded in the original form of a word. Over many years the pronunciation of these words became simplified, but the spelling did not change to reflect the new pronunciation.

For example, the letter **G** is often silent before **N** or **M**.

gnat   *phlegm*   *sign*

Similarly, **H** is often silent at the start of a word, or after **G** or **R**.

honest   *ghost*   *rhyme*

E is often silent at the end of words.

have   *give*   *love*

In fact, it has been reckoned that of the 26 letters in the alphabet, only five are never silent. These five are **F**, **J**, **Q**, **V**, and **X**.

The presence of single and double letters

All of the letters except **H**, **Q**, and **Y** can occur as both single and double letters within a word.

For example, the letter **B** occurs as a single letter in some words.

  robin   *habit*   *crab*

But in other words the **B** is doubled.

  bobbin   *rabbit*   *ebb*

When consonants are doubled, they are pronounced just the same as a single consonant. So when you hear a word you cannot always tell where a consonant sound is represented by a single letter or a double letter.

346 why you need to work at spelling

Spelling variants

Some words do not have a single spelling that is regarded as correct,
but can be spelled in two or more different ways.

Some words that come from other languages can be written in
'different ways in English because the original language uses a different
alphabet and there are different systems for representing that
alphabet in English.

veranda	*verandah*
czar	*tsar*
alleluia	*hallelujah*

Other spelling variations are simply a matter of taste.

barbecue	*Bar-B-Q*
judgment	*judgement*

The fact that such variations exist means that for some words there is
not always a single correct spelling that you can learn.

American and British spelling

One of the most common sources of variations in spelling is the fact
that some words are conventionally spelled differently in American
English and British English. Some spellings that are regarded as correct
by American speakers are not used in Britain (or in Australia and most
other English-speaking countries). Canadian English uses spellings
that match the American spellings for some words and the British
spellings for others.

The table below shows some examples of variations between British
and American spelling.

American English	British English
aluminum	*aluminium*
analyze	*analyse*
anesthetic	*anaesthetic*
ax	*axe*
behavior	*behaviour*
breathalyze	*breathalyse*
catalog	*catalogue*
center	*centre*
check	*cheque*
color	*colour*
curb	*kerb*
defense	*defence*
favorite	*favourite*
fulfill	*fulfil*
gray	*grey*
installment	*instalment*
jewelry	*jewellery*
liter	*litre*
luster	*lustre*

American English	British English
meager	meagre
mold	mould
mustache	moustache
odor	odour
percent	per cent
plow	plough
program	programme
pajamas	pyjamas
skeptic	sceptic
sulfur	sulphur
theater	theatre
tire	tyre

And now the good news

All of these factors mean that English spelling needs some work before you can become very accurate. The good news, however, is that there are things you can do to help you understand the system better and so become confident about how to spell words. We will look at these in the next two chapters.

patterns and building blocks

Patterns and building blocks

Some groups of letters appear in many different English words. Often a group of letters will indicate the same thing in every word where it appears. For example, the letters **RE** at the start of a word usually mean "again."

Because so many words are made up of these building blocks, you don't need to learn every spelling individually. Often you can spell out a word by adding together the blocks of letters that form the word. So it is important to know what these blocks are, how they are joined to the rest of a word, and what they mean.

Building blocks at the start of words

A block of letters that regularly appears at the start of words and carries a meaning is called a **prefix**. A prefix can be attached in front of another word or block of letters to create a new word with a different meaning.

For example, when the letters **UN** are added to another word (called a **root word**), they add the meaning of "not" to the sense of the other word.

     unnatural   **un**known   **un**holy

Notice that you can spell these words by splitting them into the prefix and the root word, as the spelling of the root word stays the same.

It is not always so obvious that a prefix is being added to an existing word to make a new word. Many prefixes occur in words that came to English from Latin and Greek. In these cases the blocks to which they are joined are often Latin or Greek forms rather than familiar English words. Nevertheless, it is worth studying these building blocks and noting that they occur in many English words.

The prefix **AB** means "away from" or "not."

*ab*normal   *ab*use   *ab*scond

The prefix **AD** means "toward."

*ad*dress   *ad*just   *ad*mit

The prefix **AL** means "all."

*al*together   *al*ways   *al*mighty

The prefix **ANTE** means "before." Take care not to confuse this with **ANTI**. If you remember the meaning of both these prefixes you should be able to work out the correct spelling of a word that starts with one of them.

*ante*date   *ante*room   *ante*cedent

The prefix **ANTI** means "against." Take care not to confuse this with **ANTE**. If you remember the meaning of both these prefixes you should be able to work out the correct spelling of a word that starts with one of them.

*anti*war   *anti*social   *anti*depressant

The prefix **ARCH** means "chief."

*arch*bishop   *arch*enemy   *arch*angel

The prefix **AUTO** means "self."

*auto*graph   *auto*biography   *auto*mobile

The prefix **BENE** means "good" or "well."

*bene*fit   *bene*volent   *bene*factor

The prefix **BI** means "two" or "twice."

      bicycle   **bi**monthly   **bi**focals

The prefix **CIRCUM** means "around."

      circumference   **circum**stance   **circum**navigate

The prefix **CO** means "together." There is sometimes a hyphen after this prefix to make the meaning clear.

      copilot   **co**-owner   **co**operate

The prefix **CON** means "together."

      confer   **con**stellation   **con**verge

When it is added before words beginning with **L**, the prefix **CON** is changed to **COL**.

      collaborate   **col**lateral   **col**lide

When it is added before words beginning with **B**, **M**, or **P**, the prefix **CON** is changed to **COM**.

      combat   **com**mit   **com**pact

When it is added before words beginning with **R**, the prefix **CON** is changed to **COR**.

      correct   **cor**respond   **cor**relation

The prefix **CONTRA** means "against."

      contradict   **contra**vene   **contra**band

The prefix **DE** indicates removal or reversal.

> *de*frost   *de*throne   *de*caffeinated

The prefix **DIS** indicates removal or reversal.

> *dis*agree   *dis*honest   *dis*trust

The prefix **EN** usually means "into."

> *en*rage   *en*slave   *en*danger

The prefix **EX** means "out" or "outside of."

> *ex*it   *ex*port   *ex*ternal

The prefix **EX** also means "former." The prefix is followed by a hyphen when it has this meaning.

> *ex*-wife   *ex*-partner   *ex*-president

The prefix **EXTRA** means "beyond" or "outside of."

> *extra*ordinary   *extra*terrestrial   *extra*sensory

The prefix **HYPER** means "over" or "more."

> *hyper*active   *hyper*critical   *hyper*tension

The prefix **IN** sometimes means "not."

> *in*human   *in*sufferable   *in*credible

The prefix **IN** can also mean "in" or "into."

> *in*filtrate   *in*take   *in*grown

When it is added before words beginning with **L**, the prefix **IN** is changed to **IL**.

*il*literate *il*legal *il*logical

When it is added before words beginning with **B**, **M**, or **P**, the prefix **IN** is changed to **IM**.

*im*balance *im*moral *im*possible

> Note that the word *input* is an exception to this rule.

When it is added before words beginning with **R**, the prefix **IN** is changed to **IR**.

*ir*regular *ir*responsible *ir*relevant

The prefix **INTER** means "between."

*inter*national *inter*war *inter*ruption

The prefix **INTRA** means "within."

*intra*venous *intra*net *intra*mural

The prefix **MACRO** means "very large."

*macro*economics *macro*biotic *macro*cosm

The prefix **MAL** means "bad" or "badly."

*mal*practice *mal*formed *mal*administration

The prefix **MAXI** means "big" or "biggest."

*maxi*mize *maxi*mum *maxi*dress

The prefix **MICRO** means "very small."

*micro*scope   *micro*chip   *micro*wave

The prefix **MINI** means "small."

*mini*skirt   *mini*series   *mini*bus

The prefix **MIS** means "wrong" or "false."

*mis*behave   *mis*fortune   *mis*take

The prefix **NON** means "not."

*non*sense   *non*fiction   *non*stop

The prefix **PARA** usually means "beside" or "parallel to."

*para*medic   *para*military   *para*legal

The prefix **POST** means "after."

*post*pone   *post*graduate   *post*dated

The prefix **PRE** means "before."

*pre*arranged   *pre*war   *pre*season

The prefix **PRO** means "ahead" or "forward."

*pro*rate   *pro*active   *pro*voke

The prefix **PRO** also means "in favor of." The prefix is followed by a hyphen when it has this meaning.

pro-*choice*   **pro**-*democracy*   **pro**-*European*

The prefix **RE** means "again."

    rearrange   **re**read   **re**heat

The prefix **SEMI** means "half."

    semifinal   **semi**retirement   **semi**professional

The prefix **SUB** means "under."

    submarine   **sub**soil   **sub**way

The prefix **SUPER** indicates "above," "beyond," or "extreme."

    superhuman   **super**market   **super**star

The prefix **TELE** means "distant."

    telegraph   **tele**vision   **tele**scope

The prefix **TRANS** means "across."

    transfer   **trans**plant   **trans**continental

The prefix **ULTRA** indicates "beyond" or "extreme."

    ultrasound   **ultra**modern   **ultra**conservative

Building blocks at the end of words

A block of letters that regularly appears at the end of words and carries a meaning is called a **suffix**. Just like a prefix at the start of a word, a suffix can be attached to a root word or word form to create a new word with a different meaning.

For example, when the letters **LESS** are added to the end of a root word, they add the meaning of "without" to the sense of the root word.

head**less**   child**less**   life**less**

It is worth studying these building blocks and noting that they occur at the end of many English words.

The suffix **ABLE** means "able to."

break**able**   read**able**   enjoy**able**

> It is difficult to distinguish this from the suffix **IBLE**, which occurs in many words and has the same meaning. A list of the common words with each suffix is given on pages 363–364.

The suffix **AL** means "related to."

season**al**   nation**al**   tradition**al**

The suffix **ANCE** indicates a state or quality.

accept**ance**   defi**ance**   resembl**ance**

The suffix **ANT** indicates an action or condition.

resist**ant**   toler**ant**   dorm**ant**

> It is difficult to distinguish this from the suffix **ENT**, which occurs in many words and has the same meaning. A list of the common words with each suffix is given on pages 365–366.

The suffix **ARY** means "related to."

caution**ary**   revolution**ary**   document**ary**

358 patterns and building blocks

The suffix **ATE** creates verbs indicating becoming or taking on a state.

hyphen*ate*   elev*ate*   medic*ate*

The suffix **ATION** indicates becoming or entering a state.

hyphen*ation*   elev*ation*   medic*ation*

The suffix **CRACY** means "government."

demo*cracy*   auto*cracy*   bureau*cracy*

The suffix **CRAT** means "ruler."

demo*crat*   auto*crat*   bureau*crat*

The suffix **DOM** means "state of being."

free*dom*   bore*dom*   martyr*dom*

The suffix **EE** indicates a person who is affected by or receives something.

interview*ee*   evacu*ee*   honor*ee*

The suffix **EN** means "become."

damp*en*   dead*en*   black*en*

The suffix **ENCE** indicates a state or quality.

resid*ence*   abstin*ence*   depend*ence*

The suffix **ENT** indicates an action or condition.

abstin*ent*   obedi*ent*   independ*ent*

It is difficult to distinguish this from the suffix **ANT**, which occurs in many words and has the same meaning. A list of the common words with each suffix is given on pages 365–366.

The suffix **ER** means "person from."

islan**der**   Southern**er**   New York**er**

The suffix **ER** also means "person who does a job" or "thing that does a job."

driv**er**   paint**er**   teach**er**
fasten**er**   scrap**er**   light**er**

The suffix **ESCENT** means "becoming."

adol**escent**   obsol**escent**   lumin**escent**

The suffix **ETTE** means "small."

kitchen**ette**   cigar**ette**   disk**ette**

The suffix **FUL** means "full of."

beauti**ful**   pain**ful**   resent**ful**

The suffix **HOOD** means "state of being."

child**hood**   likeli**hood**   priest**hood**

The suffix **IAN** creates nouns indicating a member of a profession.

politic**ian**   magic**ian**   mathematic**ian**

The suffix **IBLE** means "able to."

ed**ible**   terr**ible**   poss**ible**

> It is difficult to distinguish this from the suffix **ABLE**, which occurs in many words and has the same meaning. A list of the common words with each suffix is given on pages 363–364.

The suffix **IC** means "related to."

atom**ic**   period**ic**   rhythm**ic**

The suffix **IFICATION** creates nouns indicating an action.

not**ification**   class**ification**   clar**ification**

The suffix **IFY** creates verbs indicating an action.

not**ify**   class**ify**   clar**ify**

The suffix **ISH** means "fairly" or "rather."

small**ish**   young**ish**   brown**ish**

The suffix **ISH** also means "resembling."

tiger**ish**   boy**ish**   amateur**ish**

The suffix **ISM** means "action" or "condition."

critic**ism**   hero**ism**   absentee**ism**

The suffix **ISM** also creates nouns indicating a prejudice.

sex**ism**   rac**ism**   anti-Semit**ism**

The suffix **IST** means "doer of."

motorist   *soloist*   *artist*

The suffix **IST** also indicates a prejudice.

sexist   *racist*   *ageist*

The suffix **ITY** indicates a state or condition.

reality   *stupidity*   *continuity*

The suffix **IVE** indicates a tendency toward something.

explosive   *active*   *decorative*

The suffix **IZE** creates verbs indicating a change or becoming.

radicalize   *legalize*   *economize*

The suffix **LET** means "little."

booklet   *ringlet*   *piglet*

The suffix **LIKE** means "resembling."

doglike   *childlike*   *dreamlike*

The suffix **LING** means "small."

duckling   *gosling*   *foundling*

The suffix **LY** means "in this manner."

kindly   *friendly*   *properly*

The suffix **MENT** means "state of."

contentment   enjoyment   employment

The suffix **METER** means "measure."

thermometer   barometer   speedometer

The suffix **NESS** means "state of" or "quality of."

kindness   blindness   selfishness

The suffix **OLOGY** means "study of" or "science of."

biology   sociology   musicology

The suffix **SHIP** means "state of" or "condition of."

fellowship   dictatorship   horsemanship

The suffix **SION** means "action" or "state of."

confusion   decision   explosion

> It is difficult to distinguish this from the suffix **TION**, which occurs in many words and has the same meaning. A list of the common words with each suffix is given on pages 366–368.

The suffix **SOME** means "tending to."

quarrelsome   troublesome   loathsome

The suffix **TION** means "action" or "state of."

creation   production   calculation

It is difficult to distinguish this from the suffix **SION**, which occurs in many words and has the same meaning. A list of the common words with each suffix is given on pages 366–368.

The suffix **Y** means "like" or "full of."

watery   hilly   snowy

ABLE and IBLE

The suffixes **ABLE** and **IBLE** are both quite common (although **ABLE** is more common) and have the same meaning. You should be aware of the possibility of confusing these endings and check if you are not sure which one is correct.

The table below shows some common words with each ending.

Words that end in ABLE	Words that end in IBLE
adaptable	accessible
admirable	audible
adorable	compatible
advisable	convertible
agreeable	credible
allowable	divisible
arguable	eligible
available	flexible
capable	gullible
desirable	horrible
durable	illegible
enjoyable	inaudible

Words that end in ABLE	Words that end in IBLE
enviable	indelible
excitable	inedible
flammable	invisible
hospitable	irresistible
irritable	legible
lovable	negligible
movable	plausible
notable	possible
palatable	risible
probable	sensible
suitable	tangible
tolerable	terrible
wearable	visible

A useful – but not one-hundred percent reliable – rule of thumb is that when one of these endings is added to an existing word, the spelling is **ABLE**.

adapt**able**   enjoy**able**   lov**able**

Adjectives ending in **ABLE** will form related nouns ending in **ABILITY**.

cap**able**   prob**able**   suit**able**
cap**ability**   prob**ability**   suit**ability**

However, adjectives ending **IBLE** will form related nouns ending in **IBILITY**.

gull**ible**   flex**ible**   poss**ible**
gull**ibility**   flex**ibility**   poss**ibility**

ANT and ENT

The suffixes **ANT** and **ENT** are both quite common and have the same meaning. You should be aware of the possibility of confusing these endings and check if you are not sure which one is correct.

The table below shows some common words with each ending.

Words that end in ANT	Words that end in ENT
abundant	absent
adamant	accident
arrogant	adjacent
assistant	affluent
blatant	ailment
brilliant	ancient
buoyant	apparent
defiant	argument
deodorant	coherent
dominant	convenient
dormant	deficient
elegant	dependent
emigrant	descent
exuberant	efficient
fragrant	eminent
hesitant	equipment
ignorant	evident
immigrant	fluent
important	implement
incessant	lenient
indignant	negligent
irritant	nutrient
migrant	opulent
militant	parent
mutant	patient

Words that end in ANT	Words that end in ENT
occupant	permanent
pleasant	precedent
poignant	president
radiant	prominent
redundant	pungent
relevant	rodent
reluctant	salient
resistant	silent
stagnant	solvent
tenant	strident
tolerant	succulent
vacant	sufficient
valiant	turbulent
vigilant	vehement

Words ending in **ANT** will form related nouns ending in **ANCE** or **ANCY**.

defi**ant**	toler**ant**	vac**ant**
defi**ance**	toler**ance**	vac**ancy**

However, words ending in **ENT** will form related nouns ending in **ENCE** or **ENCY**.

flu**ent**	opul**ent**	suffici**ent**
flu**ency**	opul**ence**	suffici**ency**

SION and TION

The suffixes **SION** and **TION** are both quite common and have the same meaning (although **TION** is more common). You should be aware of the possibility of confusing these endings and check if you are not sure which one is correct.

The table below shows some common words with each ending.

Words that end in SION	Words that end in TION
adhesion	accusation
admission	ambition
cohesion	assumption
collision	attention
collusion	audition
conclusion	caution
confusion	collection
conversion	condition
derision	congestion
dimension	decoration
discussion	direction
division	duration
erosion	emotion
evasion	equation
exclusion	evolution
excursion	exception
expansion	fiction
explosion	intention
illusion	invention
inclusion	isolation
invasion	location
mission	mention
occasion	motion
omission	nation
permission	nutrition
persuasion	option
possession	pollution
revision	relation
session	separation
tension	solution
torsion	tuition
version	vacation

Words ending in **SION** are often related to adjectives ending in **SIVE**.

expan**sion**	persua**sion**	permi**ssion**
expan**sive**	persua**sive**	permi**ssive**

However, words ending in **TION** are often related to adjectives ending in **TIVE**.

na**tion**	rela**tion**	atten**tion**
na**tive**	rela**tive**	atten**tive**

Building blocks at the end of verbs

There is a small group of suffixes called **inflections** that are regularly added to the basic forms of verbs. These endings indicate either the time of action or the person performing the action.

The ending **S** is added to verbs to create what is called the **third person singular** form of the present tense – that is, the form used after "he," "she," "it" or a named person or thing when talking about present action.

cheat**s**	cook**s**	walk**s**

The ending **ING** is added to verbs to create the **present participle**, which is used to refer to present action. This form of the verb, when used as a noun, is called a **gerund**.

cheat**ing**	mix**ing**	walk**ing**

The ending **ED** is added to most verbs to create the **past tense** and **past participle** – forms that are used when talking about action in the past.

cheat**ed**	mix**ed**	walk**ed**

Note that some common verbs have past tenses and past participles that do not end in **ED** but that are formed in an irregular way.

bent	*spent*	*did*
gone	*done*	*fallen*

Building blocks at the end of adjectives

There are two inflection suffixes that are regularly added to the basic forms of adjectives to indicate the degree of the quality indicated by the word.

The ending **ER** is added at the end of an adjective to mean "more." This is called the **comparative** form.

smarter	*greener*	*calmer*

The ending **EST** is added at the end of an adjective to mean "most." This is called the **superlative** form.

smartest	*greenest*	*calmest*

Note that these suffixes are generally only added to words of one or two syllables. For adjectives with more than two syllables (and some adjectives with two syllables) comparative and superlative forms are created by using the words "more" and "most."

more beautiful	**more** interesting	**more** loyal
most beautiful	**most** interesting	**most** loyal

The comparative and superlative forms of the common adjectives *good* and *bad* are formed in an irregular way.

Good	*better*	*best*
Bad	*worse*	*worst*

Building blocks at the end of nouns

The inflection suffix **S** is regularly added to the basic forms of nouns to indicate the **plural** form of the word, which indicates more than one of the thing.

cats   *dogs*   *books*

> The plural form of some words is formed slightly differently, and the rules explaining how plurals are formed are given on pages 398–400.

Spelling words that contain suffixes

Adding a suffix that begins with a consonant, such as **LESS** or **SHIP**, to a root word is usually straightforward. Neither the root word nor the suffix is changed.

help + less = helpless

However, when adding a suffix that begins with a vowel, such as **ED** or **ABLE**, to a root word you need to take more care with the spelling. Depending on the ending of the root word, you may need to add an **E**, drop an **E**, double a consonant, or change a **Y** to an **I**.

cope + ed = coped
fit + ing = fitting
deny + able = deniable

> The rules for adding vowel suffixes are given in full on pages 393–394.

Double suffixes

Sometimes a suffix can have another suffix attached to it to make an even longer word.

> abuse + ive + ness = abusiveness
> soothe + ing + ness = soothingness
> avail + able + ity = availability
> care + less + ly = carelessly
> commend + able + ly = commendably
> emotion + al + ism = emotionalism
> admit + ed + ly =admittedly
> fear + less + ness = fearlessness

Greek and Latin roots

English has many words that contain Greek and Latin roots. Some of these roots appear in many different English words, and are still used regularly to create new words.

If you can get to know these roots, how to spell them, and what they mean, you will find it a great help in your reading and writing, as well as in your spelling.

AER comes from Greek *aēr*, meaning "air." It is used in a lot of words connected with air and with flying.

> **aer**ate   **aero**bics   **aero**dynamics

AMBI comes from the Latin word *ambo*, meaning "both."

> **ambi**dextrous   **ambi**valent

ANTHROP comes from the Greek word *anthrōpos*, meaning "human being."

> *anthrop*ology   phil*anthrop*ist   lyc*anthrop*y

AQUA is the Latin word for "water."

> *aqua*lung   *aqua*marine   *aqua*tic

Sometimes the second **A** in **AQUA** changes to another vowel.

> *aque*duct   *aque*ous   *aqui*fer

ASTRO comes from the Greek word *astron*, meaning "star."

> *astro*nomy   *astro*logy   *astro*naut

AUDI comes from the Latin word *audīre*, meaning "to hear."

> *audi*ence   *audi*tion   *audi*torium

BIO comes from the Greek word *bios*, meaning "life."

> *bio*logy   *bio*graphy   *bio*technology

CAPT and **CEPT** both come from the Latin word *capere*, meaning "to take."

> *capt*ure   *capt*ivate   *capt*ion
> con*cept*   inter*cept*   re*cept*ion

CEDE comes from the Latin word *cēdere*, meaning "to go."

> inter*cede*   pre*cede*   re*cede*

> Note that some words that sound like these do not have the same ending: pro*ceed*, suc*ceed*, super*sede*.

CENT comes from the Latin word *centum*, meaning "hundred." A *cent* is a monetary unit in many countries, taking its name from the fact that it is worth one hundredth of the main unit of currency.

    century   **cent**imeter   **cent**ipede

CLUDE comes from the Latin word *claudere*, meaning "to close."

    con**clude**   ex**clude**   se**clude**d

CRED comes from the Latin word *crēdere*, meaning "to believe."

    in**cred**ible   **cred**it   **cred**ulous

CYCL comes from the Latin word *cyclus*, which is derived from the Greek word *kuklos*, meaning "circle" or "wheel."

    re**cycl**able   **cycl**one   bi**cycl**e

DEC comes from the Latin word *decem*, meaning "ten."

    decimal   **dec**ibel   **dec**iliter

DICT comes from the Latin word *dīcere*, meaning "to say."

    dictionary   pre**dict**   contra**dict**

DOM comes from the Latin word *domus*, meaning "house."

    domestic   **dom**icile   **dom**e

DOMIN comes from the Latin word *dominus*, meaning "master."

    dominate   **domin**eering   con**domin**ium

DUCE and **DUCT** both come from the Latin word *ducere*, meaning "to lead."

intro**duce**	de**duce**	re**duce**
aque**duct**	con**duct**or	via**duct**

DUO is the Latin word for "two."

duo	**duo**poly	**duo**logue

EGO is the Latin word for "I."

ego	**ego**tist	**ego**centric

FACT comes from the Latin word *facere*, meaning "to make."

satis**fact**ion	**fact**ory	manu**fact**ure

FRACT comes from the Latin word *fractus*, meaning "broken."

fraction	**fract**ure	in**fract**ion

GEN comes from the Greek word *genesis*, meaning "birth."

gene	**gen**etics	**gen**esis

GEO comes from the Greek word *gē*, meaning "earth."

geology	**geo**metry	**geo**graphy

GRAPH comes from the Greek word *graphein*, meaning "to write."

graphic	auto**graph**	para**graph**

GRESS comes from the Latin word *gradī*, meaning "to go."

pro**gress**	di**gress**ion	ag**gress**ive

HYDRO comes from the Greek word *hudōr*, meaning "water."

    hydroplane   **hydro**foil   **hydro**therapy

Sometimes the **O** in **HYDRO** is dropped or changes to another vowel.

    hydrant   **hydr**aulic   de**hydr**ated

JECT comes from the Latin word *jacere*, meaning "to throw."

    in**ject**ion   de**ject**ed   re**ject**

KILO comes from the Greek word *chīlioi*, meaning "a thousand."

    kilometer   **kilo**gram   **kilo**watt

MANU comes from the Latin word *manus*, meaning "hand."

    manual   **manu**facture   **manu**script

MILLI comes from the Latin word *mille*, meaning "a thousand."

    millimeter   **milli**gram   **milli**pede

MULTI comes from the Latin word *multus*, meaning "many."

    multiplication   **multi**cultural   **multi**plex

NOV comes from the Latin word *novus*, meaning "new."

    novelty   re**nov**ate   in**nov**ation

OCT comes from the Latin word *octō*, meaning "eight." The Greek word is *oktō*.

    octagon   **oct**ave   **oct**et

PED comes from the Greek word *pais*, meaning "child."

> encyclo**ped**ia **ped**iatrician **ped**ophile

PED may also come from the Latin word *pēs*, meaning "foot."

> **ped**al **ped**estal quadru**ped**

PHIL comes from the Greek word *philos*, meaning "loving."

> **phil**anthropist **phil**osophy Anglo**phile**

PHOBIA comes from the Greek word *phobos*, meaning "fear." It appears in hundreds of words relating to the fear or hatred of certain people, animals, objects, situations, and activities.

> claustro**phobia** agora**phobia** xeno**phobia**

PHON comes from the Greek word *phōnē*, meaning "sound" or "voice."

> **phon**etic sym**phon**y micro**phone**

PHOTO comes from the Greek word *phōs*, meaning "light."

> **photo**copier **photo**graph **photo**sensitive

POLY comes from the Greek word *polus*, meaning "many" or "much."

> **poly**gon **poly**ester **poly**gamy

PORT comes from the Latin word *portāre*, meaning "to carry."

> **port**able im**port** trans**port**ation

POS comes from the Latin word *positus*, meaning "put."

> **pos**ition im**pos**e de**pos**it

PRIM comes from the Latin word *prīmus*, meaning "first."

> **prim**ary   **prim**itive   **prim**e

QUAD comes from the Latin word *quattuor*, meaning "four."

> **quad**rangle   **quad**ruped   **quad**riceps

SCOPE comes from the Greek word *skopein*, meaning "to look at."

> micro**scope**   tele**scope**   stetho**scope**

SCRIBE comes from the Latin word *scrībere*, meaning "to write."
SCRIPT comes from the Latin word *scriptus*, meaning "written," which is related to the word *scrībere*.

> **scribe**   sub**scribe**   de**scribe**
> **script**   sub**script**ion   de**script**ion

SECT comes from the Latin word *secāre*, meaning "to cut."

> **sect**ion   dis**sect**   inter**sect**ion

SENT comes from the Latin word *sentīre*, meaning "to feel."

> **sent**imental   con**sent**   dis**sent**

SOC comes from the Latin word *socius*, meaning "friend."

> **soc**ial   as**soc**iation   **soc**iology

SON comes from the Latin word *sonāre*, meaning "to sound."

> **son**ic   con**son**ant   re**son**ate

STAT comes from the Latin word *stātus*, meaning "standing," which itself comes from the verb *stāre*, meaning "to stand."

    statue   **stat**ic   **stat**us

STRICT comes from the Latin word *stringere*, meaning "to tighten."

    strictness   con**strict**   re**strict**ion

STRUCT comes from the Latin word *struere*, meaning "to build."

    structure   de**struct**ive   con**struct**ion

TACT comes from the Latin word *tangere*, meaning "to touch."

    tactile   con**tact**   in**tact**

TERR comes from the Latin word *terra*, meaning "earth."

    terrain   Medi**terr**anean   **terr**estrial

THERM comes from the Greek word *thermē*, meaning "heat."

    thermometer   **therm**al   hypo**therm**ia

TRACT comes from the Latin word *tractus*, meaning "dragged" or "pulled."

    con**tract**   sub**tract**ion   **tract**or

TRI comes from the Latin word *trēs*, meaning "three." The Greek word is *treis*.

    triangle   **tri**o   **tri**athlon

patterns and building blocks

VEN comes from the Latin word *venīre*, meaning "to come."

venue con**ven**tion inter**ven**e

VERT comes from the Latin word *vertere*, meaning "to turn."

di**vert** re**vert** con**vert**

VIS comes from the Latin word *vīsus*, meaning "sight," which itself comes from the verb *vidēre*, meaning "to see."

visual **vis**ible **vis**ion
visit super**vis**e tele**vis**ion

VOR comes from the Latin word *vorāre*, meaning "to devour."

voracious carni**vore** omni**vor**ous

Compound words

Many English words are formed simply by adding two existing words together. These are called **compound words**. It can be easy to spell these words if you break them down into their parts.

book + store = bookstore
door + mat = doormat
summer + time = summertime
tea + pot = teapot
waste + water = wastewater

Some words don't immediately seem as though they are made from two common words but in fact they are. These can also be easy to spell if you think of them in terms of their two parts.

> cup + board = cupboard
> hand + kerchief = handkerchief
> neck + lace = necklace
> pit + fall = pitfall

Commonly occurring spelling patterns

Prefixes, suffixes and root forms all can be remembered as having a particular meaning. However, there are some combinations of letters that are useful to remember when learning English spelling but that don't have any particular meaning.

The patterns in this section all appear in many different words and are not pronounced in the way you might expect. It is worth remembering these patterns and the common words in which they occur.

Some of these letter blocks were usually sounded in the original language (such as **OUGH** in Anglo-Saxon words or **IGN** in Latin words) but have lost that sound in modern English as the pronunciation of the language has gradually become simplified.

The pattern **AIN** occurs at the end of several words representing a sound that is more often spelled as **EN**. This syllable is always unstressed.

bargain	captain	certain
chaplain	curtain	fountain
mountain	porcelain	villain

The pattern **AUGHT** occurs in several words representing a sound that is more often spelled as **OT**.

aught	*caught*	*daughter*
dis*traught*	*fraught*	*haughty*
naught	*naughty*	on*slaught*
slaughter	*taught*	

It also occurs in *laughter*, representing a sound that is more often spelled as **AFT**.

The pattern **CH** occurs in many words that come from Greek representing a sound that is more often spelled as **C** or **K**.

a*ch*e	an*ch*or	bron*ch*itis
*ch*ameleon	*ch*aracter	*ch*arisma
*ch*asm	*ch*emical	*ch*emistry
*ch*imera	*ch*iropractor	*ch*lorine
*ch*olera	*ch*olesterol	*ch*ord
*ch*oreography	*ch*orus	*ch*risten
*Ch*ristmas	*ch*rome	*ch*ronic
mona*ch*	o*ch*er	psy*ch*iatry
psy*ch*ology	stoma*ch*	syn*ch*ronize

The pattern **CI** occurs before endings such as **OUS**, **ENT**, and **AL** in several words representing a sound that is more often spelled as **SH**. The root word often ends in **C** or **CE**.

artifi*ci*al	atro*ci*ous	auda*ci*ous
capri*ci*ous	commer*ci*al	cru*ci*al
defi*ci*ent	deli*ci*ous	effi*ci*ent
fa*ci*al	falla*ci*ous	fero*ci*ous
finan*ci*al	gra*ci*ous	judi*ci*ous
mali*ci*ous	offi*ci*al	offi*ci*ous
perni*ci*ous	pre*ci*ous	preco*ci*ous
profi*ci*ent	ra*ci*al	so*ci*al

spacious	*special*	*sufficient*
suspicious	*tenacious*	*vivacious*

The pattern **EA** occurs in many words representing a sound that is more often spelled as **E**.

bread	*breath*	*deaf*
dead	*dread*	*endeavor*
head	*heather*	*heaven*
heavy	*lead*	*meadow*
ready	*steady*	*sweat*
thread	*treacherous*	*tread*
treasure	*wealth*	*weather*

The pattern **EAU** occurs in several words representing a sound that is more often spelled as **OW**. These words all come from French.

beau	*bureau*	*chateau*
nouveau	*plateau*	*tableau*

It also occurs in these words representing a sound that is more often spelled as **EW**.

beautiful	*beauty*

The pattern **EIGH** occurs in several words representing a sound that is more often spelled as **AY**.

eight	*freight*	*inveigh*
neigh	*neighbor*	*sleigh*
weigh	*weight*	

Less commonly, it can represent a sound that is more often spelled as **IE**.

height	*sleight*

The pattern **EIGN** occurs in several words representing a sound that is more often spelled as **AIN**.

d**eign**   f**eign**   r**eign**

It also occurs in these words representing a sound that is more often spelled as **IN**.

for**eign**   sover**eign**

The pattern **GUE** occurs at the end of several words representing a sound that is more often spelled as **G**.

catalo**gue**	dialo**gue**	epilo**gue**
fati**gue**	haran**gue**	intri**gue**
lea**gue**	merin**gue**	monolo**gue**
pla**gue**	ro**gue**	synago**gue**
ton**gue**	va**gue**	vo**gue**

Some of the words above ending in **LOGUE** also have acceptable spellings that eliminate the unsounded **UE** at the end.

analog	catalog	dialog
epilog	monolog	travelog

The pattern **IGH** occurs in several words representing a sound that is more often spelled as **IE**.

bl**igh**t	br**igh**t	f**igh**t
fl**igh**t	fr**igh**t	h**igh**
l**igh**t	f**igh**t	m**igh**t
m**igh**ty	n**igh**t	pl**igh**t
r**igh**t	s**igh**	s**igh**t
sl**igh**t	th**igh**	t**igh**t

The pattern **IGN** occurs in several words representing a sound that is more often spelled as **INE**.

al**ign**	ass**ign**	ben**ign**
cond**ign**	cons**ign**	des**ign**
mal**ign**	res**ign**	s**ign**

The pattern **OUGH** occurs in several words representing different pronunciations.

alth**ough**	bor**ough**	b**ough**
b**ough**t	br**ough**t	c**ough**
d**ough**	d**ough**ty	dr**ough**t
en**ough**	f**ough**t	**ough**t
r**ough**	s**ough**t	th**ough**
thor**ough**	th**ough**t	thr**ough**
t**ough**	tr**ough**	wr**ough**t

The pattern **OUL** occurs in several words representing a sound that is more often spelled as **OO**.

c**oul**d	sh**oul**d	w**oul**d

The pattern **OR** occurs in several words representing a sound that is more often spelled as **ER**.

arm**or**	behavi**or**	clam**or**
col**or**	demean**or**	enam**or**ed
endeav**or**	fav**or**	ferv**or**
glam**or**	harb**or**	hon**or**
hum**or**	lab**or**	neighb**or**
parl**or**	ranc**or**	rig**or**
tum**or**	vap**or**	vig**or**

Note that the spelling *glamour*, mainly a British spelling, is also used in American English.

The pattern **OUS** occurs at the end of hundreds of words representing a sound that is more naturally spelled as **US**. Note that these words are always adjectives.

anxi**ous**	cauti**ous**	danger**ous**
fabul**ous**	furi**ous**	gener**ous**
hilari**ous**	joy**ous**	mountain**ous**
nerv**ous**	obvi**ous**	pi**ous**
previ**ous**	seri**ous**	zeal**ous**

The pattern **QUE** occurs in several words representing a sound that is more often spelled as **C** or **K**.

anti**que**	baro**que**	criti**que**
grotes**que**	mas**que**rade	mos**que**
opa**que**	pictures**que**	pla**que**
statues**que**	techni**que**	uni**que**

The pattern **SC** occurs in many words representing a sound that is more often spelled as **S**.

abs**c**ess	acquie**sc**e	a**sc**ent
coale**sc**e	cre**sc**ent	de**sc**ent
efferve**sc**ent	fa**sc**inate	ira**sc**ible
ob**sc**ene	o**sc**illate	re**sc**ind
scene	**sc**ent	**sc**ience
scimitar	**sc**intillate	**sc**issors

The pattern **SCI** occurs before a vowel in several words representing a sound that is more often spelled as **SH**.

con**sci**ence	con**sci**ous	lu**sci**ous

The pattern **TI** occurs before endings such as **OUS**, **ENT**, and **AL** in many words representing a sound that is more often spelled as **SH**.

ambitious	cautious	contentious
circumstantial	essential	facetious
infectious	nutritious	partial
patient	potential	quotient
residential	spatial	substantial

The pattern **TURE** occurs in many words representing a sound that is often spelled as **CHER**.

adventure	capture	creature
culture	denture	feature
fracture	furniture	future
gesture	lecture	mixture
moisture	nature	pasture
picture	puncture	texture
torture	venture	vulture

spelling rules

Spelling rules

English has a small number of rules that can guide you about how words and certain types of word are spelled. If you can learn these rules, you will be on your way to becoming a better and more confident speller. Don't be put off if the rule sounds complicated – look at the examples and you will see spelling patterns emerging.

Although these rules do not cover every word in the language, they can help you make a good attempt at guessing how an unfamiliar word is spelled.

Q is always followed by U

One of the simplest and most consistent rules is that the letter **Q** is always followed by **U**.

*qu*ick   *qu*ack   *qu*iet

> The only exceptions are a few unusual words that have been borrowed from other languages, especially Arabic: bur*q*a, Ira*q*i.

J and V are followed by a vowel

These letters are rarely followed by a consonant and do not usually come at the ends of words.

If you come across a sound you think might be a **J** at the end of a word or syllable, it is likely to be spelled using the letters **GE** or **DGE**.

page   *edge*   *forage*

If a word ends with the sound represented by **V**, there is likely to be a silent **E** after the **V**.

receive   *give*   *love*

Double consonants don't occur at the start of a word

If a word begins with a consonant, you can be confident that it is a single letter.

> The only exceptions are a few unusual words that have been borrowed from other languages, such as *llama*.

H, J, K, Q, V, W, X, and Y are not doubled

The consonants **B**, **C**, **D**, **F**, **G**, **L**, **M**, **N**, **P**, **R**, **S**, **T**, and **Z** are commonly doubled in the middle and at the end of words, but **H**, **J**, **K**, **Q**, **V**, **W**, **X** and **Y** are not, so you can be confident about them being single.

rejoice   *awake*   *level*

> There are occasional exceptions in compound words (such as *withhold*, *glowworm*, and *bookkeeping*), words borrowed from other languages (such as *Sukkoth and sayyid*), and informal words (such as *savvy* and *civvies*).

A, I, and U don't typically come at the end of words

In general, English avoids ending words with **A**, **I**, and **U** and adds an extra letter to stop this happening.

say   *tie*   *due*

However, there are quite a lot of exceptions to this rule, most of which are words that have been borrowed from other languages.

banana   *ravioli*   *bayou*

The three-letter rule

"Content words" (words that name and describe things and actions) have at least three letters. The only common exceptions are *go*, *do*, and *ax*. There are, however, certain informal two-letter words that are shortenings of longer words, such as *ad* (for *advertisement*), and *el* (for *elevated train*).

Note that words that do not name or describe things but exist to provide grammatical structure (prepositions, conjunctions, and determiners) can consist of one or two letters.

The three-letter rule accounts for the fact that some content words have extra or doubled letters.

buy   *bee*   *inn*

Note that these extra letters are not found in non-content words with similar sounds.

by   *be*   *in*

I before E, except after C

When the letters I and E are combined to make the "EE" sound, the I comes before the E.

br*ie*f	ch*ie*f	f*ie*ld
n*ie*ce	s*ie*ge	th*ie*f

When these same two letters follow the letter C in a word, the E comes before the I.

c*ei*ling	dec*ei*t	rec*ei*ve

There are a few exceptions to this rule.

caff*ei*ne	prot*ei*n	s*ei*ze	w*ei*rd

The rule does not hold true when the letters I and E combine to make a sound other than "**EE**."

for*ei*gn	surf*ei*t	th*ei*r

Adding a silent E usually makes a short vowel become long

As noted on page 335, the vowels **A**, **E**, **I**, **O**, and **U** each have a "short" sound when they appear on their own in short words.

cat	rat	hat
men	pen	ten
bit	hit	sit
dot	lot	got
but	nut	hut

Each of the vowels also has a characteristic "long" sound, which is created by adding an **E** to the consonant after the vowel. The **E** is not sounded in these words.

date	rate	hate
scene	cede	theme
bite	mite	like
note	lone	mole
flute	rule	brute

If there is more than one consonant after a short vowel, adding a silent **E** does not make the vowel become long.

lapse	cassette	gaffe

C and G are soft before I and E but hard before A, O, and U

The letters **C** and **G** both have two sounds: one "soft" and one "hard."

These letters always have a hard sound when they come before **A**, **O**, and **U**.

card	cot	recur
gang	gone	gum

> Note that the word *margarine* is an exception to this rule.

In general these letters have a "soft" sound before **I** and **E** (and also **Y**).

cent	circle	cycle
gentle	giraffe	gyrate

The rule is very strong for **C**, but there are a lot of exceptions for **G**.

    *gi*bbon   *gi*rl   *ge*t

Note that some words add a silent **U** after the **G** to keep the sound hard.

    *gu*ess   *gu*ide   *gu*illotine
    *gu*ilty   *gu*itar   *fatigue*

Adding endings to words ending in E

Many English words end with a silent **E**. When you add a suffix that begins with a vowel onto one of these words, you drop the **E**.

    abbreviate + ion = abbreviation
    appreciate + ive = appreciative
    desire + able = desirable
    fortune + ate = fortunate
    guide + ance = guidance
    hope + ing = hoping
    response + ible = responsible
    ventilate + ed = ventilated

Words that end in **CE** and **GE** are an exception to this rule. They keep the final **E** before adding a suffix that begins with **A**, **O**, or **U** in order to preserve the "soft" sound.

    change + able = changeable
    notice + able = noticeable
    advantage + ous = advantageous

However, you do drop the **E** in these words before adding a suffix that begins with **E**, **I**, or **Y**.

> *stage + ed = staged*
> *notice + ing = noticing*
> *chance + y = chancy*

Adding the ending LY to words ending in LE

When you make an adverb by adding the suffix **LY** to an adjective that ends with **LE**, you drop the **LE** from the adjective.

> *gentle + ly = gently*
> *idle + ly = idly*
> *subtle + ly = subtly*

Adding endings to words ending in Y

When you add a suffix to a word that ends with a consonant followed by **Y**, you change the **Y** to **I**.

> *apply + ance = appliance*
> *beauty + ful = beautiful*
> *crazy + ly = crazily*
> *happy + ness = happiness*
> *smelly + er = smellier*
> *woolly + est = woolliest*

However, in certain short adjectives that end with a consonant followed by **Y**, you keep the **Y** when you add the ending **LY** to make an adverb.

> *coy + ly = coyly*
> *shy + ly = shyly*

spry + *ly* = *spryly*
wry + *ly* = *wryly*

Adding endings to words ending in C

You add a **K** to words that end in **C** before adding a suffix that begins with **I**, **E**, or **Y** in order to preserve the "hard" sound.

mimic + *ing* = *mimicking*
frolic + *ed* = *frolicked*
panic + *y* = *panicky*

The word *arc* is an exception to this rule.

arc + *ing* = *arcing*
arc + *ed* = *arced*

When you make an adverb by adding the suffix **LY** to an adjective that ends with **IC**, you add **AL** after the **IC**.

basic + *ly* = *basically*
genetic + *ly* = *genetically*
chronic + *ly* = *chronically*

The word *public* is an exception to this rule.

public + *ly* = *publicly*

Adding endings to words ending in a single consonant

In **words of one syllable** ending in a short vowel plus a consonant, you double the final consonant when you add a suffix that begins with a vowel.

> *run + ing = running*
> *pot + ed = potted*
> *thin + est = thinnest*
> *swim + er = swimmer*

This rule does not apply to words ending in the consonants **H, J, K, Q, V, W, X** and **Y**, which are never doubled (see page 389).

> *slow + est = slowest*
> *box + er = boxer*

In **words of more than one syllable** ending in a single vowel plus a consonant, there are two rules.

(1) If the word is pronounced with the stress at the end, you usually double the final consonant when you add a suffix that begins with a vowel.

> *acquit + al = acquittal*
> *begin + ing = beginning*
> *commit + ed = committed*
> *occur + ence = occurrence*

(2) If the word does not have the stress at the end, you don't double the final consonant when you add a suffix that begins with a vowel.

> *target + ed = targeted*
> *darken + ing = darkening*
> *marvel + ous = marvelous*

The letter **L** generally follows the two rules given above.

> *cancel + ation = cancelation*
> *gambol + ing = gamboling*
> *marshal + ed = marshaled*
> *travel + er = traveler*
> *excel + ence = excellence*
> *repel + ent = repellent*
> *surveil + ant = surveillant*

In British English, however, **L** doubles before a suffix beginning with a vowel whether or not its syllable is stressed; thus British English spells all of the words above with double **L**. Double-**L** spellings such as *traveller* and *cancellation* are sometimes seen in American English and they are not considered incorrect.

Note that when you add a suffix that begins with a vowel to a word that ends in a single vowel plus **P**, you typically double the **P** regardless of the stress.

> *airdrop + ed = airdropped*
> *bootstrap + ed =bootstrapped*
> *handicap + ed = handicapped*
> *kidnap + er = kidnapper*
> *slip + age = slippage*
> *wrap + ing = wrapping*

Making plurals

The most common way to make a plural form of a word (to show that you are talking about more than one example of it) is simply to add an **S**.

> *dog + s = dogs*
> *house + s = houses*
> *bee + s = bees*
> *banana + s = bananas*

When you make a plural of a word that ends with **S**, **X**, **Z**, **SH**, or **CH**, you add **ES**.

> *bus + es = buses*
> *kiss + es = kisses*
> *lens + es = lenses*
> *fox + es = foxes*
> *jinx + es = jinxes*
> *buzz + es = buzzes*
> *rash + es = rashes*
> *match + es = matches*
> *ranch + es = ranches*

When you make a plural of a word that ends with a consonant plus **Y**, you change the **Y** to **I** and add **ES**.

> *fairy + es = fairies*
> *pantry + es = pantries*
> *quality + es = qualities*
> *spy + es = spies*
> *story + es = stories*

However, when you make a plural of a word that ends with a **vowel** plus **Y**, you simply add **S**.

> boy + s = boys
> day + s = days
> donkey + s = donkeys
> guy + s = guys

When you make a plural of a word that ends with a single **O**, you usually just add an **S**. This is true of nearly all words that come from Spanish.

> bronco + s = broncos
> memo + s = memos
> solo + s = solos
> taco + s = tacos
> zero + s = zeros

However, there are a number of words that end with a single **O** that add **ES** when they are plural.

> echo + es = echoes
> hero + es = heroes
> potato + es = potatoes
> tomato + es = tomatoes
> veto + es = vetoes

> Remember: My her**oes** eat potat**oes** and tomat**oes**.

When you make a plural of a word that ends in a single **F** (and some words that end in **FE**), you change the **F** (or **FE**) to **V** and add **ES**.

leaf + es = lea**ves**
elf + es = el**ves**
life + es = li**ves**
scarf + es = scar**ves**
self + es = sel**ves**
shelf + es = shel**ves**

There are some exceptions to this rule.

belief + s = beliefs
brief + s = briefs
chef + s = chefs
roof + s = roofs

The suffix FUL

The suffix that means "full of" is spelled **FUL** – not (as you might expect) **FULL**. When you add the suffix onto an existing word to create a new word, the new word is always spelled with just one **L**.

beautiful	cupful	faithful
grateful	hopeful	painful

The prefix AL

When *all* and another word are joined to make an unhyphenated word, you drop the second **L**.

> *all + mighty = almighty*
> *all + ready = already*
> *all + though = although*
> *all + together = altogether*

However, if the word you make by adding *all* to another word is spelled with a hyphen, you keep both **L**'s.

> *all + important = all-important*
> *all + inclusive = all-inclusive*
> *all + powerful = all-powerful*

The prefixes ANTE and ANTI

There are some English words that begin with **ANTE** and other words that begin with **ANTI**. You can usually work out how to spell the word if you think about what it means.

Words that begin with **ANTE** usually have a meaning of "before" or "in front of."

> **ante**cedent   **ante**diluvian   **ante**room

Words that begin with **ANTI** usually have a meaning of "against" or "opposite."

> **anti**septic   **anti**social   **anti**matter

The prefixes FOR and FORE

Some English words begin with **FOR** and others begin with **FORE**. You can often work out how to spell the word if you think about what it means.

Words that begin with **FORE** usually have a meaning of "before" or "in front of."

*fore*cast   *fore*father   *fore*word

If the word does not have this meaning, it is likely that it will be spelled **FOR**, and there will not be an **E** after the **R**.

*for*give   *for*get   *for*feit

The endings CE and SE

Many English words end in **CE** or **SE**. It can be easy to use the wrong spelling because **CE** and **SE** usually have the same "s" sound at the end of a word.

Here are some common words that end with a **CE** spelling.

choice   juice   niece
piece   practice   sauce
truce   vice   voice

Note that words (often adjectives) ending in **ANT** or **ENT** may have a related noun ending in **ANCE** or **ENCE**, but never in **ANSE** or **ENSE**.

defi*ant*   ignor*ant*   pati*ent*
defi*ance*   ignor*ance*   pati*ence*

Here are some common words that have **SE** at the end.

condense	defense	expanse
immense	intense	license
offense	pretense	suspense

The endings IZE and ISE

IZE is the most common suffix forming action verbs in English.

organize	realize	pulverize
stigmatize	civilize	mobilize

A few verbs sound as if they are spelled with **IZE** but in fact are spelled with **YZE**.

analyze	catalyze	paralyze

Other words are spelled with **ISE** rather than **IZE**. These are usually words where the ending is a natural part of the word and has not been added on as a suffix.

advertise	advise	chastise
comprise	compromise	despise
devise	disguise	exercise
franchise	improvise	revise
supervise	surprise	televise

Rules for using apostrophes

Showing possession

The apostrophe (') is used to show that something belongs to someone. It is usually added to the end of a word and followed by an **S**.

'S is added to the end of singular words.

> a baby**'s** diaper
> Hannah**'s** book
> a child**'s** cry

'S is added to the end of plural words not ending in **S**.

> children**'s** games
> women**'s** clothes
> people**'s** lives

An apostrophe alone is added to plural words ending in **S**.

> Your grandparents are your parents**'** parents.
> We are campaigning for workers**'** rights.
> They hired a new ladies**'** fashion guru.

'S is added to the end of names and singular words ending in **S**.

> James**'s** car
> the octopus**'s** tentacles

Note, however, that if the word ending in **S** is a historical name, an apostrophe only is sometimes preferred.

> Dickens**'** novels
> Achilles**'** heel

'S is added to the end of people or their names to indicate that you are talking about their home.

> *I'm going over to Harry's for dinner tonight.*
> *I stopped by at Mom's this afternoon, but she wasn't home.*

To test whether an apostrophe is in the right place, think about who the owner is.

> *the boy's books [= the books belonging to the boy]*
> *the boys' books [= the books belonging to the boys]*

> Note that an apostrophe is *not* used to form possessive pronouns such as *its*, *yours*, or *theirs*. Nor is it used to form the plurals of words such as *potatoes* or *tomatoes*.

Showing a contraction

An apostrophe is used in shortened forms of words to show that one or more letters have been left out. These contractions usually involve shortened forms of common verbs such as *be* and *have*.

> *I'm [short for "I am"]*
> *they've [short for "they have"]*
> *we're [short for "we are"]*

Some contractions involve the negative word *not*.

> *aren't [short for "are not"]*
> *isn't [short for "is not"]*
> *haven't [short for "have not"]*

Some contractions have two expanded forms. The context tells you which words are contracted.

he'd [short for "he had"]	*He'd already left when I got there.*
he'd [short for "he would"]	*I asked him if he'd stay.*
she's [short for "she is"]	*She's a great dancer.*
she's [short for "she has"]	*She's already eaten lunch.*

> Note that the apostrophe is always positioned at the point where the omitted letters would have been.

An apostrophe is also used in front of two digits as a way of referring to a year or decade.

China hosted the Summer Olympics in '08 [short for "2008"].
He worked as a schoolteacher during the '80s and early '90s.

Showing a plural

An apostrophe should *not* be used to form the plural of a normal word.

However, an apostrophe can be used in plurals of letters, numbers, and sometimes, in words and abbreviations spelled in all capital letters, to make them easier to read.

Mind your p's and q's.
His 2's look a bit like 7's.
She got straight A's in her exams.
There are five ATM's located on campus.

Rules for using a capital letter

A capital (or "upper-case") letter is used to mark the beginning of a sentence.

When I was 20, I dropped out of college and became a model.

Capital letters are also used for the first letter in proper nouns. These include:

- people's names
  Takesha Forbes   *William Doudi*

- days of the week
  Monday   *Wednesday*   *Saturday*

- months of the year
  August   *October*   *June*

- public holidays
  Christmas   *New Year*   *Yom Kippur*

- nationalities
  Spanish   *Iraqi*   *Argentine*

- languages
  Swahili   *Flemish*   *Gaelic*

- geographical locations
  Australia   *Lake Placid*   *Mount Everest*

- religions
  Islam   *Buddhism*   *Sikhism*

Capital letters are also used for the first letter in titles of books, magazines, newspapers, **TV** shows, films, etc. Where there are several words, a capital letter is usually used for each of the main "content words" as well as the first word of the title.

The Denver Post	*Vanity Fair*	*Twelfth Night*
The Secret Garden	*60 Minutes*	*Mamma Mia!*

tips for learning hard words

Tips for learning hard words

You can improve your spelling greatly by studying the rules and familiarizing yourself with the patterns that come up regularly. Nevertheless, knowing the principles of spelling can only get you so far. There are times when you just have to learn the order of letters in a particular word.

The tips in this chapter can help you learn tricky spellings so that they stay in your mind.

Mnemonics

A **mnemonic** is a saying or rhyme that helps you remember something. The word comes from Greek *mnēmonikos*, which itself comes from *mnēmōn*, meaning "mindful." A mnemonic can be a rhyme or sentence that helps you remember anything, not just spelling. You may already know mnemonics for other things, such as *All Cows Eat Grass*, which is often used in music as a way to remember the notes corresponding to the spaces in the bass clef (because the first letter of each word corresponds to the name of a note).

There are various types of mnemonics that can help with spelling.

Initial-letter mnemonics

In some mnemonics, the word you want to remember is spelled out by the initial letters of all the words in a sentence or phrase.

Big elephants are useful to Indians for unloading logs.

This sentence can help you to remember the word *beautiful*.

Partial initial-letter mnemonics

In some mnemonics, a phrase acts as a reminder of how to spell only the tricky parts of a word, but does not spell out the whole word.

You can use this sort of mnemonic to remember how to spell the word *accelerate*.

If it can accelerate, a car can easily lead every race.

A similar device can be used to remember the double letters in the word *accommodation*.

The accommodations have two cots and two mattresses.

Partial mnemonics

Another type of mnemonic uses words or syllables that are contained within the problem word to help you remember it.

You can use this technique to remember the beginning of the word *ascertain*.

As certain reports are verified, we will ascertain the truth.

A similar device can be used to remember the double letters at the start of the word *address*.

Add your **add**ress.

The remaining chapters of this book include many mnemonics to help you remember how to spell tricky words. Use these if you find they help you.

However, the best mnemonics are often ones that you make up yourself. If you base these phrases around words and topics that are especially meaningful to you, you are more likely to remember them. For example, you might use the names of your friends, your pets, or your family members, or you might make up sentences that relate to your hobbies. Try to make up your own mnemonics for words you find hard to remember.

Look, Say, Cover, Write, Check

Another way of learning how to spell a word is to go through five steps: look, say, cover, write, check.

- **Look** at the word carefully.

- **Say** the word aloud to yourself, listening to how it sounds.

- **Cover** the word and try to remember what it looks like.

- **Write** the word.

- **Check** what you have written to see if you got it right.

Breaking down the word into its parts

Another good way of learning a word is to break it down into its syllables, and sound them out, pronouncing even the silent letters.

> dictionary = dic + ti + on + ar + y
> ecstasy = ec + sta + sy
> handkerchief = hand + ker + chief
> material = ma + te + ri + al
> separate = se + par + ate
> Wednesday = Wed + nes + day

If you get into the habit of looking at words in this way you will find them easier to learn.

Word families

Words that come from the same root word tend to preserve the same core patterns in spelling. If you know that one word is related to another word, it can help you remember how the word is spelled.

The words below are all related to *act*.

act	*action*	*activity*
react	*reaction*	*reactive*

Sometimes knowing that words are related can help you remember which vowel to use. For example, words related to *irritate* all have an **A** after the **T**.

irritate	*irritant*	*irritable*

Word families are a very powerful way of remembering how to spell a word. However, there are just a few occasions when words that sound as though they might be related are in fact not related, or when words that are related are not spelled with the same core pattern. Some of these "false friends" that you need to watch out for are listed on pages 480–482.

words with silent letters

Words with silent letters

Some words are hard to spell because they contain letters that are not pronounced. Often these letters were pronounced in the original language from which the word came into English. Here is a list of words that it is worth learning, including ways of remembering some of them.

abscess
>There is a silent **C** after the first **S**.

acquaint, acquiesce, acquire, acquit
>There is a silent **C** before the **Q**.

aghast
>There is a silent **H** after the **G**.

> Remember: A**gh**ast at the **gh**osts.

aisle
>There is a silent **S** before the **L**.

answer
>There is a silent **W** after the **S**.

arraign
>There is a silent **G** after the **N**.

asthma
>There is a silent **TH** after the **S**.

autumn
>There is a silent **N** after the **M**.

> Remember the adjective *autumnal* (*autumn* + *al*) where you hear the **N**.

bankruptcy
>There is a silent **T** after the **P**.

> Remember that this word comes from *bankrupt* + the ending **CY**.

Buddhism
There is a silent **H** after the **DD**, just as in *Buddha*.

campaign
There is a silent **G** before the **N**.

castle
There is a silent **T** after the **S**.

chalk
There is a silent **L** before the **K**.

column
There is a silent **N** after the **M**.

comb
There is a silent **B** after the **M**.

condemn
There is a silent **N** after the **M**.

> Remember that this word is related to *condemnation*.

cupboard
There is a silent **P** before the **B**.

> Remember that the word *clapboard* also shows this pattern:
> a *cupboard* in a *clapboard* house.

debt
There is a silent **B** before the **T**.

> Remember that this word is related to *debit*.

descend
There is a silent **C** after the **S**.

> Remember: You d**esc**end on an **esc**alator.

diaphragm
There is a silent **G** before the **M**.

doubt
> There is a silent **B** before the **T**.

> Remember that this word is related to *dubious*.

dumb
> There is a silent **B** after the **M**.

exceed, excel, excellent, excess, excite
> There is a silent **C** after the **X**.

excerpt
> There is a silent **C** after the **X** and a silent **P** before the **T**.

exhaust, exhibit, exhilarate
> There is a silent **H** after the **X**.

extraordinary
> There is a silent **A** before the **O**.

> Remember that this word comes from *extra + ordinary*.

fasten
> There is a silent **T** before the **S**.

> Remember that *fasten* means "to make *fast*."

fluorescent
> There is a silent **U** before the **O** and a silent **C** after the **S**.

foreign
> There is a silent **G** before the **N**.

ghastly, gherkin, ghetto, ghost, ghoul
> There is a silent **H** after the **G**.

gnarl, gnash, gnat, gnaw, gnome, gnu
> There is a silent **G** before the **N**.

government
> There is a silent **N** before the **M**.

handkerchief, handsome
> There is a silent **D** after the **N**.

hasten
There is a silent **T** after the **S**.

> Remember that *hasten* means "to make *haste*."

heir, honest, honor, hour
There is a silent **H** at the start.

indict, indictment
There is a silent **C** before the **T**.

> Remember: **I** **n**ever **d**abble **i**n **c**riminal **t**hings.

island, isle
There is a silent **S** before the **L**.

jeopardize, jeopardy
There is a silent **O** after the **E**.

knack, knead, knee, kneel, knife, knight, knit, knob, knock, knoll, knot, know, knuckle
There is a silent **K** before the **N**.

leopard
There is a silent **O** after the **E**.

limb, lamb
There is a silent **B** after the **M**.

listen
There is a silent **T** after the **S**.

medieval
There is a silent **I** after the **D**.

miniature
There is a silent **A** before the **T**.

mnemonic
There is a silent **M** before the **N**.

> Remember: **M**y **n**ephew **E**ric **m**emorizes **o**dd **n**umbers **i**n **c**lass.

moreover
There is a silent **E** before the second **O**.

mortgage
There is a silent **T** before the **G**.

muscle
There is a silent **C** after the **S**.

parliament
There is a silent **A** after the **I**.

people
There is a silent **O** after the first **E**.

playwright
There is a silent **W** before the **R**.

pneumatic, pneumonia
There is a silent **P** before the **N** at the beginning.

psalm
There is a silent **P** before the **S**.

pseudonym, psychedelic, psychiatry, psychic, psychology
There is a silent **P** before the **S**.

rapport
There is a silent **T** before the second **R**.

> Remember that this word is related to *report*.

raspberry
There is a silent **P** after the **S**.

receipt
There is a silent **P** before the **T**.

rhapsody, rhetoric, rheumatism, rhinoceros, rhododendron, rhombus, rhubarb, rhyme, rhythm
There is a silent **H** after the **R** at the beginning.

salmon
There is a silent **L** after the **A**.

scissors
There is a silent **C** after the first **S**.

sheikh
> There is a silent **H** after the **K**.

shepherd
> There is a silent **H** after the **P**.

> Remember that a shep**herd herd**s sheep.

silhouette
> There is a silent **H** after the **L**.

solemn
> There is a silent **N** after the **M**.

sovereign
> There is a silent **G** before the **N**.

spaghetti
> There is a silent **H** after the **G**.

stalk
> There is a silent **L** before the **K**.

subpoena
> There is a silent **B** before the **P** and a silent **O** after the **P**.

subtle
> There is a silent **B** before the **T**.

> Remember: **Sub**marines move in **sub**tle ways.

sword
> There is a silent **W** after the **S**.

talk
> There is a silent **L** before the **K**.

two
> There is a silent **W** after the **T**.

viscount
> There is a silent **S** before the **C**.

> Remember: The v**iscount** gets a d**iscount**.

walk
There is a silent **L** before the **K**.
Wednesday
There is a silent **D** before the **N**.
what, when, where, whether, which, why
There is a silent **H** after the **W**.
wrangle, wrap, wrath, wreath, wreck, wrench, wrestle, wretched, wriggle, wring, wrinkle, write, wrist, wrong
There is a silent **W** before the **R**.

single and double letters

Single and double letters

Some words present a problem in spelling because it is not obvious from their pronunciation whether they have a double or single letter. Here is a list of words that it is worth learning, including ways of remembering some of them.

abbreviate
    There are two **B**'s.

> Remember: **A**lways **be b**rief when you **abb**reviate.

accelerate
    There are two **C**'s and one **L**.

> Remember: If it can **acceler**ate, **a** car can easily lead every race.

accessory
    There are two **C**'s and two **S**'s.
accident
    There are two **C**'s.

> Remember: **A c**lose **c**all can lead to an **acc**ident.

accommodate
    There are two **C**'s and two **M**'s.

> Remember: If you think that this word **accommodates** as many letters as possible, it will help you to remember that there are the maximum number of **C**'s and **M**'s!

accompany
    There are two **C**'s.
accumulate
    There are two **C**'s and one **M**.

accurate
There are two **C**'s and one **R**.

across
There is one **C** and two **S**'s.

acupuncture
There is only one **C** after the **A**.

address
There are two **D**'s and two **S**'s.

> Remember: **Add** your **add**ress.

affiliate
There are two **F**'s and one **L**.

aggravate
There are two **G**'s and one **V**.

aggressive
There are two **G**'s and two **S**'s.

allergy
There are two **L**'s.

> Remember: An **allergy** saps **all** energy.

alligator
There are two **L**'s and one **G**.

already, although, altogether
There is only one **L**.

aluminum
There are no double letters.

appall
There are two **P**'s and two **L**'s.

apparatus, apparent, appearance
There are two **P**'s and one **R**.

appendix, appliance, appreciate, apprehensive, approve, approximate
> There are two **P**'s.

assassinate, assess
> There are two double **S**'s.

associate
> There are two **S**'s and one **C**.

attitude
> There is a double **T** followed by a single **T**.

> Remember: **At ti**mes you have a bad **atti**tude.

baggage
> There is a double **G** – just the same as in *luggage*.

balloon
> There are two **L**'s and two **O**'s.

> Remember: A **ball**oon is shaped like a **ball**.

banana
> There are two single **N**'s.

battalion
> There are two **T**'s and one **L** – just the same as in *battle*.

beginner
> There is one **G** and two **N**'s.

bellicose, belligerent
> There are two **L**'s.

boycott
> There are two **T**'s.

broccoli
> There are two **C**'s and one **L**.

> Remember: Bro**cc**oli **c**ures **colic**.

bulletin
> There are two **L**'s and one **T** – just the same as in *bullet*.

carafe
> There is one **R** and one **F**.

career
> There is no double **R**.

> Remember: A **car car**eered off the road.

cassette
> There are two **S**'s and two **T**'s.

cinnamon
> There are two **N**'s and one **M**.

collaborate
> There are two **L**'s and one **B**.

colleague
> There are two **L**'s.

colonnade
> There is one **L** and two **N**'s.

colossal
> There is one **L** in the middle and two **S**'s.

> Remember: Co**loss**al **loss**es

commemorate
> There is a double **M** followed by a single **M**.

commercial
> There are two **M**'s.

commiserate
> There are two **M**'s and one **S**.

commit

There are two **M**'s and one **T**.

committee

There are two **M**'s, two **T**'s, and two **E**'s.

> If you remember that a **committee** should have as many members as possible, it may help you remember that this word has the maximum number of **M**'s, **T**'s, and **E**'s.

commotion

There are two **M**'s (unlike *locomotion*).

compel

There is only one **L** (but the **L** doubles when most inflections are added).

connotation

There are two **N**'s and two single **T**'s.

control

There is only one **L** (but the **L** doubles when most inflections are added).

coolly

There are two **L**'s.

> Remember: This word is *cool* + the ending **LY**.

correspond

There are two **R**'s.

curriculum

There are two **R**'s and one **C** in the middle.

daffodil

There are two **F**'s but no double **D** or **L**.

desiccated

There is one **S** and two **C**'s – which is the same as in *coconuts*!

deterrent

There are two **R**'s but no double **T**.

dilemma

There is one **L** and two **M**'s.

> Remember: **Emma** is in a dil**emma**.

disappear, disappoint, disapprove

There is one **S** and two **P**'s.

> Remember: Th**is** **app**le has d**isapp**eared.

dispel

There is one **S** and only one **L**.

dissatisfied

There are two **S**'s after the first **I**.

dissect

There are two **S**'s.

dissimilar

There are two **S**'s, one **M**, and one **L**.

dumbbell

There are two **B**'s.

> Remember: This is a compound of *dumb* and *bell*.

earring

There are two **R**'s.

> Remember: This is a compound of *ear* and *ring*.

effervescent

There are two **F**'s and one **S**.

eligible

There is only one **L** at the start.

> Remember: You must **el**ect the most **el**igible candidate: **Eli**.

embarrass
> There are two **R**'s and two **S**'s.

> Remember: This word has two **R**'s and two **S**'s, which is an **embarrass**ment of riches!

enroll
> There are two **L**'s.

> Remember: When you en**roll** your name will be on a **roll**.

erroneous
> There are two **R**'s and one **N**.

> Remember that this word is related to *err*.

exaggerate
> There are two **G**'s.

> Remember: I am st**agger**ed by how much you ex**agger**ate.

excellent
> There are two **L**'s.

> Remember: My **ex-cell**mate was an **excell**ent friend.

flammable
> There are two **M**'s (unlike *flame*).

fullness
> There are two **L**'s and two **S**'s.

giraffe
> There is one **R** and two **F**'s.

guerrilla
> There are two **R**'s and two **L**'s.

graffiti
> There are two **F**'s and one **T**.

hallucination
> There are two **L**'s, one **C**, and one **N**.

harass
> There is one **R** and two **S**'s.

hazard
> There is only one **Z** (unlike *blizzard*).

hideous
> There is only one **D**.

> Remember: **Hide** that **hide**ous thing away.

holiday
> There is only one **L** and one **D**.

> Remember that a holiday was originally a holy day.

horrible
> There are two **R**'s – just the same as in *terrible*.

horror
> There is a double **R** – just the same as in *terror*.

hurricane
> There are two **R**'s and one **C**.

illiterate
> There are two **L**'s and a single **T**.

imitate
> There are no double letters.

immediate
> There are two **M**'s and one **D**.

inaccurate
> There is one **N**, two **C**'s, and one **R**.

ineligible
> There are no double letters.

innocent
> There are two **N**'s and one **C**.

innocuous
> There are two **N**'s and one **C**.

intelligence, intelligent
> There are two **L**'s.

> Remember: I can **tell** the **gent** is in**tell**i**gent**.

interrogate
> There are two **R**'s and one **G**.

> Remember: In**terro**gation may cause **terro**r.

interrupt
> There are two **R**'s.

> Remember: It's **terr**ibly rude to in**terr**upt.

irascible
> There is only one **R**.

> Remember that this word is related to *irate*, which also has only one **R**.

irregular
> There are two **R**'s and one **G**.

irrelevant
> There are two **R**'s and one **L**.

irritable
> There are two **R**'s and one **T**.

limit
> There is only one **M** and one **T**.

literature
> There is only one **T**.

luggage
> There is a double **G** – just the same as in *baggage*.

macabre
> There is only one **C**.

macaroon
> There is only one **C** and one **R**.

> Remember: Ma**car**oons taste great after ma**car**oni.

mattress
> There are two **T**'s and two **S**'s.

mayonnaise
> There are two **N**'s.

> Remember: Dip **n**ice **n**ibbles in mayo**nn**aise.

Mediterranean
> There is one **D**, one **T**, and two **R**'s.

millennium
> There are two **L**'s and two **N**'s.

millionaire
> There are two **L**'s and one **N**.

misshapen
> There are two **S**'s.

misspell
> There are two **S**'s and two **L**'s.

misspent
> There are two **S**'s.

moccasin
> There are two **C**'s and one **S**.

necessary
> There is one **C** and two **S**'s.

> Remember: It is ne**cess**ary for a shirt to have **one c**ollar and **two s**leeves.

obsession, obsessive
There is a single **S** followed by a double **S**.

occasion
There are two **C**'s and one **S**.

occupy
There are two **C**'s and one **P**.

occur
There are two **C**'s and one **R**.

occurrence
There are two **C**'s and two **R**'s.

omission
There is one **M** and two **S**'s.

opinion
There is one **P** and a single **N** in the middle.

opponent, opportunity, opposite
There are two **P**'s.

overrate
There are two **R**'s – just the same as in *underrate*.

paraffin
There is one **R** and two **F**'s.

parallel
There is a double **L** in the middle and a single **L** at the end.

pastime
There is one **S** and one **T**.

pavilion
There is only one **L**.

penicillin
There are two **L**'s and no double **N**.

> Remember: You take penic**ill**in when you are **ill**.

permit
There is only one **T**.

personnel
There are two **N**'s and one **L**.

porridge

There are two **R**'s.

possess

There are two double **S**'s.

> Remember: You should po**ss**e**ss** **two** **s**hoes and **two** **s**ocks.

possible

There are two **S**'s.

preferred

There is one **F** and a double **R**.

preference

There is one **F** and no double **R**.

procedure

There is only one **E** after the **C**.

profession, professor

There is one **F** and two **S**'s.

profitable

There is one **F** and one **T**.

propel

There is a single **P** in the middle, and a single **L**.

propeller

There is a single **P** in the middle, and a double **L**.

quarrel

There are two **R**'s and one **L**.

questionnaire

There are two **N**'s.

really

There are two **L**'s.

> Remember: This word is *real* + the ending **LY**.

rebellion

There is one **B** and two **L**'s.

recommend
There is one **C** and two **M**'s.

recurrent
There is a single **C** and a double **R**.

referred
There is a single **F** and a double **R**.

remittance
There is one **M** and two **T**'s.

resurrection
There is a single **S** and a double **R**.

sapphire
There are two **P**'s.

> Remember: You would be ha**pp**y to get a sa**pp**hire.

satellite
There is one **T** and two **L**'s.

> Remember: **Tell** me about the sa**tell**ite.

scissors
There is a double **S** in the middle.

skillful
There is a double **L** and then a single **L**.

> Remember: Just as in *skill*.

solicitor
There are no double letters.

success
There is a double **C** and a double **S**.

succinct
There is a double **C**.

suddenness
There is a double **D** and a double **N**.

sufficient
    There are two **F**'s.

suffocate
    There are two **F**'s and one **C**.

supplement
    There are two **P**'s and one **M**.

suppose
    There are two **P**'s.

suppress
    There is a double **P** and a double **S**.

surplus
    There is only one **S** at the end.

symmetry
    There are two **M**'s and one **T**.

taffeta
    There are two **F**'s and no double **T**.

tattoo
    There is a double **T** and a double **O**.

terrible
    There are two **R**'s – just the same as in *horrible*.

terror
    There is a double **R** – just the same as in *horror*.

threshold
    There is no double **H**.

toffee
    There are two **F**'s and two **E**'s.

tomorrow
    There is one **M** and two **R**'s.

tranquil
    There is only one **L** at the end.

tyranny
    There is one **R** and two **N**'s.

underrate
    There are two **R**'s – just the same as in *overrate*.

until
>There is only one **L** at the end.

usually
>There are two **L**'s.

>Remember: This word is *usual* + the ending **LY**.

vacuum
>There is one **C** and two **U**'s.

vanilla
>There is one **N** and two **L**'s.

>Remember: **Vanill**a ice cream from the **van** made me **ill**.

villain
>There are two **L**'s.

walnut
>There is only one **L** and one **T**.

welcome, welfare
>There is only one **L**.

withhold
>There are two **H**'s.

words
with
foreign
spelling
patterns

Words with foreign spelling patterns

Some words present a problem in spelling because they have come into English from another language and have kept a spelling pattern found in the original language. Often these spelling patterns are quite different from the patterns you would expect to find in English words.

If you know a bit of French or Greek, for example, you will find it easier to understand why words that come from those languages are spelled the way they are. Even if you don't, you should soon get used to certain spelling patterns from these languages that appear repeatedly in English, such as **EAU** and **EUR** in French words and **PH** and **RRH** in Greek words.

Here is a list of words that it is worth learning, including ways of remembering some of them.

aficionado
> There is one **F** and the middle is **CIO**. The word comes from Spanish.

amateur
> The ending is **EUR**. The word comes from French.

apparatus
> The ending is **US** (not **OUS**). The word comes from Latin.

archaeology
> The second syllable is spelled **CHAE**. The word comes from Greek.

> Remember: Ar**chae**ology discovers **c**urious **h**ouses of **a**ncient **e**ras.

beautiful, beauty
> The beginning is **BEAU**. These words come from French.

> Remember: **B**ig **e**ars **a**re **u**seful.

beige
> The ending is **EIGE**. The word comes from French.

biscuit

The ending is **CUIT**. The word comes from French (where *cuit* means "cooked").

> Remember: If you want a bis**cuit**, I will give **u it**.

bouquet

The first vowel sound is spelled **OU**, the middle consonant is **Q**, and the ending is **ET**. The word comes from French.

> Remember: A bou**quet** for a **que**en.

bourgeois

The first vowel sound is spelled **OUR**, the consonant in the middle is **GE**, and the ending is **OIS**. The word comes from French.

Braille

The ending is **AILLE**. The word comes from a French name.

brochure

The ending is **CHURE**. The word comes from French.

brusque

The ending is **SQUE**. The word comes from French.

bureau

The ending is **EAU**. The word comes from French.

> Remember: **B**usinesses **u**sing **r**otten **e**thics **a**re **u**seless.

camaraderie

The first three vowels are **A**. Until the last two letters, the pattern *consonant + vowel* is repeated 5 times. The word comes from French.

camouflage

The vowel sound in the middle is spelled **OU**, and the ending is **AGE**. The word comes from French.

catarrh

The ending is **ARRH**. The word comes from Greek.

champagne
The opening is **CH** and the ending is **AGNE**. The word comes from a French place-name.

chaos
The opening sound is spelled **CH**. The word comes from Greek.

> Remember: **C**riminals **h**ave **a**bandoned **o**ur **s**ociety.

character
The opening sound is spelled **CH**. The word comes from Greek.

chauffeur
The opening is **CH** and the ending is **EUR**. The word comes from French.

chord, chorus
The opening sound is spelled **CH**. These words come from Greek.

chute
The opening is **CH**. The word comes from French.

connoisseur
The middle vowel sound is spelled **OI** and the final vowel sound is spelled **EUR**. The word comes from French. (Also watch out for the double **N** and double **S**!)

crochet
The ending is **CHET**. The word comes from French.

dachshund
The middle is **CHSH**. The word comes from German (where *Dachs* means "badger" and *Hund* means "dog").

> Remember: Da**chsh**un**ds** **ch**ase **sh**eep through the **und**ergrowth.

diarrhea
The middle is **RRHE**. The word comes from Greek.

etiquette
The ending is **QUETTE**. The word comes from French.

euphoria, euthanasia

The opening is **EU**. These words come from Greek (where *eu* means "well").

Fahrenheit

There is an **H** before the **R**, and the ending is **EIT**. The word comes from a German name.

fiancé, fiancée

The ending is **CÉ** when referring to a man and **CÉE** when referring to a woman. The word comes from French.

foyer

The ending is **ER**. The word comes from French.

gateau

The ending is **EAU**. The word comes from French.

grandeur

The ending is **EUR**. The word comes from French.

hemorrhage

The middle is **ORRH**. The word comes from Greek.

hierarchy, hieroglyphics

The beginning is **HIER**. These words come from Greek (where *hieros* means "holy").

> Remember: **H**idden **i**n **E**gyptian **r**uins.

hypochondriac, hypocrisy, hypocrite

The beginning is **HYPO**. These words come from Greek (where *hypo* means "under").

jodhpur

There is a silent **H** after the **D** and the ending is **UR**. The word comes from a place name in India.

> Remember: You wear jo**dh**purs when you ride a **d**appled **h**orse.

karate

The final letter is **E**. The word comes from Japanese.

khaki
> There are two **K**'s and a silent **H**. The word comes from Urdu.

larynx
> The ending is **YNX**. The word comes from Greek.

lasagne
> The ending is **AGNE**. The word comes from Italian. The spelling *lasagna* is also used.

lieutenant
> The first vowel sound is spelled **IEU**. The word comes from French (where *lieu* means "place").

liqueur
> The ending is **QUEUR**. The word comes from French.

machete
> The middle sound is spelled **CH**. The final vowel is **E**. The word comes from Spanish.

maneuver
> The vowel sound in the middle is spelled **EU**. The word comes from French.

martyr
> The ending is **YR**. The word comes from Greek.

matinée
> The ending is **ÉE** – just the same as in *fiancée*. The word comes from French.

meringue
> The ending is **INGUE**. The word comes from French.

memoir
> The ending is **OIR**. The word comes from French.

mustache
> The ending is **CHE**. The word comes from French.

naïve
> The middle of this word is **AÏ**. The word comes from French.

niche
> The ending is **ICHE**. The word comes from French.

nuance
> The vowel after **U** is **A**. The word comes from French.

omelette

There is an **E** after the **M** and the ending is **ETTE**. The word comes from French. The simpler spelling *omelet* is also used.

pseudonym

There is a silent **P** at the beginning, the first vowel sound is spelled **EU**, and the ending is **NYM**. The word comes from Greek.

psychiatry, psychic, psychology

There is a silent **P** at the beginning, the first vowel is a **Y**, and there is an **H** after the **C**. These words come from Greek (where *psychē* means "soul").

queue

The sequence of vowels is **UEUE**. The word comes from French, where it means "tail."

reconnaissance

The third vowel sound is spelled **AI**. The word comes from French. (Also watch out for the double **N** and double **S** – just the same as in *connoisseur*.)

rendezvous

The first vowel sound is spelled **E**, the second is spelled **EZ**, and the ending is **OUS**. The word comes from French.

repertoire

The middle vowel sound is spelled **ER** and the ending is **OIRE**. The word comes from French.

reservoir

The middle sound is spelled **ER** and the ending is **OIR**. The middle **R** is not always pronounced. The word comes from French.

> Remember: A **reserv**oir **reserv**es water.

restaurant

The middle vowel sound is spelled **AU** and the ending is **ANT**. The word comes from French.

restaurateur

There is no **N** before the second **T** (unlike in *restaurant*), and the ending is **EUR**. The word comes from French.

rheumatism
> The opening is **RHEU**. The word comes from Greek.

rhinoceros
> The opening is **RH**, and the ending is **OS**. The word comes from Greek.

schizophrenia
> The opening is **SCH**, and the next consonant sound is spelled with **Z**. The word comes from Greek (where *schizein* means "to split").

sheikh
> The vowel sound is spelled **EI**, and there is a silent **H** at the end. The word comes from Arabic.

silhouette
> There is a silent **H** after the **L**, the middle vowel is spelled **OU**, and the ending is **ETTE**. The word comes from French.

souvenir
> The first vowel sound is spelled **OU** and the ending is **IR**. The word comes from French.

spaghetti
> There is a silent **H** after the **G** and the ending is **ETTI**. The word comes from Italian (as does *confetti*, which has a similar ending).

suede
> The ending is **UEDE**. The word comes from French (where *de Suède* means "Swedish").

> Remember: **Sue de**manded **suede** shoes.

surveillance
> The middle vowel sound is spelled **EI**. The word comes from French.

ukulele
> The first two vowels are **U**; the last two are **E**. The word comes from Hawaiian.

yacht
> The middle is **ACH**. The word comes from Dutch.

confusable words

Confusable words

When two words have a similar or identical sound, it is easy to confuse them and use the correct spelling for the wrong word. This section lists sets of words that are easily confused and offers some ways of remembering which is which.

accept, except

To **accept** something is to receive it or agree to it. **Except** means "other than" or "apart from."

> Please **accept** my apologies
> The mayor would not **accept** their demands.
> I never wear a skirt **except** when we go out.

affect, effect

To **affect** something is to influence or change it. An **effect** is a result something gives or an impression something makes.

> Tiredness **affected** his concentration.
> discoveries that have a profound **effect** on medicine

> Remember: To **a**ffect something is to **a**lter it but the **e**ffect is the **e**nd result. Another mnemonic for this difference is the word **raven**. **R**emember, **a**ffect **v**erb, **e**ffect **n**oun.

aid, aide

Aid means "help," and to **aid** somebody is to help them. An **aide** is a person who acts as an assistant to an important person.

> bringing **aid** to victims of drought
> They used fake uniforms to **aid** them in the robbery.
> one of the President's **aides**

aloud, allowed

Aloud means "loud enough to hear." **Allowed** is the past tense of the verb **allow**, and is also used as an adjective.

> *Read your sentence **aloud** to the class.*
> *Who **allowed** them onto the property?*
> *a list of **allowed** commands.*

allude, elude

To **allude** to something is to refer to it in an indirect way. If something **eludes** you, you can't understand or remember it, and if you **elude** something, you dodge or escape from it.

> *I never **allude** to that unpleasant matter.*
> *The name of the tune **eludes** me.*
> *She managed to **elude** the police.*

> Remember: If something **e**ludes you, it **e**scapes you.

altar, alter

An **altar** is a holy table in a church or temple. To **alter** something is to change it.

> *The church has a magnificent **altar**.*
> *We may have to **alter** our plans.*

ascent, assent

An **ascent** is an upward climb. To **assent** to something is to agree to it, and **assent** means "agreement."

> *the **ascent** of Mount Everest*
> *We all **assented** to the plan.*
> *You have my whole-hearted **assent**.*

aural, oral
Something that is **aural** is to do with the ear or listening. Something that is **oral** is to do with the mouth or speaking.

> a good **aural** memory
> **oral** history

> Remember: An **au**ral examination might involve **au**dio equipment.

base, bass
The **base** of something is the bottom part of it. A **bass** voice or instrument is the one that produces the lowest musical notes.

> the **base** of the table
> a **bass** guitar

baited, bated
If something such as a hook is **baited**, it has food attached to it as a temptation. The word **bated** means "cut short," and is mainly used in the expression *bated breath*.

> The trap had been **baited**.
> I waited with **bated** breath.

berth, birth
A **berth** is a bed on a ship or train, or a place where a ship is tied up. The **birth** of someone or something is the act of it being born or created.

> a cabin with six **berths**
> the date of her **birth**
> the **birth** of jazz

board, bored
A **board** is a long piece of wood, or a group of people with authority. *Bored* means impatient and uninterested. *Bored* is also the past tense of the verb *bore*.

> *A **board** was nailed across the door.*
> *She sits on the **board** of directors.*
> *I've been feeling **bored** all afternoon.*
> *Carpenter bees **bored** holes in the wood.*

born, borne

To be **born** is to be brought into life. To be **borne** is to be accepted or carried, and when fruit or flowers are **borne** by a plant, they are produced by it. If something is **borne** out, it is confirmed.

> *Olivia was **born** in Houston.*
> *He has **borne** his illness with courage.*
> *The trees have **borne** fruit.*
> *The predictions have been **borne** out by the election results.*

boulder, bolder

A **boulder** is a large rock. The word **bolder** means "more brave" or "more daring."

> *The road was blocked by an enormous **boulder**.*
> *The victory made the soldiers feel **bolder**.*

bow, bough

To **bow** is to bend your body or head, and a *bow* is an action where you bend your body or head. A *bough* is a branch of a tree.

> *He gave a long **bow** to the king.*
> *overhanging **boughs** of elm and ash*

brake, break

A **brake** is a device for slowing down, and to **brake** is to slow down by using this device. To **break** something is to change it so that it does not work or exist.

> *I slammed on the **brakes**.*
> ***Brake** when you approach the intersection.*
> *Don't **break** that vase!*

breach, breech

To **breach** something is to break or break through it, and a **breach** is a break or a gap made. The **breech** is the lower part of a human body, a rifle, or some other thing.

> *a **breach** of the peace*
> *In a **breech** birth the baby's legs come out first.*

breath, breathe

Breath, without an **E**, is the noun, but **breathe**, with an **E**, is the verb.

> *He took a deep **breath**.*
> *I heard him **breathe** a sigh of relief.*

bridal, bridle

Bridal means "relating to a bride." A **bridle** is a piece of equipment for controlling a horse, and to **bridle** at something means to show anger about it.

> *a **bridal** dress*
> *a leather **bridle***
> *I **bridled** at the suggestion that I had been dishonest.*

broach, brooch

To **broach** a difficult subject means to introduce it into a discussion. A **brooch** is an item of jewelry.

> *Every time I **broach** the subject, he walks away.*
> *a diamond **brooch***

callous, callus

Someone who is **callous** does not take other people's feelings into account. A **callus** is a patch of hard skin.

> *He treats her with **callous** rudeness.*
> *Wearing high heels can cause **calluses**.*

cannon, canon

A **cannon** is a large gun that fires heavy balls. A **canon** is a general rule or an official collection of texts.

> *The ship fired its only* ***canvas***.
> *the* ***canon*** *of great American novels*

canvas, canvass

Canvas is strong cloth. To **canvass** is to persuade people to vote a particular way or to find out their opinions about something.

> *a* ***canvas*** *bag*
> *The store decided to* ***canvass***, *its customers.*

Remember: If you canva**ss**, you **s**eek **s**omething.

capital, capitol

A **capital** is a city that is also a seat of government. A **capitol** is a building that is a government headquarters. **Capitol** is often **capitalized** (that is, it starts with a **capital** letter).

> *What's the* ***capital*** *of Delaware?*
> *The* ***Capitol*** *is decorated with beautiful lights at Christmas.*

Remember: The **Capitol** has a r**o**und d**o**me.

cereal, serial

Cereal is food made from grain. A **serial** is something published or broadcast in a number of parts. **Serial** also describes other things that happen in a series.

> *my favorite breakfast* ***cereal***
> *a three-part* ***serial***
> *a* ***serial*** *offender*

Remember: A **seri**al is a part of a **seri**es, but a ce**real** is a **real** breakfast.

chord, cord
A **chord** is a group of three or more musical notes played together. **Cord** is strong thick string or electrical wire. Your vocal **cords** are folds in your throat that are used to produce sound.

>   major and minor **chords**
>   tied with a thick **cord**

Remember: A **chor**us often sings **chor**ds.

chute, shoot
A **chute** is a steep slope for sliding things down. To **shoot** something means to send a missile at it, and to **shoot** means to go very fast. A **shoot** is also a very young plant.

>   a laundry **chute**
>   **shooting** at pigeons
>   to **shoot** along the ground
>   bamboo **shoots**

coarse, course
Coarse means "rough" or "rude." A **course** is something that you go around, or a set of classes in which you learn something. **Course** is also used in the phrase *of course*.

>   a **coarse** fabric
>   his **coarse** jokes
>   a golf **course**
>   a meditation **course**
>   Of **course** I want to go with you.

colander, calendar
A **colander** is a bowl-shaped drainer. A **calendar** is a chart with dates on it.

*Strain the potatoes with a **colander**.*
*a **calendar** with mountain scenes*

> Remember: A col**and**er has **hand**les and drains wat**er**, while the cal**endar** marks the **end** of the ye**ar**.

complement, compliment

A **complement** is something that goes well with something else or that completes it, and to **complement** something is to go well with it or complete it. A **compliment** is a remark expressing admiration, and to **compliment** something is to express admiration for it.

*She is a perfect **complement** to her husband.*
*The host received many **compliments** on the food.*

> Remember: A compl**i**ment is the opposite of an **i**nsult and a compl**e**ment compl**e**tes something.

confidant, confident

A **confidant** is a friend you tell secrets to. **Confident** means "trusting" or "self-assured."

*a trusted **confidant***
*We are **confident** you will do a good job.*

council, counsel

A **council** is a group of people elected to look after the affairs of an area. **Counsel** is advice and to **counsel** is to give advice.

*the city **council***
*I **counseled** her to forgive him.*

> Remember: The coun**cil** members take minutes with pen**cil**s.

councilor, counselor

A **councilor** is a member of a council. A **counselor** is someone who gives advice, especially a lawyer. Both words are sometimes spelled with **LL**.

> Three **councilors** resigned after the meeting.
> The college assigns each student a **counselor**.

currant, current

A **currant** is a small berry. A **current** is a flow of water, air, or electricity. **Current** also means happening.

> a **currant** bush
> an electrical **current**

> Remember: There are currants in cakes and currents in electricity.

dairy, diary

A **dairy** is a place where milk is processed. **Dairy** products are foods made from milk. A **diary** is a book in which you write down thoughts and events.

> She worked in a **dairy**.
> an entry in her **diary**.

> Remember: The dairy next to the airport.

decease, disease

The verb **decease** means "to die." A **disease** is an unhealthy condition.

> my **deceased** father
> an infectious **disease**

> Remember that if you are deceased you have ceased to be.

defuse, diffuse
To **defuse** something is to make it less dangerous or tense. To **diffuse** something is to spread it or cause it to scatter. **Diffuse** means spread over a wide area.

> *Police **defused** a powerful bomb.*
> *The governor will try to **defuse** the crisis.*
> *The message was **diffused** widely.*
> *curtains to **diffuse** the glare of the sun*

desert, dessert
A **desert** is a region that receives little rain. To **desert** someone is to abandon them. A **dessert** is sweet food served after the main course of a meal.

> *the Mojave **Desert***
> *She **deserted** me to go shopping.*
> *We had apple pie for **dessert**.*

> Remember: A de**ss**ert is a **s**ticky **s**weet food.

device, devise
Device, with a **C**, is the noun. **Devise**, with an **S**, is the verb.

> *a safety **device***
> *The schedule that you **devise** must be flexible.*

discreet, discrete
If you are **discreet** you do not cause embarrassment with private matters. **Discrete** things are separate or distinct.

> *We made **discreet** inquiries.*
> *The job was broken down into several **discrete** tasks.*

> Remember: When discr**ete** means "separate," the **E**'s are separate.

elegy, eulogy

An **elegy** is a mournful song or poem. A **eulogy** is a speech praising someone or something, especially someone who has just died.

> *elegies of love and loss*
> *His nephew delivered a nostalgic eulogy*

elicit, illicit

To **elicit** something such as information means to draw it out. If something is **illicit**, it is not allowed.

> *I managed to elicit the man's name.*
> *illicit drugs*

eligible, illegible

Eligible means "suitable to be chosen for something." If something is difficult to read, it is **illegible**.

> *an eligible candidate*
> *illegible handwriting*

> Remember: **El**igible means suitable to be chosen, and so is related to the word **el**ect.

emigrate, immigrate

If you **emigrate**, you leave a country to live somewhere else. Someone who does this is an **emigrant**. If you **immigrate**, you enter a country to live there. Someone who does this is an **immigrant**.

> *Her parents had emigrated from Scotland.*
> *Russian immigrants living in the United States*

> Remember: **I**mmigrants come **i**n.

eminent, imminent

Someone who is **eminent** is well-known and respected. **Imminent** means "about to happen."

*an **eminent** professor*
*an **imminent** disaster*

emit, omit

If something is **emitted**, it is let out. If you **omit** something, you leave it out. Similarly, something that is let out or sent out is an **emission**, while something that is left out is an **omission**.

*cars **emitting** exhaust fumes*
*She was **omitted** from the team.*
*a program to cut carbon **emissions***
*a surprising **omission** from the list of great painters*

enquire, inquire

These are alternative spellings for the same word. You can spell this word with an **E** or an **I**, although the form **inquire** is more common. Some people use the form **enquire** to mean "ask about" and the form **inquire** to mean "investigate."

ensure, insure

To **ensure** that something happens is to make sure that it happens. To **insure** something is to take out financial cover against its loss. To **insure** against something is to do something in order to prevent it or protect yourself from it.

*His performance **ensured** victory for his team.*
*You can **insure** against identify theft.*
*Football teams cannot **insure** against the cancelation of a game.*

envelop, envelope

Envelop is the verb meaning "to cover or surround." **Envelope**, with an **E** at the end, is the noun meaning "a paper covering that holds a letter."

*Mist began to **envelop** the hills.*
*a self-addressed **envelope***

exercise, exorcize
To **exercise** means to move energetically, and **exercise** is a period of energetic movement. To **exorcize** an evil spirit means to get rid of it.

> Remember: You ex**e**rcise your l**e**gs but ex**o**rcize a gh**o**st.

faun, fawn
A **faun** is a legendary creature. A **fawn** is a baby deer. To **fawn** on or over someone is to flatter them.

> *a story about **fauns** and centaurs*
> *Bambi the **fawn***
> ***fawning** over his new boss*

faze, phase
Faze is a verb meaning "disturb" and is almost always used with "not." **Phase** is a noun that denotes a stage in a process.

> *He wasn't **fazed** by the bad news.*
> *teenagers going through a rebellious **phase***

final, finale
Final means "last of a series," and a **final** is the last game or contest in a series to decide the winner. A **finale**, with an **E** at the end, is the finish of something, especially the last part of a piece of music or a show.

> *the World Cup **Final***
> *the **finale** of a James Bond film*

flare, flair
Flair is ability. A **flare** is a bright torch used as a warning, and to **flare** is also to widen out.

> *She showed natural **flair**.*
> ***flared** jeans*

flour, flower

Flour is used in baking. A **flower** is the colored part of a plant.

> self-rising **flour**
> a basket of **flowers**

> Remember: Flour makes biscuits and dumplings.

forgo, forego

To **forgo** means to choose not to have something. To **forego** is a less common word meaning "to go before."

> I decided to **forgo** the pudding.
> I will ignore the **foregoing** remarks.

fowl, foul

Foul means dirty or unpleasant, and a **foul** is an illegal action in a sport. **Fowl** are certain types of birds that can be eaten.

> **foul** play
> called for a bad **foul**
> a butcher selling wild **fowl**

gambol, gamble

To **gambol** means to run about friskily. To **gamble** means to accept a risk, and a **gamble** is a risk that you take.

> lambs **gamboling** on the hillside
> to **gamble** on horses
> Going there would be an enormous **gamble**.

gorilla, guerrilla

A **gorilla** is a large ape. A **guerrilla** is a member of a small unofficial army fighting an official one.

> a documentary about **gorillas** and chimps
> ambushed by a band of **guerrillas**

> Remember: King Kong was a giant gorilla.

grate, great
A **grate** is a framework of metal bars, and to **grate** means to shred.
Great means "very large" or "very good."

> *the **grate** over the drain*
> ***grated** cheese*
> *a **great** expanse of water*
> *the **great** composers*

grill, grille
A **grill** is a device for cooking food, and to **grill** food is to cook it on such a device. A **grille** is a metal frame placed over an opening.

> *Cook the chicken on the **grill**.*
> ***Grill** it for ten minutes.*
> *iron **grilles** over the windows*

grisly, grizzly
Grisly means nasty and horrible. **Grizzly** means gray or streaked with gray. A **grizzly** is also a type of bear.

> ***grisly** murders*
> *a **grizzly** beard*

hangar, hanger
A **hangar** is a place where airplanes are kept. A **hanger** is a shoulder-shaped frame for storing clothes.

> *a row of disused aircraft **hangars***
> *Put your coat on a **hanger**.*

hear, here
To **hear** is to become aware of a sound with your ears. Something that is **here** is in, at or to this place or point.

> *Can you **hear** me?*
> *We come **here** every summer.*

heard, herd
Heard is the past tense of the verb **hear**. A *herd* is a group of animals that live, travel, or are grouped together.

> I **heard** that you were moving.
> We saw a **herd** of elk on the mountain this morning.

heir, air
An **heir** is someone who will inherit something. **Air** is the collection of gases that we breathe.

> His **heir** received a million dollars.
> polluted **air**

heroin, heroine
Heroin is a powerful illegal drug. The **heroine** of a story is the main female character in it.

> addicted to **heroin**
> the **heroine** of the film

hoard, horde
To **hoard** is to save things, and a **hoard** is a collection of things that have been saved. A **horde** is a large group of people, animals, or insects.

> a priceless **hoard** of modern paintings
> a **horde** of press photographers

hoarse, horse
Hoarse means "sounding rough or harsh." A **horse** is a large hoofed mammal.

> a **hoarse** voice
> a gallpoing **horse**

hour, our
An **hour** is a period of time. **Our** means "belonging to us."

> *a flight of four **hours***
> ***our** favorite coffee shop*

humus, hummus
Humus is decaying vegetable material in the soil. **Hummus** is a food made from chickpeas.

> *soil enriched with **humus***
> *a lunch of salad and **hummus***

Hungary, hungry
Hungary is a European country. It is spelled with an **A**, unlike **hungry**, which means "wanting to eat."

> Remember: **Gary** from Hun**gary** gets an**gry** when he is hun**gry**.

idol, idle, idyll
An **idol** is a famous person worshipped by fans, or a picture or statue worshipped as a god. **Idle** means "doing nothing." An idyll is a poem or text about a peaceful, quiet setting.

> *The villagers worshipped golden **idols**.*
> *He's an **idle** bum.*
> *He composed **idylls**, ballads, and elegies.*

> Remember: To be id**le** takes **l**ittle **e**nergy.

it's, its
It's, with an apostrophe, is a shortened form of *it is*. **Its**, without an apostrophe, is used when you are referring to something belonging or relating to things that have already been mentioned.

> *It's cold.*
> *The lion lifted its head.*

kernel, colonel
A **kernel** is a seed or part of a nut. A **colonel** is an army officer.

> *apricot kernels*
> *a colonel in the French army*

> Remember: The co**lonel** is a **lonel**y man.

know, now
To **know** something means to be certain that it is true. **Now** means "at this moment."

> *Do you know the way to the bus station?*
> *I'm just leaving now.*

led, lead
Led is the past tense of the verb **lead**. **Lead**, when it is pronounced like **led**, is a soft metal, or the part of a pencil that makes a mark.

> *the road that led to the house*
> *lead poisoning*

liable, libel
Liable is an adjective meaning "responsible." It is related to **liability**. **Libel** is a noun and verb about publishing lies.

> *You will be liable for the cost.*
> *a case of libel*
> *She was libeled in the newspaper.*

lightening, lightning
Lightening is a form of the verb **lighten**, and means "becoming lighter." **Lightning**, without an **E**, is bright flashes of light in the sky.

> *The sky was **lightening**.*
> *forked **lightning***

liquor, liqueur
Liquor is a general term for strong alcoholic drinks such as whiskey, gin, and vodka. A **liqueur** is a sweet, flavored alcoholic drink, usually drunk after a meal.

> *a **liquor** store*
> *a selection of **liqueurs***

loath, loathe
If you are **loath** to do something, you are very unwilling to do it. To **loathe**, with an **E** at the end, is to hate something.

> *I am **loath** to change it.*
> *I **loathe** ironing.*

> Remember: I loath**e** that **E** at the end!

lose, loose
Something **loose** is not firmly held or not close-fitting. To **lose** something is not to have it any more, and to **lose** is also to be defeated.

> ***loose** pants*
> *Why do you **lose** your temper?*
> *We win away games and **lose** home games.*

martial, marshal
Martial is an adjective meaning "military." A **marshal** is a law enforcement officer.

martial law
A sky **marshal** on the flight made an arrest.

mat, matte

A **mat** is a covering for a floor. A **matte** color or surface has a dull appearance.

> *the kitchen* **mat**
> **matte** *photo paper*

medal, meddle

A **medal** is a round object given as a prize or award. To **meddle** means to interfere in an undesirable way.

> *the winner of four gold* **medals**
> *Stop* **meddling** *with my cell phone!*

metal, mettle

A **metal** is a hard substance such as iron or bronze. **Mettle** is your ability to deal with something difficult.

> *protective coverings made of* **metal**
> *These debates will really test your* **mettle**.

miner, minor

A **miner**, ending in **ER**, works in a mine. **Minor**, ending in **OR**, means "less important" or "less serious." A **minor** is also someone under eighteen.

> *His grandfather was a* **miner**.
> *a* **minor** *incident*

morning, mourning

The **morning** is the first part of the day. **Mourning** is a form of the verb **mourn**, and means "grieving for a dead person."

morning coffee
a period of *mourning* for the victims

mucus, mucous
Mucus is a slimy substance produced by the body. **Mucous** is an adjective meaning "relating to or producing mucus."

a discharge of *mucus*
mucous membranes

navel, naval
Your **navel** is the opening on your belly just above your waist. **Naval** is an adjective meaning "pertaining to or involving a navy."

of, off
Of is pronounced as if it ended with a **V** and is used in phrases like *a cup of tea* and *a friend of his*. **Off** is pronounced as it is spelled, and is the opposite of *on*.

a bunch *of* grapes
They stepped *off* the plane.
I turned the television *off*.

palate, palette, pallet
The **palate** is the top of the inside of the mouth, and your **palate** is also your ability to judge the taste of food and wine. A **palette** is a plate on which an artist mixes colors, and a **palette** is also a range of colors. A **pallet** is a platform on which items are stored or shipped.

a coffee to please every *palate*
a natural *palette* of earthy colors
crates of lettuce stacked on *pallets*

passed, past
Passed is the past tense of the verb **pass**. To go **past** something is to go beyond it. The **past** is the time before the present or describes things that existed before it.

*He had **passed** by the window.*
*I drove **past** without stopping.*
*the **past** few years*

peace, piece

Peace is a state of calm and quiet. A **piece** is a part of something.

*I enjoy the **peace** of the woods.*
*the missing **piece** of a jigsaw*

> Remember: a **pie**ce of **pie**.

pedal, peddle, petal

A **pedal** is a lever controlled with the foot, and to **pedal** something is to move its pedals. To **peddle** something is to sell it illegally. A **petal** is one of the outer colored parts of a flower.

***pedaling** her bicycle to work*
***peddling** drugs*
*perfume made from rose **petals***

pendant, pendent

A **pendant** is something you wear around your neck. **Pendent** is a less common word meaning "hanging."

*a **pendant** with a five-pointed star*
***pendent** yellow flowers*

personal, personnel

Personal means "belonging or relating to a person." **Personnel** are the people employed to do a job.

*a **personal** bodyguard*
*a change in **personnel***

pore, pour

If you **pore** over something, you study it carefully, and a **pore** is also a small hole in the surface of your skin. To **pour** something is to let it flow out of a container, and if something **pours**, it flows.

>   *poring over a map*
>   *The rain was pouring down.*

pray, prey

To **pray** means to say words to a god. An animal's **prey** is the thing it hunts and kills to eat.

>   *praying for a good harvest*
>   *a lion in search of its prey*

precede, proceed

Something that **precedes** another thing happens before it. If you **proceed** you start or continue to do something.

>   *This is explained in the preceding chapter.*
>   *students who proceed to higher education*

prescribe, proscribe

To **prescribe** something is to recommend it. To **proscribe** something is to ban or forbid it.

>   *The doctor will prescribe the right medicine.*
>   *Two athletes were banned for taking proscribed drugs.*

principal, principle

Principal means "main" or "most important," and the **principal** of a school is the person in charge of it. A **principle** is a general rule, or a belief that you have about the way you should behave. *In principle* means "in theory."

>   *The Festival has two principal themes.*
>   *She is the principal of Pleasant View Elementary.*

the basic **principles** of Marxism
The invitation had been accepted in **principle**.

> Remember: My **pal** is the princip**al**; you must l**e**arn the princip**le**s.

prophecy, prophesy
Prophecy, with a **C**, is the noun. **Prophesy**, with an **S**, is the verb.

I will never make another **prophecy**.
I **prophesy** that Norway will win.

prophet, profit
A **prophet** is a spiritual leader who is thought to speak for a god. **Profit** is money earned from a business activity.

the **prophet** Ezekiel
Profit in the last quarter rose to $75 million.

quiet, quite
Quiet means "not noisy." **Quite** means "fairly but not very."

a **quiet** night in
He is **quite** shy.

> Remember: A qui**et** p**et** can have qu**ite** a b**ite**.

rain, reign, rein
Rain is water falling from the clouds. To **reign** is to rule a country or be the most noticeable feature of a situation. **Reins** are straps that control an animal, and to **rein in** something is to keep it under control.

torrential **rain**
She **reigned** for just nine days.
Peace **reigned** while Charlemagne lived.
Keep a tight grip on the **reins**.
She **reined** in her enthusiasm.

road, rode
A **road** is a way leading from one place to another. **Rode** is the past tense of the verb **ride**.

> a country **road**
> We **rode** in the back seat.

roll, role
A **roll** is something with a round shape, and to **roll** something means to make it move like a ball. A **role** is the part that you play.

> a **roll** of paper
> dinner **rolls** fresh from the oven
> to **roll** the dice
> He played a major **role** in the incident.

skeptic, septic
A **skeptic** is a person who expresses doubts. Something that is **septic** is infected by bacteria.

> a **skeptic** about religion
> The wound turned **septic**.

> Remember that these words are both spelled the way they are pronounced.

sight, site, cite
Sight is the power to see, and a **sight** is something that you see. A **site** is a place with a special use. **Cite** means to refer to or mention as evidence of something.

> an operation to improve his **sight**
> I can't stand the **sight** of all this mess.
> a building **site**
> The mayor **cited** several cases of misused funds.

stationary, stationery
Stationary, with an **A**, means "not moving." **Stationery**, with an **E**, is paper, pens, and other writing equipment.

> The traffic is **stationary**.
> the **stationery** cupboard

> Remember: Station**e**ry is **e**nvelopes, but station**a**ry is st**a**nding still.

stile, style
A **stile** is a step that helps you climb over a wall or fence. **Style** is the way something is done, or an attractive way of doing things.

> He clambered over the **stile**.
> cooked in genuine Chinese **style**
> She dresses with such **style**.

strait, straight
Strait means "narrow," and is found in the words *straitjacket* and *strait-laced*. A **strait** is a narrow strip of water. **Straight** means "not curved."

> the **Straits** of Gibraltar
> a **straight** line

symbol, cymbal
A **symbol** is something that represents another thing. A **cymbal** is a musical instrument.

> a **symbol** of fertility
> the clash of the **cymbals**

team, teem

A **team** is a group of people engaged in a common effort. **Teem** is a verb meaning "overly full of."

> *a basketball **team***
> *a lake **teeming** with fish*

their, there, they're

Their is the spelling used to refer to something belonging or relating to people or things that have already been mentioned. **There** is the spelling for the word that says that something does or does not exist, draws attention to something, or says that something is at, in, or going to that place. **They're**, with an apostrophe, is a shortened form of *they are*.

> *people who bite **their** nails*
> ***There** is no life on Jupiter.*
> ***There**'s Kara!*
> *They didn't want me **there**.*
> ***They're** a good team.*

through, threw

Through means "going from one side to the other." **Threw** is the past tense of the verb *throw*.

> *They walked **through** the dense undergrowth.*
> *Youths **threw** stones at passing cars.*

tide, tied

The **tide** is the regular change in sea level. **Tied** is the past tense of the verb *tie*.

> *high **tide***
> *a beautifully **tied** bow*

two, to, too

Two is the number after one. The word **to** has many uses, such as indicating direction in phrases like *to the house* and forming the infinitive of the verb, as in *to go*. **Too** means "in addition."

> *I have **two** sisters.*
> *We went **to** Barcelona.*
> *I need **to** leave soon.*
> *Will you come **too**?*

tongs, tongue

Tongs are instruments for holding and picking up things. Your **tongue** is the fleshy pink organ in your mouth.

> *curling **tongs***
> *It burned my **tongue**.*

vein, vain, vane

Vain means unsuccessful. **Vain** also means proud of your looks or abilities. **Veins** are tubes in your body through which your blood flows. A **vein** is also a mood or style. A weather **vane** is a device that shows wind direction.

> *a **vain** attempt to negotiate a truce*
> *You're so **vain**!*
> *the jugular **vein***

> Remember: To be **va**in is **v**ery **a**rrogant, but a **ve**in is a blood **ve**ssel. The weather va**ne** shows the wind coming from the **n**orth**e**ast.

waive, wave

To **waive** something is to give it up. A **wave** is a curled, moving body of water. To **wave** is also to move your hand in greeting or farewell.

> *The prisoner **waived** his right to a jury trial.*
> *Ten-foot **waves** washed onto the beach.*
> *Did you **wave** because you wanted me or just to say hi?*

waiver, waver

A **waiver** is an official document that allows an unusual action. To **waver** is to be undecided about something.

> *You must sign a **waiver** promising not to sue.*
> *I **wavered** over whether to cancel the meeting.*

wander, wonder

To **wander** is to walk around in a casual way. To **wonder** is to speculate or enquire about something.

> *She **wandered** aimlessly about the house.*
> *I **wonder** what happened*

way, weigh, whey

A **way** is a route or path, or a manner of doing something. To **weigh** something is to find out how heavy it is. **Whey** is the liquid part of milk that separates when you make cheese.

> *Is this the **way** to the beach?*
> *You're doing it the wrong **way**.*
> ***Weigh** the flour.*
> *curds and **whey***

weather, whether

The **weather** is the conditions in the atmosphere. **Whether** is a word used to introduce an alternative.

> *the **weather** forecast*
> *I'm not sure **whether** to stay or to go.*

wet, whet

Wet means "containing liquid" and to **wet** something means to add liquid. **Whet** is a verb that means "to sharpen" or "to make more intense."

Your clothes are all **wet**.
Wet *the cloth and cover the bowl with it.*
The smell of pie has **whetted** *my appetite.*

which, witch
Which is a word used to introduce a question, or to refer to something or things that have already been mentioned. A **witch** is a woman with magical powers.

Which *house is it?*
The ring, **which** *I had seen earlier, had now disappeared.*
a story about **witches** *and wizards*

whose, who's
Who's, with an apostrophe, is a shortened form of *who is*. **Whose**, without an apostrophe and with an **E** at the end, is used when you are asking who something belongs to, or referring to something belonging or relating to things that have already been mentioned.

He knows **who's** *boss.*
Who's *there?*
a little boy **whose** *nose grew every time he told a lie*
Whose *coat is this?*

wrap, rap
To **wrap** something means to put something around it, and a **wrap** is something that is folded around something else. A **rap** is a sharp blow, and **rap** is a style of music.

to **wrap** *presents*
a turkey and cream cheese **wrap**
a **rap** *on the door*
They like listening to **rap**.

wring, ring

A **ring** is the sound made by a bell, and it is also a circle or enclosure.
To **wring** something is to twist it.

> the **ring** of the doorbell
> dancing in a **ring**
> **wringing** out the wet clothes

> Remember: You **w**ring out something **w**et.

wry, rye

Wry means "mocking" or "ironic." **Rye** is a type of grass or grain.

> a **wry** smile
> a sandwich made with **rye** bread

yoke, yolk

A **yoke** is an oppressive force or burden. A **yoke** is also a wooden beam
put across two animals so that they can work together, and to **yoke**
things together is to link them. The yellow part of an egg is the **yolk**.

> a country under the **yoke** of oppression
> horses **yoked** to a plow
> I like the **yolk** to be runny.

your, you're, yore

Your, without an apostrophe, is used when you are referring to
something belonging or relating to the person or people you are
speaking to, or relating to people in general. **You're**, with an
apostrophe and with an **E** at the end, is a shortened form of you are.
Yore is a little-used word that occurs mainly in the phrase days of yore,
meaning "a time in the past."

> **Your** sister is right.
> Cigarettes can damage **your** health.
> **You're** annoying me.
> In days of **yore** I competed in marathons.

false
friends

False friends

Knowing that words are related to each other can be a great help to spelling. For example, when you spell *typical*, it can help to think of the related word *type* so that you know that the letter after the **T** is a **Y**.

But there are a few traps. Sometimes it seems logical that a word should follow a certain pattern or be spelled the same way as a word that sounds like it, but you will find that it doesn't. You will need to be alert when you spell the words listed here.

agoraphobia
There is an **O** after the **G**. Don't be confused by *agriculture*.
ancillary
There is no **I** after the **LL**. Don't be confused by *auxiliary*.
aqueduct
There is no **A** after the **U**. Don't be confused by *aquarium*.
bachelor
There is no **T** before the **CH**. Don't be confused by *batch*.

> Remember: Was **Bach** a **bach**elor?

comparison
The letter after the **R** is an **I**. Don't be confused by *comparative*.

> Remember: There is no com**paris**on with **Paris**.

contemporary, temporary
There words contain the sequence **TEMPOR**. Don't be confused by words like *temperature* and *temperament*.
curiosity
There is no **U** after the **O**. Don't be confused by *curious*.
denunciation
There is no **O** before the **U**. Don't be confused by *denounce*.
desperate, desperado
The vowel after the **P** is **E**. Don't be confused by *despair*.

develop

There is no **E** on the end. Don't be confused by the ending of *envelope*.

disastrous

There is no **E** after the **T**. Don't be confused by *disaster*.

duly

There is no **E** after the **U**. Don't be confused by *due*.

extrovert

The vowel before the **V** is **O**. Don't be confused by *extra*.

flamboyant

There is no **U** before the **O**. Don't be confused by *buoyant*.

fiery

The sequence is **ER**, not **RE**. Don't be confused by *fire*.

forty

There is no **U** after the **O**. Don't be confused by *four*.

genealogy

The vowel before the **L** is **A**. Don't be confused by words like *geology*, *biology*, *ontology*, etc.

glamorous

There is no **U** after the first **O**. Don't be confused by *glamour*.

greyhound

It is spelled with an **E**, not an **A**. Don't be confused by the color *gray*.

hindrance

There is no **E** after the **D**. Don't be confused by *hinder*.

hypochondriac

The vowel after the **P** is **O**. Don't be confused by the more common prefix *hyper*.

inoculate

There is only one **N** after the **I**. Don't be confused by *innocuous*.

Israel

The vowel sequence is **AE**. Don't be confused by *real*.

kindergarten

The ending is **TEN**. Don't be confused by *garden*.

lavender

The vowel at the end is **E**. Don't be confused by *calendar*.

liquefy

The vowel before the **F** is **E**. Don't be confused by *liquid*.

minuscule
> The vowel after the **N** is **U**. Don't be confused by *mini*, *minimum*, etc.

> Remember: This word is related to *minus*.

negligent
> The vowel after the **L** is **I**. Don't be confused by *neglect*.

ninth
> There is no **E** before the **TH**. Don't be confused by *nine*.

obscene
> There is a **C** after the **S**. Don't be confused by *obsess*.

ostracize
> The vowel in the middle is **A**. Don't be confused by *ostrich*.

personnel
> There are two **N**'s. Don't be confused by *personal*.

primitive
> The vowel after the **M** is **I**. Don't be confused by *primate*.

pronunciation
> There is no **O** before the **U**. Don't be confused by *pronounce*.

questionnaire
> There are two **N**'s. Don't be confused by *millionaire*.

refrigerator
> There is no **D** before the **G**. Don't be confused by *fridge*.

sacrament
> The middle vowel is **A**. Don't be confused by *sacred*.

sacrilegious
> There is an **I** before the **L** and an **E** after the **L**. Don't be confused by *religion*.

supersede
> The ending is **SEDE**. Don't be confused by words like *recede* and *precede*.

truly
> There is no **E** after the **U**. Don't be confused by *true*.

veterinarian
> There are **I**'s after both **R**'s. Don't be confused by *veteran*.

wondrous
> There is no **E** after the **D**. Don't be confused by *wonder*.

other commonly misspelled words

Other commonly misspelled words

The final chapter of this book includes another list of words that are often spelled incorrectly. These words do not fall clearly under any of the categories covered in the previous five chapters.

Sometimes these words are hard to spell because the sound does not match the spelling. Sometimes the problem comes from the fact that a sound has several possible spellings and you need to know which applies in this particular word. Some of the words have unusual features about them.

It is worth familiarizing yourself with these words. Helpful ways of remembering the spelling have been provided for some of them.

absence
    There is a single **S** at the beginning and a single **C** at the end – just the same as in its opposite, *presence*.
abysmal
    The vowel sound after the **B** is spelled with a **Y**.
accede
    The ending is **CEDE** – just the same as in *concede*, *precede*, and *recede*.
ache
    The consonant sound is spelled **CH** and there is an **E** at the end.

> Remember: An **ache** needs **a che**ap remedy.

acknowledge
    The second syllable is spelled **KNOW**.

> Remember: The word is made from *ac + knowledge*.

adequate
    The vowel after the **D** is an **E**.
advantageous
    There is an **E** after the **G**.

advertisement
>There is an **E** after the **S**.

>Remember: The word is made up of *advertise* and the suffix **MENT**.

aerial
>The beginning is **AE** – just the same as in *aerobic* and *aerosol*.

aesthetic
>There is an **A** before the **E**. The spelling *esthetic* is sometimes used.

amethyst
>The second vowel is **E** and the final vowel is **Y**.

analysis
>The vowel after the **L** is **Y** and the final vowel is **I**.

annihilate
>There are two **N**'s and the middle is **IHI** – just the same as in the related word *nihilism*.

anonymous
>The vowel between the **N** and **M** is a **Y**, and the ending is **OUS**.

anxious
>There is an **I** after the **X** – just as in *anxiety*.

apology
>The vowel after the **L** is **O**.

>Remember: I will **log** an apo**log**y.

architect
>There is an **H** after the **C**.

>Remember: The **arch** was designed by an **arch**itect.

argue
>The ending is **UE**.

aspartame
>The second vowel is **A**, just as in *asparagus*.

atheist
The first vowel is **A**, and the second vowel is **E**.

attendance
The ending is **ANCE**.

> Remember: You **dance** atten**dance** on someone.

atrocious
The ending is **CIOUS** – just the same as in *delicious*.

attach
There is no **T** before the **CH** – just the same as in the opposite word, *detach*.

> Remember: Atta**ch** a **c**oat **h**ook to the wall.

auxiliary
There is a single **L**, which is followed by an **I**.

awful
There is no **E** after the **W**, and a single **L** at the end.

bachelor
There is no **T** before the **CH**.

> Remember: Was **Bach** a **bach**elor?

barbecue
The correct spelling is **CUE**. The informal spelling is **Bar-B-Q**. Most people disapprove of the spelling *barbeque*.

because
The vowel sound after the **C** is spelled **AU**, and the ending is **SE**.

> Remember: **B**ig **e**lephants **c**an **a**lways **u**nderstand **s**mall **e**lephants.

beggar
> The ending is **AR**.

> Remember: There is a begg**ar** in the g**ar**den.

boundary
> There is an **A** after the **D** that is sometimes not pronounced.

breadth
> The vowel sound is spelled **EA** and there is a **D** before the **TH**.

Britain
> The final vowel is spelled **AI** – just the same as in *certain*.

> Remember: There is a lot of r**ain** in Brit**ain**.

broad
> The vowel sound is spelled **OA**.

> Remember: Some **road**s can be quite **broad**.

bronchitis
> There is an **H** after the **C**, and the ending is **ITIS**.

bruise
> The ending is **UISE** – just the same as in *cruise*.

buoy
> There is a **U** before the **O**.

> Remember: A **buoy** is a **b**ig **u**nsinkable **o**bject **y**oked in the sea.

buoyant
> There is a **U** before the **O** – just the same as in *buoy*.

bureaucracy
> The vowel in the middle is spelled **EAU** and the ending is **CY**.

> Remember that the start of this word is the same as the word *bureau*.

burglar
> The ending is **AR**.

business
> The opening is **BUSI**.

> Remember: It's none of your **busi**ness what **bus I** get!

caffeine
> This is an exception to the rule "**I** before **E** except after **C**."

calendar
> The vowel in the middle is **E** and the ending is **AR**.

carriage
> There is an **I** before **AGE** – just the same as in *marriage*.

catalogue
> The ending is **OGUE** – just the same as in *dialogue*. The spellings *catalog* and *dialog* are also used.

category
> The vowel after the **T** is an **E**.

cauliflower
> The first vowel is spelled **AU**.

ceiling
> The word begins with a **C** and the first vowel sound is spelled **EI**.

> Remember the rule: **I** before **E** *except after* **C**.

cellophane
> The first letter is **C** and there is a **PH** in the middle.

cemetery
> All of the vowels in this word are **E**'s.

> Remember: A parking **meter** at the ce**meter**y.

certain
> The final vowel is spelled **AI** – just the same as in *curtain*.

choir
> Nothing much in this word looks like it sounds: the beginning is **CH** and the vowel sound is spelled **OIR**.

> Remember: **Cho**irs sing **cho**ral music.

claustrophobia
> The first vowel sound is spelled **AU**, and there is an **O** before the **PH**.

cocoa
> The first vowel is **O** and the second vowel sound is spelled **OA**.

coconut
> There are two **O**'s – just the same as in *cocoa*.

coffee
> There is a double **F** and the ending is **EE** – just the same as in *toffee*.

competent
> The second and third vowels are both **E**.

> Remember: You must be **compete**nt in order to **compete**.

competition
> The vowel after the **P** is an **E**.

> Remember: You **compete** in a **compet**ition.

complexion
> The letter after the **E** is **X**.

concede
> The ending is **CEDE** – just the same as in *accede*, *precede*, and *recede*.

conference
> The vowel after the **F** is an **E** – just the same as in the related word *confer*.

congeal
> The letter after the **N** is a **G**, and the ending is **EAL**.

conscience

The sound after the first **N** is spelled **SCI**.

> Remember: The ending is the same as the word *science*.

conscientious

The ending is **TIOUS**. The word is related to *conscience*, but the **C** changes to a **T**.

conscious

The sound after the first **N** is spelled **SCI**.

continent

The middle vowel is **I** and the ending is **ENT**.

controversial

The vowel after the first **R** is an **O**.

convenient

The ending is **ENT**.

counterfeit

The ending is **EIT** – just the same as in *forfeit* and *surfeit*.

courteous

The first vowel sound is spelled **OUR** and there is an **E** before the **OUS**.

criticize

The letter after the second **I** is **C** – just the same as in the related word *critic*.

crocodile

The middle vowel is an **O**.

> Remember: A cro**cod**ile has eaten a **cod**.

crucial

The letter after the **U** is a **C**.

cruise

The ending is **UISE** – just the same as in *bruise*.

currency
> The vowel in the middle is an **E**.

curtain
> The final vowel sound is spelled **AI** – just the same as in *certain*.

> Remember: Always buy pl**ain** curt**ain**s.

cyber-, cycle, cylinder, cynic, cyst
> The beginning is **CY**.

decrease
> The ending is **EASE** – just the same as in *increase*.

> Remember: Decr**ease** with **ease**.

definite
> The vowel after the **F** is an **I**, and the ending is **ITE** – just the same as in the related word *finite*.

deliberate
> The first vowel is **E**, and the ending is **ATE**.

> Remember the related word *deliberation*.

delicious
> The ending is **CIOUS** – just the same as in *atrocious*.

describe
> The first vowel is **E** – just the same as in *description*.

detach
> There is no **T** before the **CH** – just the same as in the opposite word, *attach*.

deter
> The ending is **ER**.

different
> There is an **E** after the **F** that is sometimes not pronounced.

dilapidated

The beginning is **DI** (not **DE**).

> Remember: A **di**lapidated building is **di**sused.

dinosaur

The middle vowel is an **O**.

> Remember: There are **no** di**no**saurs **now**.

eccentric

There are two **C**'s at the start.

ecstasy

The ending is **ASY** – just the same as in *fantasy*.

elegant

The vowel after the **L** is an **E**.

> Remember: E**leg**ant **leg**s.

eighth

There is only one **T**, even though the word comes from *eight* + the ending **TH**.

> Remember: **E**dith **is g**oing **h**ome **t**o Henry.

either

The **E** comes before the **I** – just the same as in the related word *neither*.

emphasis, emphasize

The sound after the **M** is spelled **PH**.

emphysema

The middle vowel is **Y**.

> Remember: You'll get emph**yse**ma if **y**ou **s**moke **e**nough.

encyclopedia
> The vowel before the **P** is an **O**.

endeavor
> The middle vowel sound is spelled **EA**.

exasperate
> The beginning is **EXA** and the vowel after the **P** is an **E**.

exercise
> The beginning is **EXE** and the ending is **ISE**.

expense
> The ending is **SE** – using an **S** as in the related word *expensive*.

extension
> The ending is **SION**.

> Remember that this word is related to *extensive*.

extravagant
> The vowel after the **V** is an **A**.

> Remember: There are an extravagant number of **A**'s in extravagant.

facetious
> The ending is **TIOUS**.

> Remember: The word f**acetiou**s contains the vowels **AEIOU** in order.

family
> There is an **I** after the **M** that is sometimes not pronounced.

> Remember that you should be famil**i**ar with your famil**y**.

fascinate
> There is a **C** after the **S**.

fatigue
> The ending is **GUE**.

feasible
> The first vowel sound is spelled **EA** and the ending is **IBLE**.

February
> There is an **R** after the **B** that is often not pronounced.

feud
> The middle is spelled **EU**.

> Remember: **F**euds **e**nd **u**p **d**isastrously.

fifth
> There is an **F** before the **TH**.

foreign
> The ending is **EIGN** – just the same as in *sovereign* and *reign*.
> This is an exception to the rule "**I** before **E** except after **C**."

forfeit
> The ending is **EIT** – just the same as in *counterfeit* and *surfeit*.
> This is an exception to the rule "**I** before **E** except after **C**."

friend
> There is an **I** before the **E**.

> Remember: **I** before **E**, except after **C**.

gauge
> There is a **U** after the **A**.

> Remember: **G**reat **A**unt **U**na **g**rows **e**ggplants.

generate, generation
> The vowel after the **N** is **E**.

genuine
> The ending is **INE**.

gipsy, gypsy
>The word can be spelled with either an **I** or a **Y** after the **G**.

glimpse
>There is a **P** before the **S** that is sometimes not pronounced.

grammar
>The ending is **AR**.

> Remember that gramm**a**r is related to gramm**a**tical.

gruesome
>There is an **E** after the **U** and another at the end.

guarantee, guard, guess, guide, guillotine, guilty, guitar
>There is a **U** after the **G** in these words.

gymnasium, gymnastics
>The vowel sound after the **G** is spelled with a **Y**.

gynecology
>The beginning is **GYN** – a sequence that occurs in some other words that pertain to women, such as *misogyny*.

harangue
>The ending is **GUE** – just the same as in *meringue* and *tongue*.

hatred
>The final vowel is **E**.

hearse
>The vowel sound is spelled **EA** and there is an **E** on the end.

> Remember: I didn't **hear** the **hear**se.

heifer
>The first vowel is spelled **EI** and there is only one **F**.

height
>The middle is **EIGH** – just the same as in *weight*.

heir
>There is a silent **H** and the ending is **EIR**.

> Remember: **H**appy **E**dward **i**s **r**ich.

holocaust
The vowel after the single **L** is an **O**.

horoscope
The vowel after the **R** is an **O**.

hyacinth
The vowel after the **H** is a **Y**, and the letter after the **A** is a **C**.

hygiene
The first vowel sound is a **Y** and the second vowel sound is spelled **IE**.

hyphen
The first vowel sound is a **Y**.

hypochondriac
The letter after the **P** is **O** and this is followed by **CH**.

hypocrite
The letter after the **P** is **O** and the ending is **ITE**.

hypocrisy
The letter after the **P** is **O** and the ending is **ISY**.

hysteria
The first vowel sound is a **Y**.

idiosyncrasy
The vowel after the **D** is **I**, the vowel after the first **S** is **Y**, and the ending is **ASY**.

incense
The letter after the first **N** is **C**, but the letter after the second **N** is **S**.

incident
The letter after the **N** is **C**, which is followed by an **I**.

incongruous
There is a **U** after the **R**.

increase
The ending is **EASE** – just the same as in *decrease*.

> Remember: Incr**eas**e with **ease**.

independent
The final vowel is an **E**.

input
> The opening is **IN**. This is an exception to the rule that the prefix **IN** changes to **IM** before a **P**.

integrate
> The vowel before the **G** is **E** – just the same as in *integral*.

intrigue
> The ending is **IGUE**.

introduce
> The vowel before the **D** is **O**.

irascible
> There is a **C** after the **S** and the ending is **IBLE**.

issue
> There is a double **S** in the middle – just the same as in *tissue*.

jealous, jealousy
> The first vowel sound is spelled **EA**; the second vowel is **OU** – just the same as in *zealous*.

journey
> The first vowel sound is spelled **OUR**.

> Remember: How was y**our jour**ney?

judgment, judgement
> There is an optional **E** before the **M**, though most people prefer the shorter spelling.

knowledge
> The opening is **KNOW**.

> Remember that **know**ledge is what you **know**.

knowledgeable
> There is an **E** after the **G**.

labyrinth
> The vowel sound after the **B** is a **Y**.

lackadaisical

There is a **CK** after the first **A** and the vowel sound after the **D** is spelled **AI**.

> Remember: If you **lack a dai**ly routine you are **lackadai**sical

lacquer

There is **CQU** in the middle.

language

The **U** comes before the **A**, which is the opposite of the way the letters fall in *gauge*.

languor

The ending is **UOR**.

> Remember: Liq**uor** may cause lang**uor**.

laugh

The vowel sound is spelled **AU** and the final consonant sound is spelled **GH**.

league

The ending is **GUE**.

lecherous

There is no **T** before the **CH**.

leisure

The **E** comes before the **I**.

length

There is a **G** after the **N** that is sometimes not pronounced.

liaise, liaison

There are two **I**'s in these words.

> Remember: **L**ouise **i**s **a**lways **i**n **s**ome **o**ld **n**ightgown.

licorice
> The middle vowel is **O** and the ending is **ICE**.

> Remember: Have you ever tasted licor**ice ice** cream?

maintenance
> The vowel after the **T** is an **E**, and the ending is **ANCE**.

> Remember: He does the main**tenan**ce for his **tenan**ts.

mantelpiece
> The letters after the **T** are **EL**.

margarine
> The vowel after the **G** is an **A**. This is an exception to the rule that **G** is "hard" before **A**, **O**, and **U**.

marriage
> There is an **I** before **AGE** – just the same as in *carriage*.

massacre
> There is a double **S** and the ending is **RE**.

> Remember: A **mass** of crops in every **acre**.

mathematics
> There is an **E** after the **TH** that is sometimes not pronounced.

> Remember: I teach **them** ma**them**atics.

messenger
> The vowel after the **SS** is **E** – just the same as in *passenger*.

miscellaneous
> There is a **C** after the first **S** and a double **L**.

> Remember: Mis**cell**aneous **cell**s.

misogyny
> The ending is **GYNY**. The sequence **GYN** also occurs in some other words that pertain to women, such as *gynecology*.

money
> The vowel after the **M** is **O**, and the ending is **EY**.

monkey
> The vowel after the **M** is **O**, and the ending is **EY**.

mystery
> The vowel sound after the **M** is **Y**, and the ending is **ERY**.

mystify
> The vowel sound after the **M** is **Y** – just the same as in *mystery*.

nausea
> The vowel after the **S** is **E**.

> Remember you might get nau**sea** at **sea**.

neither
> The **E** comes before the **I** – just the same as in the related word *either*.

neural, neurotic, neutral
> The opening is **NEU**.

niece
> The **I** comes before the **E**, just as in *piece*.

nuisance
> The opening is **NUI**.

onion
> The first letter is **O**.

ophthalmologist, ophthalmology
> The beginning is the unusual sequence **OPHTH** and there is an **L** before the **M** that is often not pronounced.

> Remember: **O**ph**th**almologists **p**ractice **h**igh-**t**ech **h**ealing.

original
> The vowel after the **G** is an **I**.

> Remember: I ori**gin**ally ordered **gin**.

ornament
> The vowel after the first **N** is an **A**.

oxygen
> The vowel after the **X** is a **Y** and the ending is **GEN** – just the same as in *hydrogen* and *nitrogen*.

pageant
> There is an **E** after the **G** that makes the **G** soft. There is no **D** before the **G**.

pamphlet
> There is a **PH** after the **M**.

parachute
> The ending is **CHUTE**.

particular
> There is an **AR** at the beginning and the end.

passenger
> The vowel after **SS** is **E** – just the same as in *messenger*.

peculiar
> The ending is **AR**.

penetrate
> The vowel after the **N** is **E**. *Perpetrate* has the same vowel pattern.

permanent
> The vowel after the **M** is an **A** and the vowel after the **N** is an **E**.

> Remember: A lion's **mane** is per**mane**nt.

persistent
> The ending is **ENT**.

persuade
> The beginning is **PER** and there is a **U** after the **S**.

phenomenon
The middle part is **NOM** and the ending is **NON**.

pigeon
There is an **E** before the **O** that makes the **G** soft. There is no **D** before the **G**.

pillar
There is a double **LL** and the ending is **AR**.

plagiarize
There is a **GI** in the middle.

> Remember: The **GI** was guilty of pla**gi**arizing.

plague
The ending is **GUE**.

pneumonia
There is a silent **P** at the start and the first vowel sound is spelled **EU**.

> Remember: **P**neu**monia** **p**robably **n**ever **e**ases **u**p.

poignant
The **G** comes before the **N**.

prayer
The ending is **AYER**.

prejudice
The letter after **PRE** is **J**.

> Remember: **Prej**udice is **prej**udging things.

prerogative
The beginning is **PRER**, not **PER** (which you might think from the way most people pronounce it).

prevalent
The vowel after the **V** is **A**.

privilege

> The vowel after the **V** is **I** and the vowel after the **L** is **E**.

> Remember: It is **vile** to have no pri**vile**ges.

protein

> This is an exception to the rule "**I** before **E** except after **C**."

provocation

> The vowel after the **V** is **O**.

> Remember that this word is related to *provoke*.

pursue

> There is an **R** after the first **U**.

pyramid

> The first vowel is a **Y**.

quandary

> There is an **A** after the **D** that is often not pronounced.

recede

> The ending is **CEDE** – just the same as in *accede*, *concede*, and *precede*.

rehearsal

> The vowel sound in the middle is spelled **EAR**.

> Remember: I **hear** there is a re**hear**sal.

reign

> The ending is **EIGN** – just the same as in *sovereign* and *foreign*.

relevant

> The vowel after the **L** is an **E**, and the vowel after the **V** is **A**.

religion

> There is an **I** before the **O** and no **D** before the **G**.

reminisce

> The vowel after the **M** is an **I**, and the ending is **ISCE**.

rhythm

The beginning is **RH**, and the only vowel in this word is a **Y**.

> Remember: **R**hythm **h**elps **y**ou **t**o **h**ear **m**usic.

righteous

The ending is **EOUS**.

rogue

The ending is **OGUE** – just the same as in *vogue*.

rudimentary

There is an **A** after the **T** that is often not pronounced.

sacrifice

The vowel after the **R** is **I**. The ending is **ICE**.

sacrilege

The vowel after the **L** is **E** – just the same as in *privilege*.

sausage

The first vowel sound is spelled **AU**, and this is followed by a single **S**.

schedule

The opening is **SCH**.

> Remember: The **sch**ool **sch**edule.

science, scientific

The opening is **SC**.

scythe

The opening is **SC**, the main vowel is **Y**, and there is an **E** at the end.

secretary

The vowel before the **T** is **E**.

> Remember: The **secret**ary can keep a **secret**.

seize

This is an exception to the rule "**I** before **E** except after **C**."

separate
> The vowel after the **P** is **A**.

> Remember that this word has the word *par* contained inside it.

sergeant
> The first vowel sound is spelled **ER**, and this is followed by **GE**.

series
> The ending is **IES**.

serious
> The ending is **OUS**.

several
> There is an **E** after the **V** that is sometimes not pronounced.

shoulder
> There is a **U** after the **O**.

sieve
> There is an **E** after the **I**, and another **E** at the end.

> Remember: A **sieve** is for **sif**ting **eve**rything.

similar
> There is an **I** after the **M** that is not fully pronounced, and the ending is **AR**.

> Remember: A **simile** compares things that are **simil**ar.

simultaneous
> There is an **E** after the **N**.

skeleton
> The vowel after the **L** is **E**.

> Remember: Don't **let on** about the ske**leton** in the closet.

somersault
>The first vowel is an **O**, and the final vowel sound is spelled **AU**.

soothe
>There is an **E** at the end.

sovereign
>The ending is **EIGN** – just the same as in *foreign* and *reign*.

> Remember: A sove**reign reign**s.

spontaneous
>There is an **E** after the second **N**.

stealth, stealthy
>There is an **A** after the **E** – just the same as in *wealth* and *wealthy*.

stereo
>The vowel after the **R** is an **E**.

> Remember: Ste**re**o **re**cords.

stomach
>The first vowel is an **O**, and the ending is **ACH**.

strength
>There is a **G** after the **N** that is sometimes not pronounced.

surfeit
>The ending is **EIT** – just the same as in *counterfeit* and *forfeit*.

surgeon
>There is an **E** between the **G** and the **O**.

> Remember: Surg**eo**ns give **e**ffective **o**perations.

surprise
>There is an **R** before the **P**.

susceptible
>There is a **C** after the second **S**. The ending is **IBLE**.

sustenance
>The vowel after the **T** is **E**.

synonym
There is a **Y** after the **S** and one before the **M**.

syringe
There is a **Y** after the **S**. The ending is **GE**.

tacit
The middle consonant is a **C**.

temperament, temperature
There is an **A** after the **R** that is often not pronounced.

thorough
The final vowel sound is spelled **OUGH**.

through
The vowel sound is spelled **OUGH**.

tissue
There is a double **S** in the middle – just the same as in *issue*.

toffee
There is a double **F** and the ending is **EE** – just the same as in *coffee*.

tongue
The ending is **GUE** – just the same as in *harangue*.

tragedy
There is no **D** before the **G**.

> Remember: I **raged** at the t**raged**y of it.

twelfth
There is an **F** before the **TH** that is often not pronounced.

typical
The letter after the **T** is a **Y** – just the same as in *type*.

usual
The letter after the first **U** is **S**.

> Remember: **U**gly **s**wan **u**ses **a** **l**ipstick.

vaccinate
There is double **C** – just the same as in *access* and *accent*.

vague
The ending is **AGUE**.

varicose
The first vowel is **A**.

vegetable
The vowel after the **G** is an **E**.

> Remember: **Get** some ve**get**ables inside you!

vehement
There is an **H** after the first **E** that is often not pronounced.

vogue
The ending is **OGUE** – just the same as in *rogue*.

weird
This is an exception to the rule "**I** before **E** except after **C**."

worship
The vowel sound is spelled **OR**.

wrath
There is a silent **W**, and the vowel is an **A**.

yacht
This is a very unusual spelling: the middle part of the word is **ACH**.

zealous
The first vowel sound is spelled **EA**; the second vowel is **OU** – just the same as in *jealous*.

> Remember that this word is related to *zeal*.

index
of hard
words

3. Writing

522 contents

Preparing to write

Thinking about your writing

Whatever you are writing, it is important to think about it first.
If you plan your writing well, it will be **clear**, **logical**, **and effective**.

You may think that planning your writing is just one extra job, and a waste of time, but in fact good planning will probably **save you time** as well as making your writing better.

Planning does not necessarily take a lot of time, and you do not always need to make a **written plan**. For instance, it would be silly to make a written plan for a text message – the whole point is that texting is a quick way of communicating. However, even with a text message, you should plan **in your mind**, so that you know what you want to say.

For longer pieces of writing, such as essays, reports, and often even letters, it is very useful to make a written plan. A plan will help you:

- *organize your thoughts*
- *make sure you are clear about what you want to write*
- *make sure you have all the information you need*
- *make sure you don't leave anything out*

> **Key point to remember**
> Planning will save you time and make your writing more effective.

Before you start to write, the most important question to ask yourself is: **What am I trying to achieve?**

The best way to be clear about this is to ask three questions:

1   **Who** is this writing for?
2   **What** do I want to say?
3   **Why** do I want to say it?

Imagine, for example, that you really like animals, and you need a summer job, so you decide to write to the local zoo. In this case, the answers to the questions above could be:

1   The manager or human relations officer of the zoo.
2   That you want a summer job. That you love animals and worked on a farm last year.
3   Because you want to get a summer job in a zoo.

There are important points to remember about each of these questions:

- **Who?** Make sure that you use a suitable style and tone for your audience. Informal language and jokes are fine for your friends, but a job application needs to be more formal.
- **What?** Make sure that what you say is absolutely clear, and that you have included everything you wanted to include.
- **Why?** Make sure that your writing achieves what you want it to achieve. For instance, if you write a letter of complaint, be clear about what you want to happen: are you writing it because you want an apology, or do you want your money back?

Before starting to write, it can sometimes be helpful to make a **brief summary** of what you are trying to achieve. This can help you to concentrate on the most important points of your writing.

When you have finished your writing, you can go back to your summary and check that what you have written achieves what you wanted it to. A good summary will always answer the questions, who?, what?, and why?

Here are two examples of this kind of summary:

> *A survey of students' opinions of the food in our school cafeteria, to be used as the basis of a campaign for better school meals.*

> *A letter of complaint to the manager of the local theater to say that our recent visit was spoiled by the noise of building work going on in the lobby area, and to ask for our money back.*

Your summary can also help you resist the temptation to add too many details or extra points. Remember that many people are busy – if they do not understand your main points quickly, you may not achieve what you hope to achieve.

> **Key point to remember**
> Always be clear about the purpose of your writing.

Organizing your ideas

Whatever you are planning to write, you need to organize your ideas: either on paper, on your computer, or in your head.

There are several good things about this stage of writing:

- You do not need to think too much about grammar and spelling.
- You do not need to write whole sentences: single words, phrases, or even pictures are fine.
- You do not need to put your ideas into any kind of order to begin with – that can come later.
- The act of writing things down can give you new ideas.

It is also a good idea to write down things that you don't know!

Say, for instance, you are writing an essay about the causes of World War I, a subject you have been studying in class. You might write down the things you know about, such as the alliances between different countries, the assassination of Archduke Franz Ferdinand, and conflicts over territory in the Balkans.

Then you can add things you do not know, but think you ought to include in your essay. Examples might be: why were these alliances formed?; who killed Franz Ferdinand and why?; what role did imperialism play in the arguments between countries?

These **questions** will help you to see what **further research** you need to do.

> **Tip for success**
> If you write down your ideas, you will not forget them!

When you have written down all your ideas, you need to put them in some kind of **order**. If you have a very clear idea of what your writing will contain, it may be possible to do this right from the beginning.

One simple way to order your ideas is to list them under different **headings**.

For instance, this writer is planning an article for her student magazine about a vacation job overseas:

Reasons to work overseas	Types of work available	Practical issues
chance to travel see real life earn money make new friends work experience	voluntary v. paid teaching farm work tourist industry	legal: work permits, etc. safety cheapest way to travel there how much will I earn?

It can be useful to be able to **move your ideas around**.

One possibility is to use **Post-it® notes** (small pieces of paper with one sticky edge) and arrange them on a table or a wall.

Imagine you are writing a party invitation. You want to include the date and time of the party, what it's celebrating, that you need a reply to your invitation, that friends and partners are welcome, and that you'd like people to bring drinks.

If you write all those things individually on Post-it® notes, you can make sure you include all the points you want to, and in the best order.

A very flexible way of ordering ideas is to use **mind maps**, or **spider maps**. In these maps, you start with the most important, central idea, and work out from there, using branches leading outwards. The more detailed the idea, the further the branches are from the central point.

This writer is planning to write a leaflet about what we can do to protect the environment:

Tip for success
A good mind map will help you structure your writing by showing you how points relate to each other.

Another method that is suitable for some kinds of writing is a **flow chart**. This writer is planning a letter to the local parks authority to ask for repairs to the public basketball court:

Write my address, phone number, email address and today's date

↓

Address to proper official (phone City Hall to get a name)

↓

Say we want basketball court repaired

↓

Explain problem with court

↓

Ask for a reply and to be kept informed of progress

↓

Sign (See if any of my friends want to sign it too)

↓

Address envelope, add stamps and send

Tip for success
As well as the things you want to write, your flow chart can include things you need to do: for example, finding out a name or address, finding information (e.g., a bank account number), or filling out a form you need to enclose.

Research

For some pieces of writing, especially longer pieces, you will need to do some research. How much you need to do will depend on the information you already have and the amount of detail your writing needs.

If you are a student, your **teacher** will be able to help. They may give you a list of books or websites to use.

Think about whether there is **anybody you know** who could give you information, or at least tell you the best place to look. Perhaps you have a neighbor who works at the local museum, a relative who was alive during World War II, or a friend who is crazy about sports?

A good place to do research is the **library**. Books will be arranged by subject, so it is easy to find what you want. Most libraries also have computerized systems, which allow you to look for books in several ways, for example:

- by subject
- by keywords
  (*important words that give a clue to what the book is about*)
- by author
- by date of publication

It is often useful to ask the **librarians** for help. They will know about all the different sources of information, some of which may not be in book form. For example, many libraries have copies of old newspapers on microfilm (that is, in a photographed form) that you need a special machine to read. Many libraries also have their catalogs online. Looking here first can make your time at the library more efficient if you determine first that the library holds the books you want and you learn where they are located.

Using **the Internet** is a quick and useful way to research a topic. However, it is important to remember that **anyone** can put information on a website. You need to make sure that any source you use is suitable.

A good starting point is to ask two questions:

- **Who** wrote the information you are looking at?
- **What** is the purpose of the site where you found it?

Answering these questions will help you to think about two further questions:

- Is this information likely to be reliable?
- Is the information likely to be fair, or does the writer have a particular purpose, such as supporting an opinion or trying to make you buy something?

Using a **search engine** such as Google®, Yahoo®, or Bing® can be a start, but there is a danger: at first you may find so many sites that you miss the ones that are really important. Many teachers and professors include websites on their reading lists, so if you have been given a reading list, make sure you use it. Otherwise, think about sites that will be reliable. For instance, in the US you might look for medical information on the National Institutes of Health site (http://www.nih.gov). In the UK you could look at the National Health Service site (http://www.nhs.uk).

Tip for success
If you are using the Internet in a library, the librarian may be able to help you find suitable sites.

Making notes and summaries

When you are doing research, you will want to **make notes**. Your notes can be in whatever form suits you best. The important thing is to make sure you will still understand them when you come to use them!

Make sure that the notes you take **relate to the subject** you will be writing about. There is no point adding extra information – however interesting it is – that you will not be able to use.

Notes should be **short** – do not copy out or cut and paste huge pieces of text. In order to **summarize**, it is very important to make sure you have understood the main points. When you have read a chapter or an article, it can be useful to try to write down the most important three or four points in it.

Look for clues in what you are reading to help you:

- Are there any words that are underlined or in **heavy type**?
- Do the headings summarize the main points?
- Does the book itself include summaries or lists of main points?

Use abbreviations, shorten words, or leave out words altogether. "Vikings > N America 900CE" is much more efficient than writing "The Vikings came to North America in 900 CE."

> **Key point to remember**
> Make sure you will be able to understand your notes
> when you need to use them.

If you have a good idea of the structure of your piece of writing, it can be useful to organize your notes.

For example, if you are writing an essay about a book you have read, you may be asked to look at particular things, such as the way the author builds up characters; the style of language used; the way the plot develops; and the author's relationship with the reader.

If you divide your paper into **themes** like these, you can order your notes as you take them. This will make it easier to organize your essay, and also help you balance the amounts of material you have on each theme.

You may use your notes to record good **quotations** to use in your own writing, but be careful:

- If you use a direct quotation, you must reproduce it accurately, and you must say where it has come from.
- If you summarize what someone has said, you must change it into your **own words**. Copying the words of others is called **plagiarizing**. It is not allowed in academic work, and it can be illegal.

Tip for success
While you are making notes, keep a list of **useful words and phrases** to use in your own writing.

Outlines

For longer pieces of writing, it is useful to produce an outline before you start. An outline can have as much or as little in it as you think will be useful for you, but it should at least include a basic list of **headings**. If you have organized your ideas and notes in some of the ways suggested above, you will probably find it fairly easy to produce an outline.

Start by picking out a number of main points – these will be the framework for your writing, and will lead to more detailed points within them.

For some types of writing, such as a report, it may be appropriate to keep these headings in the final text. For others, the headings will simply be a way of organizing your writing and will not appear in your finished work.

You can use your outline to check that everything you want to write is in a **logical order**:

- Make sure that understanding one part does not rely on another part that comes later.
- If you move on to a different point, see if it needs some sort of introduction or explanation.
- Make sure that all the points connected to a particular idea are treated together.

The person who made the following outline is writing a report on the use of volunteers in a local charity:

Volunteer report

Introduction

- what this report covers
- research and methods used
- purpose of report

Summary of main points

The current situation

- number of volunteers
- what they do
- how they are managed

Problems with the current situation

- not enough volunteers
- volunteers not clear about their role
- lack of communication with paid employees

Suggestions for improvement

- better targeting of recruitment campaigns
- written handbook for volunteers
- regular employee/volunteer meetings

Conclusion

> **Key point to remember**
> Use your outline to make sure everything is included and is in the best order.

Writing a draft

A draft is a rough version of your finished writing. It can be as close to or as far away from the final text as you like. For instance, you may decide to concentrate on the content and not worry about spelling and punctuation – that is up to you. If you are writing something very long, or very important, you may write **more than one draft**.

When you have written a draft, it is useful to ask the following questions:

- Does the **order** of what you have written make sense?

- Have you **included everything** you wanted to include?

- Is all the material **relevant**? Is there anything you should cut out?

- Is the **tone** right? For instance, if it is a letter of complaint, is it firm and assertive or is it offensive and rude?

- Does any part need **more explanation**, more information or more evidence?

- Is the amount of **space given to each theme** appropriate, or is one part too long or too short?

- Does it **achieve** what you want it to achieve? (If you wrote a brief summary at the beginning, you can check against it.)

It can sometimes be useful to give a draft of your writing to **someone else**, and ask if what you have written is clear, interesting, and effective – having another person's opinion can be very valuable in giving you a different perspective. That person might make suggestions for additions or improvements, or check facts for you.

Presentation

General layout

A clear and attractive layout will make your writing both more enjoyable to read and easier to understand.

The use of computers makes it easy for everyone to present their writing in a professional way, and gives us lots of choices about how to do this. One of the most useful things about using a computer is that you can edit text and move it around as you work. You can experiment with different ways of presenting it – you do not have to decide on your layout at the beginning.

Here are some general rules:

- Almost all documents look better if there is plenty of **space** around the words.
- Do not make your **sentences or paragraphs** too long.
- Do not make the **size of type** too small.
- Whatever style you choose for the different parts of your document, make sure you **keep to the same style all the way through**.

Tip for success
Before you finish your document, look at it using the **print preview** option, to see how it will look on the page when it is printed.

Look at the following piece of text:

> To: all Little League members
> Welcome back to baseball practice! Many of you will know that we
> have new uniforms this season. Each player will need a red shirt and
> helmet; these will be available at the first practice. You also need
> the appropriate glove, and cleats, which can be of any type. Please
> remind your parents that there is a $40 fee to cover coaching and
> transportation to games. See you at practice next week,
> From: Matt (team coach)

Now see how a better layout can make the same information much
easier to read:

> To: All Little League members
>
> Welcome back to baseball practice!
>
> **New uniforms**
> Many of you will know that we have new uniforms this season.
> Each player will need:
>
> - red shirt and helmet (available at the first practice)
> - glove appropriate to your position
> - cleats (any type)
>
> **Fees**
> Please remind your parents that there is a $40 fee to cover coaching
> and transportation to games.
>
> See you at practice next week!
>
> Matt (team coach)

Most pieces of text are divided into paragraphs. Each paragraph discusses one point or idea.

The beginning of a new paragraph can be shown in two ways. The first is to **indent** the first sentence, which means starting it further to the right than the rest of the paragraph, like this:

> Additional research has shown a strong link between smoking and heart disease. In a study of more than 1,000 healthy males, it ...

The second way is to **leave a whole line of space** between paragraphs. If you do this, you do not need to indent the first sentence. Separating paragraphs in this way can help to make the structure of your writing clear by showing where each new point or idea starts and ends. Most computer word processing programs will allow you to arrange your paragraphs in either of these styles automatically.

Try not to leave a heading or a single line of a paragraph at the **end of a page**, or to have the last line of a paragraph at the **top of a page**. It is better to have a larger space than usual at the bottom of a page than to have a small part of the paragraph on its own.

You should also try to avoid having a hyphenated word as the last word on a page. To avoid this, try rewriting your sentence, or use one of the "keep" features in your word processing program to keep certain lines together on a page.

> **Key point to remember**
> Using plenty of white space will make your document easier to read.

You will need to decide how you want the **edges** of your text to look.

> You can set your computer like this, so that the ends of the sentences do not fall in a straight line. This style, called "ragged right" or left-justified, can look natural, and the spacing between each word looks better. It usually results in fewer hyphenated words.

> Alternatively, you can set your computer so that the words form a neat, straight line at both of the edges. This style, called justified, can look neater, but you may find that you get large gaps between some words in order to make them fit and you will probably have more hyphenated words.

You will also have to decide whether or not you want your document to use **hyphens** if a long word comes at the end of a line. If the lines in your document are fairly long, and you are not using extremely long words, it is usually best not to use hyphens. However, if you have short lines, you may need to use hyphens to avoid large spaces between words, especially if you are using justified text.

Hyphens must be used at a suitable breaking point in the word. Your computer will do this for you, but if you are writing by hand, you will need to decide where to put hyphens yourself. If you are not confident about this, consult a dictionary: most dictionaries show "syllabification dots" at the points in a word where you are allowed to break it, like this:

bath·y·scaphe   re·pro·duc·tion   un·im·pres·sion·a·ble

Tip for success
If you do use hyphens, check the line ends when you have finished to make sure there are no word breaks that could cause confusion, such as leg-end, or thin-king.

Fonts and typefaces

A font is the whole set of letters, numbers, and other characters that share the same design. You will be able to choose fonts when you write documents on your computer. They range from standard fonts that you might use for an essay or a letter, to very unusual and dramatic ones that you might use for a party invitation, a poster, or a sign:

Dear Ms. Hodges
    I am writing to inquire about the possibility of a job in your company ...

Come to our spooky ghost party!

The **normal font size** for general texts such as essays is 11 or 12 points. You may want to use larger fonts for headings. Sometimes smaller sizes (usually 10 or 11 points) are used for long quotations.

Fonts like this one, which have very small lines at the ends of letters, are called **serif** fonts, while fonts like this one, which have nothing at the ends, are called **sans-serif** fonts. It is best to use a serif font such as Times New Roman for long pieces of text. Headings are often displayed in a sans-serif font such as Arial or Helvetica, even when the main text is in a serif font.

You can also choose different ways of writing words, for example using *italics*, **bold (also called heavy) type**, ***bold italics***, underlining, or SMALL CAPS.

Tip for success
Avoid writing more than a few words in CAPITAL LETTERS because they are difficult to read.

Bullets

If you want to separate a list of points from the main part of your text, a simple way to do so is to use bullets. Text arranged in this way can be called a bulleted list.

Bullets are often used when the order of the list is not particularly important, e.g.:

> During this exciting week-long course, students will:
>
> - learn how to gather food in the wild
> - spend two nights in a nearby forest
> - learn how to build a shelter from earth and branches

It is not usual to use periods at the end of text that follows bullets, though if the text is more than one sentence, you may feel it looks better.

You can decide whether or not to use capital letters at the beginning of each bullet. In the example above, capital letters were not used because each bulleted item formed a complete sentence following the introductory phrase "students will ..."

> **Key point to remember**
> The most important thing to remember is that when you have decided whether or not to use capital letters and periods, you should do the same for each item.

Bullets can be introduced by any sort of symbol you think is appropriate:

- Probably the most common type is a circle like this.
- A dash is also an acceptable way to format a bulleted list.

▶ You may want to emphasize your points more with a symbol like this.

♪ Or even choose something completely different if it is relevant to your text.

It is important to make sure that the bullet text matches up grammatically with the words you use to introduce it. If you use a phrase such as "You will need the following:", it is simple to follow it by a list of items.

However, you will often find bulleted text introduced by phrases such as:

To write a successful essay, you should:
Students will have the opportunity to:

In cases like this, make sure you read through the introductory phrase and the bullet text together, to make certain they form a correct sentence. Look at the following:

Students will have the opportunity to:

- canoe in the local river
- learn how to cook on a camp fire
- making lots of new friends

The third point does not make a grammatically correct sentence. It should be "make lots of new friends."

Numbered lists

Numbered lists are used in a similar way to bulleted lists. They are often used to show that the order of items is important or where they show a ranking:

The most common girls' names in the US in 2009 were:

1   Isabella
2   Emma
3   Olivia
4   Sophia
5   Ava

You can use numbers or letters to order your points, and in some cases you may even want to do both, in order to go into more detail about a particular point:

Here is the agenda for Monday's meeting:

1   Minutes of the last meeting
2   Sales reports
    a   Europe and the Middle East
    b   Americas
    c   East Asia
3   Next year's training budget
    a   in-house training
    b   external courses

Tip for success
When you want to indent a list of points, always use a function such as the **tab key** or the bullet or numbers from the **menu bar**. Do not try to indent using the space bar because the spacing will not be even. Your word processing program may have an icon you can click on to adjust the amount of indent of text you have selected.

Headers, footers, and page numbers

Headers and footers are pieces of text that appear at the top or bottom of the pages of your document but are separate from the rest of the writing on that page.

Typical items that might be put in them include:

- document title
- chapter or section titles
- author name
- copyright information
- date
- document reference

Using headers and footers can make your work look more professional. If you have the same header and footer throughout the whole document, you only need to put the text in once and your computer will do the rest automatically.

It is also possible to use different headers and footers for different sections of a document, for example, for each new chapter or section, or on odd and even pages. This can be useful for readers.

Page numbers can also be added automatically, and placed wherever you want them: at the top or bottom of the page; on the right, left, or in the center.

You can also choose the position, size, font, etc., of your headers and footers. For example, you may want a chapter heading at the top of each page to be fairly large, but a copyright note at the bottom to be quite small.

Using images

Using images can be a great way to liven up your text. Reasons for using images may include:

- helping to explain something – sometimes an image can be clearer than words
- decorating a document such as a party invitation
- emphasizing a brand, for example, by using a company logo

A simple way to get images is to use **clip art** that is available in your word processing software, or downloadable from the Internet.

If you are using images in a more serious document, you should give them captions, and it will often be necessary to number them so that you can refer to them in the text.

Make sure that your images are an appropriate size for your document – it is easy to change the size of an image on your computer.

Key point to remember
If you use an image, make sure you are legally allowed to do so. Some images are protected by **copyright**, which means you need the owner's permission to use them, and you may have to pay.

Tables and boxes

If you want to present information in rows and columns, it is a good idea to use a table:

Course schedule

Group 1	Group 2	
9.00 -9.30 9.30 – 11.00 11.00- 11.30	Introductions Singing workshop Break	Introductions African drumming Break

You can make tables on your computer, and say how many rows and how many columns you need. You can add more rows and columns later if you need to, and you can change their size and position in the table.

You can also use tables to set out information neatly and then make the actual lines of the box disappear afterwards.

If you want to separate off one section of text from the rest, you can put a box or border around it.

> You can also put a shade or a colored tint inside a box to make it stand out, like this.

> There are many different types of boxes and borders to choose from in your computer's word processing program. This one, for example, has a shadow effect.

Charts and diagrams

Charts and diagrams can be a good way to present information, particularly numerical information, which can be much easier to understand when shown this way.

Charts and diagrams are particularly good for information that needs to be analyzed, such as information showing **comparisons**, **patterns**, **and trends**.

All charts and diagrams should be numbered and have a heading. Make sure there is plenty of space around them, and that there is always a reference to them in the text:

> As we can see from table 1 ...

> Fig. 3.8 illustrates the increase in ...

There are many different types of chart and diagram. Think about which one best suits the information you want to present.

Graphs

Graphs such as this one are a good way of showing trends in numbers:

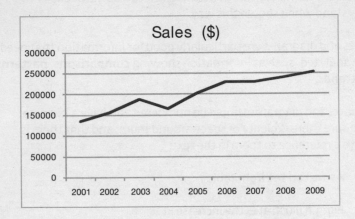

Pie charts

Pie charts are a clear way of showing the relative size of groups of things:

Venn diagrams

Venn diagrams are used to show overlapping groups:

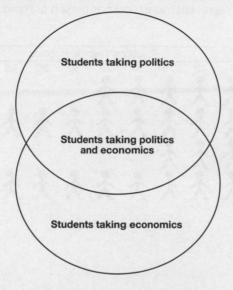

Bar charts

Bar charts also make it easy to compare numbers and amounts:

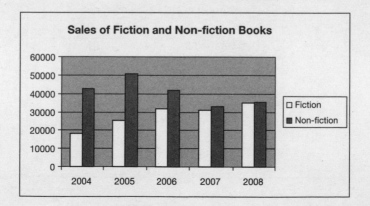

Pictograms

Pictograms are a simple way of showing numbers of people or things.
Each image can represent more than one person or thing:

Students' Favorite Hobbies									
Description	5	10	15	20	25	30	35	40	45	50

Structure

Logical ordering

If you have planned your writing well, you should have no problem writing it in a logical sequence.

Make sure that your **points lead into each other** in such a way that your reader is guided through your argument. Remember that you should move from general points to more specific, detailed points.

Never include a point without the necessary **background or explanation**, or one that relies on reading something later in the text. Unless you actually refer to other sources, or unless you know that your reader possesses certain knowledge, the text should include all the information needed to understand it.

Make sure that all points of discussion about a particular area of your text come together – **do not change from one topic to another** and then back again.

An essay should **start with an introduction and end with a conclusion**, and in fact there are many types of writing where this is a useful principle, even if it is not done in such a formal way. For instance, if you are writing a formal letter, it can sometimes be helpful to include a short title after the greeting. This acts as an introduction.

Introductions

When you write an essay, you should start with an **introduction** and end with a **conclusion**.

Your introduction will give your readers the information they need to lead them into the main part of the essay.

The introduction should do the following things:

- **Introduce the topic**: briefly describe what the essay is about, providing any necessary explanation of the background and context of the topic.

- **Explain the purpose of the essay**: say what you will discuss, making sure that it fits exactly with the title of your essay. If you have been given a title, be careful to look for words like "examine," "contrast," "describe," or "analyze," and make sure that this is what your essay does.

- **Define your terms**: if there is any possibility of doubt, say exactly what you mean by words and phrases, both in the title and throughout the essay. For instance, if your essay is about childhood diabetes, you should say what age range you consider to be covered by the term *childhood*.

In the same way, if there is any possible doubt about the meaning of the title, you should say very clearly what you understand by it, and how this understanding will form the basis of what follows.

- **Explain how your points are organized**: give a brief summary of the structure of your essay.

An introduction can be more than one paragraph, if necessary. As a general rule, it should be around 10% of the total length of your essay. Remember though, it should not be a summary of the whole thing – if it is, the reader will not bother reading to the end!

Other points you may want to cover in your introduction include:

- **A statement of why your topic is particularly interesting or important.**

- **An explanation of how your work fits into a wider context**: for example, how it relates to research being done by others, or how it is affected by current events or attitudes.

- **A discussion of areas of your topic where there is a lack of knowledge.**

> **Tip for success**
> While a short quotation can be an interesting way to start an essay, avoid long quotations or detailed examples in your introduction.

Conclusions

The introduction and conclusion form a frame for your essay. The conclusion brings together all the ideas and information you have discussed. It shows the reader that the essay is complete and that the aims of the essay have been achieved.

When you write your conclusion, always look back at the introduction. Make sure that your conclusion shows your essay has really done what you said it would do.

A conclusion does two main things:

- **Summarizes** the main points and ideas.

- **Reaches conclusions** by saying what the consequences of your writing are.

By summarizing the main points, you provide your reader with a brief, clear statement of the most important points you have discussed. You should also include a brief reminder of the purpose of this discussion.

Everything that you summarize must be fully covered in the main part of the essay – you should not add any new information here.

As well as summarizing *what* you have discussed, you should summarize what you have said your evidence suggests.

> **Key point to remember**
> Never add any new points or ideas in your conclusion.

The type of conclusions you reach will depend on the question you were dealing with in the essay. You might:

- **Achieve a task set in the title**: For instance, if you were asked to contrast the characters of the Bennet sisters in the novel *Pride and Prejudice*, you would simply summarize the main differences you found.

- **Give your opinion**: For instance, if you were asked to say whether or not nuclear power is a good form of fuel, you would express your opinion and explain briefly how the evidence you have presented supports it.

- **Show what you have learned from looking at evidence**: For instance, if you are asked to analyze the results of a research project on the effects of diet on rates of heart disease, you would summarize the main facts you have discovered from the survey.

- **Make recommendations**: For instance, if you are writing a report on the best way to encourage recycling, you would suggest actions that could be taken.

Often you will find that issues you discuss in essays are complicated and you cannot find a simple answer or give a definite opinion. This is fine – you should simply explain why this is the case by summarizing the main points.

Headings

Headings are often used in long documents. They can **make the presentation more effective and attractive** by breaking up long pieces of text.

Headings are **useful for your readers**. They reveal the structure of your document and enable the reader to find a particular topic easily.

It is best to **start with headings and then write your text**. If you do it like this, your essay will be better organized than if you simply write it and try to add headings afterwards. If you have written an outline, you can often use the points in your outline as headings, modifying them as you work if necessary.

You can use **different levels of heading**. The lower levels are called subheadings. In a long document, main headings mark the major sections and subheadings then divide these sections.

Try not to use too many headings. As a general rule, 2 or 3 headings per letter-size page would be enough. Sometimes you cannot avoid having a very short section under a heading – there may simply be very little to say about that particular point. That is fine, but try not to break up the text too much.

> **Key point to remember**
> Start with your headings, then write your text.

If you are using subheadings, it is even more important to plan your heading structure before you write, so that you have a consistent framework for the whole document. Sections of similar importance should have the same level of heading.

It is usually a good idea to number headings, especially if you want to make a table of contents. It is up to you how you number them, but a common way would be to use a system of numbers and points:

1. **Main heading**
   1.1 **subheading**
      1.1.1 **sub-subheading**

Once you have decided on a structure, you need to choose a style for your headings. Make sure the style is the same throughout the whole document.

You will need to think about the following:

- the **font type and font size** for each level of heading
- are your headings **numbered**, and if so how?
- are your headings **bold**, *italic*, <u>underlined</u>, etc.?
- do they start with a **capital letter**?
- do they include **punctuation**?
- how much **space** is there before and after the surrounding text?

> **Tip for success**
> Computer programs like Word® have built-in headings that you can use. You can change the style if you want, then you can simply choose the heading type when you need it.

Try to make your headings as specific as possible. Instead of the heading "Background," for example, try to express what sort of background information you are giving in this section. Make sure that your headings accurately describe the information they include.

Try to think about your headings from the point of view of the reader and the purpose of your document.

For instance, if you are writing an explanation of how to do something, headings with verbs can be effective, e.g.:

* **Planning your vegetable garden**
* **Deciding what to grow**
* **Preparing your soil**

Sometimes it is appropriate to use questions as headings, e.g.:

* **What is a carbon footprint?**
* **How can I reduce my carbon footprint?**

The reader should be able to read separately from the headings. Do not use pronouns in the first sentence that refer back to the heading. For example, if your heading is "Principles of the carbon cycle" do not begin the next sentence "This is the process ...."

Tip for success
Before you print your document, check to make sure that there are no headings on their own at the bottom of pages.

Paragraphs

In a long piece of writing, such as an essay or a report, each paragraph should contain one separate point or idea.

The **first sentence** of each paragraph usually introduces what the paragraph is about:

- *Smith's views have, however, been challenged by several experts.*
  (Continue by explaining what the experts say.)

- *This new law gave greater protection to workers.*
  (Continue by describing how it did so.)

Here are some useful phrases to link your paragraphs:

- **As a result of** *this research, scientists have decided ...*
- **Meanwhile**, *my brothers had been busy ...*
- **Despite** *these problems, they carried on trying to ...*
- **Nevertheless**, *she was forced to ...*
- **However**, *we did not allow ourselves to ...*
- **On the other hand**, *many people say that ...*
- **In addition to** *this work on dolphins, he ...*

Tip for success
Try not to make your paragraphs too long. If they are very long, you will probably find that they can be divided into separate points.

Style

What is good style?

When people write with good style, their writing is clear, interesting, elegant and appropriate for their audience.

The best style to use will vary according to the type of document you are writing: the kind of original, descriptive writing you would use for a piece of creative writing would not be appropriate for a factual report.

There are many aspects to writing with good style, which are discussed in this section.

However, one simple rule applies to all your work:

Avoid repeating words.

Whatever you are writing, it will sound dull and clumsy if you use the same words over and over again. If you read your work aloud, you will notice when you have done this.

Too much repetition	Better ...
Team A discovered ..., Team B discovered ..., Team C discovered ...	Team A discovered ..., Team B found ..., Team C's results showed ...

Sometimes the easiest way to avoid repetition is simply to replace one of the words with a pronoun:

Too much repetition	Better ...
We intend to invite all our friends and ask each friend to bring some food.	We intend to invite all our friends and ask each of them to bring some food.

However: just as you avoid repetition, you should avoid the habit called "elegant variation," which is using a difficult and unfamiliar synonym just because you don't want to use a simpler word again. The best way to avoid elegant variation is to avoid using a word that is not familiar to you – perhaps one that you have found in a list of synonyms in a thesaurus. Such a word will probably stand out awkwardly in your text and will not do the job you want it to do.

Writing in sentences

Sentences are the building blocks of texts. The length of your sentences will depend on who you are writing for. Very long sentences can be confusing, while very short sentences can sound childish and can be irritating to the reader. If your sentence is longer than about 15–20 words, see if you can divide it.

The basic rule is that each sentence should have **a subject and a predicate**:

> *The vase smashed on the floor.*
> (vase = subject, smashed on the floor = predicate)
> *My Mom plays the violin.*
> (My Mom = subject, plays the violin = predicate)

Note that the predicate of a sentence always contains a verb.

Some people think it is bad style to end a sentence with a preposition such as *on*, *up* or *in*. However, avoiding this can sometimes lead to a rather formal style. Compare the following:

> *We were shocked to see the conditions they live in.*
> *We were shocked to see the conditions in which they live.*

As always, think about the reader and the purpose of your document to help you choose the appropriate style and tone.

> **Tip for success**
> Try reading your work aloud; if your sentences work well, it will be easy to read. See where you make natural pauses, and think about whether you need to add commas, semicolons, or other punctuation.

Do not string lots of sentence parts together using commas. This is a common mistake, and can be confusing.

Look at the following:

> First we went to the Statue of Liberty, which was fantastic, our tour guide was excellent, and we saw Ellis Island, later we had our picnic on the lawn outside the museum.

This sentence would be much better using dashes and splitting it into separate sentences, like this:

> First we went to the Statue of Liberty, which was fantastic – our tour guide was excellent. After that we saw Ellis Island, and later we had a picnic on the lawn outside the museum.

However, make sure you use commas where they are needed, as they can help the reader understand your sentences better.

For instance, commas are needed if a subordinate clause (less important part of a sentence) comes before the main clause, e.g.:

> If the flight is late, call before you take off.

They are also needed for adding small pieces of information about someone or something in your sentence, e.g.:

> My sister, who is a vet, has three children.

Tip for success
Take care with punctuation. There is a detailed explanation of how to use commas and other punctuation marks in the punctuation section of this book.

Using plain English

It is important to write in plain English. Plain English is easier to write, and certainly easier to understand. Try to follow these rules:

- **Avoid unnecessary jargon.** Don't talk about "interfacing" with someone when you mean "communicating" with them, or simply "talking" to them. Don't say "design solution" – it's just a design.

Of course, there are times when technical and specialist terms *are* appropriate. If your audience consists only of people who work in a particular field, they will expect you to use the terms they are familiar with. And if you are writing a scientific or technical essay, you must use the correct terminology. As always, think of your reader.

- **Avoid unnecessary formality.** Ask yourself if there is a simpler word or phrase that would be appropriate for your reader.

very formal	simpler ...
prior to	before
in excess of	more than
in the vicinity of	near

- **Try to use active verbs instead of nouns.** This will make your sentences sound less complex and formal.

noun form	active verb form
give encouragement to	encourage
ensure the completion of	complete
make provision for	provide
make utilization of	use

Active or passive verbs?

It is usually better to use active verbs in your writing because the structure is simpler. Passive verbs can sometimes sound formal. Compare these two sentences, for example:

> *New recycling methods have been introduced by the county.* (Passive.)
> *The county has introduced new recycling methods.* (Active.)

However, the passive can be useful in certain cases. For instance, you may use the passive if you do not want to appear to be blaming someone or criticizing someone:

> *You have not paid the fine.* (Active and accusing.)
> *The fine has not been paid.* (Passive and more neutral.)

You may also want to use the passive if you do not want your reader to blame you:

> *I'm sorry to report that I have lost your documents.* (Active and admitting fault.)
> *I'm sorry to report that your documents have been lost.* (Passive and implying that it may have been someone else's fault.)

The passive is also used when you do not know who carried out an action or it is irrelevant who carried out the action. This will often happen in academic writing in which the slightly more formal style is appropriate:

> *The results were analyzed in the laboratory.*
> *The buildings were knocked down in 1989.*

Avoiding clichés

A cliché is a word or phrase that has been used too often. If you use clichés, your writing may be boring or irritating. When readers find too many clichés, they may lose interest and miss your main message. They may think that if your writing is not original, your ideas cannot be original either.

You may find that clichés slip into the first draft of your writing – after all, it is because they are so well known and come so easily to mind that they have become clichés. Read through your document and try to identify any phrases that seem to fit into this category. If English is not your first language, it may be difficult to do this. In this case, it may be a good idea to ask a native English speaker for advice.

Then ask yourself: what does this phrase actually mean? It may not really have much meaning at all, in which case you can probably delete it. Examples of this sort of cliché are:

> *when all is said and done*
> *at this point in time*
> *with all due respect*
> *in any way, shape, or form*
> *going forward*

Or it may be that the phrase has been used so much that it has lost all its power, and may well annoy your reader. Examples of this sort of cliché are:

> *move the goalposts*
> *reinvent the wheel*
> *the best thing since sliced bread*

Sometimes a simple **combination of adjective and noun** can be so overused that it becomes a cliché, e.g.:

> *roaring fire*
> *vise-like grip*
> *long-lost friend*

This does not mean that such combinations should never be used, but try not to use too many obvious combinations, and choose something more original if you can.

One area of language where it is very easy to fall into the trap of using a cliché is the **simile**.

Look at the following similes:

> *as cold as ice*
> *as fresh as a daisy*

They are so overused that they are not powerful descriptions. Now look at the following similes, all found in real writing:

> *as cold as a Siberian winter*
> *as cold as a stone statue*
> *as fresh as green shoots in the morning*

Of course, imaginative similes like these are not suitable for all types of writing. In formal writing, it may be best to avoid similes altogether. In more creative writing, you should aim to be descriptive and original, but your similes should fit into the overall style of the text.

Avoiding redundancy (unnecessary words)

It is very easy to use more words than you need, and too many words will make your writing less effective and may annoy your readers.

Compare the following:

> *Jack and I are of the same opinion on this matter.*
> *Jack and I agree.*

> *Due to the fact that the train was delayed, we were late for the concert.*
> *We were late for the concert because the train was delayed.*

Avoid "empty" words and phrases that do not add meaning to your sentences, e.g., *in terms of, the fact of the matter*.

Avoid saying the same things twice. This is known as **tautology**. Consider the following:

9 a.m. in the morning	a.m. means "in the morning" – choose one or the other
reexamine again	just say "reexamine" – the "again" is expressed in the prefix "re-"
my personal opinion	if it's your opinion, it's personal – you don't need to say so
mutual cooperation	you can't cooperate on your own, so it must be mutual

Avoid adding illogical extra words. Consider the following:

in actual fact	if it is a fact, it must be "actual" – just say "in fact"
very unique	something unique is the *only* one of its kind – there are no degrees of uniqueness

Avoiding ambiguity

Ambiguity is when something could possibly be understood in more than one way. It is an easy trap to fall into because *you* know what you mean when you write, but try to put yourself in the reader's place and make sure there is no room for doubt.

Be careful with **words that have more than one meaning**. Often the context will be enough to make it clear which meaning is intended. If you write that you are going to the bank, nobody is likely to think you are going to a river bank. However, consider the following:

> *My teacher is really funny.*
> (Is the teacher humorous or strange?)

> *The food was very hot.*
> (Was it a high temperature, or was it spicy?)

Make it clear whether you are using words and phrases in a **literal or figurative** sense:

> *He was in debt to his friend.*
> (Did he owe his friend money or simply feel grateful?)

> *There was a chasm between us.*
> (Was there a hole in the ground, or a big difference of opinion?)

Use pronouns carefully to make sure it is clear who or what they refer to:

> *Rosie had an argument with Sarah, and she started crying.*
> (Who cried, Rosie or Sarah?)

*I couldn't attach the bird boxes to the posts in the field because
they weren't strong enough.*
(Was it the posts or the bird boxes that weren't strong?)

Check the structure of your sentence to make sure it is clear how
the parts relate to each other. Compare the following:

We talked about bullying at work.
(Ambiguous – were we at work or not?)

We talked about the issue of workplace bullying.
At work, we talked about bullying.

They told us about the murder at 11 o'clock.
(Ambiguous – did the murder happen at 11 o'clock?)

At 11 o'clock, they told us about the murder.
They told us about the murder that occurred at 11 o'clock.

Make sure it is clear what your adjectives are describing:

a large woman's handbag
(Is it the woman or the handbag that is large?)

a formal English test
(Is the test formal, or is it a test of formal English?)

Be clear about the purpose of your writing. Imagine that you receive
a memo that includes the following:

*It would be a good idea for all employees to take at least 30 minutes
for lunch.*

It would not be clear whether the memo is saying that you *must* take
30 minutes or simply that it would be a nice thing if possible.

Register

The word 'register' refers to aspects of language such as how formal or informal it is. Compare the following:

> *They furnished us with the requisite implements.* (Very formal.)
> *They gave us the necessary tools.* (Neutral.)
> *They let us have the gear we needed.* (Informal.)

You should match the register of your language to the type of writing you are doing. Using the wrong register can make your writing sound odd and can even cause offense.

Register can often be shown by the choice of words or phrases:

formal or literary	neutral	informal
wax lyrical	speak enthusiastically	rattle on
precisely	exactly	on the nose
in ascendancy	becoming successful	climbing up

Dictionaries mark words that are formal or informal, so you can check if you are not sure. Many idioms and phrasal verbs are either informal or slightly informal, so take care to use them appropriately.

Informal language is fine for personal letters, emails, texts, etc., but for most forms of writing, a neutral style is more appropriate. You may want to use a slightly formal style when writing for an audience older than you or for an audience that you have some obligation to. Remember, though, that formal does not mean pompous. Do not use very formal language to try to impress – it is more important to put your ideas across clearly.

Tip for success
Do not use different registers within the same piece of writing.

Sometimes words and phrases with a particular register are needed for specific types of writing. For instance, **legal documents** often contain extremely formal language, such as *hereunder* or Latin words such as *ex gratia*, which would be out of place in most other types of writing.

Similarly, some types of writing need to use very specific **technical terms**. For example, a document for medical professionals might use a word such as *suprarenal* instead of saying "above the kidneys" because this word will be understood by its readers. In scientific documents, the use of technical terms can be necessary to avoid any ambiguity.

At the other end of the scale, **literary or poetic language** such as *lovelorn*, *flaxen* or *the gloaming* may be appropriate in some types of creative writing.

Your choice of **grammar** and the way you **structure** your sentences can also affect register. Compare the following:

> *The man to whom I gave my ticket.*
> *The man I gave my ticket to.*

In the first sentence, the use of *whom* gives a formal feel to the sentence. In the second sentence, the preposition is used at the end. In the past this was considered incorrect, but it is now widely accepted, and would be appropriate for most types of writing.

It is not usually considered appropriate to use contractions (e.g., don't, he'd, wouldn't) in formal writing because they make the text sound informal.

Tone

The tone of your writing expresses your **attitude** towards the reader, and it is important that you be careful about this.

For instance, if you are writing to complain about a product or service, you need to come across as being assertive and clear about your facts. You must decide for yourself whether you want to be rude or threatening too – but if you are, make sure it is on purpose and not because you have chosen your words badly!

It can be useful to **imagine that you are talking to your reader**. What sort of tone do you want to take? For example, you might be:

chatty	authoritative	sincere	sympathetic
grateful	serious	assertive	humorous
persuasive	practical	unfriendly	offended
efficient	angry		

If you **think about what you want to achieve** with your writing, it will help you decide what tone to take. For example, if you are writing a letter to accept a job, you will probably want your tone to be friendly yet professional and show that you are pleased to have been chosen.

It is important to use language that is the **right level of difficulty** for your reader. If you use difficult words, you may sound as if you are showing off, but if you use very simple language, your reader might feel you are talking down to them.

An important issue that influences tone is the **relationship of the writer to the reader**. For instance, a suggestion for changes to working practices might have a very different tone coming from a junior employee than if it comes from a senior manager.

You should always take into account **how well you know the person** who will read your document. If you do not know them at all, you must be aware that they may be offended by an informal tone that is too familiar, or by expressing views that they may not share. Humor can also be difficult – if your readers do not know you, they may be unsure whether you are joking or not.

Compare the following letters:

> Dear Emma
>   Tom told me you broke your leg skiing – after I'd stopped laughing, it occurred to me that you must be a bit out of it, so I'm sending you these chocolates to cheer you up. See you when (if ???) you can walk again,
> Lizzie, x

> Dear Emma
>   I'm so sorry to hear about your skiing accident. Your mother told me you are likely to be in a cast for weeks, and I know how hard that will be for you. Do take good care of yourself, and I hope to hear some better news of you soon,
> with love from
> Aunt Bea

In the first letter, the tone is chatty and humorous, and while it might make Emma smile, if her injury is serious she might be offended that her friend is joking about it. However, if Lizzie is a very close friend, she will probably have judged the tone of the note appropriately. The second letter is much more sincere and serious and the tone shows that the writer is really concerned about Emma.

If you are angry about something, it can be very easy to let it show, sometimes without intending to. For example, look at this email:

> *Thanks for your offer of database training, but I really don't feel it's necessary, and I wouldn't want to distract you from your work, which is already behind schedule.*

The tone of the email makes it clear that the writer was offended by the offer of help and takes revenge by implying that the person offering help cannot manage their own work.

This may be what the writer intends, but if you would prefer to keep a good relationship with your colleague, something like the following would be better:

> *Thanks for the offer of database training, but I think I've managed to get to grips with it now, and I wouldn't want to take up your time unnecessarily as I know you are very busy.*

You should always think twice about expressing anger or other negative emotions in your writing: things you say aloud may be forgotten, but once you have written something you have created a record that may live far beyond anyone's memory of it.

> **Key point to remember**
> The tone you choose is up to you, but if your writing expresses an attitude, make sure this is what you intend.

Emphasis

We use emphasis to draw a reader's attention to the points that are most important. There are several ways of doing this:

- **Order within the document**. It is usual to start with the most important points.

- **Order within a sentence or paragraph**. The first part of the sentence will usually be seen as the most important. Compare the following:

  > A thorough safety assessment is needed urgently, following a number of accidents on the site.
  > Following a number of accidents on the site, a thorough safety assessment is needed urgently.

In the first example, the fact that the safety assessment is needed is emphasized by coming first in the sentence. In the second example, the fact that there have been some accidents comes across as the more important point. If you want to give special emphasis to a subject, consider writing your sentence in a way that isolates the most important thing at the end. For example:

> Following a number of accidents on the site it became clear that one thing was urgently needed: a thorough safety assessment.

- **A summary of main points**. This can be done in the conclusion of a document, or even as a list. For example, a detailed report might start with a section on "key findings" or "key recommendations" – simply a list of the main points the author wishes to make.

- **Amount of text**. The more important a point, the more space you are likely to use discussing it. If you add too much detail about minor points, readers may be confused about what is most important.

- **Blank space around a key phrase or sentence.** This is a somewhat dramatic way of emphasizing a key point but it may be appropriate in some kinds of writing:

  > *The evidence led to one clear conclusion:*
  > *He did not kill his wife.*

- **Typeface**. It is very simple to highlight words and phrases by using different forms of typeface such as **bold**, *italics* or <u>underlining</u>. Italics are probably the most commonly used:

  > Students should not bring cell phones to class *at any time*.
  > Make sure you take *all* your belongings with you.

Fonts can also be made larger or smaller for emphasis, or a different color may be used to make certain parts of a document stand out. Do not use color for emphasis, however, unless you are sure that your document will always be reproduced in color.

- **Repetition**. Repetition can be used in several ways to emphasize points. You could make a point and then repeat it immediately, using phrases such as:

  > *In other words ...*
  > *Put more simply ...*

This is a useful way to stress the point you are making and also to explain it in a different way so that you can be certain that all your readers will understand it.

If you are writing a long document, you may want to repeat certain points throughout it, using phrases such as:

  > *This demonstrates yet again ...*
  > *Again we see ...*

Repetition can also be a useful stylistic advice, in writing as well as in speech. You might repeat a word, a phrase, or part of a phrase:

> *They said local businesses would close – not true. They claimed jobs would be lost – not true. They claimed traffic would increase – not true.*

- **Headings**. Headings can be used to reinforce the main point that will be made in the parts they refer to.

- **Sudden change of style**. If readers are surprised by a sudden change of style, they may pay more attention to what is being said. One example would be to use a very short, snappy sentence after one or more longer, more flowing sentences:

> *Architects and engineers had assured officials and residents that the techniques used in constructing the bridge would ensure that it remained solid during an earthquake. It did not.*

- **Emphatic words and phrases**. These can highlight the most important points, e.g.:

> *Our priority now is ...*
> *The crucial advantage that this plan offers is ...*

In a similar way, sentence adverbs such as *crucially* or *above all* signal the importance of what follows, as do adjectives such as *urgent*, *vital*, or *essential*.

- **Punctuation.** The most obvious way to emphasize a sentence is to end it with an exclamation point:

> *We won over a thousand dollars!*

Be careful with exclamation points, though. It is fine to use them in informal letters, emails, etc., but do not use them too often. It is not usually appropriate to use them in more formal writing.

Structuring a sentence with a dash or a colon can also emphasize part of it. See, for example, how the second of these two sentences has more emphasis:

Critics described his performance as terrible.
Critics had one word for his performance: terrible.

Avoiding offense

A simple rule for avoiding offense is this:

Treat everyone equally in your writing, regardless of age, sex, race, sexual orientation or physical difference.

Always make sure that you are **aware of the customs and values of your readers**. For instance, for some readers it may be insensitive to assume that couples, even married couples, consist of a man and a woman. Another audience might be offended by the idea that a couple consists of anything except a man and a woman; so it is not always easy to find the correct balance.

Check that the terms you use for sensitive issues such as race and disability are the **modern**, **accepted terms**, and not old-fashioned terms that might be considered offensive.

Race and religion

It goes without saying that offensive racial or religious insults or stereotypes should never be used.

However, it can sometimes be easy to display discrimination without meaning to, simply because of our cultural background. Make sure you follow these general rules:

- **Only mention race or religion if it is relevant to your writing.** If you mention someone's race or religion, ask yourself if you would have mentioned it if it was the same as yours.

- **Make sure you use accepted modern terms,** not old-fashioned ones that many now consider offensive. For instance, a term such as *Red Indian* belongs only in old Westerns – for writing today, use *American Indian* or *Native American*. Similarly, the term *African American* is the preferred description for Americans of African origin.

- **Be aware of different cultures.** For instance, don't assume that everyone celebrates Christmas, or that July and August are always the hottest months of the year.

The accepted current term for people whose parent or ancestors are from different races is *mixed-race*. If you are in doubt about any terms connected with race or religion, check a good, recent dictionary.

Sexism

Here are some rules for avoiding sexism in your writing:

- **Use job titles that refer to both men and women**. For example, use *police officer* rather than *policeman*; *chair* or *chairperson* instead of *chairman*; *letter carrier* rather than *mailman*.

- **Avoid the suffix –ess on jobs.** Words like *authoress* and *poetess* are old-fashioned and patronizing, and should not be used. It is best to avoid the *–ess* suffix for jobs altogether: while the words *actress* and *waitress* are still used, many women in these professions prefer *actor* and *server*. Today there are preferred alternatives for most such words, such as *flight attendant* instead of *stewardess*.

- **Do not mention a person's sex if it is not relevant.** It is usually best to avoid terms such as *male nurse* or *lady doctor*.

- **Do not make assumptions about the sex of people in a particular profession.** Do not write things like "*businessmen and their wives.*"

- **Avoid stereotypes of roles and characteristics.** It's not necessarily Mom who cooks the dinner and Dad who fixes the car.

- **Avoid using masculine pronouns.** Sentences such as "Each traveler must present his documents" sound old-fashioned and sexist. Most people now consider it acceptable to use the pronoun *their* in such cases.

- **If you write to someone whose sex you do not know, do not begin your letter** *Dear Sir/s*. You could use *Dear Sir/Madam* in very formal situations, or choose another form of address altogether, e.g., *Dear Friends/Dear Supporters*.

Disability

When writing about illness and disability, there are several points to bear in mind:

- **Be sure to use current, accepted terms.** Use *bipolar disorder* rather than *manic depression*, for example.

- **Do not describe someone only by their illness.** Remember that they are a person first of all, so say *someone with epilepsy* rather than *an epileptic*.

- **Try not to portray someone with a disability as a victim.** Avoid words like *victim*, *afflicted with*, *suffering from*. Say *using a wheelchair* rather than *wheelchair-bound*.

- **Do not refer to people without a disability as** *normal*. Say *not handicapped* or *able-bodied* instead.

Increasing your vocabulary

The best way to increase your vocabulary is to **read a lot**. Be sure that your reading includes material that requires you to think and that contains some words that you will have to use a dictionary to understand better.

If you find a word you do not know, you will sometimes be able to get a good idea of its meaning from the other words around it. If not, **look it up in a dictionary**. It is not always a good idea to look up every new word as you find it, because it can be distracting, but you could **underline or highlight** some of the words and look them up later.

It can be useful to **keep a vocabulary notebook**, to record new words you have learned. You can arrange the words in whatever way is best for you: by alphabetical order or by subject.

Try to develop an interest in words, and ask yourself questions about them. For instance, you can widen your vocabulary by learning **words in groups**. If you know that *canine* refers to dogs, see if you know a word of the same kind that relates to cats (*feline*) or to cows (*bovine*). Similarly, if you know that *carnivorous* means "meat-eating," do you know the word for "plant-eating" (*herbivorous*) or for creatures that eat anything (*omnivorous*)?

Notice the context that words are in. You can often make your writing more elegant by choosing which words go together, such as the interesting verbs with the common nouns in these examples:

> *abandon* an attempt
> *draw* to a close
> *adopt* a method

Word games such as **crossword puzzles** can help to develop an interest in words and can introduce words you did not know before.

Using a thesaurus

A thesaurus is a reference book that shows lists of words with similar meanings. Some word processing systems have a thesaurus built into them, so that you can click on a word for suggestions of different words with similar meanings, and there are also many thesauruses online. Look at very common words in your writing and see if there are any more interesting or specific words you could use instead. You can use a thesaurus for this, but be careful to avoid the use of words completely unknown to you; you might well use them incorrectly:

if you have written ...	consider whether you could use ...
difficult	ambitious, demanding, grueling, knotty, laborious
eat	bolt, consume, gulp, sample, wolf down
boring	bland, characterless, dreary, insipid, soul-destroying

Using a dictionary

A good dictionary will help a lot with your writing. Try to use a
dictionary that is **suitable for you**. For instance, if you are in school,
a special **dictionary aimed at your level of study** should have all the
words you need for all your subjects, but not be too big to carry
around. If English is not your first language, try to use a **learner's**
dictionary, which will have simple definitions, lots of example
sentences, and all the grammar information you need.

Digital dictionaries

There are many types of digital dictionary available now. Tiny
handheld ones are easy to carry around, and may be useful for spelling
or quick look-ups, but the screens may be too small to show lots of
useful information.

A lot of book dictionaries come with either a **CD-ROM** or with a code
that gives you access to an **Internet dictionary**. You can use these
easily while you are working on the computer. Some of them will even
look up words for you if you put the cursor over the word you want.

CD-ROM and Internet dictionaries can be extremely useful because
they can do things that are impossible in paper books. For instance,
if you don't know how to spell a word, you can just type in the letters
you are sure of, and all the words containing those letters will be
found. Many of these dictionaries have extra information such as
synonyms and antonyms, the ability to search for vocabulary in topics,
and extra examples. You can also hear spoken pronunciations, rather
than trying to work them out from symbols.

Information in dictionaries

Dictionaries are not just for meanings and spelling, although of course these are very important uses. Dictionaries can give you information on:

- **Irregular inflections**. If words do not have regular patterns, this will be shown. For instance, you can see that the plural of *genus* is *genera* or that the past participle of *sink* is *sunk*.

- **Variant spellings**. You can see which words have more than one spelling, e.g., *caftan* and *kaftan*.

- **Regional information**. You can see when words and spellings are used in a particular variety of English, e.g., *courgette* is used in British English, but Americans say *zucchini* for the same vegetable.

- **Example sentences**. Many dictionaries give example sentences, showing how to use a word in context.

- **Etymology**. Large dictionaries often give information about the origins of words and phrases. This can be a very useful tool for helping you to remember which words are related to each other through a common ancestor.

- **Register**. A dictionary will tell you if a word is formal, informal, etc.

- **Pronunciation**. This is usually shown using a set of symbols that indicate sounds and stress.

- **Syllabification**. American dictionaries usually show the places in a word that divide syllables; this can be useful if you are writing by hand and need to know where a word can break.

Terms used in writing English

The following are important terms that refer to different styles of writing and types of words and phrases. You need to know them for studying literature, and also to be aware of them for use in your own writing.

Antonym

An antonym is a word with an opposite meaning. *Legal* and *illegal* are antonyms, as are *mature* and *immature*.

Alliteration

Alliteration is the use of the same letter or sound (especially consonants) at the beginning of two or more words that are close together in a sentence:

>   *droplets of dew at dawn*

Assonance

Assonance is the repetition of vowel sounds in two or more words that are close together in a sentence:

>   *I laughed, but my heart was torn apart.*

Euphemism

A euphemism is a word or phrase that is used to avoid talking directly about something that is embarrassing, upsetting, or offensive.

Euphemisms can be used in personal writing to show tact to your reader. For instance, in a letter of sympathy, some people prefer to use the euphemism *passed away* rather than *died*. Euphemisms can be used to avoid embarrassment to readers who are uncomfortable with words connected with sex or bodily functions.

Euphemisms are sometimes used in formal writing to deliberately disguise an unpleasant truth. For instance, a company press release might talk about *restructuring* or *downsizing* rather than *laying off employees*. In war, the terms *collateral damage* or *friendly fire* sound much less terrible than the reality of what they describe.

There is no place for euphemism in scientific or technical writing.

Figurative language

Figurative language is where an extra, more imaginative meaning comes from a literal meaning. For instance, the literal meaning of the word *chasm* is "a large hole in the ground," whereas the figurative meaning refers to a fundamental difference of opinion between people.

Idioms

Idioms are phrases such as *give someone a hand* and *be over the moon*, where the meaning is not the same as the literal meaning of all the words in the phrase.

Metaphor

Metaphor is the use of a particular word or phrase – usually a concrete noun – to describe the characteristics of something else. For instance, we might say *She has a heart of ice*, meaning that she shows no sympathy or emotion.

Proverbs

Proverbs are short sentences that many people know, often expressing advice, or something that many people believe to be true. Examples of proverbs are *A stitch in time saves nine* and *Spare the rod and spoil the child*.

Similes

Similes are phrases such as *as red as a beet* or *sing like an angel*, which compare one thing to another. The difference between a simile and a metaphor is that similes say that something is *like* something else, whereas a metaphor says something *is* something else.

Synonyms

Synonyms are words with the same or similar meanings. For instance, *smart* is a synonym of *intelligent*. However, it is important to note that words with similar meanings often have subtle differences in register or tone. *Purchase* is more formal than *buy*, for instance, while *slim* is a much more positive description than *skinny*.

Special information

Speech

There are two ways of writing about what someone said:

- In **direct speech**, we repeat the actual words used:

  "There is nothing we can do about it," Mona said.

- In **reported speech** (also called **indirect speech**), we make the words part of our own sentence, usually using a verb such as *say*, *tell*, or *explain*:

  Mona said that there was nothing we could do about it.

Direct speech

Direct speech is common in fiction and other writing where the actual words of speakers are quoted. The reporting verb (e.g., *say*, *tell*, *explain*) may come before the words that were spoken, or after them, or at a natural pause inside the reported sentence:

> ***Mona said**, "There is nothing we can do about it."*
> *"There is nothing we can do about it," **Mona said**.*
> *"It's no good," **Mona said**, "We'll just have to ask for help."*

The words spoken must be written inside double quotation marks. In British English, single quotation marks are usually used.

The words spoken always begin with a capital letter as long as the sentence is not divided by a reporting verb. The comma comes inside the quotation marks:

> *"Give her a chance," Jamie begged.*
> *"There is," Mona said, "nothing we can do about it."*

If the words spoken are a question or an exclamation, there is no comma but instead a question mark or an exclamation point, which comes inside the quotation marks:

> *"Why did you do it?" she asked.*
> *"Oh, mind your own business!" he snapped.*

The subject and reporting verb can be used either way around:

> *"There is nothing we can do about it,"* **Mona said**.
> *"There is nothing we can do about it,"* **said Mona**.

Tip for success
If you are writing a long stretch of direct speech between two characters, it is not always necessary to use reporting verbs each time. As long as it is clear which character is speaking, you can just start a new line within new quotation marks each time a different person speaks.

Reported speech

When you use reported speech, the words put into the reported clause do not exactly match the words actually spoken. For example, you will need to change pronouns, words like *here* and *there*, or the tense of the sentence:

> *"I believe* **you**.*"*
> *She said that she believed* **us**.
> *"I've been* **here** *before."*
> *He said that he had been* **there** *before.*
> *"* **I've done** *the housework."*
> *He said* **he had done** *the housework.*

Reported speech always has two clauses: the **reported clause**, which contains the words that were spoken, usually in a slightly different form; and the **main clause**, which contains the reporting verb. The main clause usually comes first:

> *Katie told me* that Marie is going to resign.
> *Sara asked* whether Hardeep was feeling better.

If the main reported clause is a statement, the main clause is linked to the reported clause by *that*:

> *Monique said **that** her favorite actor was Ben Kingsley.*
> *John replied **that** he preferred Scarlett Johansson.*

The linking word *that* can be left out after most reporting verbs except those that mean "answer":

> *She told me **(that)** she was going to leave.*
> *I replied **that** I was very sorry to hear that.*

If the reported clause is a question, the main verb will be a question word such as *ask, inquire, wonder, query*. The link between the main clause will be *if* or *whether*:

> *She asked me **if** I was comfortable.*
> *He inquired **whether** the changes had been made.*

Reported clauses can also be used to express what someone is thinking as well as what is actually spoken:

> *Hussain **wondered** whether **the concert would be sold out**.*
> *Charlotte **thought** that **she had better go and see her family**.*

> **Key point to remember**
> Speech in a reported clause is not separated from the reporting verb by a comma, is not enclosed in quotation marks, and does not begin with a capital letter unless it is a proper noun. Reported questions are not followed by question marks.

Questions

There are three main ways of making questions in English:

- With a **question word**, such as *who*, *why*, *how*:

    Who *won the race?*
    Which *team was it?*

- With an **auxiliary verb** (*do*, *have*, or *be*):

    Do *your children like sports?*
    Have *you seen her latest movie?*

- With a modal verb, such as *can* or *may*:

    Can *Mahmoud come too?*
    May *I see the letter?*

Occasionally, we express sentences by our tone of voice, but this would only be appropriate for written English if you are writing direct speech:

*"**She's left her job?** I thought she was happy there."*

Negative forms of questions almost always use contractions:

Doesn't *he like talking about his childhood?*
Can't *Peter have one too?*

If the full *not* form is used, it comes immediately after the subject. The full form is very formal:

Does *he* ***not*** *like talking about his childhood?*
Can *Peter* ***not*** *have one too?*

Questions should always have a question mark at the end, even if they are headings. The only time that a question does not have a question mark is if it is written in reported speech:

> *Do you like cats?*
> *He asked me if I liked cats.*

Sentence tags

Sentence tags look like short questions and are used at the end of sentences. They are sometimes called **question tags**, but many sentences ending with a tag are not real questions.

Tags are usually used to check if the listener or reader agrees with what the speaker or writer has said. Sentence tags are used very commonly in speech and in informal writing such as a chatty email, but rarely in formal written English.

If you need to write them, either in a piece of informal writing, or if you are quoting direct speech, remember that they have a comma before them, and a question mark at the end:

> *You've seen the program, haven't you?*
> *Well, we can't jump over it, can we?*
> *You aren't listening, are you?*

Quotations

There are many reasons to use quotations in your writing:

- To show how the **ideas and research of others** have contributed to your own work.

- To **add evidence** to your arguments, particularly from respected sources.

- To **show different opinions**, sometimes ones that conflict with yours.

- To **add interest or humor** to your writing. If someone has said something particularly clever or witty about your subject, it can liven up your text to quote it.

- In writing about literary works, to give **samples of text for analysis**.

However, do not include too many quotations. You are the author, and your ideas and analysis are the most important part of your writing. Your writing should not rely too heavily on quotations – they should be there to support your work but not to form the main part of it.

Make sure that any quotations you add are there for a good reason – do not put them in simply to make your document longer. Too many quotations can interrupt the flow of your writing and make the text seem cluttered.

Remember that there is a big difference between quoting and **plagiarizing**, which means using the work of others as if it were your own. Even if you use different words rather than quoting directly, if you are using someone else's ideas, you should say so.

Always make sure your quotations are **accurate**. If you have found your quotation as a quotation in someone else's work, you should go back to the original source, if possible, to check it.

It is **not necessary to use whole sentences** in quotes – in fact it is usually best to use only the parts that are relevant to your argument. However, if you take a sentence out of a paragraph, or a word or phrase out of a sentence, make sure that you do not change the author or speaker's intended meaning.

If you use a quote, you must always **explain why you have used it** and what you think its importance is. This can be done very simply. For example, if the quotation clearly backs up a point you have just made, you could use a phrase like:

> As Dr. X says ...

Other quotations may need more **analysis and explanation**. You cannot assume that your reader will draw the same conclusions from a quotation as you do, so you must make it very clear what you think its significance is. You might start your next sentence with phrases such as:

> This shows that ...
> [The author] is clearly of the opinion that ...
> Put more simply, this means ...

It is often useful to give a **context** for your quotation, for example, by explaining when and where it was written or spoken, or the situation that the writer or speaker was in.

How to show quotations

For long quotations (around 60 words or more), it is common to use a separate paragraph, indented slightly from the rest of the text and often using a slightly smaller font.

Shorter quotations are usually shown as part of a sentence:

> *Greenberg argued that "the law is the expression of underlying values of culture."*
> *She described the children as "motivated and alert."*

Quotations can also follow an introductory clause, using a colon or a comma before the inverted comma:

> *Charles made a pronouncement: "There will be no more discussion on this matter."*
> *Oscar Wilde once said, "Always forgive your enemies; nothing annoys them so much."*

If you are quoting lines of poetry, you can break the lines as they are in the original poem or show the ends of lines with a slash (/):

> *As an unperfect actor on the stage,/Who with his fear is put beside his part*

If you want to **omit part of a quotation**, you can use an ellipsis inside brackets, like this: [...]

> *She described the play as "racist in a way that was typical of that time, and deeply upsetting."*
> *She described the play as "racist [...] and deeply upsetting."*

If you want to add something to a quotation to make its meaning clearer, put the words you add inside brackets:

> *Giving evidence, the officer said, "I went to his house with Al [Albert Flynn, brother of the accused]."*

If a quotation contains an error, for instance of spelling or grammar, or if it contains something that is surprising, shocking or offensive, and you want to stress that this is *really* what the person said or wrote, use [*sic*], which is Latin for *thus*:

Clarke wrote that he "could of [sic] done it."
(This should be "could have done it.")

Quoting or paraphrasing?

Sometimes you may want to use your own words to explain what someone else has said. This is called paraphrasing. There could be several reasons for this:

- The original quote might be too long, so you need to summarize.
- The original quote might be written in language that is too difficult, so you need to simplify it.
- You might not want to break up your own text with too many direct quotes.
- You need to make a slight change to the original quotation (a verb tense, for example) in order to make it read correctly in your sentence.

Think about the purpose of your quotations. For example, in an essay on literature, it may be necessary to have a lot of quotations so that you can discuss and analyze the actual language of the author. For a science essay, it may be more appropriate to paraphrase most of the ideas you discuss.

If you do paraphrase, you must still make it clear whose work you are using. Make sure that your paraphrase does not change the meaning of the original in any way – if you want to add your own comments, or disagree, you must make it clear which are your ideas and which are the ideas of the person you are paraphrasing.

Referencing quotations

If you use a quotation, you should always say who the speaker or author is, and – if at all possible – what the source was.

This can be done **within the text**, using your own words to introduce the quotation:

> As Juliet says in Shakespeare's Romeo and Juliet, "Parting is such sweet sorrow."
> In a speech during his visit to Berlin in 1963, President John F. Kennedy famously said "Ich bin ein Berliner."

In **academic writing**, it is usual to refer to a footnote or a bibliography (list of books you used) to reference a quotation. Styles for this can vary, so it is a good idea to ask your teacher if there is a recommended style. A common way is to show the author and the date of the publication in parentheses in the main text, then show the whole source in the bibliography.

In the text:

> As Prof. Williams points out: "There is a measurable difference between the amount people claim to eat and the amount they actually eat." (Williams, 2007, p. 25)

In the bibliography:

> Williams, J. (2007) The Causes of Obesity. Newtown: Newtown University Press.

If you use a **quotation from a website**, you must reference it in a similar way. Again, there are different styles for this, but a common way is:

> Author, A (date) Title of article or web page. Available at: article. com. Accessed on 10/04/2010

Proper nouns

Names of people

Names of people should always begin with capital letters:

> *Ivan Gorecki*
> *Julia Jones*

Titles, such as *Mr.*, *Mrs.*, *Ms.*, *Dr.* are written with periods in American English, but *often* without them in other varieties of English:

> *Ms. Hooper*
> *Prof. McCarthy*

Geographical terms

Remember to use capital letters for all of the following:

- Countries and other political divisions, e.g., *Japan*, *Denver*, *Sierra County*, *Chicago's Pullman neighborhood*, *Halsted Street*
- Nationalities, e.g., *Japanese*, *Swedish*
- Other geographical locations, e.g., *Mount Everest*, *Lake Tahoe*, *the Ohio River*
- Languages, e.g., *French*, *Swahili*

When writing geographical names that begin with *the*, it is more common to use a lower case:

> *the United States*
> *the Alps*

Names of companies and products

Names of companies and products usually have capital letters:

> *Nokia*®
> *Coca-Cola*®

Be careful to spell the name of companies and products exactly as they are spelled by their owners. For instance, the name of the publisher of this book is *HarperCollins*, with no space before the second capital letter.

In formal writing or writing that is to be published, you need to find out if a company name or product name is a registered trademark, and if it is, to put a trademark symbol (® or ™) after the word.

Names of books, plays, movies, etc.

Capital letters are used for the first letter in titles of books, magazines, newspapers, TV shows, movies, etc. Where there are several words, capitals are usually used for the main content words. This means that short prepositions and articles typically begin with a small letter, but longer prepositions and pronouns, even short ones, usually begin with a capital:

> *The Wall Street Journal*
> *The Merchant of Venice*
> *Gone with the Wind*
> *All About My Mother*

If you mention titles such as these in your text, they should be in italic:

> He decided to write a letter to *The Times*.
> Her last book, *Diary of a Wife*, deals with the subject of domestic violence.

The exceptions to this rule are the Bible and the Koran, which remain in ordinary type.

Abbreviations

It can sometimes be difficult to decide when to use periods in abbreviations. In British English, it is becoming more common to use abbreviations without periods, while in American English, they are used more often. In both varieties of English, there are some forms of abbreviation where it is more common to use periods than others.

In some cases, you may make your decision based on the need to avoid ambiguity, e.g., *a.m.* rather than *am*. Make sure that you treat each form consistently throughout your text.

You must be certain that your readers will understand any abbreviations you use. It is safe to use widely understood abbreviations like *NBC* or *FBI*, though even in these cases, if your audience is not American, you may need to add an explanation. However, less common abbreviations could puzzle your readers, so it is best either to avoid them, or to put the full form in parentheses the first time you use them.

There are a few abbreviations that are so widely used that it is not necessary to give the full forms at all. Examples include *USA*, *DNA*, *HIV*, *ATM* and the abbreviations for the main North American time zone designations such as *EDT* and *PST*.

Abbreviations formed from the first letter of all the words can be spelled with or without periods, though it is now more common to omit them:

> *NBC (National Broadcasting Corporation)*
> *FBI (Federal Bureau of Investigation)*

Abbreviations formed from the first part of a word usually need periods:

> *Prof. (Professor)*
> *Oct. (October)*

Abbreviations formed from the first and last letters of a word have a period in American English but usually not in British English:

> St. *(street or saint)*
> Dr. *(doctor)*

Abbreviations formed from Latin words use periods:

> e.g. *(exempli gratia = for example)*
> i.e. *(id est = that is to say)*
> etc. *(et cetera = and the other things)*

However, the common Latin abbreviation *AD (anno domini = in the year of the lord)* and its earlier partner *BC (= before Christ)* are now more commonly used without periods.

Abbreviations for metric scientific measurements are often formed from the first letter of each of the parts of a compound word. They do not use periods, and you do not add an *s* to form their plurals:

> kg **(k**ilo**g**ram *or kilograms)*
> ml **(m**illi**l**iter *or milliliters)*

Abbreviations for imperial measurements are often very irregular, and usually have periods. Like metric abbreviations, they do not add *s* in the plural:

> oz. *(ounce or ounces)* Comes from the Italian word *onza*
> lb. *(pound or pounds, in weight)* Comes from the Latin word *libra*

Acronyms

Acronyms are words formed from the first letters of several words or from parts of words. If the word is formed only from the first letter of several words, it is properly called an initialism, though most people call these acronyms as well. The difference between acronyms and other abbreviations is that acronyms are pronounced as words themselves, rather than as individual letters:

> *NATO (North Atlantic Treaty Organization)*
> *GUI (graphical user interface)*

Acronyms are not usually written with periods. In fact, many acronyms make a journey from being abbreviations to becoming words in their own right. Nobody really thinks of words like *laser* (*Light Amplification by Stimulated Emission of Radiation*) or *scuba* (*self contained underwater breathing apparatus*) as being abbreviations at all, but they did start out that way.

Numbers

Numbers can be written using figures or letters:

1   *one*
350   *three hundred and fifty*
1,299   *one thousand, two hundred and ninety-nine*

Note that you put a comma or, less usually, a space between each group of three figures, counting from the right:

3,490
2 350 100

In mathematical and scientific writing, numbers are always written as figures. In general writing, you can use words or figures:

480 coulombs is equivalent to 0.005 faradays.
About two hundred people attended the meeting.
We'll need 50 chairs.

It is quite common to use words for numbers less than 10, and figures for larger numbers. Whatever you decide, be consistent throughout your writing.

However, if you have two numbers together, you may use a combination to avoid confusion:

Three 5-year-olds were hurt in a car accident near Lexington.

Very large numbers in the millions, billions or even higher are usually written like this:

40 million
3 billion

Notice that there is no *s* on the end of *million* and *billion* here.

When there has been more than one king or queen with the same name, or sometimes when a man has the same name as his father, grandfather, etc., their names are followed by an ordinal number, usually written in roman numerals:

> *Henry VIII*
> *George Hamilton IV*

Tip for success
Take care with spelling the number *forty* – there is no *u* in it.

Dates

There are several accepted ways of writing dates:

> June 11, 1961
> 11 June 1961
> 6.11.61
> 06/11/1961

The style you choose will depend on what you are writing – the longer styles are suitable for essays, polite letters or other formal writing, while the shorter styles are used in quick emails, filling in forms, etc. Note that the American style of writing dates is different from most other countries'. The usual American style is in the order: month – day – year. British English, and many other languages, prefer to use the order: day – month – year.

If you are writing about centuries, the most common style is:

> *During the 15th century ...*

Remember that the name of the century is always the number above the beginning of the years in it, so for instance 1492 is in the 15th century, and 1997 is in the 20th century.

When we are writing about history, the abbreviations *BC* and *AD* are used for dates before and after the birth of Christ.

AH (for Latin *anno Hegirae*, year of the Hegira) designates years in the Muslim calendar. AH 1 is the equivalent of AD 622.

Tip for success
Note that non-Christian writers often prefer to avoid the abbreviations *BC* and *AD* and use the equivalents *BCE* (*before the common era*) and *CE* (*of the common era*) instead.

Foreign words and phrases

There are many words in English that come from other languages originally, but then become so absorbed into English that we do not think of them as being foreign any more. Examples are *bazaar* from Persian, *karate* from Japanese and *intelligentsia* from Russian. These words are used in just the same way as any other English words.

However, for a word or phrase that is not fully naturalized as English, *italics* are often used:

> The same complaint was repeated *ad nauseam*.
> (Latin = until we were sickened.)
> *Entre nous*, his finances are in a perilous state.
> (French = between ourselves.)
> Her writings displayed a bleak *Weltanschauung*.
> (German = view of life and the world.)

Sometimes it can be difficult to decide if a word has entered mainstream English. If you are unsure whether or not to use italics, consider whether your reader is likely to think of the word or phrase as being part of normal English.

For instance, if you know a lot about yoga, terms such as *chi* (vital energy) and *chakra* (one of the points of physical or spiritual energy) will probably be well known to you. If you are writing for an audience which is also knowledgeable about yoga, you can probably use them without italics and without explanation. However, if your writing is for a general audience, it is best to use italics to indicate that these are words of foreign origin (Chinese and Sanskrit), and also to explain them, at least the first time they are used.

Many foreign words and phrases will only be suitable in very formal or intellectual forms of writing.

Checking your work

General checks

It is important to **leave time to check your work**, so that the finished quality is as high as possible. Checking falls into two main areas:

- **Overall structure and content**.

- **Detailed points of spelling, grammar, punctuation, etc.**

If you have planned your work carefully and written one or more drafts, as described in the section on Planning in this book, your work should already be logical and well structured. However, even for a short piece of writing, such as a letter or work email, it is worth asking yourself the following questions:

- Has my writing achieved what I wanted it to achieve?
- Have I expressed my points clearly?
- Do my ideas or pieces of information come in a logical sequence?
- Do I have enough evidence to support my points?
- Is the tone of my writing what I wanted it to be?
- Have I included everything I wanted to include?

It can often be a good idea to **ask someone else** to correct your work – your eyes will see what you *intended* to write, whereas someone else may spot errors more easily.

> **Tip for success**
> Many people find it easier to check their work on paper rather than on a computer screen, so if it is important that it is correct, consider printing it out.

Checking spelling

It is important to make sure your spelling is correct. There is a section on spelling in this book that gives general rules, and also a section on words that are often misspelled.

Use your instinct: if a word looks wrong, check it in a dictionary. You can also use a spellchecker on your computer, but make sure that it is set to the variety of English you want: most word processing programs have spelling dictionaries for several varieties of English.

General points to look out for include:

- **Homophones**. These are words that sound the same but are spelled differently, e.g., their/there, witch/which, bare/bear. Remember that the spellchecker on your computer will not be able to find errors in homophones because they are both correct words.

- **Letters that are the wrong way around**. It is very easy to make this kind of error when you are typing your work, for instance typing "form" instead of "from." Since both of these are correct spellings of English words, your spellchecker will not flag them.

- **Missing letters**. Make sure you do not leave out silent letters in words such as *government*, or forget to double the consonant in words such as *swimming*.

> **Tip for success**
> Take particular care with typed writing – it is much easier to make a mistake with fingers on keys than with a pen.

Checking grammar and punctuation

There are sections on grammar and punctuation in this book that give general rules, and also a section on common errors.

General points to look out for include:

- **Apostrophes**. Make sure you have put them in where they are needed and left them out where they are not.

- **Capital letters**. Make sure that all proper nouns have capital letters. It is also a common error to put a lower case "i" where the upper case pronoun "I" is needed.

- **Repeated words**. These are often found at the end of one line and the beginning of another.

- **Missing words**. It can be very easy to leave out little words such as "of" or "in," and equally difficult to spot that they are missing, since your mind can compensate by adding them in unconsciously when you read.

- **Agreement.** This means making sure that all the parts of a sentence relate correctly to each other, avoiding mistakes such as *"We was asked to contribute."* (Should be: *We were asked to contribute.*)

Be especially careful to read sentences that you have changed at some point in your writing. See below under "Checking work written on a computer."

If you are using your computer to write, you will probably have a grammar checker available. This will pick up some common problems, but you should still check your work yourself.

> **Tip for success**
> Do not try to correct huge pieces of text in one go –
> you need to be fresh to be able to spot errors.

Other things to check

- **Facts and information.** If there is any doubt about the source of your information, for instance if it came from a website you are not sure is reliable, make sure you can confirm it in another, more reliable source.

- **Numbers.** Always check numbers, especially long ones such as telephone numbers. It is very easy to make a mistake when you type these.

- **Dates**. If you tell people a meeting is on Thursday the 6th, but the 6th is a Wednesday, you will cause confusion.

- **Repetition of words and phrases**. As you were writing, you may not have realized that you used the same word or phrase over and over again, but when you check at the end – especially if you read your work aloud – you will notice this, and can vary your words if you want to.

- **References**. If you have referred to another book, paper, etc., make sure you have acknowledged it and referenced it properly. In the same way, if you have used charts, diagrams, etc., make sure there are references to them all in the text.

- **Cross-references.** If you have a long document, with many different, numbered sections, you may want to cross-refer from one to another. It is best to do this at the end, when your section headings will not change. If you are writing on a computer, you will be able to set up your document so that cross-references change automatically if the heading numbers change.

Checking work written on a computer

In many ways, computers have made all sorts of writing much easier, especially because we can correct mistakes and move around sections of text without having to write everything out again. However, this also means that it is very easy to introduce mistakes.

If you correct one word in a sentence or one part of a sentence, take great care to make sure that the whole sentence is still correct. For instance, it is very easy to leave in words that are not needed. Look at the following example:

> *She had an important role in his career.*
> *His mother played had an important role in his career.*

The writer only deleted "*she*" instead of "*she had*" when making this correction, leading to an extra verb in the sentence.

Remember, too, to make sure that agreement within a sentence is not affected by a change to part of it:

> *I gave my passport to the officer, who looked at it closely.*
> *I gave my passport and driver's license to the officer, who looked at it closely.*

In this case, the writer has added the words "and driver's license" but has forgotten to change the pronoun *it* later in the sentence to *them*.

> **Tip for success**
> If you decide to move a section of text, make sure that you have deleted it from where it was originally.

Marking your corrections

Printing out your work and reading through it on paper can be a helpful way of spotting mistakes. It is usually best to **mark up a whole document or section of a document** on paper before you actually make the changes on the computer. Making each change as you spot it will probably be inefficient and distracting.

When people do **proofreading** in a formal way, there is a set of standard marks that they use. It is unlikely that you will need to learn formal proofreading marks, but some of them can be useful, as they are a clear way of showing your changes, particularly if you are **correcting someone else's writing**.

For example, the mark ^ shows *where* something is to be added, and the text in the margin shows *what* is to be added. The symbol # shows where a space should be added and the symbol ⌐ in the margin indicates that the words in the text with a line through them should be deleted.

There are several books and websites that explain how to use proofreading symbols.

If you are **correcting someone else's work on screen**, it can be useful to use a system that shows the changes you suggest, rather than simply making the changes yourself. That way, an author or editor can decide whether to accept or reject your corrections. You can also leave explanations, comments, and suggestions that another reader can delete later.

Writing

Formal or work emails

Email is much faster than writing letters. You can receive a reply to an email within seconds – or minutes – of sending one. In this way, email is more **like conversation** than paper-based writing. This is its great advantage: email communication, like conversation, can be **two-way** and **almost immediate**. This speed can also be its weakness when people do not take enough care writing emails, especially formal or work emails.

First, here are some general points about email to keep in mind:

- Email tends to be brief.
- Email is generally less formal than communication on paper.
- Email does not communicate emotions as successfully as face-to-face or even telephone conversations. The reader of your email may not be able to tell from your words if you are serious or joking, angry or just surprised.
- Emails, especially very short emails, can sound angry, unfriendly or rude when this is not intended by the writer.

> **Key point to remember**
> Emails that are written very quickly and carelessly can sound unfriendly and rude.

The **rules are less strict** for writing formal or work *emails* than for writing formal *letters*. People have been writing letters for many hundreds of years so rules have had time to develop. Email, as a more recent form of communication, is much less fixed in its rules.

The **rules are** also **different** in different countries and cultures and in different places of work. This point is worth remembering. What is right for one group of people may not be right for all people.

It is also true to say that **everyone** has **their own style** of writing email. Even within the same company, two people may take very different approaches to this form of communication.

The points laid out in this unit are therefore a **guide to writing formal emails**. By following these generally accepted rules, you will get the most out of email. You will also avoid some of the most frequent problems that arise from this form of communication.

> **Tip for success**
> When you join a new company, notice how your colleagues write their emails and consider changing your style to fit in with the company style.

Salutations for formal emails
(Words or phrases used for saying hello)

It is generally a good idea to **start an email with a greeting** rather than beginning the message immediately. Just like a face-to-face exchange of greetings, email greetings:

- show that you are friendly and pleasant
- show respect for the reader

In addition, a greeting allows the reader to pause for a moment before reading the message itself.

If, however, you and a colleague are writing a series of short emails to each other on a particular subject, the rules are different. It is generally acceptable after the first exchange of emails to include only the information, without greetings.

Note that if you are using **instant messaging**, which is an even faster method of communication, you only need to add a salutation to the first in a series of messages that you send to someone.

There are no fixed rules for the type of greeting that you use. Generally, if you are emailing someone that you work with or even someone that you do not know, it is acceptable to **start the email** with a simple "**Hello**" or "**Hello James.**" (If you know the colleague well, "**Hi**" or "**Hi James**" might also be fine.)

You may want to **show more respect** in your greeting, perhaps if the person is much older than you, has a higher rank than you in the same company, or is from a country or culture that is more formal than yours. If you are in any doubt about this, you could address the person, "**Dear Mr. Sanchez**" or "**Dear Ms. Sanchez.**"

If you receive an email and the sender of the message has used his or her first name only, it is **acceptable to use their first name** when you reply.

> **Key point to remember**
> If you decide to use the more formal salutation "Dear Mr. Sanchez" or "Dear Ms. Sanchez," make sure that you use the correct title. If the person you are emailing is a doctor, for example, be sure to include that in the salutation.

Subject lines

People who use email for work often complain that they receive too much email and that it takes up too much of their time dealing with it.

You can help with this situation by **making full use of the subject line**. The subject line gives you the chance to tell the reader of your email **why you are emailing them** before they have even opened your message.

For example, if you are emailing a company to ask for information about a product, in the subject line, write the name of the product and the fact that you need information:

> Subject: Balance bike (ref: N765) info required

The subject line gives you the chance to **show the main points** of your email. If you start to type "Hi" or "Another thing" in the subject line, think for a moment whether you can replace it with something more useful.

Look at the following subject lines and see how, in only a few words, you can show the main points of an email:

> Subject: Meeting Room changed to 307

> Subject: Lunch (Fri 9 Oct) canceled

> Subject: REQ: Feb sales figures

> Subject: Reminder: conference agenda due

Tip for Success
Write a useful subject line that says in just a few words what your email is about and what, if any, action you need the reader to take.

Content and length

Before you even start to type your message, make sure you can answer the following two questions:

- Why am I writing this?
- What do I want the reader of this email to do?

Remember that most people receive a lot of email in the course of a working day. For this reason, they do not welcome long emails! Your job is therefore to **tell them your point or points quickly and clearly**. Here are a few tips to help you do this:

- Make the first sentence count. Introduce the topic of the email clearly and in a few words.

- Write in short paragraphs. Separate paragraphs, each relating to a different point, will make the information easier to understand. Do not allow important points to get lost in one long paragraph.

- Consider using headings within the body of your message if the message relates to several different subjects.

- Consider numbering your points. The reader will find this useful when responding to particular points.

- Leave a space between each paragraph.

- Use short sentences. Try to keep your sentences to a maximum of 20 words. These can be quickly read and understood.

- If possible, try to fit your message onto one screen so that the reader does not have to scroll down to see the rest of it.

Read the following email. Consider:

- Is the information presented in the clearest way?

- Did the writer think about the needs of the reader as she wrote her email?

Subject: conference dinner
From: "Hill, Lucy" <Lucy.Hill@bigbooks.co.uk>
To: "Ollie Walsh"

Hi Ollie

Thanks again for offering to help out with the arrangements for the conference dinner. I appreciate it. I met with David yesterday to finalize details and here's what we decided: The venue (Carmichael Hall) is reserved for Dec 18th, 7:00–12:00. Your contact there is Julia Winters (354 638-9761). Invitations should go out to all conference delegates the week starting November 3rd. The invitations are currently with the printers, btw, and when they are returned to us (this Friday) will need checking against the original delegate list which I'll get Sujata to send to you. Hallidays, the caterers, will need to know final numbers by Dec. 10th at the latest. Please call them to let them know. Last, could you please check with Sujata over the timing of the speeches and let the relevant people know when their slot is.

Many thanks,
Lucy

Now see how much clearer the same message looks when the writer considers what will be most helpful to the reader and has:

• broken the text up into separate, short paragraphs

• given each paragraph a heading

• allowed plenty of white space

Subject: conference dinner
From: "Hill, Lucy" <Lucy.Hill@bigbooks.com>
To: "Ollie Walsh"

Hi Ollie

Thanks again for offering to help out with the arrangements for the conference dinner. I appreciate it. I met with David yesterday to finalize details and here's what we decided:

Venue
The venue (Carmichael Hall) is reserved for Dec 18th, 7:00–12:00. Your contact there is Julia Winters (354 638-9761)

Invitations
The invitations are currently with the printers. When they are returned to us (this Friday) they will need checking against the original delegate list, which I'll get Sujata to send to you. Invitations should go out to all conference delegates the week starting November 3rd.

The caterers
Hallidays, the caterers, will need to know final numbers by Dec. 10th. Please call them to let them know.

Speeches
Last of all, could you please check with Sujata over the timing of the speeches and let the relevant people know when their slot is.

Many thanks,
Lucy

Tone

Read the following email and ask yourself how the writer was feeling when he wrote it:

Subject: conference dinner
From: "Walsh, Ollie" <Ollie.Walsh@bigbooks.com>
To: "Lucy Hill"

Lucy,

There are problems re the arrangements for the conference dinner:

1. The invitations just arrived this morning so I will be late sending them out.

2. Julia Winters called late yesterday. She was under the impression that 150 people were attending. Sujata's list says it's 170. Which of these is right?

3. Re the speeches, Alice and David are fine with 10 minutes each but Michael wants 15 minutes. Is he allowed 15 minutes? Also, you didn't ask Sandra to speak and she's offended. Did you mean not to ask her or is this an oversight?

Ollie

Perhaps the writer of this email was angry or stressed. That is certainly the impression that his email gives. However, it is possible that he was neither angry not stressed: he simply needed advice from Lucy about how to act. Supposing he was not angry, how might he have written exactly the same questions but in a polite and pleasant way?

Now compare the tone of the previous email with this email:

Dear Lucy,

I'm afraid[1] there are a few problems re the arrangements for the conference dinner: (This shouldn't make too much difference.[2])

1. FYI, the invitations only arrived this morning so I'm afraid I will be a day late sending them out.

2. Julia Winters called late yesterday. She was under the impression that 150 people were attending. Sujata's list says it's 170. Do you know[3] which of these figures is right?

3. Re the speeches, Alice and David are fine with 10 minutes each but Michael would prefer[4] 15 minutes. Is this possible? Also, I have heard that Sandra Winters would like to speak too. This may not be possible but I thought I'd let you know.[5]

Best,
Ollie

Here the writer explains the same problems and asks the same questions without making the reader feel that the problems are all her fault. Notice how:

[1] Before he tells her about a problem, he writes "I'm afraid ..."
[2] He tells her about a problem but lets her know that it is not serious.
[3] He adds "Do you know" to the question, which softens it.
[4] He uses the polite phrase "would prefer" rather than the direct verb "wants."
[5] In the first version of the email he blames the reader (you didn't ask Sandra to speak and she's offended). Here, he simply lets the reader know that there is a problem. She can then decide what to do.

Generally, people intend their emails to be **polite and pleasant** –
or at least neutral. However, because emails are often brief and
quickly written, they can sometimes sound slightly demanding,
angry, or even rude.

Remember that the reader of your email **cannot see you smile** and
cannot hear that your voice is friendly. Try to be aware of this
potential problem and to develop ways of showing that you are polite
and friendly through the words that you write. This is *especially* true if
the person you are emailing has never met you.

If you are emailing someone that you have spoken or written to before,
consider starting your message by saying "**I hope you are well**." Again,
this lets the reader know that you are friendly and pleasant.

It is fine to keep your emails brief, but **not too brief**. You want to
communicate quickly and efficiently but you still need to show respect
to the reader and to show that you have considered their feelings. This
can be difficult, especially when you are in a hurry, but it is important.
If, for example, you are giving a piece of bad news, start your sentence
with "I'm afraid ..." or "I'm sorry ..." rather than just stating the problem.

Be aware that verbs used in **the passive can sound a little formal**.
For example "The sales report that you were sent in February" (passive)
sounds slightly formal (whereas "the sales report that I sent you in
February" (active) does not). This is fine if you want to write a slightly
formal email. If you are emailing a colleague that you know well,
and want to write a friendlier email, however, you may want to avoid
this structure.

Do not write using all UPPER-CASE LETTERS. People sometimes use
upper-case letters to show the difference between their own writing
and someone else's. This may make the reader think that you are angry
and shouting. Upper-case letters are also more difficult to read than
lower-case letters.

Always read an email that you have written before you send it, especially if you are writing to disagree with someone. **Imagine that you are the reader** and try to **read the email as they will read it**. Does it sound angry, aggressive, or demanding and, if so, is that *really* what you intended? If you are in any doubt, do not send the email immediately. Save it and read it later in the day when you are feeling calm and can judge whether you need to change it.

> **Tip for success**
> Before you send an email, read it to check that the tone
> of it is what you intended.

Punctuation and abbreviations

Generally, the rules for spelling, grammar, and punctuation that apply to letter-writing also apply to formal or work emails:

- Bad spelling, grammar, and punctuation may give the reader a bad opinion of you and of your company, if you work for one.
- In addition, they may make your message unclear or confusing. In particular, emails that lack periods or commas are difficult to read.

It is generally agreed that **contractions** (I'm, he's, can't, etc.) **are acceptable** in most formal or work emails. In formal *letters*, the full form of the words should be used but, as we have said before, formal emails are less formal than formal letters.

Other abbreviations, such as "U" for "you," "plz" for "please," and "thx" for "thanks," though often used in personal email, are generally not acceptable in formal or work emails.

Likewise, emoticons or smileys ☺ are not generally used in formal or work emails:

- They are considered too informal or familiar.

- There is a risk that the reader will not understand what you mean by these symbols.

> **Tip for success**
> Always read an email before you send it, to check for errors.

Ending a formal email

Between the main part of the email and the signoff, (the part that says goodbye), there is often a line linking the two.

What you write at this point will, of course, depend on the purpose of your email, but here are a few typical sentences that are often used:

- *I hope to hear from you soon.*
- *I look forward to hearing from you.*
- *I look forward to your response.*
- *Many thanks for your time.*
- *Thanks again for this.*
- *Many thanks in advance.*
- *Thank you for taking the time to answer my questions.*
- *I hope this helps.*
- *Please get in touch if you have any more queries.*
- *Please do not hesitate to get in touch if you have any questions.*
- *Let me know what you think.*

Just as it is a good idea to start an email with a greeting, it is also **polite to finish an email with a signoff**. Not everyone does this: some people end an email by typing their name alone. But an email that ends without a signoff can sound a little rude, especially if the content of the email has included a disagreement or problem.

A number of signoffs are commonly used in formal or work emails. Again, there are no fixed rules for the type of signoff that you use. The phrases below are some of the most common.

- *Many thanks*
- *Thank you*
- *Thanks again*
- *Best*
- *Regards*
- *Best regards*
- *Kind regards*
- *Warm regards*
- *Best wishes*
- *With best wishes*

Below is an example of a slightly formal email. The sender of the email (an artist), is replying to a person who has made an enquiry about her work. They have never met each other. Notice the tone, which is polite and friendly but still slightly formal.

Subject: paintings
From: "Lewis, Lara" <lara.lewis@macp.com>
To: "Michael Peters"

Hello Michael,

Thank you for your inquiry.

I am a studio artist at Multnomah Arts Center in Portland. You are welcome to visit me there anytime and have a look at the paintings I have available (no obligation of course!).

I also attend events around the country as you can see in the 2010 Events page on my website.

Prices start at $250 for the small paintings (approx. 8" x 12"). The larger paintings are about $600 (12" x 15") depending on the piece.

I also undertake commissions if you have something specific in mind.

Please give me a call on (503) 459-8253 if you would like to come to my studio and we can arrange a suitable time.

Kind regards,
Lara

This email is sent from one colleague to another. This time, as the sender and reader know each other, the tone is slightly less formal, though it is still formal enough to be suitable for work.

Subject: minutes (meeting 03/20/10)
From: "Rose, Andrew" <andrew.rose@wentworths.com>
To: "Helena Ghiotto"

Hi Helena,

I'm attaching the minutes from yesterday's meeting.

Thanks very much for coming to the meeting. I think we all found it very useful to have your sales perspective on the various issues. Sophia and I agreed that it would be good to have you or Chris present at such meetings in the future. Perhaps we could discuss this over coffee sometime?

Would you mind emailing me a copy of Jeanne's report? Thanks in advance.

Have a good trip – and please say hi to Carlo from me.

Best,
Andrew

Informal or social emails

The rules for writing informal or social emails are very relaxed. Generally, when people email their friends, **they write as they speak**. They use the same words as they would use in speech and they put those words together in much the same way.

Salutations
(Words or phrases used for saying hello, also called greetings.)

People generally **start informal emails with a greeting** in order to sound friendly. There are no fixed rules for the type of greeting used. Generally, people write "**Hi**" or "**Hi Julia**" or "**Hello**" or "**Hello Julia**." Sometimes there is no greeting and the name of the reader alone is used.

Tone

As we have said before, email does not communicate emotions very clearly. The reader of an email cannot see the sender's face or hear their voice and they may struggle to work out how they are feeling. This is especially true when an email has been written very quickly or with little care. One solution to this problem is the **smiley** or **emoticon**, a typed symbol representing a face. Smileys are used either to show how the sender feels or to show the tone of an email when the words alone do not make this clear. The most common of these smileys are shown below:

☺ or ☻	I am happy/pleased/friendly.
☹ or ☺	I am sad, disappointed, or fed up.
☺	I am enthusiastic/eager.
☺	I am surprised or shocked.
☺	I am joking/being sarcastic.

Punctuation and abbreviations

Some people take care to punctuate their informal emails correctly but many do not. For example, it is quite common to see informal emails written completely in lower-case letters. Generally, people do not expect perfect punctuation in this type of email.

Emails **often include abbreviations**. Some of the most common abbreviations are shown below. It is worth remembering when you use one of these that not everyone knows what all these abbreviations mean.

AFAIK	As Far As I Know	IMHO	In My Humble Opinion
AKA	Also Known As	IOW	In Other Words
ASAP	As Soon As Possible	IRL	In Real Life
B4	Before	L8R	Later
BTW	By The Way	LOL	Laughing Out Loud
CUL8R	See You Later	NSFW	Not Safe For Work
CYA	See Ya	OTOH	On The Other Hand
CYU	See You	POV	Point Of View
FWIW	For What It's Worth	ROTFL	Rolling On The Floor Laughing
FYA	For Your Amusement	TAFN	That's All For Now
FYI	For Your Information	TIA	Thanks In Advance
HTH	Hope This Helps	TTYL	Talk To You Later
IGWS	It Goes Without Saying	TTFN	Ta Ta For Now
IMO	In My Opinion	THX	Thanks

Ending an informal email

As with email openings, there are no fixed rules for how to end informal emails. In a very quickly written email there may be no signoff (the part before the name that says goodbye), or just the name of the sender. Sometimes, people write only the first letter of their name instead of their whole name. However, **most people like to use a signoff** because it is friendly. Additionally, between the main part of the email and the signoff, there is often an extra line linking the two. Below are some examples:

- *Talk to you later.*
- *Hope you're doing okay/well.*
- *Hope you're all well.*
- *See you soon.*
- *Better go now.*
- *Tell you more when we speak.*
- *Have a good weekend.*
- *Hope to see you soon.*

A number of signoffs are commonly used in informal emails before the name of the sender. The phrases below are some of the most frequent:

- *Love*
- *Lots of love*
- *Take care*
- *Ciao*
- *Later*
- *See you*
- *See ya!*
- *Cheers!*

Text messages

Texting (more formally, text messaging) between cell phones is an extremely popular form of communication. Its great advantage is that it allows people to communicate almost as quickly as spoken language in situations where speech is not suitable.

Text messages (or informally, texts) are **short** as there is a limit to the number of characters that can be used in each message. Because of this, a special language of **text abbreviations** has developed. Some of these abbreviations include numbers as well as letters. Here are some of the most common text abbreviations with their meanings:

@	at	gr8	great	tx/thx	thanks
2	to, too or two	ic	I see	u	you
2day	today	l8	late	w8	wait
2moro	tomorrow	l8r	later	wan2	want to
4	for	lo	hello	wk	week
aml	all my love	m8	mate	wrk	work
b4	before	pls	please	xlnt	excellent
btw	by the way	r	are	y	why
c	see	some1	someone		
cm	call me	spk	speak		
cu	see you	sry	sorry		
cul	see you later	syl	see you later		

Sometimes people also use **smileys** or **emoticons** in their texts. These are typed symbols representing a face, as shown in the previous section under "Tone."

Formal or work letters

Nowadays so much communication is done through email and the telephone that the skill of formal letter writing can get forgotten. However, letters are still used in some situations.

Here is a general layout for a formal letter. Note that the layout of formal letters varies but that this format is generally accepted.

[1]**Anthony Johnson**

5130 Molden Road	Phone 410 360 5625
Waldorf MD 20601	Cell 443 532 5437
	E-mail tonyrjohnson@lycos.com

[2]November 18, 2010

[3]Ms. Harriet Jones
Planning Officer
St. Mary's County Planning Board
Waldorf MD 20601

[4]Dear Ms. Jones:

[5]**Planning Application Ref. No. 09/291/XUL**

Thank you for your letter informing us of this application. As the owners and occupiers of 5130 Molden Road, we are concerned that the building of five new houses will create an unacceptable degree of noise and disturbance in the area.

We are also anxious about the amount of traffic that this development will generate. As parents who cycle on Molden Road with our children, we feel that the extra volume of traffic will make the road unsafe.

For these reasons, we believe that this is a highly unsuitable proposal for development in this area, and hope that the Zoning Board will reject the application.

[6]Yours sincerely,

Anthony Johnson   *Sylvie Johnson*

[7]Mr. Anthony & Mrs. Sylvie Johnson

1. Most people today write letters on letterhead, which is special stationery that shows the sender's name and address. Companies use professionally printed letterhead with their logo and other information on it. Computer programs have templates that make it easy for you to create your own personal letterhead. If you do not use letterhead, you can write your address at the top of the letter.

2. Write the date on the left, under the letterhead. Write the month in full as a word.

3. Write the address of the person that you are writing to on the left, under the date.

4. If you know the name of the person you are writing to, use a courtesy title and the family name to address them. If you do not know the name of the person you are writing to, write "Dear Sir or Madam." In a business letter you normally use a colon after this line; in other kinds of letters, a comma is preferred.

5. The heading goes here in bold, giving the subject matter of the letter. This will not be appropriate for all formal letters but it is useful in cases where the letter clearly relates to a particular subject.

6. Write "Yours sincerely," "Sincerely yours," or just "Sincerely" at the end of the letter. Remember to start the first word with a capital letter.

7. Write your signature by hand and then type your name under it. Put your given name first and family name second.

> **Key point to remember**
> If you know that the person you are sending the letter to is a woman but you do not know how she prefers to be addressed, use the title, Ms. Ms. is used for both married and single women.

Most formal letters have a similar structure, having an introduction, a main part and a conclusion.

In your first paragraph, introduce the reason that you are writing. This should be brief – a line or two is usually enough.

> *On June 20th, 2009, I bought a self-assembly children's scooter (model: XR36) from you for $40 which I paid for with cash.*

In the main part of the letter **give details which explain the reason that you are writing**. Keep this as brief as you can. Say everything that you need to say but no more. Present the facts in a logical order that can easily be understood.

> *The next day I unpacked and assembled the scooter and my son rode it to the park. After half an hour of using the scooter, I noticed that the middle of the rear wheel was cracked. I immediately stopped my son from riding on the scooter as I was worried that it was unsafe.*

In the conclusion to your letter, **tell the reader what you would like them to do** as a result of your letter:

> *I am not at all happy with the quality of this scooter and am therefore requesting a full refund.*

The language that you use in a formal letter must be appropriate. It should be polite, whatever subject you are writing about. It does not need to be very formal but it **must not be *informal***. Therefore, you should:

- avoid slang or informal language
- avoid contractions, such as *I'm, he's, they've*, etc.

Make sure that you **spell the name of the person that you are writing to correctly**. People can feel offended when their names are misspelled.

It is helpful to **write a clear heading** before the main part of your letter. This tells the reader exactly what the letter is about. There is a greater chance that the reader will pay attention to your letter if they know from the start what they are dealing with.

Take care over the appearance of your letter. Present the text in short blocks and leave plenty of white space between them. Prepare a letter that looks easy to read.

If at all possible, make your letter no longer than one page. People who have to deal with many letters are much more likely to deal immediately with a letter that is simple, short, and to the point.

> **Key point to remember**
> Make sure that you use the reader's correct title. For example, do not write *Mr.* ...' if the reader has some other more specific title that is appropriate, such as *Dr.* or *Prof.*

When you are planning your letter, try to **think of the contents of that letter from the point of view of the reader**. Most working people read a great deal of text every day, whether it is email, text messages or printed matter. Most people are also very busy in their jobs and have only a limited amount of time to read a message in whatever form it is sent.

You – the letter writer – must therefore try to help the reader by making the message of the letter as clear as possible. You can do this by:

- giving the main point (or points) first. Your reader will immediately want to know why you are writing to them and may feel impatient with your letter if they have to read through a lot of text in order to find this out.

- not including too much information. Only write what the reader needs to know. Do not include a lot of details or the reader may struggle to understand the main point of the letter.

- not including irrelevant information. This might confuse the reader or make them impatient.

- keeping your sentences short and simple. Short sentences with a simple structure are easier to understand.

> **Tip for success**
> Write a clear letter that can be easily understood,
> no longer than one page if possible.

Look at this letter written by the parent of a child to the child's teacher:

362 Maple Street
Hanover, PA 17331

13 December 2010

West Manheim Elementary School
670 Baltimore Street
Hanover, PA 17331

Dear Ms. Lennon,

I am writing to clarify the situation regarding Millie's nut allergy as I know this has recently caused some confusion and concern. Millie has a slight allergy to almonds and hazelnuts. The allergy is mild and not life-threatening but it does cause swelling of the mouth, which Millie finds distressing. Our doctor has recommended that Millie avoids eating all foods containing these nuts. If any of the children brings birthday cake or cookies to school, could Millie please not be given any in case the food sets off an allergic reaction. In the event of Millie accidentally eating food that contains almonds or hazelnuts, please administer the medicine that the school nurse now has in her office. This will immediately alleviate the symptoms. The medicine is clearly marked with Millie's name. I hope this clarifies the situation. If you have any questions, please call me at (717) 729-3045. Many thanks for your help.

Yours sincerely,
Anna Green

Now see how much clearer and easier to read the letter is when:

- a heading is used, giving the reason for the letter
- the text is broken up into short paragraphs
- there is plenty of white space around those paragraphs

---

362 Maple Street
Hanover, PA 17331

13 December 2010

West Manheim Elementary School
670 Baltimore Street
Hanover, PA 17331

Dear Ms. Lennon,

Millie Green's nut allergy

I am writing to clarify the situation regarding Millie's nut allergy as I know this has recently caused some confusion and concern.

Millie has a slight allergy to almonds and hazelnuts. The allergy is mild and not life-threatening but it does cause swelling of the mouth, which Millie finds distressing. Our doctor has recommended that Millie avoids eating all foods containing these nuts.

If any of the children brings birthday cake or cookies to school, could Millie please not be given any in case the food sets off an allergic reaction.

In the event of Millie accidentally eating food that contains almonds or hazelnuts, please administer the medicine that the school nurse now has in her office. This will immediately alleviate the symptoms. The medicine is clearly marked with Millie's name.

I hope this clarifies the situation. If you have any questions, please call me at (717) 729-3045.

Many thanks for your help.

Yours sincerely,
Anna Green

Letters of complaint

Letters are sometimes written to make complaints, for example, about the quality of goods or services. The following letter is written by a woman who is unhappy with the service that she recently received in a restaurant:

Carla Sylva
1452 Calle Amapolas Apt 103
Carolina PR 00979-1126

Phone 939 384 6937
Cell 939 382 6021
E-mail csylva@Yahoo.com

17 June 2010

Maria's
Urb Las Gladiolas
150 Calle A
San Juan PR 00926

Dear Sir or Madam:

[1] I am writing to complain about the poor service I received in your restaurant, where my friend and I had lunch last Saturday (June 13th).

[2] Having requested over the phone a table by the window, we were disappointed to find ourselves seated instead at the back of the restaurant. Our food took over an hour to come and when it arrived, my friend's main course was cold. We complained about this and our waitress returned the food to the kitchen for reheating. Unfortunately, she forgot to bring the food back to us and, when we reminded her, she was discourteous. Neither dessert that we chose from the menu was available and, although we asked for our coffee to arrive with dessert, it came ten minutes later.

[3] As a result of all this, we did not enjoy our meal. Your restaurant had been recommended to us by a friend but we were extremely disappointed by what we found.

[4] I am enclosing a copy of the bill and would like to receive a refund of at least half of it.

I look forward to hearing from you soon.

Yours faithfully,

Carla Sylva.

Carla Sylva

1. In the opening paragraph, explain briefly what you are complaining about.
2. In the main paragraph explain the problem, giving particular examples of what you are dissatisfied with. Include relevant details, such as dates and places. Give enough information here but not so much that the important parts are lost.
3. Tell the reader what the result of all these problems was.
4. Tell the reader what you would like them to do about the problem.

Be polite. Keep the tone of your letter polite and as pleasant as possible. You may feel that the reader is to blame for your situation but do not be rude because of this. If the reader is offended by what you write, he or she will probably not want to help you with your problem. In any case, the person reading your letter will probably not have caused your problem.

Stay calm. You may be angry but try not to let this show. Never use an aggressive or insulting tone. Avoid adjectives such as "terrible" and "appalling" that cause or show strong emotion; use calmer, more neutral words instead. If you are obviously angry in your letter, it will probably make the person reading it not at all enthusiastic about helping you

Job-related letters

People often apply for a job by sending their résumé to a company, together with a job application letter, which is often called a cover letter. With a well-written cover letter you can:

*   point out the most important parts of your résumé

*   show a potential employer that you can write effectively

*   show a potential employer that you are a pleasant person

2nd floor, OKW Osaka Bldg,
1-6-2 Awajimachi, Chuo-ku,
Osaka 541-0047

18 October 2010

Ms. Helena Sano
10th floor, Sakae East Bldg,
4-2-7 Sakae, Naka-ku,
Nagoya 460-0008

Dear Ms. Sano:

[1] **RE: Editorial assistant**

[2] I am writing to apply for the above post as advertised in the Evening Sun on October 16. I am enclosing my résumé, as requested.

[3] I am currently working in a publishing company that specializes in children's books. [4] I have been working on various aspects of publishing, including editing, in cooperation with freelance editors and checking manuscripts.

I have worked in this company for two years and have gained considerable experience and knowledge. [5] I now feel that it is time to take my career to the next step. I am looking for a position that will provide new challenges and engage me more fully in the publishing process. [6] I am organized and energetic and I enjoy meeting and working with a range of people.

[7] I would welcome the opportunity to discuss my skills and experience with you.

I look forward to hearing from you.

Yours sincerely,

Thomas Maruako

Thomas Maruako

1. Give the title of the job that you are applying for here.
2. Give details of the job that you are applying for and say how you found out about it.
3. Describe the job that you are doing now, including details of tasks and responsibilities.
4. Tell the reader what skills and knowledge you have gained in your current job.
5. Tell the reader why you want to leave your current job for the new job.
6. Describe the qualities that make you suitable for the new job.
7. Say that you would be pleased to provide the reader with more information.

Do not write too much in your cover letter. The main part of the letter should have two or three short paragraphs only. Ideally, the whole letter should fit on one page.

Write a cover letter for each new job that you apply for. Do not assume that a general letter will be enough. Write specifically about the job that you are applying for and keep in mind the skills and qualities that are right for that job.

> **Tip for success**
> Always address a cover letter to a particular person.
> If you know the title of their job but not the person's
> name, call the company and ask for the name.

The following is a letter of inquiry, written by a person who is looking for work. It is not a response to a job advertisement. Instead it is the sort of letter that a person who wants work sends to several potential employers, hoping that one of them will require their services:

Sophia Pylas
3 Victoria Street
Wellington 6011

6 August 2010

Hotel Grand
26 Quay Street
Auckland 1021
BR2 4UT

Dear Sir or Madam:

I am writing to inquire about the possibility of work in your hotel this summer. I am especially interested in reception duties but would seriously consider any other type of work that you could offer me.

I am a twenty-year-old student and for the last three years have spent every summer working in hotels in Wellington. I have worked as a receptionist, a waitress and a cleaner. This summer I intend staying with relations in Auckland from December 5th till January 31st and am hoping to find employment for this period.

I enclose a résumé giving details of my work experience and very much look forward to hearing from you.

With thanks

Yours faithfully

Sophia Pylas

Sophia Pylas

Informal letters

Again, so much communication is done through email and the telephone these days that informal letters between friends are becoming quite rare. Still, some people like to write letters – or at least notes – to their friends. There are also some occasions when, even between good friends, a letter seems more appropriate than an email.

[1] *December 18th, 2010*

[2] *Dear Sara,*

[3] *It was great to speak to you last week – thanks for calling. I'm so sorry I haven't been in touch this year. It's been quite hectic with one thing and another!*

[4] *We're both really excited that you're coming to see us in the new year – it's been far too long. I just thought I'd better remind you to bring your hiking shoes. There are some fantastic walks we can do around here (if we have the energy!) Also, make sure you bring warm sweaters and coats. The scenery here is gorgeous but it is <u>very</u> cold, especially in January (and I seem to remember from our college days that you feel the cold!)*

Did I mention I bumped into Steve Washington in Albany earlier this year? He looked so different I almost didn't recognize him. Anyway, I'll tell you more when I see you …

[5] *Really looking forward to seeing you both. I'll call you nearer the time with directions.*

[6] *Much love,*
Emma [7] *xxx*

[8] *P.S. Can't wait to see you with short hair!*

1 You do not need to write your address here, although some people do. If you want to give the reader a new or different address, you can write it here. If you sometimes write from one place and sometimes another, you may show which of these addresses you are writing from by putting, for example:

> *Chicago*
> *December 18th, 2010*

2 You can use the traditional greeting for an informal letter, which is "Dear Paolo/Greta, etc." or you may like to write simply, "Hi Paolo/Greta, etc.," followed by a comma.

3 You can start an informal letter by referring to a previous communication with the reader. You can also start by asking about the health of the reader or by saying sorry for not having written to or telephoned the reader recently:

- *How are you?*
- *How are you doing?*
- *I hope you're both well.*
- *I'm sorry it's been so long since my last letter.*

4 The tone of an informal letter is very often conversational. Just as in conversation, you can use informal words and phrases freely. You can use contractions (e.g., *I'm, won't,* etc) too and you do not have to write in full sentences.

5 You can end a letter by saying how pleased you are that you are going to see the reader soon. You may also encourage the reader to write or to call you:

- *It'll be great to see you.*
- *It would be great to meet up one of these days.*
- *Can't wait to see you.*

- *Hope to hear from you soon.*
- *Stay in touch.*
- *Write soon.*

6   If you are writing to a close friend, before you sign your name, you will want to show affection by using a word or phrase such as:

- *Love,*
- *Lots of love,*
- *Much love,*
- *All my love,*
- *Love from,*

If you are writing to a friend that you do not know so well, you may prefer:

- *Best wishes,*
- *All the best,*
- *Kind regards,*
- *Regards,*

7   If you are very close to the reader, you can add a kiss or kisses after your name (x or xxx) or a hug or hugs (o or ooo).

8   If, when you have finished writing your letter, you think of something else that you want to add, you can put it after the letters, "P.S." (an abbreviation for post script).

Letters are still sometimes written to mark special occasions. For example, here is a letter congratulating the reader on getting a new job:

Mexico City
July 3rd

Hi Channa,

How are you doing? I'm just dropping you a line because I wanted to say congratulations on landing your exciting new job!

Norberto and I are both very pleased for you. You told us last time we met up that you were looking around but didn't seem very optimistic about the opportunities. I know there are a lot of people out there chasing not many jobs. You must have been pretty impressive in interview!

Anyway, I just wanted to congratulate you. I hope the job is everything you want it to be and that you get to work with a great bunch of people.

Well done, Channa!

Lots of love, Marta and Norberto

Notice that the letter, though informal, follows the basic structure for formal letters. It has:

- an introduction, where the writer says why she is writing the letter, i.e., to congratulate the reader on getting her job
- a main part, where the writer puts background information, writing that she knew the reader was looking for a new job and that she knew finding work was difficult
- a conclusion, where the writer congratulates the reader again and adds two specific wishes of her own

Another occasion which often makes people feel that they should write letters is the death of a person loved by the reader. People often feel that the seriousness of the occasion deserves a proper letter and not a quickly written email. A letter, rather than a phone call, also gives the writer time to think about what they want to say and how they are going to say it. This can be a very hard letter to write.

San Diego
June 13, 2010

Dear Polly,

I'm writing because I've just heard the very sad news about your Dad. I just wanted to tell you how sorry I am and to let you know that I am thinking of you.

I have very fond memories of Colin. He was a very kind, warm man and always so welcoming when I came to visit. You enjoyed such a good relationship with him and remained so close throughout your adult life. I know you will be devastated by his death. I am very sorry. I know Ben will be a great comfort to you at this difficult time.

Thinking of you, Polly, and sending you all my love.

Julia

Again, this letter follows the introduction – main part – conclusion format.

- An introduction, where the writer says that she has been told that the person has died.
- A main part, where the writer relates good memories of the dead person and says they know how important the person was to the reader. This part also often includes something that the writer hopes will comfort the reader.
- A conclusion, where the writer usually says that they are thinking of the reader.

Blogs

A blog is a website where someone regularly writes their thoughts and opinions in the form of a *post*, that is, a text that appears all at one time – often daily. Blogs usually contain text, images and links to other websites.

Blogs are written for various reasons. Many people write blogs in order to comment on political issues or stories in the news. Some bloggers write about particular activities and all the issues that relate to them, while other people write blogs in order to sell a product or service. Some blogs, meanwhile, just describe what the blogger does in daily life.

The style and tone of a blog will depend very much on its content. A cycling blog written by an avid cyclist might have an informative and factual tone. The blog writer (*blogger*) wants to provide useful information for other cyclists and to share experiences with them. They may not be so interested in entertaining their readers.

A political blog, on the other hand, might be very funny, using humor in order to criticize politicians.

The blog that someone writes about their daily life will probably have an informal tone and be written in the style of a conversation, chatting to readers as if they were friends.

Whatever the content or subject matter of the blog that you are writing, there are a few general rules.

The first – and possibly the most important – is to **consider your reader**. **Who** do you intend to read this? What are their interests and opinions, and **what do they want from your blog**? Do they want:

- information on a particular subject?
- entertainment?
- to hear your opinions?
- all of the above?

It is only by providing what your reader wants that you will keep them coming back for more.

It might help to **think of your blog as a *resource*** for the reader. For example, if you are writing a blog about a particular sport, you might like to **share tips** with the reader about techniques that you have discovered that have improved your performance. Or you might **provide links** to websites that sell equipment that you have found useful. Give your reader the advantages of your experience and knowledge.

> **Key point to remember**
> If you give links to other blogs or websites, make sure you have visited them first and are certain of their content.

Talk to your reader. Most blogs are written in a slightly informal, conversational English. This is what readers expect. It gives them the feeling that they have formed a relationship with the writer and are connecting with them. Try to imagine that you are *chatting* to your reader. **Use the sort of words and phrases that you would naturally use in conversation** with a friend. This may include words and phrases that you would not use in other forms of writing.

Be yourself. People want to read blogs with original writing and original ideas. If they come back to your blog, it is because they like reading about what *you* have to say and they want to see how *you* say it. Be confident in your style and never try to write like someone else.

Do not be afraid to start your sentences with *I*. Generally, people do not expect blogs to read like newspapers. In other words, they do not visit a blog to read a report of facts. Most people read blogs because they give them a chance to learn about other people. They want to know *what the writer has done* and *how the writer feels* about things. **Tell your reader in the first person about your experiences and opinions**.

> **Tip for success**
> Once you have developed a style of writing that you are
> happy with, keep using that style.

Keep your blog short. Most people spend only a few minutes of their day or week reading blogs. They do not have time to read a lot, no matter how interesting or amusing the writing is. Do not fill the screen with text. Leave some white space and create a clean, simple screen that the reader knows they can deal with quickly.

Write a post that readers can scan. Remember that many people who visit a blog do not read the whole text word for word. Instead they *scan* the screen to get an idea of what the post is about or what information it might contain. They may want to get the general idea of what you have written or they may want only to find particular information. Present your blog in such a way that people scanning the text can get the most from it. You can do this by:

* writing in **short paragraphs**. It is much easier to scan a text that is broken up into many short *chunks* rather than one long block of text.

* providing **lists of information**, introduced by bullets. Lists are quick and easy to understand.

* providing a number of **relevant titles** to break up your text. Titles naturally attract the eye and can help guide the reader to a particular part of the post.

* highlighting important text in bold, color, or by formatting it as a hyperlink.

Communicate your message quickly. Whatever message or information you are trying to communicate in your post, make sure you do it within the first few lines. Do not assume that the reader has the time or the interest to read through a long introduction. Start your point immediately you start writing.

Make use of pictures. Select attractive and relevant images to break up blocks of text. Even if your images are only for decoration, they will still make the screen look more professional and more appealing.

Finally, when you have finished writing your post, **edit your writing**. The tone of your blog might be relaxed and informal but you still need the writing itself to be correct. Some readers will stop visiting a blog because it is poorly written even though they are interested in the topic. Take time to:

- remove phrases or words that are not needed
- change the order of paragraphs if this improves the post
- correct errors
- correct punctuation

> **Key point to remember**
> Get your reader's attention by saying what is most important within the first few lines.

Essays

Writing essays requires effort and a lot of people struggle with some aspect of it. However, it is a worthwhile skill to develop and practice. The ability to write an effective essay will help you in many other kinds of informational or persuasive writing. There are a number of things that you can do to make the task easier.

Give yourself enough time. In order to write the best essay possible you will probably need to read about the essay topic and research it. All of this takes time. Writing an essay hours before you have to hand it in is very stressful and rarely results in an excellent essay. Help yourself by starting your essay well before the deadline.

Learn from others. Read essays that other people have written on a range of subjects. Consider:

- How does the writer introduce the topic?
- What phrases do they use to present their points?
- How have they linked those points?
- Do they present their points in a logical order?
- Does the conclusion successfully bring together all the ideas and points presented in the essay?

Has the writer succeeded in any of the above and, if so, what can you learn from this?

Never plagiarize. If you use someone else's words, always give the name of the person who wrote or said those words and the title of the work in which the words appeared. Never pretend that someone else's words are your own. If you plagiarize you will cancel the good effect of any of your own work in an essay because your readers will not respect your ability or opinions.

If you have been given a specific essay title or topic, **read and then reread it**. Before you start even to plan your essay make absolutely sure that you **understand the title or topic** and what it is asking you to do. Remember that this is one of the main points on which your essay will be judged. This point may sound obvious, but failure to follow instructions is one of the commonest reasons for essays receiving a low grade.

As you write more essays, you will notice that certain verbs are used again and again in essay assignments. Here are some of the most common of these, together with their meanings. Make sure that you know exactly what each verb means in the context of an essay title:

- **analyze**: to examine something in detail for the purposes of explaining it
- **assess**: to judge how valuable, important, or successful something is
- **compare**: to look for similarities between
- **contrast**: to look for differences between
- **evaluate**: to judge how valuable, important, or successful something is
- **illustrate**: to explain something by using examples
- **outline**: to describe the most important points
- **relate**: to show how two or more issues are connected
- **summarize**: to describe the most important points

> **Key point to remember**
> No matter how well written your essay is, if you fail to address the subject of your essay properly, you will lose points.

Take time to **plan your essay**. Proper planning will help you to organize and develop your thoughts so that you are clear about what you want to write. It will also ensure that you do not leave anything out. Planning does not need to take a lot of time, and there are a number of helpful and imaginative ways that you can do it. There is a section on planning your work on pp. 524–537.

Keep to the point. Do not introduce unrelated subjects or aspects of a subject that are not relevant. Even if your points are interesting, you will not gain points for them! Ask yourself before you introduce a subject or make a point, how does this contribute to the essay assignment?

Make every word count. Write clearly and concisely, avoiding overlong sentences, meaningless phrases, and unnecessary adjectives. You will want to show that you have a varied vocabulary but do not be tempted to use a lot of words where a few well-chosen words will do!

Remember paragraphs. As a general rule, every time you make a separate point, start a new paragraph. Do not make your paragraphs too long. If a paragraph is very long, consider dividing it into separate points.

Remember that the type of English that is right for essays is a **slightly formal English**. It is more formal than the English that we usually use for speaking and writing emails. The English generally used in essays does not:

- include informal or slang words (unless you are quoting someone)
- include contractions, such as *isn't* and *won't*
- generally include phrases that use the words *I*, *me*, or *my*

Finally, when you have finished your essay, make sure you **read it carefully at least twice**. Be prepared at this point to make changes to it. Consider:

- the order of the points that you make. Is this logical and does your argument flow?
- your choice of language. Is it clear and does it say exactly what you intended it to say?

Look out too for:

- spelling errors
- typing mistakes (the informal name for this is typo)
- repetition of particular words. If you find you have used a word many times, consider replacing it with a synonym (a word with a similar meaning).

Tip for success

Use your computer's spellchecker to check your finished work but make sure that you read your essay for spelling errors too. You are more likely to find these if you read your essay aloud. Remember that a spellchecker will not find a typo such as "from" where the intended word is "form."

Essay phrases and words

There are **different stages to an essay** and each stage of the essay requires you to do different things. Under the relevant heading below, you will see a range of words and phrases that can be used at a particular stage or for a particular purpose. Use these words and phrases to express your ideas in a way that is more precise and more varied.

Introductions

The following notes will help you with many of the issues you need to cover in your introduction:

Introducing the topic and purpose of an essay
Here you **say briefly what you will discuss,** making sure that the title of your essay reflects this:

- *This essay will examine/look at …*
- *This essay focuses on/discusses …*
- *This essay considers/explores …*
- *The aim of this essay is to assess/examine …*
- *This essay seeks to evaluate/examine …*

Defining key terms used in the essay
If there is any doubt about the meaning of a word or phrase that is important in your essay, **explain** in your introduction **what** *you* **mean** by that word or phrase:

- *Throughout this essay the term "x" will refer to …*
- *The term "x" refers here to …*
- *For the purposes of this essay, the term "x" is used to mean …*

Explaining how the essay is organized
You may like to give a very **brief summary of the structure** of your essay. This shows the teacher/professor that you have arranged your

thoughts and arguments in an organized way. It will also make it easier for them to understand exactly what you are saying:

- *This essay is divided into three parts. The first part looks at ...*
- *There are three parts to this essay. The first part deals ...*
- *This essay has been structured in the following way.*
- *This essay begins by ... It then looks at ...*
- *The first part of this essay examines/looks at ...*

Saying why the topic is particularly interesting or important
You may like to **put the topic in context**, especially if the topic is of particular relevance now:

- *It is often said that ...*
- *We live in a world in which ...*
- *The issue of x is one that affects everyone ...*
- *Recent years have seen an increasing interest in ...*
- *The past decade has seen the rapid growth of ...*
- *One of the most important developments in recent years is ...*

Raising an area of your topic where there is disagreement or controversy
You might want to **offer arguments against** an idea suggested by your essay title, especially if you know of recent findings that seem to contradict it. If your essay title includes a question, it is always a good idea to do this.

- *This is not always true, however.*
- *This is not always the case, however.*
- *However, recent evidence suggests that this may not be the case.*
- *More recently, research has emerged that seems to contradict ...*
- *Concerns have been recently been raised about ...*
- *There is increasing concern about ...*
- *Not everyone agrees with this statement, however ...*
- *Not everyone is in favor of x, however ...*

Mentioning an area of your topic where there is a lack of knowledge

Again, this offers you the opportunity to introduce an argument against a statement or question in the essay title or to at least to **show that there is doubt** about the subject.

- *Less is known, however, about the effects of ...*
- *So far there has been little discussion of ...*
- *However, very little attention has been paid to ...*
- *We hear a lot about x but we hear less about y.*

The main part of the essay

This is the part of the essay where you **discuss and develop the ideas** that you outlined in your introduction. In this part of the essay, you will need to do several things. For example, you need to give facts and make statements; justify or disagree with statements; give reasons; and suggest causes. The following notes will help you with many of the issues you need to cover in the main part of your essay:

Stating what is generally considered to be true

You will probably want to **introduce a statement that everyone** – or most people – **agree is true**. (You might then develop the point or go on to argue against that point.)

- *It is often said that ...*
- *It is certainly true that ...*
- *It can be demonstrated that ...*
- *It is certainly the case that ...*
- *It is undoubtedly the case that ...*
- *No one would argue that ...*
- *Few people would argue that ...*
- *Few would argue that ...*

Stating that something is partly true

You may **only partly agree** with a statement:

- *There is an element of truth in this statement.*
- *There is some degree of truth in this.*
- *This is to some extent true.*
- *This is to some degree true.*

Key point to remember

When giving personal opinions in academic essays, it is generally better to avoid phrases that use the words *I*, *me*, or *my*:

✗ *I think that keeping animals in captivity is wrong for the following reasons:*
✗ *It's my opinion that keeping animals in captivity is wrong for the following reasons:*
✔ *Keeping animals in captivity is wrong for the following reasons:*

Providing facts

You might like to **refer to some new information** or statistics that relate to your topic:

- *Recent research clearly indicates/shows …*
- *Recent research suggests …*
- *A new study confirms that …*
- *A recent report revealed …*
- *It has recently emerged that …*

Useful words and phrases

The verbs *seem* and *appear* can be used to make these claims less definite, for example:

Government-funded research into this area appears to/seems to confirm this theory.

Suggesting reasons for something
You might want to **suggest an explanation** – or more than one
explanation – for a situation or problem that you have described:

- *Perhaps this is because ...*
- *It might be that this is caused ...*
- *This may be because of/caused by ...*
- *This may be a result/consequence of ...*
- *It is likely/possible that ...*
- *We might assume from this that ...*
- *One possible explanation is that ...*
- *We might deduce from this that ...*

Describing the result of something
If you have stated the cause of something, you might want to **say what
the result is**. These words can be used to start sentences that link the
cause of something with the outcome.

- *Consequently ...*
- *As a result/consequence ...*
- *The result is ...*
- *The consequence is ...*
- *It follows that ...*
- *Therefore ...*

Adding to a point that you made before
You might like to **add to a previous point**, either by saying something
that you think is **equally important**:

- *Besides, ...*
- *In addition, ...*
- *Similarly, ...*
- *In the same way, ...*

or by giving a point that is **even more important**:

- *What is more, ...*
- *Furthermore, ...*
- *Moreover, ...*
- *More importantly, ...*

Introducing examples

You will almost certainly want to **provide examples of what you are claiming**. Examples provide proof for your claim and can be introduced with the following words:

- *For example ...*
- *For instance ...*
- *A good example of this is ...*
- *This can be demonstrated by ...*
- *As evidence of this, ...*
- *An illustration/instance of this is ...*

> **Useful words and phrases**
> Alternatives to the phrase *good example* are *notable example* and *prime example*.

Note that you can vary the structure of your sentences by sometimes using the phrases *for example* and *for instance* in the middle of a sentence, with commas before and after:

- *Paper recycling, **for example**, is now common practice in most countries.*

- *Cycling to work, **for instance**, can significantly reduce your carbon footprint.*

You may want to highlight the importance of one particular example, in the following way:

- Environmental issues, ***particularly/in particular*** global warming, dominate the news.

- Environmental issues, *notably/chiefly* climate change and recycling, are at last being addressed.

Giving different opinions
Whatever your view on a subject, you will probably need to **show that you are aware of different views**, with phrases such as:

- *It could/might be argued that ...*
- *It is sometimes said that ...*
- *There are those who claim that ...*
- *Some claim that ...*
- *Another way of looking at/viewing this is ...*

Discussing differences
You may want to **highlight the differences** between two things:

- *There is a marked/sharp contrast between ...*
- *X is in sharp/stark contrast to y*
- *There is a clear distinction between x and y*
- *There are significant differences between x and y*
- *This contrasts sharply with ...*
- *X differs/varies widely*
- *By/In contrast, ...*
- *By/In comparison, ...*
- *Conversely, ...*

> **Key point to remember**
> Remember that the phrases *in contrast*, *by comparison*, and *conversely* can appear in the middle of a sentence, (with commas before and after), as well as at the start of a sentence, e.g.:
>
> *Carlos was clever, handsome, and charismatic. His brother, in contrast, was a plain, shy man.*
> *Carlos was clever, handsome, and charismatic. In contrast, his brother was a plain, shy man.*

Reporting what someone else has said

You will sometimes want to **quote what someone else has said or written**. There are many reasons for doing this. You might want to provide support for own opinion or you may want to introduce an opinion that you can then disagree with.

- *Smith asserts/claims/proposes/suggests that ...*
- *Smith maintains/states that ...*
- *Jones comments/observes//remarks/reports/writes that ...*
- *Jones concludes that ...*
- *According to Jones, ...*
- *As Jones states/points out, ...*
- *In Jones's view/opinion, ...*
- *Jones's view/opinion is that ...*

> **Key point to remember**
> Note that the present tense is usually used in such phrases.

Introducing quotations

Often, you will need to **name not only the author of a quotation, but also the text** that the quotation comes from. This can be done in a number of ways, so it is a good idea to ask your teacher if there is a recommended style:

- *Blake (1998, p. 62) asserts that "Walker hated his mother."*
- *Blake[1] claims that "Walker hated his mother."*
- *As Blake (1998, p. 62) points out, Walker had a difficult relationship with his mother.*
- *Blake (1998, p. 62) maintains that Walker had a difficult relationship with his mother.*

Saying the same thing in a different way
You will sometimes want to **make clear exactly what it is that you are saying** by repeating your point in a way that is briefer and simpler.

- *In other words, …*
- *To put it simply, …*
- *To put it more simply, …*
- *That is to say, …*
- *To look at this another way, …*

Conclusions
The conclusion brings together all the ideas and information you have discussed. It shows the reader that the essay is complete and that the aims of the essay have been achieved. In a conclusion, you **summarize the main points** and say what the consequences of your evidence are:

- *In summary, …*
- *To summarize, …*
- *To sum up briefly, …*
- *In conclusion, …*
- *To conclude, …*
- *It can be concluded that …*
- *We can therefore conclude that …*

Papers, theses, and dissertations

A paper is a piece of writing on a particular subject that is usually longer than an essay, especially one that a student does as a requirement for course work. A thesis (plural *theses*) is a longer paper based on a student's personal research that is submitted as an important requirement for a college or university degree (usually a bachelor's or master's degree). A dissertation is an even longer paper, based on original research, that is typically written as the main requirement for a doctoral degree (Ph.D.). Theses and dissertations are usually divided into a series of numbered chapters.

All of these texts are like an essay in that they are **formal in style**. The type of language that is suitable for essays is suitable for these kinds of papers. They do not:

• include informal or slang words
• include contractions, such as *isn't* and *won't*
• generally include phrases that use the words *I*, *me*, or *my*

For help with formal writing, especially phrases and words to use in these longer texts, see the part in this book on writing essays.

If you are assigned a paper to write or you have to write one as part of a degree requirement, you will probably be given a target length. Both a thesis and a dissertation are **very much longer than a normal paper**. They can be anything up to 10,000 words long and some dissertations are as long as books – in fact many are published as books if there is sufficient interest in them.

Theses and dissertations have a **more complicated structure** than an essay or a shorter paper. This is partly because they are so much longer and partly because they examine their subjects in greater depth. It is important to note that the *exact* structure of a thesis or dissertation will vary depending on:

- the area of study of the dissertation. Different subjects require different structures.
- the school you attend, or the department within that school. Different colleges and universities have different rules on how to structure a dissertation.

> **Key point to remember**
> Before you even start to plan your thesis or dissertation, make sure you have a copy of your department's rules on how to structure it.

As we have said, the structure of a thesis or dissertation will vary, depending on the university and the subject. It is your responsibility to make sure you know exactly what your university or subject requires. The general features of the structure that are given here are therefore only a rough guide:

Title Page
Among other details, this page will include:

- the title of the work
- the name of the writer
- the qualification for which the dissertation has been written
- the relevant university or other place of study
- the date that the dissertation was submitted

Table of contents
This is an index of everything that is contained in the paper except the title page and the table of contents itself.

Abstract
This will say in general terms what the dissertation is about. An appropriate length is generally agreed to be about 300-500 words.

Main part of the work

This will be divided into sections or chapters. The sections or chapters will each have an introduction, a main part and a conclusion. However, it is very important that there is a link between these subsections. When you are writing this part of your work, try to remember that the reader must at all times understand how one part relates to another.

Conclusion

This is where you help the reader to understand the significance of your conclusions, rather than just restating your conclusions. It can be a challenging part of your paper to write. Some people find it helpful to write this part a little time after the main body of the text. This allows them to think more clearly about everything that they have written and to make judgments about it.

Bibliography

This should be a complete list of the books, articles, and other references that you have used in your paper.

Tip for success
Do not delay preparing your bibliography until the end of your work. Prepare it as you are writing, keeping track of the books and other sources that you use.

Theses and dissertations are complicated pieces of work and are not easy to write. You can help yourself with this challenging task by **planning the structure of your work very thoroughly**. You will want to show the plan to your supervisor before you start to write it. Your discussions with your supervisor will very often result in changes to your plan so **allow yourself plenty of time for the planning stage** of the process.

For general help with planning a piece of writing, see the section on planning on pp. 524–537.

When you are ready to start writing, **do not assume that you must start at the first chapter and finish with the last**. Many people find that there is an area of the work that they are more confident about. Consider starting with that area of the subject.

Most colleges and universities have a set of rules about how to present advanced papers. These rules concern, for example, the type and size of font used, the type of paper written on and the layout of the page. **Make sure that you have a copy of the presentation guidelines for your university and that you follow them.**

The **rules for good writing apply to papers, theses, and dissertations** as they do to any other form of written work. For general help with formal writing, see the chapters in this book on writing essays and writing reports. It is worth repeating some of these rules here as they are especially true of long, complicated pieces of writing.

Write clearly. You know what you mean by your writing but if you do not express yourself clearly your reader may not. Make sure your reader does not have to struggle to understand your English.

Write concisely, avoiding overlong sentences and unnecessary adjectives. These will make your English difficult to follow.

Avoid repetition. If you find you have used a word many times, consider replacing it with a synonym (a word with a similar meaning).

Remember paragraphs. Text should never appear as a long block. As general rule, every time you make a separate point, start a new paragraph.

Write paragraphs of the right length. They should not be too long or too short. Never write a paragraph of only one sentence.

> **Tip for success**
> Remember your reader at all times. Try to write English that is a pleasure to read.

You will almost certainly want to **write more than one draft of your work**. Rewriting is an extremely valuable part of the process. It can be hard to see where the problems are while you are writing a piece of text. It is only when you come back to the text that you see where changes need to be made. You may find at this stage that you need to:

- explain a point more clearly
- remove a point that is not relevant
- change the order of the points that you are making

The above changes all relate to the content of your work. As well as examining the content of your work, you will also need to **check it thoroughly for errors**.

Remember that a supervisor who has read parts of your work will only have commented on its content or structure. They will not have brought to your attention spelling or grammatical errors. Use your computer's spellchecker to check your finished work but make sure that you **read your work for spelling errors too**. Remember that a spellchecker will not find a typo such as *from* where the intended word is *form*.

> **Tip for success**
> Read your work through once simply in order to check for grammatical errors and spelling errors.

Reports

A report is a **written document that presents information about a particular subject** to a particular reader or group of readers. The writer of the report has usually been asked by the reader to prepare the report.

Reports are written by people who work in many areas, for example, business, government and education. Many jobs will require you to write a report at some time, even if writing is not a usual part of the job. This is one reason that it is important to develop competent writing skills, no matter what your line of work.

All **reports present a number of facts** that the writer examines in detail. The writer then makes judgments based on those facts. Many reports also make recommendations about things that should be done because of the facts that they have described.

Before you start writing a report, make sure that you **know exactly what it is that you want to achieve**. It may help you to form a clearer idea if you write a short paragraph describing the purpose of it.

Make sure too that you **know exactly who you are writing the report for**. You may be writing for readers with the same understanding of the subject and the same interests, or you may be writing for different types of reader. Your report will need to cover everything that your readers are expecting.

Like an essay, a report is a **formal piece of writing**. The type of English that is right for reports does not:

- include informal or slang words

- include contractions, such as *isn't* and *won't*

- include words that imply a moral judgment, such as *horrible* and *atrocious*

- generally include phrases that include the words *I*, *me*, or *my*. (However, note that if the report includes recommendations, this part of the report may use such phrases.)

Although the English in your report should be formal, it should also be **clear and *readable***. "Formal" is not the same as "difficult." You want your reader **to understand quickly** what you have written without having to make a lot of effort. Although it may not be possible to write a report that your reader actively enjoys reading, you do not want the reader to struggle to get through it!

Do not use long, difficult words in order to impress the reader. The use of a lot of hard words can have the effect of making your writing less readable. Most readers prefer plainer, more direct English. For example, if you find yourself writing the verb *utilize*, consider whether the simpler verb *use* could be used instead. Likewise, if you write *dwelling*, ask yourself whether *home* would in fact be better.

Do not write long sentences. Of course you will want to write some longer and some shorter sentences in order to provide some variety in your English. However, you should try to avoid very long, complicated sentences as they are difficult to understand. Look at the following sentence:

> In terms of numbers, this is essentially an increase, albeit a small increase, and we look forward to seeing this trend continue over the forthcoming weeks and months.

Now see how a shorter sentence can say the same thing much more clearly:

> This is an increase, albeit a small one, and we look forward to seeing this trend continue.

Notice in the first sentence, the phrases and words:

- in terms of
- essentially
- over the forthcoming weeks and months

These words and phrases have little or no meaning in this sentence. In the second sentence, the writer has removed them without changing the meaning. If you have written a long sentence, examine the various parts of that sentence and consider whether any of the words are not needed.

As we have said, the main purpose of a report is to present facts about a subject. The purpose is *not* to describe the writer's opinions or feelings on the subject. For this reason, **do not use the words** *I*, *me*, **or** *my* **in your writing.** You may need to suggest ideas and give possible explanations for certain facts, but you should not do so with phrases such as "it seems to me" and "in my opinion." Compare the sentences below:

> ✗ *The same quarter saw sales in these markets rise by 13 percent, a development that I am convinced is due to better marketing of these products.*

> ✔ *The same quarter saw sales in these markets rise by 13 percent, almost certainly as a result of better marketing of these products.*

Similarly, the language that you use in your report:

- should not show your feelings
- should make appeals to strong feelings in your readers

For this reason, avoid words such as *appalling*, *terrible*, and *fantastic*. Instead use adjectives that express the same idea but in a calmer, more formal way, without suggesting an emotional reaction. Compare these sentences:

✗ *Sales for the last quarter of the year were terrible.*
✓ *Sales for the last quarter of the year were very disappointing.*

✗ *This was a fantastic achievement.*
✓ *This was a remarkable achievement.*

Remember that some people will not want to read the whole report, word for word. Instead they will want to *scan* it, getting the general idea of what you have written or looking for particular information. Present your report in a way that **allows people to read it quickly**. Consider:

- writing in **short paragraphs**. It is much easier to scan a text that is made of many short *chunks* rather than one long block of text.

- giving information in the form of **bullets**. Bulleted lists are quick to understand and are an acceptable way of presenting information in reports.

- breaking up your text with **headings**. Headings will guide the reader to the parts of the report that they are interested in.

The main purpose of a report is to present information. Unlike an essay, a report need not always present information in the form of written paragraphs. You can show information very effectively in the form of **bulleted lists, tables, diagrams and charts**. Label any tables and diagrams, etc., clearly. Information shown in this way should relate to the writing in your report, for example:

> *Figure 1 shows that overall sales increased by 3% in the third quarter.*
> *Overall sales increased by 3% in the third quarter (see Figure 1).*

The structure of a report

The **structure of your report** will partly depend on what is contained in it. However, most reports have a fairly similar structure:

1 Title page
2 Contents list
3 Executive summary or abstract
4 Introduction
5 Main part of the report
6 Conclusions
7 Recommendations
8 Appendices
9 Bibliography

1 Title Page
Include the following formation in your title page:

- The title of the report.
- The purpose of the report.
- Your name and the name of the person or group that you have written the report for.
- The date that you sent or gave the report to the reader(s).

2 Contents list
If you have written a long report, you will need to provide a contents list. This gives the main sections and chapters of the report and the pages on which the reader will find those sections and chapters. If your report contains many charts, tables, or illustrations, it is helpful to provide separate lists for these at the beginning of the report.

3 Executive summary or abstract
You need to give a **summary of the report** – often called an executive summary rather than an abstract when you are writing a report. Here you describe briefly the most important information that is in the report. The summary should not be long – no more than ten percent of the total report. As a rough guide, write one sentence for every main

section of your report. It is helpful to summarize your conclusions in this part of a report for readers who will read only the summary, and not the whole report.

4 Introduction
Here, you should give the following information:

- Any background information relating to the subject that the reader should be aware of.
- The purpose of the report.
- Exactly which areas of your subject you deal with in the report.

5 Body of the report
This is the longest part of the report, where you say:

- what you discovered when you examined this subject
- what you decided was true after considering all the facts (the conclusions)

You will probably need to divide this part of the report into sections. Each paragraph or group of paragraphs on the same subject is a section. It is likely that each section will also need dividing into subsections. These sections and subsections will need to be numbered. The system used by most report writers is as follows:

- Each section in the main part of the report is numbered 1,2,3, etc.
- Sections within those main sections (subsections) are then numbered 1.1, 1.2, 1.3, 1.4, etc.
- If there are any subsections of those subsections, they appear as 1.1.1, 1.1.2, etc.

6 Conclusions
This is the stage at which you bring together all the conclusions that you reached in the main part of your report. Present these conclusions in the order in which they appeared. **Do not include any new information** here.

7 Recommendations

Some reports do not include recommendations. They present and examine facts but do not make suggestions about what should be done because of those facts. Some reports do include recommendations and set them out here, in a separate part of the report. Note that some reports include recommendations in the conclusion or even in the executive summary.

8 Appendices

This is the place to put information which is referred to in the report but is too detailed or complicated to include in the main part of the report. The sort of information you would put here includes:

- questionnaires
- long, detailed tables or other small points of information that most people would think it a chore to read
- any instructions for research referred to in the report
- a glossary (that is, a list of technical terms with their definitions that are used in the report)

9 Bibliography

If you refer to other people's work in your report, give the following information here:

- the author's or authors' name(s)
- the work's full title
- the name of the publisher and place where it was published
- the year it was first published or, the number of the edition and the date it was published

Finally, when you have finished writing your report, **read it carefully from beginning to end**. Be prepared at this point to make changes to it. Consider:

- the order in which you have given the facts. Is it logical?

- the conclusions that you have reached. Are they reasonable, considering the evidence that you have given?

- your choice of language. Is it clear and does it say exactly what you intended it to say?

If possible, leave your corrected report and come back to it a day later. Are you still satisfied with every part of it? Is there any part that you now feel you need to change? **Many people write several drafts of a report** before they are happy with it.

While you are rereading your report, look out too for:

- typos and spelling errors

- repetition of particular words. If you find you have used a word many times, consider replacing it with a synonym (a word with a similar meaning).

- Unnecessary words. Look out for words which mean nothing. For example, a word such as *basically* may have no meaning in a sentence.

Report phrases and words

There are **different stages to a report** and each stage of the report
requires you to do different things. Under the relevant headings below,
you will see a range of words and phrases that can be used at a particular
stage or for a particular purpose. Use these words and phrases to
express your ideas in a way that is more precise and more varied.

Introductions

Introducing the topic and purpose of the report
Here you **explain the purpose of your report** and say exactly which
areas of the subject your report deals with:

- *This report will examine/look at ...*
- *This report aims to/sets out to examine ...*
- *This report focuses on ...*
- *This report considers/explores ...*
- *The aim/purpose of this report is to assess/examine ...*
- *This report seeks to evaluate/examine ...*
- *This report begins by ... It then looks at ...*
- *The first part of this report examines/looks at ...*

Defining key terms used in the report
If there is any doubt about the meaning of a word or phrase that is
important in your report, **explain** in your introduction **what *you* mean**
by that word or phrase:

- *Throughout this report the term 'x' will refer to ...*
- *The term 'x' refers here to ...*
- *For the purposes of this report, the term 'x' is used to mean ...*

If your report has many technical terms that will need explaining
to some readers, consider putting them in a glossary within your
appendix (see above).

Raising an area of the subject where there is disagreement or controversy

You might like to **offer arguments against** something that people generally think is true.

- *This is not always true, however.*
- *This is not always the case, however.*
- *However, recent evidence suggests that this may not be the case.*
- *More recently, research has emerged that seems to contradict ...*
- *Concerns have been recently been raised about ...*
- *There is increasing concern about ...*
- *Not everyone agrees with this statement, however ...*
- *Not everyone is in favor of x, however ...*

Mentioning an area of the subject where there is a lack of knowledge

You might want to **raise an area of your report's subject that little is known about**:

- *Less is known, however, about the effects of ...*
- *So far there has been little discussion of ...*
- *However, very little attention has been paid to ...*
- *We hear a lot about x but we hear less about y.*

Referring to new information

You might like to **refer to some new information or statistics** that relate to the subject of the report:

- *Recent research clearly indicates/shows ...*
- *Recent research suggests ...*
- *Recent findings suggest ...*
- *A new study confirms that ...*
- *A recent report revealed ...*
- *It has recently emerged that ...*

> **Useful words and phrases**
> The verbs *seem* and *appear* can be used to make these
> claims less definite, for example:
>
> *These recent findings appear to/seem to confirm this theory.*

Main part of the report

This is where you describe exactly what you discovered when you
examined the report's subject:

Suggesting reasons for something
You might want to **suggest an explanation** – or more than one
explanation – for a situation or problem that you have described:

- *Perhaps this is because ...*
- *It might be that this is caused ...*
- *This may be because of/caused by ...*
- *This may be a result/consequence of ...*
- *It is likely/possible that ...*
- *We might assume from this that ...*
- *One possible explanation is that ...*
- *We might deduce from this that ...*

Describing the result of something
If you have stated the cause of something, you might want to **say
what the result is**. These words can be used to start sentences that
link the cause of something with the outcome:

- *Consequently ...*
- *As a result/consequence ...*
- *The result is ...*
- *The consequence is ...*
- *It follows that ...*
- *Therefore ...*

Adding to a point that you made before
You might like to **add to a previous point**, either by saying something that you think is **equally important**:

- *Besides, ...*
- *In addition, ...*
- *Similarly, ...*
- *In the same way, ...*

or by giving a point that is **even more important**:

- *What is more, ...*
- *Furthermore, ...*
- *Moreover, ...*
- *More importantly, ...*

Discussing differences
You may want to **highlight the differences** between two things

- *There is a marked/sharp contrast between ...*
- *There is a clear distinction between x and y*
- *There are significant differences between x and y*
- *This contrasts sharply with ...*
- *X differs/varies widely*
- *By/In contrast, ...*
- *By/In comparison, ...*
- *Conversely, ...*

> **Key point to remember**
> Remember that the phrases *in contrast*, *by comparison*
> and *conversely* can appear in the middle of a sentence,
> (with commas before and after), as well as at the start
> of a sentence, e.g.:
> *Group A suffered few colds and infections. Group B, in contrast,*
> *reported constant ill-health.*
> *Group A suffered few colds and infections. In contrast, Group B*
> *reported constant ill-health.*

Reporting what someone else has said
You will sometimes want to **quote what someone else has said or written**:

- *Smith asserts/claims/proposes/suggests that ...*
- *Smith maintains/states that ...*
- *Jones comments/observes//remarks/reports/writes that ...*
- *Jones concludes that ...*
- *According to Jones, ...*
- *As Jones states/points out, ...*
- *In Jones's view/opinion, ...*
- *Jones's view/opinion is that ...*

> **Key point to remember**
> Note that the present tense is usually used in such phrases.

Introducing quotations
Often, you will need to **name not only the author of a quotation, but also the piece of writing** that the quotation comes from. This can be done in a number of ways:

- *Blake (1998, p. 62) asserts that "Rogers was at fault here."*
- *Blake¹ claims that "Rogers was at fault here."*
- *As Blake (1998, p. 62) points out, Rogers was at fault here.*
- *Blake (1998, p. 62) maintains that Rogers was at fault here.*

Conclusions

Summarizing

You will want to **summarize the main points of your report**:

- *In summary, ...*
- *To summarize, ...*
- *In conclusion, ...*
- *To conclude, ...*
- *It can be concluded that ...*
- *We can therefore conclude that ...*
- *The following points summarize our key findings:*
- *The key findings are outlined below:*
- *It is clear that ...*
- *No conclusions were reached regarding ...*

Recommending

You may want to **advise the reader that something should be done**:

- *We strongly recommend that ...*
- *It is my recommendation that ...*
- *It is essential that ...*
- *It would be advisable to ...*
- *I urge x to ...*

Presentations

A presentation is a speech in which you provide information to an audience about a subject that you have researched, written about, or that you know more about than they do. Most presentations are accompanied by visual aids such as slides.

Why write a presentation?

The process of writing your presentation will help you to **decide** the **key points** of your material so that you know exactly what you want to say. Deciding what to include – and what *not* to include – is very important and the key to a successful presentation.

As you write your presentation, you will think of the most **logical order** in which to present your main points.

You will also make sensible decisions about what **slides**, **objects**, or other **visual aids** you need for your talk.

By writing the whole of your presentation in advance, you can make sure that your talk is the **right length**. It is no use preparing a brilliant talk that you cannot possibly give in the time allowed. On the other hand, you do not want to finish your talk 20 minutes early!

Giving presentations can be stressful and many people feel anxious about talking to large groups of people. If you know that you have **prepared your presentation properly**, it will give you confidence on the day.

> **Key point to remember**
> Don't leave it to the last minute to prepare your presentation. Have your presentation finished at least 24 hours in advance.

Deciding the content

Whatever your presentation is about, before you start writing it, ask yourself the following question: **What am I trying to achieve with this talk?**

The best way to be clear about this is to ask two questions:

1 **Who** is this presentation for?
2 **What** is my key message?

Who?
Always write a presentation that is suitable for your audience. Try to find out in advance as much as possible about the audience and what they will **expect from you**. If possible, speak to someone else who has given a presentation to the same audience, or at least speak to the person who has organized the talk. It will help you to plan your talk if you know the following about your audience:

- how much knowledge of your subject they have
- their level of education
- how old they are
- how long they are able or willing to listen to a speaker

What?
The **key message** is the main thing that you want your audience to learn from your presentation – or very often, the main two or three things. Before you even start to write your talk, decide what your key message is.

While you are thinking of the **purpose of the presentation**, consider these questions. Is the purpose:

- to **give your audience information**?
- to **persuade your audience to do something, for example to buy something**?
- to **entertain**?
- to **allow the audience to get to know you**?

Most presentations are intended to give the audience information. If this is your main purpose, make sure you **give the right amount of information**: too much and your audience will be unable to take it in; too little and your audience may feel that they have wasted their time.

It may not be appropriate to entertain your audience – this will, of course, depend on the subject that you are speaking about. However, when you are planning your talk, keep in mind that most people find it hard to concentrate when a speaker makes no attempt to keep their interest.

> **Key point to remember**
> Remember that if you entertain your audience, you will be more likely to persuade them or inform them!

When planning a presentation, it is useful to break it down into three parts: **the beginning, the middle, and the end**.

In the beginning part of your presentation, try to get your audience's attention. You might ask them to do a short activity or perhaps ask them a question. Choose something that will wake them up and involve them. **Make your audience listen to you!**

In the middle part of the presentation, **tell them the facts** that they need to know. Keep it simple and limit yourself to what is really important. Do not tell your audience more than they can understand and remember.

Be aware that the last part of your presentation is possibly the most important part. The audience are more likely to remember what you tell them at the end of your presentation than in the middle. Whatever your **key message** is, make sure that you **say it – or repeat it – at the end**.

> **Key points to remember**
> Involve your audience.
> Repeat your key message in the last part of your presentation.

Writing notes for a presentation

Make good notes to help you give your presentation. Very few people can give a full presentation without looking at their notes now and then. Audiences do not expect speakers to be able to do this. Write only the **main points** of your talk on **numbered index cards or prompt cards**. Write one or two key points on each card and make the writing bigger and clearer than your usual handwriting. There are several good things about prompt cards:

* They remind or "prompt" you to say your next point but you do not read from them. Audiences like you to **look at them** and **speak to them**. A speaker who looks down and reads notes will not keep the audience's attention.

* They allow you to **see your next point very clearly**. (When you have finished saying one point, put the card to the bottom of the pile and you will see your next point.)

* They are **small**. The audience will not notice them, even if you look at them several times.

* You can **write the time** that you should get to each point **on each card**. This way you can make sure that you say everything you want to say in the time that is allowed.

Alternatively, rather than using prompt cards, you may want to use your slides as prompts for what you are going to talk about. These are described in the next section.

> **Tip for success**
> If you use prompt cards, number them and write the time that you should get to each point on the cards.

Writing slides for a presentation

Always **prepare your own slides**. Do not be tempted to use someone else's slides. There are several reasons for this:

- The process of preparing your own slides will help you to decide on your key points.

- It will also help you to present those points in a logical order.

- If you know exactly what is on each slide you will able to talk about each slide with confidence and authority.

Keep the **text** on your slides **simple and brief**. Do not put too much information on a slide (a very common mistake). Remember that although *you* will know your slides very well, *your audience* is looking at them for the first time. Make sure they can make sense of them very quickly. Remember too that they will only have a short time to understand what they are looking at. Limit the amount of text on a slide to **six or seven words on each line** and to **six or seven lines of text** per slide. The slide below, for example, gives as bulleted points the advantages of a new product, in this case a cleaning fluid:

Keener Cleaner

- effective
- economical
- good for the environment
- pleasant-smelling
- pleasant color
- recyclable bottle

It is important also to write the text of your slides **big enough to be seen**. Remember that if you are speaking to a lot of people in a large room, the people sitting at the back will need to be able to read your slides too.

It is a good idea to write a short **title** on each slide. This should be a single word or a short phrase. The purpose is to let your audience see immediately the subject of the slide. Make sure that your **titles** are **large** – larger than the rest of the text.

Edit your slides carefully. Look over them several times, checking the spelling and the phrasing. It is embarrassing to be told by a member of the audience that there is an error on one of your slides!

Tip for success
Limit the amount of text on a slide to **six or seven words on each line** and to **six or seven lines of text** per slide.

Presentation phrases

There are **different stages to a presentation** and each stage of the presentation requires you to do different things. Under the relevant heading below, you will see a range of words and phrases that can be used at a particular stage or for a particular purpose. Use these words and phrases to express your ideas in a way that is more precise and more varied.

Introducing yourself (and thanking your audience)

If you are new to presentations, it is a good idea to **write your introduction out in full on a prompt card**. Of course, you know this information yourself, but you may be very nervous at the start of your talk. It is easy to forget what you are saying when you are nervous. A written reminder of your first few lines will give you confidence:

- *Thank you very much for coming here today.*
- *First of all, I'd like to thank you all for coming here today.*
- *I'd like to start by thanking X, who invited me here to give this talk today.*
- *My name is Paola Sanchez and I'm the marketing manager for Now Systems.*
- *My name is Paola Sanchez and I'm here today to talk to you about ...*
- *Let me introduce myself. My name is Paola Sanchez and ...*

Introducing your talk

It is a good idea at the start of a presentation to tell your audience in a few words **what you are going to talk about**. If your audience have a clear understanding of what you are talking about from the start, it will help them to understand the whole of the talk:

- *Today/This afternoon I'm going to be talking about ...*
- *My subject today is ...*
- *The topic of my talk is ...*
- *I'm here today to tell you about ...*
- *My aim this afternoon is to ...*

You might then **tell your audience about the structure of your talk**. Again, this will help with their understanding:

- First, we're going to take a look at ...
- After that, we'll be considering...
- Finally, we'll be thinking about ...
- I'm going to divide this talk into four parts. The first part deals with ... The second part looks at ... etc.

> **Useful words and phrases**
> Notice that a speaker will often say "**We're** going to consider/look at," etc. This makes the audience feel involved in what the speaker is saying.

"Reminding" people
You will be stating facts in your presentation. Your **audience may already know** some of those facts. It is a good idea to show that you are aware of this:

- As you know...
- You may be aware that ...
- You may have heard of ...
- I'm sure many of you will already know ...
- It's often said ...

Referring to slides and other visual aids
It is likely that you will use slides or other visual aids as a part of a presentation. Try to **make a clear link between the slide and what you are saying**. The following phrases will help with this.

- If you could just take a look at this slide ...
- This slide shows you ...
- This slide represents ...
- As you can see from this graph ...
- Looking at these figures, we can see that ...

Giving more details

Often, in a presentation you make one point and then want to **give further details about that particular point**:

- *I'd like to say a little more about this point …*
- *I'd like to add at this point that …*
- *Another relevant point here is …*
- *While we're on the subject of x, it's worth also saying …*
- *Let's consider/look at this in more detail…*
- *I'd like us to think about this for a moment …*

Changing the subject

At various points in your presentation, you will want to make a new point. **Introduce each new point clearly**:

- *I'd like to move on now to the issue of …*
- *Moving on now to the subject of …*
- *Turning to the issue of…*
- *Let's turn now to the subject of …*
- *The next thing I'd like to think about/focus on is …*
- *Now we'll move on to the subject of …*
- *Let's look now at the question of …*

Using questions to make a point

You can **introduce a point by asking a question**. This might be a general point or a point that will especially interest the audience:

- *So, how does this relate to us?*
- *So why is this of interest?*
- *So why have I brought this to your attention?*
- *So why is this an advantage/a benefit?*
- *How much will all of this cost?*
- *What does this mean for …?*
- *And why is this important/significant?*
- *So where does this lead/take us?*

> **Key point to remember:**
> Introduce each new point that you make clearly.

Paraphrasing (saying something in a different way)

You may want to make a point clear by **expressing something in a different way**. These phrases will help:

- *In other words ...*
- *So what I'm saying is....*
- *To put it another way ...*
- *To put it more simply ...*
- *Another way of putting this is ...*

Returning to a point you made earlier

You might want to **show how a new point relates to an earlier point** in the presentation:

- *As I said before ...*
- *Going back to what I said earlier ...*
- *To return to a point I made earlier ...*
- *Earlier in the talk, I mentioned ...*
- *You'll recall I mentioned x earlier ...*
- *This relates to a point I made earlier about ...*
- *Let's look back at something I said earlier ...*

> **Tip for success:**
> Linking a new point with something you said earlier will
> help your audience to understand your presentation.

Summarizing your presentation

Towards the end of your talk, you may like to **remind your audience of the main points** you have made:

- *We've covered a lot of ground today. Let me quickly summarize the main points ...*

- *Let's summarize briefly what we've looked at today ...*
- *I'd like to quickly go over the main points of today's presentation ...*
- *If I can just sum up the main points of the presentation ...*
- *To finish, I'd just like to remind you of some of the issues we've covered today ...*

Concluding

Now is the time to **tell your audience the thing – or the things – that you want them to remember**:

- *I'll conclude very briefly by saying that ...*
- *I'll finish by saying ...*
- *Let me end by ...*
- *I'd like to leave you with this thought ...*

Finishing a presentation

Most speakers like to **let their audience know that they have finished their presentation**:

- *I think that's everything I wanted to say today.*
- *I think I've covered everything I wanted to say today.*
- *I think that's about it.*

You will then want to **thank your audience** and, if there is time, **invite them to ask you questions** relating to the subject:

- *Thank you all very much for taking the time to listen to this presentation.*
- *Does anyone have any questions (or comments)?*
- *Would anyone like to ask any questions?*
- *Please feel free to ask questions.*
- *If anyone has any questions, I'd be very happy to answer them.*
- *We have ten minutes left now if anyone has any questions they would like to ask.*

> **Tip for success**
> Always let your audience know that you have finished your presentation and remember to thank them for listening.

Your work qualifications

When you apply for a job it is customary to submit a standard document that gives details of your work experience, education, and background. It also gives your full name and contact details. For most jobs, this document is called a résumé in American English. The word is properly written with accents but you will often see it without accents, as *resume*, because the context makes it clear that this is not the verb *resume*. In British English this document is called a CV (short for Latin *curriculum vitae*). The term CV and the short form *vitae* are also used in American English, but usually only for certain professions such as academia and medicine. In American usage, a CV is much more detailed, longer, and presented in a different format than a résumé.

People usually send a cover letter with their résumé or CV. You will find help with this type of letter in the part of this book on writing letters.

A résumé should be as short as possible without leaving out essential information. Job advertisements sometimes specify the maximum length of résumé that is acceptable, but in any case your résumé should rarely be longer than three pages, and if you can get everything important on one or two pages that is best.

Whether you are writing a one-page document or a two- to three-page document, there are a number of things that you must keep in mind. The first of these is that the reader of your résumé or CV will probably assess it along with *many* others. They will probably have limited time to do this. Therefore, your information must be:

- quick and easy to read
- clear and concise
- pleasant to look at

> **Key point to remember**
> Keep your résumé concise. The reader will not have time
> to read through five or six pages, no matter how
> impressive the details.

Remember that if your information is poorly presented, the reader will
be more likely to reject it even if your skills and experience make you
the perfect candidate for the job. Your résumé must therefore have:

- a **clear structure**. Be sure to organize the information under
  headings such as *education* and *experience*.

- **plenty of white space**. A dense page with too much text is difficult
  and unpleasant to read.

Make sure too that you print your résumé or CV on **good quality,
clean paper**. Remember that the reader does not know you. The only
evidence that they have of your character and your suitability for the
job is the paper they have in their hand. Make it look impressive. You
should also have an electronic version of your résumé that looks
equally impressive, and does not look simply like a paper version of
your information put on the screen. Many companies today do not
even accept paper résumés and prefer to receive information in
electronic format so that they can evaluate it computationally.

Remember that the information you include must be **relevant** to the
work. Do not be tempted to include facts that do not directly relate to
the job that you are applying for. A reader with little time to assess
several résumés might be distracted by this and may not actually see
the important information.

> **Key point to remember**
> Presentation is extremely important in résumé and CV
> writing. Two documents with the same information will be
> judged differently by the reader if one of them is more
> attractively presented and better organized than the other.

Here is a general layout for a résumé. The structure and layout of résumés varies but this format is generally accepted. Notice the clear headings and the white space around the paragraphs. If you need to write a résumé, look at one by someone who is in the same profession as you in order to learn how your information should be presented.

---

[1] **Mark Ortega**   [2] 382 Danvers Court, Indianapolis, IN 46219
(317) 923-7102 [3] markort@lycos.com

[4] **Objective**   A senior sales management position with a Fortune 500 company in the Midwestern or Mid-Atlantic states

[5] **Experience**   2006–2010   Trellis Components,   Louisville, KY
National Sales Manager
- Increased sales from $50 million to $100 million.
- Doubled sales per representative from $5 million to $10 million.
- Suggested new products that increased earnings by 23%.

2003–2006   Massey and Barrett Castings   Bowling Green, KY
District Sales Manager
- Increased regional sales from $25 million to $350 million.
- Managed 250 sales representatives in 10 Midwestern states.
- Implemented training course for new recruits – speeding profitability.

1997–2003   Doublair Ventilation Systems   Nashville, TN
Senior Sales Representative
- Expanded sales team from 50 to 100 representatives.
- Tripled division revenues for each sales associate.
- Expanded sales to include mass market accounts.

1994–1997   DuraWare, Inc.   Nashville, TN
Sales Representative
- Expanded territorial sales by 400%.
- Received company's highest sales award four years in a row.
- Developed Excellence In Sales training course.

[6] **Expertise**   HVAC architecture
CAD design specification
JIT inventory management systems

[7] **Education**   1995–1997   Phoenix University Online   MBA
1991–1995   Vanderbilt University   BA

[8] **Interests**   digital photography, NASCAR, soccer, genealogy

1   Give your name in full at the top of the résumé where it can easily be seen.
2   Also provide your contact details prominently at the top.
3   Always provide your email address.
4   Write your objective at the top of your résumé. Summarize what you want your next job to be.
5   Always provide details of your most recent employment first and then work backwards.
6   If you can summarize skills that will be of interest to potential employers it is a good idea to isolate these for easy reading. This is especially true for any software and other technical skills you possess.
7   Your education background should also be listed with the most recent/highest accomplishments first.
8   It is not essential to list your personal interests but for candidates who are otherwise equal, some personal information about you might make your résumé stand out – and having common interests with potential employers or colleagues may be to your benefit.

Instructions

You will see instructions on signs in public places, in recipe books, in operating manuals, on packets of food, and a variety of other places.

Instructions are generally **written using the imperative form** of the verb. The imperative is formed by using the infinitive form of the verb without *to*:

> *Keep off the grass*
> *Stop at the white line when light shows red*
> *Now add the garlic and tomatoes*
> *Shake before use*
> *Reconnect the plug to the power outlet*

Negative imperatives are generally formed by putting *do not* or *never* before the verb:

> *Do not open door while machine is operating.*
> *Do not leave in bright sunlight.*
> *Never leave small children unattended.*

Notice that sentences that give instructions often leave out words that you would find in ordinary sentences. For example, they sometimes do not include articles (*the* or *a*). Sometimes they leave out objects. For example, the sentence above reads, "Do not leave in bright sunlight." It does not say "Do not leave *this item* in bright sunlight."

Key point to remember
Instructions are generally not written as complete sentences and they do not show *who* must follow the instruction.

Think carefully about your readers before you start to write your instructions. Consider:

- How much or how little do they know about the task for which you are writing instructions?

- How old are they?

The answers to these two questions will help you to decide:

- The level of your instructions and **how many steps you include**. If the reader knows little or nothing about the task that you are describing, you may need to give instructions for every action that is required, even if some of the instructions seem very simple to you.

- How **simple or difficult the language of your instructions is**. Will they, for example, understand technical terms? If not, you will have to find a way of giving instructions that involves simple language that anyone could understand.

- Whether you need to **add warnings to your instructions** for younger readers. For example, in a recipe you may need to warn the reader that a food is hot at a particular point and they must not touch it. Or you may decide to tell the younger reader to ask an adult for help with a particular action.

When you are writing instructions, make sure that they are **easy to follow**. Make them as **clear** and as **simple** as possible. Remember that the reader will be using your instructions because they have not done a particular task before.

Use **short, simple sentences**. Long sentences are hard to follow and can confuse the reader. Compare the following instructions for making chocolate refrigerator cake:

Recipe 1 ✗

Melt butter in pan and add cocoa, sugar, and syrup, bringing to a boil, then remove from heat and stir in broken cookies, mixing well. Press mixture into pan then melt chocolate in microwave, (medium power for 15 seconds), spreading the chocolate when melted evenly over the surface using a knife and refrigerate before slicing.

Recipe 2 ✓

1   Melt butter in pan.
2   Add cocoa, sugar, and syrup to pan and bring mixture to a boil.
3   Remove from heat and stir in broken cookies. Mix well.
4   Press mixture into pan.
5   Melt chocolate in a microwave (medium power for 15 seconds).
6   Spread melted chocolate evenly over the surface using a knife and refrigerate before slicing.

Recipe 1 is confusing and difficult to follow for the following reasons:

• It uses long sentences. It gives you ten instructions in just two sentences. This is too much information for the reader to take in.

• It gives some instructions in a form that is not the imperative. For example, it uses the -ing form of the verb *bring* in "bringing to a boil" and not the clearer "bring to a boil."

• It relies on words such as *then* and *and* to tell the reader the order in which they should do different things. This is hard for the reader to understand and remember.

Recipe 2 is clear and easy to follow:

- It breaks up the ten instructions into seven short sentences in a numbered sequence.

- The reader can easily see the order of those instructions as each new step starts a new line.

- It uses the imperative form (melt the butter, remove from heat, press mixture, etc.), for every instruction.

Key point to remember

Avoid using the passive form ("be verb-ed") when writing instructions. The active form is clearer:

✗ The red button is pressed to start the wash cycle.
✓ Press the red button to start the wash cycle.

It is helpful to **give instructions as a list** rather than a paragraph. A list clearly separates the different actions that the reader must do and makes the instructions easier to follow. Your list may be numbered, or may have bullets:

Bake from frozen in 15 minutes
1 *Preheat oven to 400°F.*
2 *Remove all packaging.*
3 *Place in the middle of oven and bake for 12-15 minutes.*

Planting your seeds
- *Fill a pot with compost.*
- *Spread the seed over the compost surface.*
- *Water the compost generously.*

Think about the order of the actions that you are describing.
Always give instructions for actions in the order in which you would
perform them. This is not always as obvious or as easy as it sounds!
Some actions can be performed at different stages of a task. Try to
work out the most logical point at which to perform such actions.
It can be helpful to write each step of a task on a different Post-it®
note. You can then move the notes around until you have decided
the most sensible order.

Consider **giving a title to your list of instructions**. The title should
explain what the reader will achieve by following your instructions.
You may want to make this sound exciting and appealing, especially
if you are writing for children:

> *How to make the best chocolate brownies ever!*
> *How to make a mask that will scare your mom and dad!*

You may be writing instructions for a number of different but related
tasks, for example, the different functions of a piece of equipment. It is
useful here to **give short titles** for the various tasks, explaining what
your instructions will help the reader to do. Note that the *-ing* form of
the verb is usually used for titles like these:

> *Setting the gentle wash cycle*
> *Resetting/Changing the cycle*
> *Cleaning the appliance*

If the reader needs any items in order to perform your instructions,
it is useful to **give a list of these items** before the instructions:

> You will need:
> 2 pieces poster board (8" x 10")
> glue
> 2 lengths thin ribbon (width 1/4")
> sequins

Use helpful pictures or diagrams. Pictures and diagrams are especially useful:

- if the task for which you are giving instructions needs the reader to use different pieces of equipment or complicated equipment

- if you are writing for children

Choose your **pictures carefully**. Pictures or diagrams that are well-chosen and clearly labeled will show the reader immediately what things look like. (It can be difficult to describe in words the appearance of a particular thing or part.) They will also show how big or small one thing is compared with another thing. This can help to make sense of instructions. Make sure that your pictures or diagrams are:

- **clear and large enough** for the reader to see all the important parts

- **clearly labeled**. If you are using lines to point to different parts of a picture, make sure the reader can see exactly which parts of the picture the lines are pointing to.

> **Tip for success**
> Give the right number of labels. Label the parts that the reader needs to know about but do not label every part.

You may find it helpful to **test your instructions** to make sure that they work. Test your instructions on people who have not seen your instructions before or have not done the task that you are describing. This will show you:

- where your instructions are not clear

- where you have left out an important step or piece of information

Choose the people to test your instructions carefully – they should be typical of the sort of person who will be using your instructions. To learn the most from this activity:

- ask the person or people to read through your instructions carefully and then ask them if they have any questions or comments

- ask questions that will show whether they have understood your instructions

- if possible, watch the group try to perform the task by following your instructions. Afterwards, ask them how easy they found the task. Were there any instructions that they found confusing?

You can then rewrite any part of your instructions that was not clear or give instructions for any part of the task that was missing.

Leaflets and flyers

A leaflet or flyer is a printed sheet of paper that gives information about something. Leaflets are given to a large number of people free of charge.

Leaflets do a variety of things. They may simply give information, for example, on a particular health problem, on an event or sale, or on garbage collection in a particular area. They may try to persuade people to buy a particular product or service, or they may try to persuade people to have a particular belief.

Whatever the purpose of a leaflet, all leaflets have a few features in common. **Leaflets are small**. Most are just one sheet of paper, sometimes folded in two or three. (This is necessary as they will be picked up, quickly read, and often then put in a pocket or bag.) Consequently, leaflets generally contain **only the most important facts** on a particular subject and they **communicate those facts in just a few words**.

When you are writing and designing a leaflet, keep in mind that people generally **look at a leaflet very quickly**. Remember:

- Use large type to convey the most important information in a few words.
- Do not include information that is not important.
- Keep the text – or texts – short.
- Express your points clearly so that they are easy to understand.
- Include a telephone number/website address or other contact information.

Before you start to write your leaflet, **draw a rough sketch** of how you want it to look. Plan where you are going to put the title, the words, and any pictures you are using.

Try to make the leaflet look attractive and choose an image or images that will capture people's attention. **The right image or images** will also **help to communicate your message**.

Do not put too much in your leaflet. Remember that people need to be able to read a leaflet quickly. If they think that your leaflet will take them too long to read, they may not even pick it up! **Leave plenty of white space** around the text and images.

You can design your leaflet in a number of ways, even if it is a single-page leaflet. For example, you could put just a title and image on the front of the leaflet and the words themselves on the back. You may decide to put both images and text on both sides of the leaflet. **Make these important decisions before you even start to write the text.**

Tip for success
Before you do anything else, plan the overall design of your leaflet.

When you have prepared an overall design for your leaflet, it is time to choose the words. The best way to do this is to try to **see those words through the reader's eyes**. Imagine the questions the reader might ask when they pick up your leaflet.

Your first task, therefore, is to work out **who your typical reader is**. It is only when you have worked this out that you can start to work on the words.

For example, imagine you are preparing a leaflet for a cooperative that delivers boxes of organic fruit and vegetables to people's houses. The typical reader is a person who has at some point considered having a box like this delivered. The reader now wants to find out how your particular cooperative would provide such a service. You can assume that the reader is interested in this type of service because one or more of these is true:

- They like good quality food.
- They care about the environment.
- They want to support small, independent companies.

They will therefore probably want answers to the following questions:

- How good is the food?
- Is it truly organic?
- How eco-friendly is the cooperative?
- Who runs this cooperative?

On the basis of these questions, the facts that you would want to include in your leaflet are:

- The food is of the highest standard – fresh and delicious.
- The food is grown according to strict organic standards, without pesticides.
- The cooperative respects the environment in everything it does, for example in using only crops grown locally and in using very little packaging.
- This is a small, locally organized cooperative.

Other facts that *any* reader will want to know are:

- How much does it cost? (Are there different prices for different size boxes?)
- How convenient is it? (Can I choose what fruit and vegetables I have in my box?)

What is important is that you **remember to keep the reader's needs in mind**. *Only* include information that is interesting and useful to them. *Do not* be tempted to give a lot of detailed information.

> **Tip for success**
> Before you include information in your leaflet, ask yourself these two questions:
>
> Will the reader want to know this?
> Will the reader understand this?

When you know what information you want to include in your leaflet, you must decide how you are going to present that information. A bulleted list **is a very clear way of presenting key information**. Look at the text in the following leaflet:

Greener Gardening – Local Garden Service

We do all types of gardening tasks, including garden design, hedge trimming, garden maintenance, lawn maintenance, flower beds, tree & shrub planting and grass cutting.

Now see how a bulleted list can make the same information much clearer:

Greener Gardening – Local Garden Service

We do:
- Garden design
- Hedge trimming
- Garden maintenance
- Lawn maintenance
- Flower beds
- Tree & shrub planting
- Grass cutting

Your leaflet may include the type of information that you cannot present in a list. For example, you may need to explain a number of facts, requiring you to write a series of paragraphs. If you are including a lot of information, remember to **break up the text with titles** for the different paragraphs.

Look at the text in the following medical leaflet:

Symptoms of the virus may include a sore throat, headache, fever, loss of appetite or extreme tiredness. Call your doctor immediately if you are pregnant or your condition suddenly gets much worse. Some people are more at risk of serious illness if they catch the virus. At risk are people with long-term lung disease, heart disease, and kidney disease.

Now see how titles can make the same information much clearer:

Common symptoms
Symptoms of the virus may include a sore throat, headache, fever, loss of appetite, or extreme tiredness.

Call your doctor immediately if:
You are pregnant or your condition suddenly gets much worse.

High-risk groups
Some people are more at risk of serious illness if they catch the virus. At risk are people with long-term lung disease, heart disease, and kidney disease.

Get your reader's attention from the start. Make the first line of your leaflet count. For example, rather than starting the text by describing your company, you could present the reader with the problem that your product or service will solve. Look how one home-delivery pizza company starts their leaflet:

Sandro's Pizzas
We deliver hot, tasty pizzas within a two-mile radius of Lockport.

Now see how effective it can be to take a different approach, talking directly to the reader:

> ## Paolo's Pizzas
> Hungry but had enough of cooking? We deliver hot, tasty pizzas ...

Include quotations. If you are trying to sell a product or service with your leaflet, you may like to include quotations from previous satisfied customers (though first check with the customer that they are happy for this to happen!):

> *"The most delicious, authentically Italian pizzas I've ever eaten in this country!" (K Santini, Lockport)*

Use simple language. Keep the language of your leaflet simple. Never include technical terms that your readers may not know. Make the sentences short so that the leaflet can be read and understood quickly.

Provide the right contact details. Will the readers of your leaflet want to call you or go to your website? Do they need to know where your office is or how to email you? Make sure you provide the contact details that your reader needs. Include an area code with any telephone number, and full address details. Even if your leaflet is to be distributed locally; you don't know who might pick it up, or where it might travel to.

Make your contact details clearly visible. Write them where the reader will see them. The top or bottom of a leaflet is usually clearer than the middle of a piece of text. Consider writing them on *both* sides of the leaflet.

Edit your leaflet. Remember that your leaflet is going to be read by members of the public and you need to create the best possible impression. The spelling, grammar, and punctuation in your leaflet must therefore be perfect. Read and reread your finished leaflet. If possible, have someone else check it.

Test your leaflet on a friend or colleague. Show them your leaflet for ten seconds only. Now ask them two questions (getting the answer for the first question before you ask the second):

1 What was the main purpose of the leaflet?
2 Tell me three things you have learned from the leaflet.

Could your friend/colleague tell you the main purpose of the leaflet? Were the three things they learned from the leaflet the three *key* things that you want your readers to notice? If their answers were not what you were hoping for, consider rewriting parts of your leaflet.

> **Tip for success**
> Take time to prepare your leaflet properly. A badly written leaflet may do more harm than good, no matter how many people read it.

Common mistakes and controversial issues

Words that are often confused

Homophones

Homophones are words that sound the same but are spelled differently, and it is easy to become confused by them:

affect Affect is a *verb*: *How will this new law affect me?*	*effect* Effect is a *noun*: *What will the effect of the new law be?*
already Already is an *adverb*. If something has already happened, it has happened before the present time: *I've already called an ambulance.*	*all ready* In the phrase "all ready," *all* is a *quantifier* meaning the whole of a group or a thing, and ready is an *adjective*: *Are you all ready to go?*
alter Alter is a verb, meaning "to change": *Nothing in the house had altered since 1960.*	*altar* An altar is the holy table in a church: *The priest stood in front of the altar.*
anyone Anyone is a pronoun and always refers to people: *Has anyone seen my hat?*	*any one* In the phrase "any one", *one* is a pronoun or a determiner that can refer to a person or a thing, depending on the context: *We never stay long in any one place.* *It could have happened to any one of us.*
bare Bare is an adjective meaning "not covered" or "not wearing any clothes": *We ran along the beach with bare feet.*	*bear* A bear is a wild animal: *There are bears in the woods.*

board	**bored**
A board is a flat piece of wood: *They nailed a board over the window.*	If you are bored, you are not interested by something: *I was so bored at school today.*
capital	**capitol**
Capital is usually a *noun*. It has several meanings, including a city that is also a seat of government: *Denver is the capital of Colorado.*	Capitol is also a *noun*. It is a building where a legislature meets: *We took a tour of the capitol and other buildings at the civic center.*
cereal	**serial**
Cereal it is another name for grain, or for a food made from grain: *Do you eat cereal for breakfast?*	A serial is something that happens in or contains a series: *We watched a three-part serial about the life of Lincoln.*
chord	**cord**
A chord is a group of three or more notes played together: *Was that an A-minor chord?*	Cord is strong or heavy string: *Tie the package with some cord.*
coarse	**course**
Coarse is an *adjective* meaning "having a rough texture" or "talking and behaving in a rude way": *The sand was very coarse.* *His manners are coarse.*	Course is a *noun* with several meanings, including "a series of lessons" and "a route or path": *The plane changed course.* *I did a course in art history.*
compliment	**complement**
A compliment is a nice thing that someone says about someone or something. Compliment can also be used as a verb: *They paid him a lot of compliments.* *She complimented me on my roses.*	If people or things complement each other, they have different qualities that go well together: *The dry wine complements this rich sauce perfectly.*

counselor A counselor gives people advice, often on personal matters, as a job: *They went to see a marriage counselor.*	**councilor** A councilor is a member of a council: *She was elected as a councilor last year.*
discreet If you are discreet, you are careful to avoid attracting attention or revealing private information: *I made a few discreet inquiries about her.*	**discrete** If things are discrete, they are not joined or connected in any way: *I met him on three discrete occasions.*
everyone Everyone is a pronoun and always refers to people: *Everyone enjoyed the show.*	**every one** In the phrase "every one," one is a pronoun or a determiner that can refer to a person or a thing, depending on the context: *They have talked to every one of my classmates.* *We have eaten every one of the cookies.*
hoard If you hoard things, you save or store them for yourself: *She hoarded jars of fruit in the cellar.* Hoard can also be a *noun*: *We found a hoard of guns under the floorboards.*	**horde** A horde is a large crowd of people: *Hordes of shoppers crowded outside the store.*
hole A hole is an opening or a hollow space in something: *There's a hole in my shoe.*	**whole** Whole is a quantifier meaning "all of something": *He ate the whole loaf.*

its Its means "belonging to it": *The dog wagged its tail.*	**it's** It's means "it is" *It's going to be difficult to fit in all this work.*
led Led is the past participle of the verb *lead*: *He led me into a small room.*	**lead** Lead is a *noun*, meaning "a soft, gray metal": *The roof is covered with lead.* Lead is also a *verb*, but it has a different pronunciation.
libel Libel is a *noun* that denotes the crime of publishing lies about someone: *They sued the newspaper for libel.*	**liable** Liable is an *adjective* that means "legally responsible": *We are not liable for damage done to personal property.*
maybe *Maybe* is an adverb that modifies a verb, a predicate, or a whole sentence. There should always be a verb in a sentence that contains *maybe*: *Maybe I'll stay till they finish this set.* *I was standing maybe 30 yards away from the accident.*	**may be** *May be* is a verb phrase or part of the verb phrase in a clause; it is the modal verb *may* plus the infinitive *be*: *There may be other reasons for changing the date.* *You may be asked to provide a reason.*
pedal Pedal is a *noun* meaning the part of a bike you press with your foot, or a *verb* meaning to press that part: *Put your foot on the pedal.* *You'll have to pedal harder.*	**peddle** If you peddle something, you sell it: *He was caught peddling drugs.*

pray Pray is a *verb* that means "to speak to a god": *I prayed that they would arrive safely.*	**prey** Prey is a *noun* that denotes an animal eaten by another: *The lions are searching for prey.*
principle Principle is a *noun* meaning "a belief about what is right or wrong" or "a basic rule": *Eating meat is against my principles.* *We learned the basic principles of* *yoga.*	**principal** Principal is an *adjective* meaning "most important": *Bad weather was the principal* *reason for the failure of the* *expedition.* Principal can also be a noun meaning "the person in charge of a school": *She was sent to the principal's office.*
site A site is an area that is used for a particular purpose or where something happens: *He works on a building site.* *This is the site of the explosion.*	**sight** Sight is the ability to see, and a sight is something you can see: *She lost her sight in an accident.* *I faint at the sight of blood.*
stationery Stationery is a *noun* meaning "paper, envelopes and writing equipment": *Envelopes are kept in the stationery* *cupboard.*	**stationary** Stationary is an *adjective* meaning "not moving": *I drove into a stationary vehicle.*
straight Straight is an adjective meaning "not curved": *The road is straight for 20 miles,* *till the mountains start.*	**strait** Strait is a noun that denotes a narrow strip of water: *The ship was attacked in the Strait* *of Malacca.*

whether Whether is a *conjunction* used to talk about a choice or doubt between two or more alternative: *I can't decide whether to have soup or salad.*	**weather** Weather is a *noun* we use to talk about rain, snow, sun, etc.: *The weather was great in Florida.*
whose Whose is a *pronoun* and a *determiner* used to ask questions about who something belongs to, or to talk about things connected to a particular person: *Whose shoes are these?* *He helped a woman whose face was covered with blood.*	**who's** Who's means "who is" or "who has": *Who's going to do the dishes?* *Who's been sleeping in my bed?*
witch Witch is a *noun*, meaning an evil magic woman: *We painted a witch on a broomstick.*	**which** Which is a *pronoun* and a *determiner* used to ask questions when there are two or more possible alternatives, or to talk about things connected to a particular person: *Which is your cabin?* *I took the coat which looked warmest.*
your Your is a *pronoun* showing that something belongs to you or relates to you: *Where is your car?*	**you're** You're means "you are": *You're late again.*

Other words that are often confused

These words do not sound the same, but they are spelled in a similar way or related to each other, and often cause confusion:

accept Accept is a *verb* and means "agree to have": *I cannot accept money from you.*	**except** Except is a *preposition* and a *conjunction* meaning "not including": *Everyone was invited except Flora.*
adverse Adverse is a formal *adjective* meaning "bad" or "negative": *Do not attempt the climb in adverse weather conditions.*	**averse** If you are averse to something, you do not like it: *I'm not averse to a sing-along now and then.*
advice Advice is a *noun*: *Can you give me some advice about growing roses?*	**advise** Advise is a *verb*: *I advised him to wait a bit longer.*
beside Beside means "next to": *Put the chair beside the window.*	**besides** Besides means "as well" or "in addition to": *I don't need any help. Besides, I've nearly finished.* *He designed houses, office buildings, and much else besides.*
censure Censure is a formal verb, meaning "to criticize strongly." It is also a noun meaning the criticism: *They were censured for their failure to implement safety measures.* *The company received censure for its poor safety record.*	**censor** Censor is a verb meaning "to cut out parts of speech or writing." It is also a noun meaning the person who does this: *His letters home from the war were heavily censored.* *Government censors cut out much of what he wrote.*

continual Continual is used to mean that something happens without interruption, and also that something happens repeatedly: *I'm fed up with this continual noise.* *There have been continual demands for action.*	**continuous** Continuous is only used for things that happen without interruption and do not stop at all: *He has a continuous buzzing sound in his ear.*
definite If something is definite, it is firm and clear and not likely to be changed: *Do we have a definite date for the meeting?*	**definitive** Something that is definitive provides a firm, unquestionable conclusion: *No one has come up with a definitive answer.*
dessert A dessert is the sweet dish you eat at the end of a meal: *Shall we have a dessert?*	**desert** A desert is a large, dry sandy area: *We traveled through the Sahara Desert.* Desert (with the same pronunciation as dessert) is also a verb meaning "to abandon." *Settlers deserted the valley after one winter.*
elder Elder is used when you are saying which of two people was born first. It is not used with *than*: *I live with my elder sister.* *He is the elder of the two.*	**older** Older simply means "more old," and can be used of people or things, and can be followed by *than*: *My car is older than yours.*
flout If you flout a law or a rule, you do not obey it: *He accused the president of flouting international law.*	**flaunt** If you flaunt something, you show it off in an obvious way: *I saw her at the party, flaunting her jewelry.*

infer If you infer something, you draw a conclusion from what you have seen, heard or read: *From his resignation letter, I inferred that he had been forced to leave.*	**imply** If you imply something, you say it in an indirect way: *She implied that he owed her money.*
lay Lay is a *transitive* verb meaning "to put something somewhere carefully", and must have an object: *Mothers often lay babies on their backs to sleep.* It is not correct to say "I'm going to lay down" – you should use *lie* for this. Lay is also the past tense of *lie*: *We lay on the floor.*	**lie** Lie is an *intransitive* verb meaning "to be in a horizontal position": *I want to lie down.*
loose Loose is an *adjective* meaning "not firmly fixed": *The bolts had worked loose.*	**lose** Lose is a *verb* meaning "to not have something any more" or "to be defeated": *I'm always losing my keys.* *I think we're going to lose the match.*
personal Personal is an *adjective* meaning "private" or "relating to a particular person": *He asked me some very personal questions.* *She has her own personal helicopter.*	**personnel** Personnel is a *noun* meaning "the people who work in an organization": *All military personnel must report to base.*
quite Quite is a qualifying *adverb* that is used mainly in set expressions: *I haven't seen her for quite a while.* *Dinner is not quite ready.*	**quiet** Quiet is an *adjective* and describes things or people that do not make much noise: *She had a very quiet voice.*

These groups of three words are among the most commonly misused words in English. They are all extremely frequent, so it is important that you are confident about using them correctly.

they're	They're means "they are": *They're going to come on the train, I'll be angry if they're late again.*
their	Their is the possessive pronoun from "they": *They forgot to bring their coats.* *Their faces were white and tear-stained.*
there	There is a pronoun and adverb used to show position or direction, to show that something exists, and at the beginning of many sentences and phrases: *There's your jacket.* *Can you see the lion over there?* *The old buildings are still there today.* *There must be another way of doing this.* *There are three churches in our town.*
too	Too is used before adjectives to mean "more than is good": *It's too hot in here.* It also means "as well": *I want some too.*
to	To is a preposition that is used in many ways, but the main ones are showing direction, showing who receives something, and forming the infinitive: *We went to the zoo.* *I gave it to John.* *I need to buy a new coat.*
two	Two is the word for the number 2: *I have two brothers.*

we're	We're means "we are": *We're having a party.* *I'll phone you when we're there.*
were	Were is the past tense of *be* when the subject is plural: *We were very happy.* *They were going to tell you.*
where	Where is used to talk about the location of things or to ask questions about the location of things: *Where do you live?* *I left the keys where Kabelo would be sure to find them.*

Words that are often misspelled

These are words which people often misspell. A few of them are difficult words, but most of them are quite common, and it is important to spell them correctly.

accidentally	Don't forget -*ally* at the end, not just -ly.
accommodation	Double *c* and double *m*. This is one of the most commonly misspelled words in English.
acquire	Don't forget the *c* before the *q*.
advertisement	Don't forget the *e* after the *s*.
apparent	Double *p* but only one *r*.
beautiful	Learn the group of vowels – *eau* – at the beginning.
because	Remember *au* after the *c*.
believe	Remember *ie*, not ei.
Caribbean	Only one *r*, but double *b*.
catastrophe	Unusually for English, the final *e* is pronounced, but remember it is only one *e* – don't be tempted to write y or ee.
category	Remember it's *e* in the middle, not i or a.
cemetery	Remember that the first three vowels are *e*, there is no *a*.
definite/definitely	Remember that there are two *i*'s and no a's in this word.
desperate	The second vowel is *e*, not a (unlike *separate*).

different	Double *f* and don't forget the *e* after them.
discipline	Don't forget the *c* after the *s*, or the *e* at the end.
embarrassing	Double *r* and double *s*.
environment	Don't forget the *n* in the middle of this word.
especially	Remember that this word starts with *e*.
existence	This word ends -*ence*, not -ance.
foreign	Remember *ei* in the second syllable, and don't forget the *g*.
forty	Unlike *four*, there is no *u* in this word.
gauge	Remember the vowel sound is *au*.
government	Don't forget the *n* in the middle of this word. Remember that it comes from the word *govern*.
grammar	Remember that this word ends -*ar*, not -er.
guarantee	Remember the *u* in the first syllable of this word.
harrass	Remember: one *r*, double *s*.
independent	Remember that this word ends -*ent*, not -ant.
island	Don't forget the *s*.
leisure	Remember that in this word, *e* comes before *i*, which is the other way around from the usual rule.
library	Don't forget the *r* after the *b*.

lightning	Do not be tempted to add an e after *light*.
maintenance	Remember that the second vowel sound is made by *e* (even though the related verb is *maintain*).
maneuver	The vowel sequence *eu* has an unusual pronunciation in this word and it is easy to forget the *e*.
millennium	Double *l* and double *n*.
miniature	Don't forget the second *i*.
minuscule	Note that the second vowel is *u*, not i. Try to think of it as beginning with *minus-*, not mini-.
occurrence	Double *c* and double *r*.
opportunity	Double *p* and don't forget the *r* before the *t*.
possess/possession	Two lots of double *s*.
privilege	This is the most frequently misspelled word in English. Remember that the middle vowel is *i*, the last vowel is *e*, and there is no *d* (as there is in *knowledge*, for example). There are no a's in this word.
profession/professional/ professor	Remember there is only one *f* in these words.
pronunciation	Do not be tempted to add an o in the second syllable.
questionnaire	Remember to write double *n* in the middle.
receipt	Remember *ei* in the second syllable, and don't forget the silent *p*.

receive	Remember *ei* in the second syllable.
recommend	Only one *c* but double *m*.
relevant	Remember that the second vowel is *e*, not a.
restaurant	Remember to write *au* after the first *t*.
rhythm	This word is unusual in having two syllables, and none of the usual vowels. It's best to memorize the whole word.
seize	Remember *ei*, here not ie.
separate	Remember that the second vowel is *a*, not e.
truly	Do not be tempted to add an e after *tru*.
weird	Remember *ei*, not ie.

Common mistakes and controversial issues

The English language arouses strong emotions. Many people have very fixed ideas about what is wrong and what is right. It is important when you write – apart from very informal texts, emails, etc. – that you use a correct, standard form of English.

If you make mistakes such as putting apostrophes in the wrong place, or using the wrong form of a verb, your readers might be distracted from your message, and even take it less seriously.

It is important to remember that there are different customs for written and spoken English. While it might be acceptable in some situations to say something like "Jane and me are going shopping," nonstandard uses should be avoided in writing.

Several customs of English grammar have come about as a result of people applying the grammar of Latin to English. However, many people are inconsistent about this. For instance, someone who objects to the use of the word *data* as a singular noun (because it is plural in Latin), may be quite happy to use the words *agenda* and *stamina* as singular nouns, even though they are Latin plurals too.

Another important thing to bear in mind is that language changes. The language used by E. M. Forster writing in the 20th century is very different from that of Shakespeare writing in the 16th century, but nobody would say that Forster's English was incorrect.

New words and phrases come into the language all the time, and even the grammar and structure of our sentences changes. Today many more people speak English as a second language than as a first language and the ways that they speak and write are beginning to have an influence on the way that English is developing.

In the notes that follow, you will find guidance on what is acceptable and what is not acceptable in current American English. However, there are many issues where people disagree, and as always, it is important to think of your audience. The most important thing is to avoid slang, informal expressions, and loose grammar when you are writing reports, papers, or material for publication.

All right or alright?

Some people consider that *alright* is not a real word, and that *all right* should always be used. However, *alright* is very commonly used, particularly when representing speech. It may be best to avoid it in very formal writing.

Among or between?

If we are talking, for example, of dividing or sharing things, *between* is usually used when there are only two people or things, and *among* when there are more than two:

> *Nora and Doyin shared the bread between them.*
> *We distributed leaflets among the crowd.*

However, many people use *between* no matter how many things there are, especially after the verb *choose*:

> *It is difficult to choose between all the different styles.*

Amount and quantity

In formal writing, it is best to use these nouns only with uncountable or mass nouns:

> *There was a large amount of mud on the carpet.*
> *We bought a small quantity of gold.*

It is not good style in formal writing to say things like: *I've got a huge amount of apples*. For countable nouns, it is best to use *number*, or to rephrase the sentence, for example: *I've got a lot of apples*.

Awhile

Because it is an adverb, *awhile* normally works as an adverbial and takes the place of the phrase "for a while":

> *We waited awhile and then two buses came.*

Many people, however, use *awhile* as the object of the prepositions *for* and *after*. This usage is acceptable in fiction and informal writing but should probably be avoided in formal writing:

> *It looked like rain for awhile but then it cleared.*
> *After awhile we left the beach and went to the movies.*

Comprise

Comprise is a formal word, and should not be used with the preposition *of*, even though the similar words *consist* or *be composed* are followed by *of*:

> *The grounds comprise a large lawn and 20 acres of woodland.*
> *My cold remedy consists of lemon, honey and garlic.*
> *The committee is composed of members of the legal profession.*

Could of/should of, etc.

It is a very common error to write *of* after modal verbs such as *could*, *might*, *should*, or *would*. This is because in speech, it sounds as if that is what we are saying. However, the sound is really a contracted form of the verb *have* (*could've*, *might've*, *should've*, etc.). In formal writing it is best to avoid the contractions all together:

> *We could have helped you if you had asked.*
> *You should have called for a taxi.*

Dangling participles

Dangling participles occur when the subject of the main clause is not the subject of the modifying clause that contains a participle (usually a word ending in -*ing* or -*ed*).

Look at the following sentence:

> *Coming home from work, my hat blew off.*

Coming is a dangling participle here because its subject is not *my hat*. In formal writing, it would be better to say something like:

> *As I was coming home from work, my hat blew off.*

Here is an example of a dangling past participle:

> *Loathed by his colleagues, we understood why he had been fired.*

This is incorrect in formal writing, because the subject of the main clause is *we*, but the subject of the participle is *he*. It would be better to write something like:

> *He was loathed by his colleagues, so we understood why he had been fired.*

It is fine to use clauses with participles as long as the subject of the main clause matches:

> *Having seen the play before, I was happy to go again.*

Data

Strictly speaking, data is the plural form of the Latin *datum*. Some people insist that it should be used with a plural verb:

> *The data were collected over several years.*

However, data is often used as a singular noun, and most people would accept that as a valid use. There is some logic to this too, since data is often used as a synonym for *information* or *evidence*, which would take singular verbs:

> *All the data was uploaded to the new server.*

Data tends to be used as a plural more commonly in scientific or academic writing. Whether you decide to use a singular or a plural verb with data, make sure that you are consistent throughout your document.

Decimate

This word originated from the Roman custom of killing one in ten of a group of soldiers guilty of crimes such as mutiny. A few people, therefore, prefer to use decimate very specifically to mean "to reduce by one tenth."

However, in modern English, decimate is used to mean "to destroy a large amount or number of something" and this is widely acceptable:

> *Troops were decimated by illness.*

Note that it is best not to use decimate – as many people do – to mean "to destroy completely." It is better to use a word like *destroy* or *annihilate* for this.

Different

The safest preposition to use with different is *from*, which is the same use as the related verb *differ from*:

> *These biscuits taste different from the other ones.*

In American English, but not British English, *than* can be used:

> *He has a different job than me.*

It is also considered acceptable in British, but not American English to use *to*:

> *Your circumstances are different to mine.*

Dilemma

The word dilemma comes from the Greek prefix *di-* meaning "two." Therefore, purists argue that it should only be used to describe a situation where there are two alternatives, and not where there are a wider range of alternatives:

> *To support my husband or my son: that was my dilemma.*

In formal writing, dilemma should not be used simply as a synonym of *problem*, but only for situations where some sort of choice or decision is to be made.

Because the original Greek word referred to two unpleasant alternatives, some people also believe that it should still only be used in this way, and not for a choice between two pleasant things.

Disinterested or uninterested?

In formal, modern English, uninterested is used to mean "not interested" and disinterested to mean "unbiased" or "impartial":

> *The audience seemed completely uninterested in what she had to say.*
> *We need a disinterested person to make a decision for us.*

However, in reality, the two words are used so interchangeably that even if you try to make the distinction, it is probably best to avoid *disinterested* altogether to avoid ambiguity, and use *unbiased* or *impartial* instead.

Double negatives

A double negative is the use of two negative words in the same sentence. These are common in some dialects of spoken English, but should never be used in writing.

> *I haven't got no money.* (Double negative.)
> *I haven't got any money.* (Standard English.)
> *She didn't tell me nothing.* (Double negative.)
> *She didn't tell me anything.* (Standard English.)

Equally

It is common to see sentences such as the following:

> *Their work was equally as good.*
> *His house is equally as large as Ava's.*

However, you should not use the word *as* with equally. Equally should come directly before the adjective:

> *Their work was equally good.*
> *His house and Ava's house are equally large.*

Farther/farthest or further/furthest?

If you use further/furthest all the time you can avoid any difficulty here. Some people, however, prefer to use farther when they are talking about literal distances:

> *We traveled farther into the mountains.*
> *Which car can go the farthest on a full tank of gas?*

Fewer or less?

Fewer should be used before plural nouns and less before uncountable nouns:

> *There are fewer pupils in her class than last year.*
> *I hope you'll have fewer problems this time.*
> *I'm trying to use less butter in my cooking.*
> *I had even less information about it than you.*

In formal writing, it is best to stick to this rule, but in more informal contexts it is common to see less used before plural nouns:

> *There were less people there than I expected.*
> *This checkout is for people with 10 items or less.*

It is acceptable even in formal English to use less before numbers:

> *I had seen him less than five times in my life.*

Hopefully

In current English it is common to see the word *hopefully* "it is hoped," usually at the beginning of a sentence, when what the speaker or writer really means is "I hope that":

> *Hopefully we won't have to wait long.*
> *Hopefully they'll pay us for the time we spent.*

However, some people object to this, saying that hopefully should only be used to mean "in a hopeful way":

> *He looked at her hopefully.*
> *We waited hopefully to see if she would appear.*

It is best to avoid overusing hopefully in formal writing as a sentence adverb because it provides an opportunity for others to criticize.

I or me?

You should avoid writing sentences such as *Tim and me cooked a meal*.

When you use two pronouns or a personal name and a pronoun together, think about whether they are the subject or the object of the sentence:

> *Tom and I went to the football match.* (Subject.)
> *He asked Jo and me to sweep all the floors.* (Object.)

If you are not sure whether to use I or me, imagine you were only writing about yourself and not the other person. For instance, you would say *I went to the football game*, so that is the form to use when you add the other person too.

Irregardless

This is not a word in standard English, so do not use it in your writing. The word you need is *regardless*.

Lend, loan and borrow

If you lend someone something, you let them use it for a while. If you borrow something, you take it from someone else to use for a while. In American English you can use *loan* as a verb, especially for amounts of money, in the same way you use *lend* for things. However, idioms always use lend; for example, *lend a hand* (=help) and *lend me your ears* (=listen)

> *Can you lend me a pen?*
> *Can you loan me 50 bucks till payday?*
> *Can I borrow your pen?*

Literally

This word should be used only to emphasize that what follows is exact fact, and is not being said in an exaggerated or figurative way:

> *The waves were literally as high as a house.*
> *She was literally penniless.*

It is common for literally to be used simply to emphasize what follows, but examples like this should be avoided in formal writing:

> *I literally jumped out of my skin.*
> *We literally had to wait for hours.*

Media

Strictly speaking, media is the plural form of the Latin *medium*.
Some people insist that it should be used with a plural verb:

>*The media were guilty of invading her privacy.*

However, media is often used as a singular noun in current English:

>*The media is making the most of this scandal.*

If you want to talk about one particular form of communication
though, you should use the singular *medium*:

>*She is of the view that television is a dangerous medium.*

Off (of)

The preposition *off* may or may not be followed by *of* in American
English:

>*It fell off of the table.*
>*It fell off the table.*

Ought

Unlike with the other modal verbs (*can*, *might*, *must*, etc.), *ought*,
is normally followed by a *to* infinitive. Some speakers, however, leave
off the *to* when *ought* is used with a negative:

>*You ought to visit Margie while you're here.*
>*Oughtn't we see if he's all right?*
>*You ought not to leave your keys in the door.*

Out

The word *out* is usually an adverb:

> *I dropped my bag and all my money fell out.*
> *I'm not going to go out today.*

You can use *out* as a preposition, but it is considered informal without *of* after it:

> *She threw the bag out the window.* (Informal.)
> *I walked out of the room.*

Per

The most common use of this preposition is to show a mathematical relationship between quantities or numbers:

> *They were paid $100 per performance.*
> *The speed limit here is 40 miles per hour.*

In business jargon it is used as a shorthand substitute for "with reference to" or "concerning," but you should avoid this use in formal writing:

> *Per your request yesterday I have sent out three cases.*
> (Business jargon.)

Phenomena

Remember that phenomena is the plural of phenomenon. Do not use phenomena as a singular:

> *Lightning is a natural phenomena.* (Incorrect.)
> *Lightning is a natural phenomenon.* (Correct.)

Plus

Plus is mainly a preposition whose meaning is similar to the conjunction *and* (as in "three plus two equals five"). *Plus* can also be used as a conjunction with a meaning similar to *and*. When it joins clauses rather than phrases, however, some people object to its use and so you should avoid it in formal writing:

> *He came in late, plus he didn't have a ticket.* (Informal.)

The reason being

Do not use the verb *is* after this phrase, because it does not relate grammatically. You should use *that*:

> *We had to sell the business, the reason being that my husband was ill.*

Refute

This word is often used simply to mean "deny," but this is not correct, standard use. Refute means to prove something wrong with evidence.

> *With these documents, he was able to refute the allegations.*

So

So is one of the commonest adverbs in English and most of its uses are not controversial. It has recently developed a new use as an intensifying or emphatic adverb that modifies the predicate of a sentence and many people disapprove of this usage, so it is best to avoid it in all except informal writing.

> *She so doesn't need to have another kid.* (Informal.)
> *That is so what I wanted you to tell me.* (Informal.)

Split infinitives

A split infinitive happens when you write an adverb between *to* and a verb, e.g., *to finally agree*.

A lot of people do not like this, although plenty of great writers such as Donne, Eliot and Browning have used it.

> *We were asked to carefully look inside the box.* (Split infinitive.)
> *We were asked to look carefully inside the box.*

In a few cases, a split infinitive is necessary to avoid a change in meaning:

> *He failed to completely understand my point.* (Split infinitive, but means that he did not understand everything about the point.)
> *He completely failed to understand my point.* (This has a different meaning – that he was unable to understand the point at all.)
> *He failed to understand my point completely.* (This could have either meaning, and is therefore ambiguous.)

Sure and surely

Both these words can be used as adverbs but their meaning and register is not the same. In general, *sure* is more informal and is used when the speaker or writer expects agreement:

> *The children sure like the new jungle gym in the playground.*
> *You sure are late!*

Surely is more likely to be used in formal contexts, and where the writer or speaker is trying to persuade:

> *I surely didn't mean to cause any offense.*
> *Surely you don't think that he'll actually answer the letter.*

Try

It is acceptable to use *and* or *to* after try, though *and* is slightly less formal:

> *Try and find the coin.*
> *We will try to help you.*

Used to

Note that when using the negative and question forms with used to, you need to drop the *d* from *used*. This is because the tense marker is now carried by whatever form of the verb *do* is used:

> *Years ago, children used to be more polite.*
> *I used to hate broccoli, but now I like it.*
> *Children didn't use to have TVs in their bedrooms.*
> *Did you use to play football when you were a child?*

In a very formal style, we could write:

> *I used not to have a car.*

Way

Way as an adverb is often used before a preposition or another adverb for emphasis, and is somewhat more informal than *far* would be in the same context:

> *You're driving way over the speed limit.*
> *There is way too much sugar in these children's diet.*

Some people use *way* as an intensifying adverb before an adjective. This use is regarded as slang by many people and should be avoided in all except informal writing:

> *That was a way stupid thing to do.* (Informal.)
> *Her Mom's really strict but her Dad is way cool.* (Informal.)

Who or whom?

Who is now commonly used as the object where in the past it was only considered correct to use whom:

> *Who do you work for?*

If you use whom in sentences like this, your writing will sound extremely formal:

> *For whom do you work?*

However, you must use whom directly after a preposition:

> *The woman to whom I spoke was a local nurse.*
> *There were twenty masked prisoners, many of whom were armed.*

Index

More fantastic titles in the Collins Webster's Easy Learning range

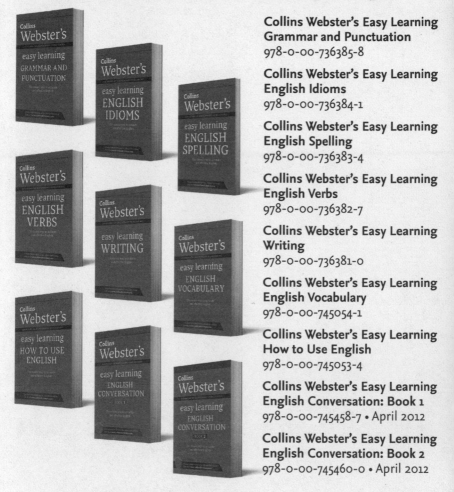

Collins Webster's Easy Learning
Grammar and Punctuation
978-0-00-736385-8

Collins Webster's Easy Learning
English Idioms
978-0-00-736384-1

Collins Webster's Easy Learning
English Spelling
978-0-00-736383-4

Collins Webster's Easy Learning
English Verbs
978-0-00-736382-7

Collins Webster's Easy Learning
Writing
978-0-00-736381-0

Collins Webster's Easy Learning
English Vocabulary
978-0-00-745054-1

Collins Webster's Easy Learning
How to Use English
978-0-00-745053-4

Collins Webster's Easy Learning
English Conversation: Book 1
978-0-00-745458-7 • April 2012

Collins Webster's Easy Learning
English Conversation: Book 2
978-0-00-745460-0 • April 2012

Selected titles now available as eBooks for Kindle and iPad.

To place an order for Collins Webster's Easy Learning titles
contact our sales team at international@harpercollins.co.uk

Collins   www.collinslanguage.com